where
(to)
weekend
around
CHICAGO
Fodo

Fodor's Travel Publications   New York   Toronto   London   Sydney   Auckland

917.73
EOD

Fodor's Where to Weekend Around Chicago

Editor: William Travis
Editorial Production: Tom Holton
Editorial Contributors: Joanne Cleaver, Kevin Cunningham, Jenn Q. Goddu, Rick Marzec, Linda Packer, Jennifer Vanasco
Maps: David Lindroth, *cartographer;* Bob Blake and Rebecca Baer, *map editors*
Cover Art: Jessie Hartland
Book Design: Fabrizio La Rocca, *creative director;* Guido Caroti, *art director;* Sophie Ye Chin, *designer*
Production/Manufacturing: Robert B. Shields

Copyright

First Edition

ISBN 1–4000–1303–8
ISSN 1547–6758

917.73

Special Sales

PRINTED IN THE UNITED STATES OF AMERICA

10 9 8 7 6 5 4 3 2 1

Where to Weekend Around Chicago

What are you doing this weekend? Just the word *weekend* implies such promise—a break from the workaday rhythm, a bit of downtime, a chance to see friends and family, a good time to be had by all. Two things are certain: there aren't enough weekends, and they're always too short. You can make them feel longer, however, by going away, seeing someplace different, and really leaving the concerns of home life behind. And, surprise, planning a weekend getaway doesn't have to be stressful, regardless of whether you're deciding where to go next month or next weekend. That's where this book comes in.

Where to Weekend Around Chicago helps you plan trips to 25 destinations within 350 mi of the city. In the dozens of towns we describe, you'll find hundreds of places to explore. Some may be places you know; others may be new to you. This book makes sure you know your options so that you don't miss something that's right around the next bend—even practically in your backyard—just because you didn't know it was there. Maybe you usually spend summer weekends in Madison or South Haven. Why not consider Door County or Amish Country for a change, or go in May or October instead? Perhaps your favorite inn is booked solid and you can't wait to get away, or you're tired of eating at the same three restaurants in Milwaukee. With the practical information in this book, you can easily call to confirm the details that matter and study up on what you'll want to see and do and where you'll want to eat and sleep. Then toss *Where to Weekend Around Chicago* in your bag for the journey.

Although there's no substitute for travel advice from a good friend who knows your style and taste, our contributors are the next best thing—the kind of people you would poll for weekend ideas if you knew them.

Joanne Cleaver has been exploring the outer reaches of the Chicago metro area for nearly 20 years. Sometimes she does it on assignment for the *Chicago Tribune* or while researching her three family-travel guidebooks. The rest of the time, she is just having fun.

Kevin Cunningham is a Big Ten alum and writer-editor. Like any good native of the Midwest, his interests are diners and severe weather watches/warnings. He has written for industry publications, newspapers, and educational publishers. Travel writing once led him to jump into a subarctic sea despite not being able to swim, and he has enjoyed an $800 meal in Paris. He lives in Chicago.

Jenn Goddu is a full-time freelance journalist in the Chicago area. She reviews theater regularly for the *Chicago Reader* and is a frequent contributor of arts and news features to the *Chicago Tribune's RedEye, Performink, Digital City Chicago* and other regional publications. Her previous travel writing has appeared in the *Post-Tribune* in northwest Indiana. She is a graduate of Smith College and has a master's degree in journalism.

A lifelong Chicago resident, **Rick Marzec** is co-founder of Hear Spot Run, Inc., a marketing/advertising agency that creates everything from humorous radio ads to marketing strategies for a wide variety of clients. Though he's traveled overseas, he loves taking road trips with his partner and dog. Rick's freelance travel writing work has appeared in *Travel Your Way, Endless Travel,* and *travelbyus.* He holds a master's degree in communications/advertising from the University of Illinois.

Abandoning her addiction to Stephen Sondheim, good wine, and cats, **Linda Packer** gave in to her travel addiction and made it her profession. She has written for Mobile Travel Guides, the British Tourist Authority, and the *Chicago Tribune,* and contributed to "In Search of Adventure," a travel anthology. She created and was editor of *Travel Your Way*, a magazine distributed through the New York Times. She works and lives in Chicago, but when she travels she does drink good wine, catches a Sondheim production whenever possible, and always misses her cats.

Freelance writer **Jennifer Vanasco** has lived by the lake in Chicago for 10 years, spending much of that time exploring the other side of the lake—Michigan. She writes about Chicago theater and local culture, among other things, for the *Chicago Reader, Chicago Free Press,* and *Chicago Tribune.* Her award-winning column on gay and lesbian social issues is syndicated around the country. It has won the Peter Lisagor Award three times—given by the local chapter of the Society of Professional Journalists.

Contents

How to Use This Book

Our goal is to cover the best sights, activities, lodgings, and restaurants in their category within each weekend-getaway destination. Alphabetical organization makes it easy to navigate through these pages. Still, we've made certain decisions and used certain terms that you need to know about. For starters you can go on the assumption that everything you read about in this book is recommended by our writers and editors. It goes without saying that no property mentioned in the book has paid to be included.

ORGANIZATION
Bullets on the map, which follows How to Use This Book, correspond to the chapter numbers. Each chapter focuses on one getaway destination; the directional line at the start of each chapter tells you how far it is from the city. The information in each chapter's What to See & Do section is arranged in alphabetical order, broken up by town in many cases. Parks and forests are sometimes listed under the main access point. Where to Stay and Where to Eat follow, with suggestions for places for all budgets, also arranged alphabetically and usually by town as well. The Essentials section provides information about how to get there and other logistical details.

For ideas about the best places for hiking, antiquing, and wine tasting, flip to the Fodor's Choice listings, which follow the map. Pit Stops are places to pull off the highway, stretch your legs, and grab a snack.

WHAT TO SEE & DO
This book is loaded with sights and activities for all seasons, budgets, lifestyles, and interests, which means that whether you want to check out a local gallery or bike walk along a lakeside path, you'll find plenty of places to explore. Admission prices given apply to adults; substantially reduced fees are almost always available for children, students, and senior citizens.

Where they're available, sightseeing tours are listed in their own section. Sports are limited to area highlights. Biking is an option most everywhere, so we give details only when facilities are extensive or otherwise notable. The same can be said of shopping, but we tell you about shopping standouts such the boutiques in downtown Woodstock, the Dane County Farmer's Market in Madison, or Michigan Avenue in Chicago. Use Save the Date as a timing tool, for events you wish to attend (and perhaps crowds you'd prefer to avoid).

WHERE TO STAY
The places we list—including homey B&Bs, mom-and-pop motels, grand inns, chain hotels, and luxury retreats—are the cream of the crop in each price and lodging category.

Baths: You'll find private bathrooms unless noted otherwise.

Credit cards: AE, D, DC, MC, V following lodging listings indicate whether American Express, Discover, Diner's Club, MasterCard, or Visa are accepted.

Facilities: We list what's available but we don't specify what costs extra. When pricing accommodations, always ask what's included. The term *hot tub* denotes hot tubs, whirlpools, and Jacuzzis. Assume that lodgings have phones, TVs, and air-conditioning and that they permit smoking, unless we note otherwise.

Closings: Assume that hostelries are open all year unless otherwise noted.

Meal plans: Hostelries operate on the European Plan (EP, with no meals) unless we specify that they use the Continental Plan (CP, with a Continental breakfast) or Breakfast Plan (BP, with a full breakfast).

Prices: Price categories are based on the price range for a standard double room during high season, excluding service charges and tax. Price categories for all-suites properties are based on prices for standard suites.

WHAT IT COSTS

$$$$	over $200
$$$	$160–$200
$$	$120–$160
$	$80–$120
¢	under $80

WHERE TO EAT
We make a point of including local food-lovers' hot spots as well as neighborhood options for all budgets.
Credit cards: AE, D, DC, MC, V following restaurant listings indicate whether American Express, Discover, Diner's Club, MasterCard, or Visa are accepted.
Dress: Assume that no jackets or ties are required for men unless otherwise noted.
Meals and hours: Assume that restaurants are open for lunch and dinner unless otherwise noted. We always specify days closed and meals not available. When traveling in the off-season, be sure to call ahead.
Reservations: They're always a good idea, but we don't mention them unless they're essential or are not accepted.
Prices: The price categories listed are based on the cost per person for a main course at dinner or, when dinner isn't available, the next most expensive meal.

WHAT IT COSTS

$$$$	over $25
$$$	$18–$25
$$	$12–$18
$	$8–$12
¢	under $8

ESSENTIALS
Details about transportation and other logistical information end each chapter. Be sure to check Web sites or call for particulars.

AN IMPORTANT TIP
Although all prices, opening times, and other details in this book are based on information supplied to us at press time, changes occur all the time in the travel world, especially in seasonal destinations, and Fodor's cannot accept responsibility for facts that become outdated or for inadvertent errors or omissions. So always confirm information when it matters, especially if you're making a detour to visit a specific place.

Let Us Hear from You
Keeping a travel guide fresh and up-to-date is a big job, and we welcome any and all comments. We'd love to have your thoughts on places we've listed, and we're interested in hearing about your own special finds. Our guides are thoroughly updated for each new edition, and we're always adding new information, so your feedback is vital. Contact us via e-mail in care of editors@fodors.com (specifying *Where to Weekend Around Chicago* on the subject line) or via snail mail in care of *Where to Weekend Around Chicago*, at Fodor's, 1745 Broadway, New York, NY 10019. We look forward to hearing from you. And in the meantime, have a great weekend.

—The Editors

Pit Stops

Off the major thoroughfares outside the city and beyond the highway rest stops, these places offer a quick bite (and a bathroom).

I-43

Dockside Deli
5 mi east of Exit 93, Port Washington
Enjoy the harbor view while eating breakfast, lunch, or a sweet snack in this sleek café. The menu has sandwiches deli-style or grilled, soup or salad, and six hot or cold breakfast options. Box lunches are available. > 222 E. Main St., Port Washington, tel. 262/284–9440. D, MC, V. Closed Sun. No dinner.

Jumes
4 mi east of Exit 126, Sheboygan
This neon pink downtown diner has an old-style neon sign outside that still says "air-conditioned." This family restaurant has been open since 1928 serving breakfast all day, burgers, shakes, and daily specials. > 504 N. 8th St., Sheboygan, tel. 920/452–4914. AE, DC, MC, V.

U.S. 31

Loaf and Mug
4 mi west of Exit 36, Saugatuck
Grab a few tasty sandwiches for an impromptu picnic on the beach or sit a spell in one of two charming dining areas, one inside and one out. Soups and pastas are served in round homemade bread bowls. The specialties are the ribbon sandwich, which layers egg and tuna salad sandwiches on top of each other, and the whitefish Reuben. The garden patio seats up to 70. > 236 Culver St., Saugatuck, tel. 616/857–3793. AE, D, MC, V. No dinner Sun.–Thurs.

Dee-Lite Bar and Grill
1 mi off U.S. 31, Grand Haven
The weekend Bloody Mary bar alone is worth coming to this 1950s-style diner housed next to an abandoned movie theater. Or, if you'd prefer, have a burger accompanied by something from Dee-Lite's venerable martini bar. Their pancakes and sandwiches are pretty good, too. > 24 Washington St., Grand Haven, tel. 616/844–5055. AE, MC, V.

I-65

Shapiro's Delicatessen Cafeteria
5 mi off Exit 17, Indianapolis
The strawberry cheesecake and huge corned-beef sandwiches on rye are signature items at this nationally known deli, an Indianapolis institution since 1904. Eight blocks south of downtown, it's convenient for lunch when attending events there. > 808 S. Meridian St., Indianapolis, tel. 317/631–4041. No credit cards.

I-90/94

Radical Rye
6 mi off Exit 142A, Madison
You can fill out your own order slip for huge sandwiches loaded with fresh-sliced deli meats and vegetables, and have them smothered with toppings of your choosing. There's also always vegetarian chili and a soup of the day. Big windows looking out onto State Street are great for people-watching. > 231 State St., Madison, tel. 608/256–1200. AE, MC, V.

Fodor's Choice

The towns, sights, activities, and other travel experiences listed on this page are Fodor's editors' and writers' top picks for each category.

BEACHES
Indiana Dunes National Lakeshore, Michigan City > chapter 2
Geneva Lake Lake Geneva > chapter 4
Bradford Beach, Milwaukee > chapter 7
Grand Haven State Park, Grand Haven > chapter 12
Whitefish Dunes State Park, Sturgeon Bay > chapter 22

DAY TRIPS
Woodstock, Illinois > chapter 3
Milwaukee Art Museum, Milwaukee > chapter 7
Lake of the Woods County Park, Mahomet > chapter 11
Historic Downtown Cedarburg, Cedarburg > chapter 13
State Street, Madison > chapter 14

EVENTS
Chicago Blues Festival, Downtown Chicago > chapter 1
Summerfest, Milwaukee > chapter 7
Tulip Time Festival, Holland > chapter 12
Fish Day Port Washington > chapter 13
Ann Arbor Blues and Jazz Festival, Ann Arbor > chapter 23

FALL FOLIAGE
Starved Rock State Park, Utica > chapter 6
Door County, Wisconsin > chapter 22
Brown County State Park, Indiana > chapter 24

FAMILY FUN
John G. Shedd Aquarium, Downtown Chicago > chapter 1
Field Museum of Natural History, Downtown Chicago > chapter 1
Milwaukee County Zoo, Milwaukee > chapter 7

Amish Acres, Nappanee > chapter 9
National Cherry Festival, Traverse City > chapter 25

HIKING
Starved Rock State Park, Utica > chapter 6
Allegan State Forest, Allegan > chapter 10
Devil's Lake State Park, Baraboo > chapter 20
Rock Island State Park, Washington Island > chapter 22
Sleeping Bear Dunes National Lakeshore, Glen Arbor > chapter 25

HISTORIC HOMES
Timm House, Elkhart Lake > chapter 13
Belvedere Mansion and Gardens, Galena > chapter 15
Marshall Historic District, Marshall > chapter 16
Taliesin, Spring Green > chapter 18
Lincoln Home National Historic Site, Springfield > chapter 19

MUSEUMS
Museum of Contemporary Art, Downtown Chicago > chapter 1
College Football Hall of Fame, South Bend > chapter 5
National New York Central Railroad Museum, Elkhart > chapter 9
Children's Museum of Indianapolis, Indianapolis > chapter 10
University of Michigan Museum of Art, Ann Arbor > chapter 23

STATE PARKS
Castle Rock State Park, Oregon > chapter 8
White River State Park, Indianapolis > chapter 17
Blue Mound State Park, Blue Mounds > chapter 18
Hoosier National Forest, Bedford > chapter 21

Peninsula State Park, Fish Creek
> chapter 22
**Sleeping Bear Dunes National
Lakeshore,** Glen Arbor > chapter 25

WINERIES
Tabor Hill Winery&Restaurant,
Saugatuck > chapter 10

Butler Winery, Bloomington > chapter 21
Chateau de Leelanau, Suttons Bay
> chapter 25
Shady Lane Cellars, Suttons Bay
> chapter 25
Peninsula Cellars, Traverse City
> chapter 25

Downtown Chicago

1

By Joanne Cleaver

DOWNTOWN CHICAGO IS FULL OF TREASURES FOR CITY LOVERS. Known as the Loop since the cable cars of the 1880s looped around the central business district (on tracks now traversed by El trains), downtown comprises the area south of the Chicago River, west of Lake Michigan, and north of the Congress Parkway–Eisenhower Expressway. Downtown Chicago's western boundary used to be the Chicago River, but the boundary continues to push westward.

The dynamic area known as the Loop is a living architectural museum where you can stroll past shimmering modern towers side by side with renovated 19th-century buildings that snap you back in time. There are striking sculptures by Picasso, Miró, Chagall, and others; wide plazas lively with music and other entertainment in summer; noisy, mesmerizing trading centers; gigantic department stores that are determined holdouts in the malling of America; and globally known museums that soothe the senses. The Sears Tower—still one of the world's tallest buildings—adds an exclamation point to the Loop skyline.

Immediately north of the Chicago River is River North. It encompasses the tony shopping areas of the Magnificent Mile and Oak Street, Navy Pier, and the high-end gallery district to the west of the Magnificent Mile. The Mag Mile, a stretch of Michigan Avenue between the Chicago River and Oak Street, owes its name to the swanky shops that line both sides of the street—and to its once-elegant low-rise profile, which used to contrast sharply with the urban canyons of the Loop. Key landmarks here are the Water Tower and the John Hancock Tower.

Shopaholics are bound to become addicted to the Loop and Near North, if they aren't already. In the Loop, the highlights are the grand old department stores, especially Marshall Field's. The Near North glitters with enormous installations of national chain department and specialty stores, from Nike to Tiffany. Oak Street is tony and exclusive, and the Magnificent Mile, from the river to Lake Shore Drive, is fringed with streets jammed with galleries of art, antiques, handicrafts, home furnishings, and just about anything else. Except bargains. This is an exclusive shopping neighborhood. Those who refuse to pay retail will have to hunt hard for reduced-price goods, though the persistent and sharp-eyed may capture some deals.

Chicago's entertainment varies from loud and loose to sophisticated and sedate. You'll find the classic Chicago corner bar in most neighborhoods, along with trendier alternatives such as wine bars. The famous Chicago bar scene known as Rush Street has faded into the mists of time, although the street has found resurgent energy with the opening of a string of upscale restaurants and outdoor cafés. For the vestiges of the old Rush Street, continue north (if you dare) to Division Street between Clark and State streets.

The strains of blues and jazz provide much of the backbeat to the city's groove. The House of Blues, in the Marina City complex on Wacker Drive, has big-time acts and big-time prices. If you're in search of the heart and soul of Chicago, a short taxi ride takes you to clubs such as Buddy Guy's Legends in the South Loop and Blue Chicago on North Clark Street. As far as dancing is concerned, the action has switched from cavernous clubs to smaller spots with DJs spinning dance tunes; there's everything from hip-hop to swing. In the past few years, Wicker Park and Bucktown have been the hottest nightlife neighborhoods, but prime spots are spread throughout the city.

With just a weekend downtown, consider choosing a hotel within walking distance of the main destinations you want to visit. If you live and work in the suburbs, try to settle on one theme per weekend visit. Nibble on a bite-size slice of downtown culture and life, and know that you can always come back for seconds.

WHAT TO SEE & DO

LOOP & DOWNTOWN SOUTH

Adler Planetarium Interactive and state-of-the-art exhibits hold appeal for traditionalists as well as for technology-savvy kids and adults who can be their own navigators through the solar system. The high-tech Sky Pavilion is a glass structure that wraps around the old building and traditional dome and contains the interactive StarRider Theater. Also in this building are a telescope terrace and interactive exhibition galleries that include 3-D computer animations of the Milky Way. Additional charges apply for the Sky Theater planetarium shows and the StarRider interactive shows. > 1300 S. Lake Shore Dr., Downtown South, tel. 312/922–7827, www.adlerplanetarium.org. $5. Labor Day–Memorial Day, Mon.–Thurs. 9–5, Fri. 9–9, weekends 9–6; Memorial Day–Labor Day, Sat.–Wed. 9–6, Thurs. and Fri. 9–9.

Art Institute of Chicago Some of the world's most famous paintings are housed in this museum, including a collection of impressionist and postimpressionist paintings, with seminal works by Monet, Renoir, Gauguin, and van Gogh, among others. The museum also houses collections of medieval, Renaissance, and modern art. Less well-known are its fine holdings in Asian art and photography. Especially helpful for first-time visitors is the 45-minute Introduction to the Collections tour, Tuesday and Saturday at 2. If you have a youngster with you, make an early stop at the **Kraft Education Center** downstairs. > 111 S. Michigan Ave., Loop, tel. 312/443–3600, www.artic.edu. $10, free Tues. Mon. and Wed.–Fri. 10:30–4:30, Tues. 10:30–8, weekends 10–5.

Buckingham Fountain A centerpiece in Grant Park since 1927, this decorative tiered fountain has intricate designs of pink marble seashells, water-spouting fish, and bronze sculptures of sea horses. It was patterned after a fountain at Versailles but is about twice as large as its model. Thanks to its size, the 25-foot-tall fountain can propel water 150 feet high and circulate 14,000 gallons a minute. > Grant Park between Columbus and Lake Shore Drs. east of Congress Plaza, Downtown South. Free. May 1–Oct. 1.

Chicago Cultural Center Visit just to marvel at the world's largest Tiffany stained-glass dome and elaborate ornamentation. The Cultural Center hosts free concerts and performances of all kinds nearly daily, including live music at 1 PM every weekday in the Randolph Cafe. The **Chicago Office of Tourism Visitor Information Center** is near the Randolph Street entrance. The **Museum of Broadcast Communications,** also housed here, displays TV and radio exhibits and has a large archive of programs and commercials. Building tours are given Tuesday–Saturday at 1:15 PM. > 78 E. Washington St., Loop, tel. 312/346–3278. Free. Mon.–Wed. 10–7, Thurs. 10–9, Fri. 10–6, Sat. 10–5, Sun. 11–5.

Civic Opera House The art nouveau home of the Lyric Opera is grand indeed, with crystal chandeliers and a sweeping staircase to the second floor. Lyric Opera performances sell out every year, but the hopeful may be able to purchase returned tickets. > 20 N. Wacker Dr., Loop, tel. Civic Opera House 312/372–7800, Lyric Opera 312/332–2244.

Field Museum of Natural History More than 6 acres of exhibits fill this museum, which explores cultures and environments from around the world. The interactive exhibits are stimulating, exploring Earth and its people, including the secrets of Egyptian mummies, the peoples of Africa and the Pacific Northwest, and the living creatures in the soil. Don't miss the Life over Time: DNA to Dinosaurs exhibit, which traces the evolution of life on Earth from one-cell organisms to the great reptiles. Kids may especially enjoy the 65-million-year-old "Sue," the largest and most complete Tyrannosaurus rex fossil ever found. More than 600 other fossils are on exhibit, including gigantic posed dinosaur skeletons. > 1400 S. Lake Shore Dr., Downtown South, tel. 312/922–9410, www.fieldmuseum.org. $8, free Wed. Weekdays 10–5, weekends 9–5.

Grant Park Chicago's front yard provides some elbow room between the Loop and the lake. The site of enormous warm-weather festivals, the park is a beautiful place for a stroll at any time of year. In summer, it's a tradition to visit Buckingham Fountain in the evening when it is illuminated with colored lights. It's one of the best free things to do. > Downtown South.

John G. Shedd Aquarium Take a plunge into an underwater world at the world's largest indoor aquarium. Interactive walk-through environments allow you to travel from the flooded forests of the Amazon to the coral reefs of the Indo-Pacific and a shark habitat. Built in 1930, the Shedd houses more than 8,000 aquatic animals. In the Oceanarium you can have a stare-down with one of the knobby-headed beluga whales, observe Pacific white-sided dolphins at play, and explore the simulated Pacific Northwest nature trail. An educational dolphin presentation is scheduled daily. Be sure to check out the underwater viewing windows for the dolphins and whales. > 1200 S. Lake Shore Dr., Downtown South, tel. 312/939–2438, www.sheddaquarium.org. $15 includes the Oceanarium; $7 Mon. and Tues. for Oceanarium and Aquarium. Memorial Day–Labor Day, Fri.–Wed. 9–6, Thurs. 9 AM–10 PM; Labor Day–Memorial Day, weekdays 9–5, weekends 9–6.

Millennium Park Built on top of a former rail yard, the approximately 24-acre park, at the northwest corner of Grant Park, is finally complete. In winter, you can take a spin on the McCormick Tribune ice rink, and in warm weather you can take in a concert at renowned architect Frank Gehry's stunning music pavilion. This pavilion replaces Grant Park's Petrillo band shell and hosts the Grant Park Music Festival as well as free summer concerts. > Bounded by Michigan Ave., Columbus Dr., Randolph Dr., and Monroe St., Loop.

Museum of Broadcast Communications Relive great moments in radio and television or watch or listen to your favorite hit shows from the past. The museum's extensive archives—available to the public—are augmented by hands-on exhibits that let you read from teleprompters, anchor your own newscast, and even tape the whole thing. > 78 E. Washington St., Loop, tel. 312/629–6000, www.museum.tv. $10. Mon.–Sat. 10–4:40, Sun. noon–5.

Museum of Contemporary Photography This museum, part of Columbia College Chicago, focuses on American-born and American-resident photographers. "Contemporary" is defined as anything after 1959, the date of Robert Frank's seminal work *The Americans*, which is on display here and portrays Americans in a way that they had not seen themselves—or wanted to see themselves—before. The permanent collection contains works from Dorothea Lange, Ansel Adams, and Nicholas Nixon. > 600

S. Michigan Ave., Downtown South, tel. 312/663–5554, www.mocp.org. Free. Mon.–Wed. and Fri. 10–5, Thurs. 10–8, Sat. noon–5.

Sears Tower This soaring 110-story skyscraper, designed by Skidmore, Owings & Merrill in 1974, was the world's tallest building until 1996 when the Petronas Towers in Kuala Lumpur, Malaysia, claimed the title. However, the folks at the Sears Tower are quick to point out that the Petronas Towers counts its spire as part of the building. But if you were to measure the 1,454-foot-tall Sears Tower in terms of highest occupied floor, highest roof, or highest antenna, the Sears Tower would win hands down. To get to the **Skydeck,** enter on Jackson Boulevard. On a clear day you can see Michigan, Wisconsin, and Indiana. (Check the visibility ratings at the security desk before you decide to ride up and take in the view.) Computer kiosks in six languages help international travelers key into Chicago hot spots. The lower level has a food court, rotating exhibits on the city's culture, and an eight-minute movie about the city. Security is very tight, so figure in a little extra time for your visit to the Skydeck. Before you leave, don't miss the spiraling Calder mobile sculpture, *The Universe,* in the ground-floor lobby on the Wacker Drive side. > 233 S. Wacker Dr., Loop, tel. 312/875–9696, www.theskydeck.com. $9.50. May–Sept., daily 10–10; Oct.–Apr, daily 10–8.

Soldier Field Home of the Chicago Bears since 1971, Soldier Field opened in 1924 and has been the site of many events besides football games, including a heavy-weight-title boxing match in 1927 between Jack Dempsey and Gene Tunney, and rock concerts by the Rolling Stones and other mega-bands. Its enormous and controversial renovation, likened by some critics to a space ship that landed on the neoclassical stadium, is scheduled to be completed in late 2003. > 425 E. McFetridge Dr., Downtown South, tel. 312/747–1285, www.soldierfield.net.

Spertus Museum Of special interest in this museum are many ritual objects from Jewish life and a poignant Holocaust memorial with many photos and a tattered concentration camp uniform. The artifacts and works of art make up the most comprehensive Judaic collection in the Midwest. A hands-on children's museum called the **Rosenbaum ARTiFACT Center** has a simulated archaeological dig, in which junior archaeologists can search for pottery underneath the sand. > 618 S. Michigan Ave., Downtown South, tel. 312/322–1747, www.spertus.edu. $5, free Fri. Sun.–Wed. 10–5, Thurs. 10–8, Fri. 10–3; children's museum Sun.–Thurs. 1–4:30.

Symphony Center Orchestra Hall, home to the acclaimed Chicago Symphony Orchestra, lies at the heart of this music center. The Georgian building has a symmetrical facade of pink brick with limestone quoins, lintels, and other decorative elements. Many music lovers buy tickets for Sunday afternoon rehearsals. > 220 S. Michigan Ave., Downtown South, tel. 312/294–3000, www.chicagosymphony.org.

NEAR NORTH

Chicago Children's Museum "Hands-on" is the operative concept for this brightly colored, 57,000-square-foot Navy Pier anchor, which encourages kids to play educational video games, climb through multilevel tunnels, run their own television stations, and, if their parents allow it, get all wet. Some favorites are an early childhood exhibit with a child-size neighborhood complete with a bakery, service station, and construction site; an art studio; and science exhibits on such subjects as recycling and inventing. > 700 E. Grand Ave., Near North, tel. 312/527–1000, www.chichildrensmuseum.org. $6.50. Tues.–Sun. 10–5.

John Hancock Center The crisscross braces in this 1,107-foot-tall building help keep it from swaying in the high winds that come off the lake. Completed in 1970, Big John was the first building of such massive height on Michigan Avenue. The 94th floor has an observation deck; you can enjoy the same view while having an exorbitantly priced drink in the bar that adjoins the Signature Room at the 95th-floor restaurant. There are restaurants, shops, and a waterfall in the lower-level public plaza. > 875 N. Michigan Ave., Near North, tel. 312/751–3681, www.hancock-observatory.com. Observation deck $9.50. Daily 9 AM–11 PM.

Michigan Avenue Bridge Completed in 1920, this bridge at the south end of the Magnificent Mile has impressive sculptures on its four pylons representing major Chicago events: its exploration by Marquette and Joliet, its settlement by trader Jean Baptiste Point du Sable, the Fort Dearborn Massacre of 1812, and the rebuilding of the city after the fire of 1871. The site of the fort, at the southeast end of the bridge, is marked by a commemorative plaque erected there by the city. The bridge has two decks for traffic and can be opened to allow tall-masted boats to pass. > 400 N. Michigan Ave., Near North.

Museum of Contemporary Art Founded in 1967 by a group of art patrons who felt the great Art Institute was unresponsive to modern work, the MCA's growing 7,000-piece collection includes work by René Magritte, Alexander Calder, Bruce Nauman, Sol LeWitt, Franz Kline, and June Leaf. Among the museum's highlights are four barrel-vaulted galleries on the fourth floor and a terraced sculpture garden with outdoor café tables overlooking Lake Michigan. The museum hosts a party ($14) with live music and hors d'oeuvres from 6 PM to 10 PM on the first Friday of every month. > 220 E. Chicago Ave., Near North, tel. 312/280–2660, www.mcachicago.org. $8, free Tues. Tues. 10–8, Wed.–Sun. 10–5.

Navy Pier No matter the season, Navy Pier is a fun place to spend a few hours. Constructed in 1916 as a commercial-shipping pier, the once-deserted pier now contains shopping promenades; an outdoor landscaped area with gardens, a fountain, a carousel, a 15-story Ferris wheel (which charges $5 per person for a once-around ride), and an ice-skating rink; the lakefront **Skyline Stage** (tel. 312/595–7437), a 1,500-seat vault-roof theater; the **Chicago Shakespeare Theatre** (tel. 312/595–5600), in an elegant round building with a bright neon sign; Crystal Gardens, one of the country's largest indoor botanical parks; an IMAX Theater; an outdoor beer garden; the **Chicago Children's Museum**; and myriad shops, restaurants, and bars. Navy Pier is also the home port for a number of tour and dinner cruises. Prices are premium for these cruises, and the food's better on land, but the voyage can be pleasant on a hot summer night. > Grand Ave. at the lakefront, Near North, tel. 312/595–7437, www.navypier.com. Daily 6 AM–11 PM.

Terra Museum of American Art Daniel Terra, ambassador-at-large for cultural affairs under Ronald Reagan, made his collection of American art available to Chicago in 1980. The collections highlight American impressionism and folk art. Look for works by Whistler, Sargent, Winslow Homer, Cassatt, and three generations of Wyeths. > 664 N. Michigan Ave., Near North, tel. 312/664–3939, www.terramuseum.org. $7, free Tues. and 1st Sun. of month. Tues. 10–8, Wed.–Sat. 10–6, Sun. noon–5.

Water Tower & Pumping Station Water is still pumped to 390,000 city residents at a rate of about 250 million gallons per day from this Gothic-style structure, which, along with the similar Water Tower across the street, survived the fire of 1871. The pumping station is also a drop-in tourist information center, open daily 7:30 AM–7 PM, which includes a coffee stand, and a gift shop. This is where you can start a tour on an ever-circulating double-decker tour bus. > 811 N. Michigan Ave., Near North.

Tours

Chicago Architecture Foundation This dedicated group conducts excellent boat, bus, walking, and bike tours for everyone from neophytes to Frank Lloyd Wright fans.

The boat tour, which goes down the Chicago River, is especially fun. Prices of tours vary. > 224 S. Michigan Ave., Loop, tel. 312/922–3432, www.architecture.org.

Mercury Chicago Skyline Cruise Embark on a cruise of the lake or river. You can choose from several canned themes, including the river architecture tour and the lake skyline tour. Daily tours are 60 to 90 minutes long and cost $17 to $19. You must buy tickets a half hour before your tour. > Michigan Ave. at Wacker Dr., Loop, tel. 312/332–1353.

Wendella Sightseeing Boats Climb aboard and see the skyline close up from the river or on the horizon from the lake. These daily architecture tours last 60 to 90 minutes and cost $16 to $18. You must buy tickets a half hour before your tour. > Lower Michigan Ave. at the Wrigley Bldg., Loop, tel. 312/337–1446, www.wendellaboats.com.

Save the Date

MARCH

St. Patrick's Day Parade The Chicago River is dyed green, shamrocks decorate the street, and the center stripe of Dearborn Street is painted the color of the Irish from Wacker Drive to Van Buren Street. > Tel. 312/942–9188.

JUNE

Chicago Blues Festival This is a popular four-day, three-stage event starring blues greats from Chicago and around the country. > Grant Park, tel. 312/744–3315.

Printer's Row Book Fair One of the largest literary events and book sales in the Midwest, this two-day event in the historic Printer's Row district presents programs and displays on the printer's and binder's arts. > Dearborn St. between Congress Pkwy. and Polk St., tel. 312/222–4778.

Taste of Chicago Pizza, cheesecake, and other Chicago specialties are served to 3.5 million people over a 10-day period that includes entertainment. Grant Park, Columbus Dr. between Jackson and Randolph Sts., tel. 312/744–3315.

SEPTEMBER

Chicago Jazz Festival This festival holds sway for four days during Labor Day weekend at the Petrillo Music Shell. > Grant Park, tel. 312/744–3315.

OCTOBER

Chicago International Film Festival For two weeks in October, this festival screens more than 100 films, including premieres of Hollywood films, international releases, documentaries, short subjects, animation, videos, and student films. Movie stars usually make appearances at the opening events. > Tel. 312/332–3456, www.chicagofilmfestival.org.

WHERE TO STAY

LOOP & DOWNTOWN SOUTH

Fairmont All rooms at this 45-story pink granite tower, a few blocks from the Loop, have marble bathrooms with oversize tubs and separate shower stalls. The suites, all of which have views of Lake Michigan, are filled with plants and marble-top darkwood furniture and have living and dining rooms. Grand suites on the top floor pamper guests with fireplaces, libraries, and kitchenettes. On Friday and Saturday evenings, live entertainment in **Entre Nous**, keeps the hotel's French-influenced restaurant festive. > 200 N. Columbus Dr., Loop 60601, tel. 312/565–8000 or 800/526–2008, fax 312/856–1032, www.fairmont.com. 626 rooms, 66 suites. 2 restaurants, room service, in-room data ports, in-room fax, minibars, cable TV, some in-room VCRs, golf privileges, 3 bars, lobby lounge, cabaret, dry cleaning, laundry service, concierge, business services, meeting rooms, parking (fee), no-smoking rooms. AE, D, DC, MC, V. $$$–$$$$

Hilton Chicago Squarely facing Lake Michigan and the museum campus, this bustling convention hotel retains its 1920s heritage in a Renaissance-inspired entrance hall and gold-and-gilt Grand Ballroom. As with many older hotels, the rooms differ in size and Renaissance-style decor. Families should ask for one of the rooms with two double beds and two baths. The hotel is convenient to McCormick Place and museums, but can feel isolated at night. > 720 S. Michigan Ave., Downtown South 60605, tel. 312/922–4400 or 800/445–8667, fax 312/922–5240, www.chicagohilton.com. 1,410 rooms, 67 suites. 2 restaurants, snack bar, room service, in-room data ports, minibars, indoor pool, health club, hair salon, hot tub, massage, sauna, 2 bars, pub, dry cleaning, laundry service, concierge, concierge floor, business services, meeting rooms, helipad, parking (fee), no-smoking floors. AE, D, DC, MC, V. $$$–$$$$

Hotel Allegro Chicago Throughout this art deco structure are bold patterns and splashes of color—rooms mix coral, Tuscan yellow, and sea-foam green; window treatments resemble the entrance to a sheik's tent. Suites have whirlpool tubs, CD players, VCRs, and robes. The Palace Theater is an appropriate neighbor for this music-themed hotel: witness the clefs on the shower curtains, a music room off the lobby, and the *High Society*–inspired watercolor mural by the lobby stairs at the entrance. A complimentary lobby wine reception is hosted every evening. > 171 W. Randolph, Loop 60601, tel. 312/236–0123 or 800/643–1500, fax 312/236–0197, www.allegrochicago.com. 451 rooms, 32 suites. Room service, in-room data ports, in-room fax, minibars, cable TVs with movies, health club, hair salon, shop, laundry service, concierge, business services, meeting rooms, parking (fee), no-smoking rooms. AE, D, DC, MC, V. $$–$$$$

Hotel Burnham The attraction here is staying in a building—the Reliance Building—that was originally designed by seminal Chicago architect D. H. Burnham and built in 1895. The interior retains such original details as Carrara marble wainscoting and ceilings, terrazzo floors, and mahogany trim. Lavish guest rooms, which were once the building's offices, are bathed in golds and navy blues and are outfitted with deep-blue velvet headboards. > 1 W. Washington St., Loop 60602, tel. 312/782–1111 or 877/294–9712, fax 312/782–0899, www.burnhamhotel.com. 122 rooms. Restaurant, room service, in-room data ports, in-room fax, minibars, cable TV, gym, bar, dry cleaning, concierge, business services, parking (fee), no-smoking floor. AE, D, DC, MC, V. $$$–$$$$

Hotel Monaco A French deco–inspired look contributes to this hotel's travel theme, as do the registration desk—fashioned after a classic steamer trunk—and meeting rooms named for international destinations such as Tokyo and Paris. In brightly colored guest rooms, turndown is accompanied by such surprise amenities as lottery tickets or Pixy Stix candy. > 225 N. Wabash St., Loop 60601, tel. 312/960–8500 or 800/397–7661, fax 312/960–1883, www.monaco-chicago.com. 170 rooms, 22 suites. Restaurant, room service, in-room data ports, minibars, cable TV, some in-room VCRs, gym, bar, dry cleaning, laundry service, concierge, business services, meeting rooms, parking (fee), some pets allowed, no-smoking floors. AE, D, DC, MC, V. $$$$

Hyatt Regency Chicago Ficus trees, palms, and gushing fountains fill the two-story greenhouse lobby. This is one of the largest hotels in the world, with illuminated signs that guide you through the labyrinth of halls and escalators throughout the two towers. It's integrated into the enormous Illinois Center complex on the eastern fringe of the Loop, just south of the Chicago River, and steps from the Michigan Avenue bridge that marks the foot of the Magnificent Mile. In the comfortable-size guest rooms, black-and-white photographs of Chicago landmarks add to the contemporary look. > 151 E. Wacker Dr., Loop 60601, tel. 312/565–1234 or 800/233–1234, fax 312/565–2966, www.hyatt.com. 2,019 rooms, 175 suites. 4 restaurants, café, snack bar, room service, in-room data ports, minibars, some refrigerators, cable TV, some in-room VCRs, hair salon, hot tubs, massage, bar, sports bar, shops, dry cleaning, laundry service, concierge, concierge floor, business services, convention center, meeting rooms, parking (fee), no-smoking rooms, no-smoking floor. AE, D, DC, MC, V. $$–$$$$

Palmer House Hilton This landmark hotel in the heart of the Loop—convenient to the theater district, Art Institute, museum campus, and shopping—is the essence of grand style. Ornate and elegant public areas include the opulent lobby, with its ceiling murals. Rooms are spacious but furnishings are older. Trader Vic's restaurant in the basement is so retro it's almost cool . . . almost. > 17 E. Monroe St., Loop 60603, tel. 312/726–7500 or 800/445–8667, fax 312/263–2556, www.hilton.com. 1,551 rooms, 88 suites. 3 restaurants, coffee shop, room service, in-room data ports, minibars, some refrigerators, cable TV, indoor pool, gym, health club, hair salon, hot tub, massage, sauna, steam room, bar, shops, dry cleaning, laundry service, concierge, concierge floor, business services, meeting rooms, parking (fee), some pets allowed, no-smoking floor. AE, D, DC, MC, V. $$$–$$$$

Swissôtel The Swissôtel's triangular Harry Weese design ensures panoramic vistas of either the city, lake, or river. The comfortable, contemporary-style guest rooms have two-line phones and marble bathrooms. The 42nd-floor fitness center and pool take the sting out of sweating with its views of the city, lake, and river. The hotel has four dining options including **The Palm** restaurant, a cousin of the New York steak house of the same name. > 323 Wacker Dr., Loop 60601, tel. 312/565–0565 or 888/737–9477, fax 312/565–0540, www.swissotel.com. 632 rooms, 36 suites. Restaurant, café, patisserie, room service, in-room data ports, in-room fax, minibars, cable TV, some in-room VCRs, indoor pool, gym, hot tub, massage, sauna, spa, steam room, 2 bars, dry cleaning, laundry service, concierge, business services, meeting rooms, parking (fee), no-smoking floor. AE, D, DC, MC, V. $$$$

NEAR NORTH

Drake Hotel Built in 1920, the grand dame of Chicago hotels presides over the northernmost end of Michigan Avenue. The lobby, inspired by an Italian Renaissance palace, envelops you in its deep-red walls and glimmering crystal. The sounds of a fountain and harpist beckon you to the Palm Court, a lovely setting for afternoon tea. There's piano music in the Coq d'Or most nights and a jazz trio in the Palm Court five nights a week. Rooms and suites have city or lake views and are filled with neoclassic furnishings. > 140 E. Walton Pl., Near North 60611, tel. 312/787–2200 or 800/553–7253, fax 312/787–1431, www.thedrakehotel.com. 482 rooms, 55 suites. Restaurant, room service, in-room data ports, some minibars, some microwaves, cable TV, some in-room VCRs, exercise equipment, gym, hair salon, bar, lobby lounge, piano bar, shops, dry cleaning, laundry service, concierge, concierge floor, business services, meeting rooms, parking (fee), no-smoking floors. AE, D, DC, MC, V. $$$$

Hotel Inter-Continental Chicago Extensive renovations completed in 2002 brought back many historic touches of this architecturally significant hotel, built in 1929. Self-guided audio tours of this landmark building with its over-the-top Egyptian theme decor are available. Rooms have rich mahogany furniture and marble bathrooms. The new lobby is bright and open with a custom-designed mosaic floor and a grand spiral staircase. The international restaurant, **Zest,** is the only street-level dining option facing North Michigan Avenue. An excellent tea is served in the cozy hotel lobby that overlooks the avenue and affords discreet people-watching. Take a swim or just admire the junior Olympic-size pool surrounded by tile walls and stained-glass windows. > 505 N. Michigan Ave., Near North 60611, tel. 312/944–4100 or 800/628–2112, fax 312/944–3050, www.chicago.interconti.com. 814 rooms, 90 suites. Restaurant, room service, in-room data ports, some in-room faxes, in-room safes, minibars, cable TV, indoor pool, gym, health club, massage, sauna, bar, lobby lounge, dry cleaning, laundry service, concierge, Internet, business services, meeting rooms, parking (fee), no-smoking floors. AE, D, DC, MC, V. **$$$$**

Park Hyatt Superior service and luxurious accommodations highlight this hotel just off Chicago's Magnificent Mile. Neutral-color rooms have contemporary, custom-designed furnishings and high-tech amenities such as flat-screen televisions, and DVD and CD players. Two-person tubs have sliding cherrywood doors, which open into the bedrooms. Many rooms have window seats with views of Lake Michigan or the Chicago skyline. > 800 N. Michigan Ave., Near North 60611, tel. 312/239–4011 or 800/778–7477, fax 312/239–4000, www.parkhyatt.com. 202 rooms, 8 suites. Restaurant, room service, in-room data ports, in-room safes, minibars, indoor pool, health club, spa, bar, dry cleaning, laundry service, concierge, business services, meeting rooms, parking (fee), no-smoking rooms, no-smoking floor. AE, D, DC, MC, V. **$$$$**

Ritz-Carlton The Ritz-Carlton, run by Four Seasons Hotels and Resorts and not the Ritz-Carlton chain, is perched above Water Tower Place. The two-story greenhouse lobby serves a delicious afternoon tea, and the **Dining Room**'s chef, Sarah Stegner, has earned a top-notch reputation. Rooms are spacious, with high ceilings, walk-in closets, and large dressing areas. All-marble bathrooms have both tubs and separate glass-enclosed showers. > 160 E. Pearson St., Near North 60611, tel. 312/266–1000, 800/621–6906 outside IL, fax 312/266–1194, www.fourseasons.com. 435 rooms, 90 suites. 3 restaurants, room service, in-room data ports, in-room safes, minibars, refrigerators, cable TV, some in-room VCRs, indoor pool, gym, health club, hot tub, massage, spa, bar, lobby lounge, dry cleaning, laundry service, concierge, business services, meeting rooms, parking (fee), some pets allowed, no-smoking floors. AE, D, DC, MC, V. **$$$$**

W Chicago Lakeshore Men and women in black dominate in this chic, high-energy hotel. The lobby is part lounge, part club scene, with velvety couches and panoramic lakeshore views. Minimalist rooms have bathrooms with shutters that open for views of either Lake Michigan or downtown Chicago. The hotel's "whatever/whenever" desk is at your service 24 hours a day. > 644 N. Lake Shore Dr., Near North 60611, tel. 312/943–9200 or 800/541–3223, fax 312/255–4411, www.starwood.com/whotels. 569 rooms, 9 suites. Restaurant, room service, in-room data ports, in-room safes, cable TV, indoor pool, exercise equipment, gym, hair salon, bar, lounge, dry cleaning, laundry facilities, laundry service, business services, meeting rooms, airport shuttle, parking (fee), no-smoking floors. AE, D, DC, MC, V. **$$$–$$$$**

Whitehall Hotel This small, luxury hotel provides peace and quiet, and friendly attentive service. The rooms evoke an old-world style, and many come with four-poster beds. Bar and restaurant, **Molive,** serves California cuisine with a Mediterranean flair. > 105 E. Delaware Pl., Near North 60611, tel. 312/944–6300 or 800/948–4255, fax 312/944–8552. 213 rooms, 8 suites. Restaurant, outdoor café, room service, in-room data ports, in-room safes, minibars, cable TV, exercise equipment, gym, bar, dry cleaning, laundry service, concierge, concierge floor, business services, meeting rooms, parking (fee), no-smoking floor. AE, D, DC, MC, V. **$$$–$$$$**

WHERE TO EAT

LOOP & DOWNTOWN SOUTH

Atwood Cafe Mahogany columns, cherrywood floors, gold café curtains, and curvy light-blue banquettes set the stage for an American menu with such reliable dishes as chicken potpie, along with contemporary dishes such as duck and manchego quesadillas. > Hotel Burnham, 1 W. Washington St., Loop, tel. 312/368–1900. AE, D, DC, MC, V. $$–$$$

The Berghoff This Chicago institution has been serving its signature beer since the end of Prohibition; in fact, the restaurant holds liquor license No. 1. The handsome oak-panel interiors evoke an authentic Old Chicago feel. Lines are long but move quickly. German classics (Wiener schnitzel, sauerbraten) are accompanied by hearty sides (creamed spinach). Desserts are best skipped. > 17 W. Adams, Loop, tel. 312/427–3170. AE, MC, V. Closed Sun. $–$$

Costa's Amid a colorful, multilevel interior with terra-cotta tile work and rough-textured white walls and archways, this noisy Greektown restaurant serves some of the best Mediterranean seafood in town. Start with an assortment of *mezes* (tapaslike Greek appetizers), then move on to fresh fish, such as excellent whole snapper or sea bass. > 340 S. Halsted, Near West Side, tel. 312/263–9700. AE, D, DC, MC, V. $–$$$

Everest Everest's highs include its perch at 40 stories above ground with sweeping views of the city's West Side. Chef Jean Joho takes humble ingredients (particularly those from his native Alsace) and transforms them into memorable dishes such as risotto with edible gold leaf. The wine list has tremendous depth, particularly in its representation of Alsatian vintages. Service is discreet and professional. > 440 S. LaSalle St., Loop, tel. 312/663–8920. Reservations essential. Jacket required. AE, D, DC, MC, V. $$$$

Francesca's on Taylor Inexpensive and with lots of pastas on the menu—kind of like an Italian mom's kitchen management—this restaurant serves seafood and imaginative pastas. Folks heading to the United Center for a Bulls game, Blackhawks game, or special event make this a popular early-dining spot. > 1400 W. Taylor St., Near South Side, tel. 312/829–2828. AE, DC, MC, V. No lunch weekends. $–$$$

Lou Mitchell's The diner, a destination since 1923, specializes in comfort food lunches. Hash browns don't get any better than this. Though out-the-door waits are common, tables turn rapidly. > 565 W. Jackson Blvd., Loop, tel. 312/939–3111. Reservations not accepted. AE, V. No dinner. $–$$

New Rosebud Cafe This extremely busy restaurant specializes in old-fashioned southern Italian cuisine; its red sauce is one of the best in town. The wait for a table can stretch to an hour or more, despite confirmed reservations, but those with patience—and tolerance for the extreme noise level—will find that the meal more than compensates. > 1500 S. Taylor St., Near South Side, tel. 312/942–1117. Reservations essential. AE, D, DC, MC, V. No lunch weekends. $$–$$$$

Prairie The wood-trimmed interior is inspired by the architecture of Frank Lloyd Wright and the updated food by the flavors of the midwestern states. Specialties include horseradish-crusted sturgeon, grilled buffalo with sweet-potato risotto, and Lake Superior whitefish. > 500 S. Dearborn, Downtown South, tel. 312/663–1143. AE, D, DC, MC, V. $$$–$$$$

Printer's Row The American regional menu at this stylish restaurant is famous for its game meats, such as grilled venison with dried cherries and grilled peppered duck breast with almond-raisin couscous. A well-chosen, fairly priced wine list is a plus.

> 550 S. Dearborn St., Downtown South, tel. 312/461–0780. AE, D, DC, MC, V. **$$–$$$$**

Red Light Chinese, Thai, Vietnamese, and Indonesian dishes commingle happily on this varied menu, which is heavily weighted with appetizers. Standout dishes include gingered pork dumplings and Taiwanese catfish. > 820 W. Randolph St., Near West Side, tel. 312/733–8880. AE, DC, MC, V. **$$$–$$$$**

Rhapsody Adjacent to Symphony Center, this is more than just a handy spot for a preconcert dinner. Seafood and lamb are served with signature terrines. The handsome bar, pouring an expansive wine-by-the-glass selection, makes a popular post-performance hangout. > 65 E. Adams St., Loop, tel. 312/786–9911. AE, D, DC, MC, V. **$$$–$$$$**

Russian Tea Room This delightful gem neighbors Symphony Center and is steps away from the Art Institute. Mahogany trim, samovars, and balalaika music set the stage for a menu of authentic dishes from Russia and neighboring republics (the owners hail from Uzbekistan). Highlights include Ukrainian borscht, *blinis* (small, savory pancakes) with caviar and salmon, and *shashlik* (lamb kebabs). > 77 E. Adams, Loop, tel. 312/360–0000. Reservations essential. AE, D, DC, MC, V. **$$–$$$$**

NEAR NORTH

Billy Goat Tavern Behind and one level down from the Wrigley Building is this subterranean hole-in-the-wall, where local journalists eat "cheezborgers" and jaw about politics and current events. > 430 N. Michigan Ave., Near North, tel. 312/222–1525. No credit cards. **¢**

Eli's the Place for Steak Clubby and inviting in leather and warm wood, this restaurant serves prime aged steaks, which are among the best in Chicago. For dessert, order Eli's renowned cheesecake, now sold nationally. > 215 E. Chicago Ave., Near North, tel. 312/642–1393. AE, D, DC, MC, V. No lunch weekends. **$$$–$$$$**

Morton's of Chicago This is Chicago's best steak house. Excellent service and a very good wine list add to the principal attraction: beautiful, hefty steaks cooked to perfection. White tablecloths, chandeliers, and off-white walls create a classy feel despite the subterranean locale. > 1050 N. State St., Near North, tel. 312/266–4820. AE, D, DC, MC, V. No lunch. **$$$–$$$$**

Pizzeria Uno Chicago deep-dish pizza got its start at Uno in 1943. It exudes old-fashioned charm, from the paneled walls to the reproduction light fixtures. Plan on only two slices of the thick and cheesy Chicago-style pie as a full meal. Unless you're really hungry, skip the pre-pizza salad or appetizer and plan to postpone dessert. > 29 E. Ohio St., Near North, tel. 312/321–1000. AE, D, DC, MC, V. **$$–$$$**

Pump Room A Chicago classic since opening in 1938, the room long thrived on its celebrity. Booth One is off-limits to all but A-list celebs, but everyone gets served the updated classics that are on the menu. Such contemporary dishes as seared tuna stand alongside steak and potatoes here. > 1301 N. State Pkwy., Near North, tel. 312/266–0360. AE, D, DC, MC, V. **$$$–$$$$**

Signature Room at the 95th Best known for its skyline view from the John Hancock's 95th floor, this is the place for a formal dinner highlighted by superb service and such classics as rack of lamb. But one of the best deals in town is its $13.95 lunch buffet served weekdays: choose from roasts, prepared entrées, vegetable sides, soup, and a full salad bar. Its Sunday brunch is lavish and pricey. > John Hancock Center, 875 N. Michigan Ave., Near North, tel. 312/787–9596. AE, D, DC, MC, V. **$$$–$$$$**

Spiaggia Refined Italian cooking dished alongside three-story picture-window views of Lake Michigan make Spiaggia one of the city's top eateries. The hallmark is simple seasonal dishes, including pancetta-wrapped rabbit and the lightest gnocchi on the planet. The scholarly wine list is no place for bargain hunters, but there are some remarkable bottles. You can also sample Spiaggia's wonders next door at Cafe Spiaggia, a lower-priced, casual sidekick serving lunch and dinner daily. > 980 N. Michigan Ave., Near North, tel. 312/280–2750. Reservations essential. Jacket required. AE, D, DC, MC, V. No lunch Sun.–Thurs. **$$$$**

TRU Quite serious food is leavened by humorous presentations, such as between-course sorbets in cones. The dining room resembles an art gallery, with white walls and carefully chosen art, including an Andy Warhol. The menu starts with a basic three-course prix-fixe ($75); from there, you can add courses. > 676 N. St. Clair St., Near North, tel. 312/202–0001. Reservations essential. Jacket required. AE, D, DC, MC, V. Closed Sun. No lunch. **$$$$**

ESSENTIALS

Getting Here

The best way to see the Loop and Near North Chicago is on foot, supplemented by public transportation or taxi. Streets are laid out in a grid, the center of which is the intersection of Madison Street, which runs east–west, and State Street, which runs north–south.

Driving both to and around can be difficult and slow. Public transportation is inexpensive and convenient; consider the train or El, if stations and stops are near your home. However, if you're traveling with kids or you're coming to shop, driving in is your best option. Lake Shore Drive is the prettiest route in and out, and isn't usually much more congested than the side streets or I–94.

BY BUS

Chicago is connected with many small towns, including its own suburbs, via Greyhound. The Chicago Transit Authority and the Regional Transportation Authority provide information on how to get around on city bus lines and suburban bus lines; the base fare is $1.50. Buses accept either cash (exact change only) or fare cards.

BUS DEPOT **Greyhound Bus Station,** > 630 W. Harrison 60607, tel. 312/408–5883.

BUS LINES **Chicago Transit Authority/Regional Transportation Authority,** > Tel. 312/836–7000, www.transitchicago.com. **Greyhound,** > Tel. 312/408–5980 or 800/231–2222, www.greyhound.com.

BY CAR

From the east, the Indiana Toll Road (I–80 [I–90]) leads to the Chicago Skyway (also a toll road), which runs into the Dan Ryan Expressway (I–90 [I–94]). Take the Dan Ryan west to any downtown exit. From the south, take I–57 to the Dan Ryan. From the west follow I–80 to I–55, which is the major artery from the southwest and leads into Lake Shore Drive. From the north I–94 and I–90 eastbound merge about 10 mi north of downtown to form the John F. Kennedy Expressway (I–90 [I–94]).

If shopping is one of your main reasons for visiting, you may need your car to get all your bags home. Driving in the Loop and Near North is not hard but it is slow. Although streets are logically organized and traffic flows smoothly, it is a congested area and short distances can often take longer than anticipated.

Even on a Sunday morning, street parking is hard to come by in the Loop and Near North. Expect to give up the car to a valet or a self-park lot, and expect that to cost you $40 or $25 a day, respectively. Although it's a short drive from the north end of Michigan Avenue to the museum campus southeast of the Loop, parking costs nearly the same as the round-trip cab fare. Most hotels offer valet parking, but expect to pay the standard rate for it.

BY TAXI

Taxis are metered. The base fare is $1.60, plus $1.40 for each additional mile or minute of waiting time. Taxi drivers expect a 15% tip.

TAXI COMPANIES **American United Cab,** > Tel. 773/248–7600. **Checker Taxi Association,** > Tel. 312/243–2537. **Yellow Cab,** > Tel. 312/829–4222.

BY TRAIN

Amtrak serves Chicago's Union Station. Metra, the regional commuter line, not only serves four stations in the Loop but offers numerous special deals for families, weekend travel, and even those bringing their bikes to the Loop. You can use its Web site to create a customized itinerary. The Chicago Transit Authority and the Regional Transportation Authority provide information on how to get around on city rapid-transit lines; the base fare is $1.50. On the subway and the El, you must use a fare card, which can be purchased at the station.

TRAIN INFORMATION **Amtrak,** > 225 S. Canal St., tel. 800/872–7245, www.amtrak.com. **Chicago Transit Authority/Regional Transportation Authority,** > Tel. 312/836–7000, www.transitchicago.com. **Metra,** > 547 W. Jackson., tel. 312/322–6777, www.metrarail.com.

TRAIN STATIONS **Ogilvie Transportation Center,** > 500 W. Madison, tel. 312/496–4777. **Union Station,** > 210 S. Canal St., tel. 312/322–4269.

Visitor Information

CONTACTS **Chicago Office of Tourism,** > Visitor Information Center, 77 E. Randolph St., 60602, tel. 312/744–2400 or 800/226–6632, www.ci.chi.il.us/tourism. **Mayor's Office of Special Events,** > 1212 N. LaSalle St. Room 703, 60602, tel. 312/744–3315, www.ci.chi.il.us/specialevents.

Michigan City

60 mi east of Chicago

2

By Jenn Q. Goddu

THE FIRST SETTLERS TO ARRIVE IN MICHIGAN CITY IN 1833 were unde-
terred by the low, swampy town site and the huge sand dunes that dominated the
lakefront. They envisioned Michigan City would become a great port city, serving the
entire Midwest.

Although Chicago would soon overshadow its Indiana neighbor as the dominant
Midwest port, Michigan City continued to develop its harbor and prospered throughout the mid-1800s with "car shops" turning out more than 1,000 freight cars a day by
1879. The city had also become a destination point for out-of-towners. However, it
wasn't until an industrial slump in the 1920s that Michigan City's city leaders turned
their attention anew to advertising their hometown as a tourist resort. The city soon
became packed with summer cottages owned by wealthy Chicagoans looking to escape the bustle of the city. Visitors came for the social activities in Washington Park,
which had a dance hall, skating pavilion, and baseball field, and to climb the remaining dunes. The tallest of Michigan City's dunes, called the Hoosier Slide, was visible
all the way from Chicago before it was flattened between 1890 and 1920, when 13.5
million tons of sand were shipped to glass factories and to the Illinois Central Railroad to provide fill for its right-of-way.

Today it is still the dunes, the maritime history, and modern attractions such as an outlet mall or casino that keep a steady stream of visitors coming to Michigan City looking for a shoreside escape. Although the city has seen its share of the problems
plaguing urban areas, renewal and revitalization projects have continued apace. When
driving through downtown you can still see pockets that need work, but once you
reach the southern shore of Lake Michigan, a magnificent beachfront unfolds. Maybe
it's the sight of the city's 1907 lighthouse, the only public operating lighthouse in the
state, perched at the end of a catwalk and pier that is a favored spot for fishing; maybe
it's simply watching the sunset and whiling the day away. Or maybe it's the visual appeal of the sandy dunes stretching out in the distance. At nearly 200 feet, they have a
certain majesty. The 123-foot Mount Baldy, a "live" dune that cannot be held in place
by grass or trees, is part of the Indiana Dunes National Lakeshore; the 192-foot Mount
Tom is found in the Indiana Dunes State Park to the west. Most of all, it's the more relaxed pace not found on Chicago's beaches. Even the seagull's squawking song
sounds more attractive here. You should keep your ears attuned for other sounds as
well: the combination of quartz crystals, moisture, and pressure and friction from your
feet can create a clear ringing sound as you stroll along the water's edge by the dunes.

The panoramic view from the shoreline is not unblemished. On a clear day, the
smokestacks of northwest Indiana's many steel mills in the distance are easy to spot.
And even though the Northern Indiana Public Service Company power plant looms
to the west of Washington Park, its inoffensive little smoking icon is a cold reminder
of the city's industry. Nevertheless, this lakefront and the 90-acre Washington Park
continue to be a deserved source of pride for Michigan City residents.

Michigan City's forefathers may have misjudged this harbor's allure as a hub for manufacturing and lumber boats, but the city still provides a brief respite to Chicagoans. With the options of spending time sitting on the beach, hiking up a sandy dune, exploring the mansions of railroad barons or industrialists who lived here in the city's heyday, finding bargains in the outlet mall, or placing bets aboard a riverboat casino, Michigan City has made itself into a safe harbor from the buzz and rush of life in the big city.

WHAT TO SEE & DO

Barker Mansion Called "the house that freight cars built," this turn-of-the-20th-century mansion, built by millionaire railroad industrialist John H. Barker, is exquisitely fitted out with rare woods, fine art, and original furniture. This lavish English manor home is listed on the National Register of Historic Places. > 631 Washington St., Michigan City, tel. 219/873–1520. $4. June–Oct., daily 10–5, tours weekdays at 10, 11:30, and 1, weekends at noon and 2; Nov.–May, tours weekdays at 10, 11:30, and 1.

Blue Chip Casino This riverboat casino has more than 1,500 slot machines and more than 45 table games such as blackjack, craps, roulette, Caribbean stud poker, three-card poker, and mini-baccarat. The casino also houses two restaurants, a snack bar and lounge, and a 188-room hotel on board. > 2 Easy St., Michigan City, tel. 888/879–7711, www.bluechip-casino.com. Boards every 2 hrs, Mon.–Thurs. 9 AM–1 AM, Fri. and Sat. 9 AM–3 AM.

Great Lakes Museum of Military History Uniforms, photos, weapons, posters, medals, firearms, a World War II declaration of war, and a 1905 cannon are on display at this military history museum, which also houses a research library. The museum covers historical periods from the Revolutionary War to the present, and considers the military heritage of this nation as well as others. > 360 Dunes Plaza, Michigan City, tel. 219/872–2702 or 800/726–5912, www.militaryhistorymuseum.org. $3. Tues.–Fri. 9–4, Sat. 10–4, Sun. noon–4 (summer only).

Indiana Dunes National Lakeshore The park's beaches, bird-filled marshes, oak and maple forests, and sand dunes are open to swimming, hiking, camping, fishing, boating, picnicking, horseback riding, cross-country skiing, and snowshoeing. Inside its boundaries stands Mount Baldy, a 123-foot sand dune. The dunes are subject to erosion so hiking or climbing is allowed only on "climbing dunes" such as this one. The park is about 2 mi west of Michigan City. > 1101 N. Mineral Springs Rd., Michigan City, tel. 219/926–7561, www.nps.gov/indu. Free. Daily.

International Friendship Gardens These ornamental gardens represent nations from across the world. The French Garden, for example, is patterned in a maze characteristic of France and the Persian Garden is laden with roses. Surrounded by trails within 100 wooded acres, the gardens are still in various stages of restoration by volunteers. > 601 Marquette Trail, Michigan City, tel. 219/878–9885, www.friendshipgardens.org. Free. May–Oct., weekends 10–4.

Jack and Shirley Lubeznik Center for the Arts The former John G. Blank Center for the Arts has been renamed and is scheduled to move into a new building at 101 W. 2nd Street, near Washington Park, in spring 2004. In the interim, the gallery complex has moved to 720 Franklin Square. The former bank building is home to the center's gift shop and offices as well as exhibitions until the move to its permanent home. The center continues to exhibit paintings, sculpture, and other works by regional artists. > 720 Franklin Sq., Michigan City, tel. 219/874–4900, www.lubeznikcenter.org. $3. Feb.–Nov., Tues.–Fri. 10–4, Sat. 10–2; Dec., Tues. and Sat. 10–2; Jan., Tues. 10–2.

Washington Park Washington Park was opened in 1893 with every citizen invited to bring a tree to plant in the new park. Today the park's 90 acres on the lakefront include picnic areas shaded by now-tall trees, as well as a public-access marina and a swimming beach. The Old Bandstand dates from 1911 and even today is the site of open-air public concerts in summer. The park is on the National Register of Historic Places. Indiana's only lighthouse, built in 1858, is now the **Old Lighthouse Museum** (tel. 219/872–6133 or 219/872–3273, $2, Tues.–Sun. 1–4). Seven rooms of exhibits trace the Great Lakes' shipping history with shipbuilding tools, nautical artifacts, and photographs. The **Washington Park Zoo** (tel. 219/873–1510, $4, Apr.–Oct., daily 10:30–4) has a feline house, monkey island, and petting barn within a wooded dune area. The reptile collection is housed in a historic stone castle. If the art deco–style observation tower is open, you can enjoy a spectacular view of the city from 220 steps above street level. > 115 Lakeshore Dr., Michigan City, tel. 219/873–1506. Free. Daily; band concerts July and Aug., Thurs.–Sat. at 8 PM.

Sports

BIRD-WATCHING
Michigan City is nestled in the heart of one of the most unique wildlife spots in Indiana. The prairies, wetlands, inland lakes, and prairies provide prime bird-watching opportunities. Bright red cardinals are easily spotted, but keep your binoculars trained for the chirp or call of migrating ducks, shorebirds, scarlet tanagers, hawks, and wood thrushes. Endangered black terns occasionally visit Stone, Pine, and Lily lakes in La Porte.

In spring and autumn birders can witness the migration along the Lake Michigan shoreline. At Mount Baldy in the Indiana Dunes you can see the spring hawk migration. In summer many species nest in area marshes, woodlots, fields, and prairie remnants. Even in winter more than 50 species have been spotted by those who brave the elements as part of the county's holiday bird count. For more information about the best birding seasons and spots contact the **Powatomi Audubon Society of La Porte County** (tel. 219/324–0649).

FISHING
Searching for that "big one" on the big lake is a popular way to pass the time. Full-day, half-day, and sunset charters for salmon and trout fishing are available on Lake Michigan. Washington Park has public-access sites to Lake Michigan, and Michigan Boulevard is the access point for Trail Creek.

Crorkindill Captain Steve Kreighbaum begins his charters in March and continues through fall aboard his 32-foot boat. Find your fill with this experienced fisherman. > 405 Trail, Michigan City, tel. 219/879–8885.
Friendly Gesture Charter Captain Mike Hampel has been leading charters since 1986. You can fish for spring coho, steelhead, lake trout, or chinook. > 220 Meadowlark Dr., Michigan City, tel. 219/874–7506, www.mikehampel.homestead.com.
Ironsides Morning or evening trips are given aboard a 37-foot Hatteras. Salmon and trout are the specialty find for Captain Michael Caplis. > 118 E. 8th St., Suite 100, Michigan City, tel. 800/223–4549.

Shopping

Lighthouse Place Premium Outlets This sprawling outlet mall in downtown Michigan City is always busy on weekends with people shopping for bargains in the 120 apparel, shoes, accessory, home furnishings, gift, and specialty stores. This Indiana location is owned by Chelsea Premium Outlets and has many of the chain retailer tenants such as J. Crew, Tommy Hilfiger, Burberry, Nine West, Bass, OshKosh B'Gosh, Oilily, Mikasa, and Crate and Barrel offering savings of 25% to 65%. The entire outlet mall resembles a nautical village. > 601 Wabash St., Michigan City, tel. 219/879–6506, www.premiumoutlets.com.

Save the Date

JUNE

Music Fest Various musical acts, many local talents, perform in the amphitheater in Washington Park over three days, usually on the last weekend of the month. > 115 Lakeshore Dr., Michigan City, tel. 800/634–2650.

JULY

Summer Festival A traditional Fourth of July weekend patriotic program, a parade, a drum-and-bugle-corps show, a cardboard boat race, a Jet Ski race, and a fireworks display are highlights of this downtown festival, now in its fourth decade. > Tel. 219/874–3630 or 800/634–2650.

AUGUST

Lakefront Art Festival Washington Park becomes a gallery for artists both local and from around the country for this annual festival held the second week of August. > Tel. 219/874–3630 or 800/634–2650.

In-Water Boat Show Boats fill the harbor on the third weekend of August. Kids may not be ready for the party barge but they may want to watch Twiggy, a water-skiing squirrel wearing mini skis and a life jacket, cruise around a 25-foot circular pool. Food and refreshments round out the weekend. > Tel. 219/874–3630 or 800/634–2650.

DECEMBER

Washington Park Festival of Lights You can drive through the park's holiday light displays or stop by Zooltide in the park's zoo and hear holiday carolers and visit with Santa Claus. The lights are turned on the first Saturday of the month. The festival runs through early January. > Tel. 219/873–1510 or 800/634–2650.

WHERE TO STAY

Al and Sally's This single-story strip motel is in the heart of the Indiana Dunes National Lakeshore, 3 mi from downtown on U.S. 12. > 3221 W. Dunes Hwy., Michigan City 46360, tel. 219/872–9131. 16 rooms. Picnic area, refrigerators, cable TV, tennis court, pool, playground. AE, D, MC, V. ¢

Brickstone Bed & Breakfast This 1880 Queen Anne home is a half block from the Prime Outlets shopping mall, six blocks from Lake Michigan, and ½ mi from the Blue Chip Casino. Rooms are themed around the seasons: the winter room has a white canopy bed, the spring room has a fencelike headboard laced with silk flowers, and the fall room is decorated in burgundy and brown. The summer suite has a pull-out couch and its own sitting room and library. > 215 W. 6th St., Michigan City 46360, tel. 219/878–1819. 4 rooms. No room phones. MC, V. BP. **$–$$**

Comfort Inn Two miles from the Lighthouse Outlet Mall and ½ mi from I–94, Exit 34B, this two-story chain hostelry has one suite with an outdoor hot tub. > 3801 N. Frontage Rd., Michigan City 46360, tel. 219/879–9190, fax 219/879–0373, www.comfortinn.com. 50 rooms, 1 suite. In-room data ports, some in-room hot tubs, some kitchenettes, cable TV, some in-room VCRs, indoor pool, laundry facilities, business services. AE, D, DC, MC, V. CP. **¢–$**

Yours for the Picking

THE FERTILE FIELDS OF LA PORTE COUNTY *have given generations of farmers around Michigan City the means to make a living. Today they are willing to share the fantastic bounty of fruits and vegetables with city folk looking to experience country life for a couple of hours. Living in Chicago may put too much distance between you and Mother Nature, but it's not hard to pick up the skills needed for a pick-your-own adventure at one of the the area's nearly 30 orchards, farms, and gardens.*

A visit to the Michigan City Farmers' Market on Saturday mornings (701 Washington St., 800/634–2650) is surely a far easier way to get that fresh-from-the-field taste, but being out in the open air and doing a little work of your own can help build up a healthy appetite and a happy sense of accomplishment. The primary crops in the area are asparagus, strawberries, cherries, blueberries, raspberries, grapes, apples, peaches, nectarines, plums, and pears. Prime picking season runs from May to October. To find out when your favorite is ripe for the picking call 800/572–3740.

And you needn't worry if you miss the weekend market and have no interest in stooping or stretching to pick your own foods: many of these farms, nurseries, and greenhouses are happy to sell you homegrown vegetables or fruits that have already been picked.

A map of orchards, farms, and gardens in the area is available from the tourism board. For blueberries, try Billy Boy's Blueberry Barn (650 Freyer Rd., Michigan City, tel. 219/872–7477) or Blueberry Dune Farm (10352 N. Rte. 39, La Porte, tel. 219/362–3393). Pick your own apples or pumpkins at Garwood Orchard (5911 W. 50 S, La Porte, tel. 219/362–4385). You can pick vegetables at Miller's Orchard (2134 N. Wozniak Rd., Michigan City, tel. 219/874–6060) or fresh fruits at Pavolka Fruit Farm (1776 N. Wozniak Rd., Michigan City, tel. 219/874–6056).

Creekwood Inn Willow Creek runs through 30 acres of oaks, pines, and walnut trees surrounding this 1930s Tudor-style country estate. Some guest rooms have fireplaces, others have French doors that open onto private terraces. The property is 3 mi from Michigan City off I–94, Exit 40B (U.S. 20 [U.S. 35]). Inventive American cuisine is served at the Ferns restaurant on-site. > 5727 N. 600 W, Michigan City 46360, tel. 219/872–8357, fax 219/872–6986, www.creekwoodinn.com. 13 rooms. Refrigerators, fishing, bicycles, croquet, hiking, business services. AE, MC, V. Closed early Jan. CP. **$$**

Duneland Beach Inn Originally built in 1920 as a 23-room one-bath hotel, the inn was remodeled to include a private bath in each room. Each room has its own theme. For a nautical theme, book the Captain's Quarters; if you're a nature lover, try the Woodland View or Dune Grass room. You can have breakfast on the enclosed veranda, which looks out into the woods. A restaurant serves a dinner of chops, pasta, steaks, and seafood Tuesday through Saturday from 5 PM to 9 PM. The inn is a block from Lake Michigan. > 3311 Pottawattamie Terr., Michigan City 46360, tel. 219/874–7729 or 800/423–7729, www.dunelandbeachinn.com. 7 rooms, 2 suites. Cable TV, in-room VCRs, hot tub; no smoking, no pets, no kids under 7. MC, V. BP. **$–$$**

Hidden Pond This country home, 14 mi south of Michigan City on Route 35, is nestled on 10 acres with perennial gardens and a pond. The four rooms are decorated with antiques and heirlooms. The beds are covered with quilts from the owner's collection. > 402 E. 8th St., La Porte 46360, tel. 219/879–8200, fax 219/879–1770. 4 rooms. Pool, hot tub; no room phones, no room TVs. MC, V. BP. **$–$$**

Historic 1866 Feallock House On the old north end of Michigan City, near Lake Michigan's beaches, this cozy 1866 home is thought to be the oldest in the district. Each of the four rooms is distinctly decorated; some have only a semiprivate bath. Henrietta's Hideaway, named for the last Feallock to live in the house, is a bright cheery room with a rocking chair and wrought-iron bed. The Moore room has a wood sleigh bed and country charm. > 402 E. 8th St., Michigan City 46360, tel. 219/878–9543, fax 219/878–9543, www.feallock.com. 4 rooms. MC, V. BP. ¢–$

Holiday Inn Executive Conference Center This complex is ¼ mi from I–94, Exit 34B. Although the hotel is on a main thoroughfare, the rooms are quiet. Decorated with colorful bedspreads and framed posters, rooms are reached via an interior corridor. Damon's restaurant serves an eclectic menu in a light and airy dining room. > 5820 S. Franklin St., Michigan City 46360, tel. 219/879–0311 or 800/465–4329, fax 219/879–2536, www.holiday-inn.com. 165 rooms. Restaurant, room service, some in-room hot tubs, some refrigerators, cable TV, indoor-outdoor pool, exercise equipment, bar, recreation room, business services. AE, D, DC, MC, V. CP. $–$$

Hutchinson Mansion Inn The stately redbrick Hutchinson Mansion Inn presides over the town's historic residential and commercial district, spanning nearly one city block, less than 1 mi from the lakefront, off I–94, Exit 34B. William Hutchinson—lumber baron, world traveler, and onetime Michigan City mayor—built this elegant Queen Anne–style mansion in 1876 and outfitted it with stained-glass windows, dark-wood paneling, and tall beamed ceilings with ornate moldings. The bedrooms are accented with antiques such as an 8-foot Renaissance-revival bed with inlaid burl wood and a rare four-poster Jenny Lind bed. Carriage-house suites have a private terrace and a porch with a swing. > 220 W. 10th St., Michigan City 46360, tel. 219/879–1700, www.bbonline.com/in/hutchinson. 5 rooms, 5 suites. In-room data ports, hot tub; no smoking. MC, V. $–$$

CAMPING

Michigan City Campground Five miles from Lake Michigan, this campground has 40 shady scenic acres with sites available for tent and RV camping. Although a creek runs through the property, no hiking trails exist. Reservations are recommended for holiday weekends. > 1601 N. U.S. 421, Michigan City 46360, tel. 219/872–7600. 12 full hook-ups, 70 partial hook-ups, 45 tent sites. Dump stations, drinking water, showers, picnic tables, general store, pool, playground. MC, V. ¢

WHERE TO EAT

Basil's Named after its owner, this upbeat bistro serves inventive fare such as fresh fish with a signature champagne sauce seasoned with tarragon, honey, and cream, as well as chops, seafood, and steak. You can have a drink at the mahogany bar before getting seated. If the company you're with isn't exciting enough, you can entertain yourself by watching the cooks at work in the open kitchen. > 521 Franklin St., Michigan City, tel. 219/872–4500. AE, D, DC, MC, V. Closed Sun. $–$$$

Galveston Steakhouse Steaks, chicken, chops, and ribs are the menu staples in this rustic family restaurant. For a cozy night, start or finish your meal with a cocktail by the bar's fireplace. Blues bands enliven the crowd on weekends. > 10 Commerce Sq., Michigan City, tel. 219/879–5555. AE, D, MC, V. No lunch weekends. $–$$$

Matey's Restaurant and Beer Garden Just before the bridge, at the entrance to Washington Park, this bustling joint specializes in Cajun seafood chowder. You can gorge on tavern oysters, wrapped in bacon and fried; farm-raised oysters on the half shell; or the all-you-can-eat lake perch dinner. For a good view of the lake, ask to be seated in the rooftop patio. Chicago Bears paraphernalia adorns the bar. > 110 Franklin St., Michigan City, tel. 219/872–9471. AE, D, DC, MC, V. $–$$$

Pullman Café Everything has a railroad theme here—the hot rail appetizers, side track sandwiches, Union Pacific dinner, and club-car lounge cocktail specials. The special house steak can be ordered Oskar-style, topped with béarnaise sauce and crabmeat, or as a sandwich, with toast points underneath and onion rings on top. You can also get pasta, chicken, fish, and other meats. The restaurant is housed in a former factory that produced railroad boxcars until 1970. The servers can be curt, but if you're there when the jazz is playing in the lounge you may be relaxed enough to ignore this. > 711 Wabash St., Michigan City, tel. 219/879–3393. D, MC, V. $–$$$

Rodini Lounge In the front window of this restaurant, a stained-glass image of the nearby lighthouse welcomes diners who come ready for the fish, which is prepared to order—broiled, panfried, or deep-fried. The seafood platter is also popular. You can also get pasta, chicken, fish, and other meats. > 4125 Franklin St., Michigan City, tel. 219/879–7388. AE, D, DC, MC, V. $$–$$$$

LA PORTE

Cafe L'Amour Duck, lamb, steaks, or seafood are served with French or Mediterranean flair in this cozy restaurant in downtown La Porte. The 1867 First National Bank and 1885 Phoenix Theater have been remodeled to conjure up a European setting. > 701 Lincolnway, La Porte, tel. 219/324–5683. AE, D, DC, MC, V. Closed Sun. No dinner Mon. $$–$$$

Heston Bar Restaurant & Lounge Prime rib with cuts up to 40 ounces are served up at this roadside steak house. Combo seafood-beef plates, chops, and fresh fish are also options. Save room for the homemade desserts. > 2003 1000 N, La Porte, tel. 219/778–2938. AE, DC, MC, V. No lunch. $$–$$$$

Trattoria Enzo Pastas, fresh fish, steaks, and specialty pizzas are among the Italian-American fare available here, served under the stencils and tea lights that hang from the walls of the dining room and bar. > 601 Michigan Ave., La Porte, tel. 219/326–8000. AE, DC, MC, V. Closed Sun. and Mon. No lunch. ¢–$$$

Ye Olde Benny's It may not be fancy but there's a little bit of everything on the menu here. The name may evoke Olde English but the house specialty is the lasagna made from an original Italian family recipe. Ribs, steak, shrimp scampi, and hot sandwiches round out the menu. This isn't exactly fine dining but the candles on the table and green tablecloths help spruce up this family restaurant. > 3101 E. U.S. 12, La Porte, tel. 219/874–3663. AE, D, DC, MC, V. ¢–$$$

ESSENTIALS

Getting Here

Only 60 mi from Chicago, Michigan City is quick and easy to get to by car, bus, or train. Choosing which way you want to come here depends on whether you want speed or scenery. The bus will double your travel time. The train also takes a little longer but the South Shore Line goes right through the Indiana Dunes National Lakeshore and is cheap and comfortable.

BY BUS

Greyhound departs daily from Chicago for Michigan City at 8:15 AM and returns from Indiana at 8:50 AM or 4:20 PM. The trip is 1 hour and 55 minutes. The round-trip fare is $14.25.

BUS DEPOT **Greyhound** > 124 W. 11th St., Michigan City 46360, tel. 219/879–5050.

BUS LINE **Greyhound** > Tel. 800/229–9424, www.greyhound.com.

BY CAR

From Chicago take I–94 into Indiana and exit at 40B. Follow U.S. 35 (U.S. 20) north and it will lead you directly into downtown Michigan City. You can also travel via I–80 (I–90; the Indiana Toll Road or Chicago Skyway) into Indiana and take Exit 39 to U.S. 421. Follow this north until it becomes Franklin Street, which will take you straight through the city toward the lakefront. For a scenic detour, get off I–94 or the toll road at Route 49, just outside Porter, and head north until you reach U.S. 12. Take U.S. 12 East through the Indiana Dunes National Lakeshore. La Porte is 15 mi south of Michigan City on Route 35.

Once you get into Michigan City, free parking is plentiful at Washington Park, Blue Chip, or Lighthouse Place Premium Outlets. Most main streets have metered or free parking.

BY TRAIN

Taking the train from Chicago to Michigan City is simple. The South Shore Line leaves from Randolph Street Station and gets you to Michigan City in just under 2½ hours (the return trip is only 2 hours). The train departs for Michigan City every 2 hours from 8 AM to 8 PM and returns to Chicago every 2 hours from 5:20 AM to 9:20 PM. The train follows Lake Michigan through northwest Indiana. It makes two stops in Michigan City; the main station is at Carroll Avenue. A one-way fare is $6.85.

Amtrak runs a daily train that departs Chicago at 1:15 PM and arrives in Michigan City an hour later. A train returning to Chicago leaves Michigan City daily at 3:19 PM. The fare is $16–$42 round-trip, depending on how far in advance you book. The Michigan City station has no attendant.

TRAIN LINES **Amtrak** > Tel. 800/872–7245, www.amtrak.com. **South Shore Line** > Tel. 800/356–2079, www.nictd.com.

TRAIN STATIONS **Amtrak** > 100 Washington St., Michigan City, tel. 800/872–7245. **South Shore Line** > 503 N. Carroll Ave., Michigan City, tel. 219/874–4221 Ext. 247, www.nictd.com.

Visitor Information

CONTACTS **La Porte County Convention and Visitors Bureau** > 1503 S. Meer Rd., La Porte 46360, tel. 219/872–5055 or 800/685–7174, www.laportecountycvb.com. **Michigan City Chamber of Commerce** > 200 E. Michigan Blvd., Michigan City 46360, tel. 219/874–6221, www.michigancitychamber.com.

Woodstock

65 mi northwest of Chicago

3

By Joanne Cleaver

WOODSTOCK IS AMERICA'S EVERY SMALL TOWN as reflected in a rose-color rear-view mirror. A visit here is like taking a step back to a simpler time. With its 19th-centry town square—complete with a white gazebo and ringed with shops and an 1890s opera house—surrounded by historic Victorian homes, its a perfect weekend getaway. With its tidy shops and homey traditions, it's almost like walking into a movie set.

The directors of *Groundhog Day* thought so, too, which is why they picked Woodstock as the town where an irascible TV weatherman played by Bill Murray is doomed to repeat the same day over and over and over. Every Groundhog Day since, the local Chamber of Commerce has hosted tours of the sites where key scenes of the movie were played. Visitors on the other 364 days of the year can self-tour, courtesy of the plaques on key buildings that tip off the initiated as to the significance of each site.

But the town is more than the movie. The historic Woodstock Square is listed on the National Register of Historic Places. It's also the site of many festivals, weekly summer band concerts, car shows, craft and art fairs. Antiques buffs have found Woodstock and its environs emerge as a haven for everything from architectural artifacts to French imports, which are sold in shops on the square and on the city's outskirts.

Anchoring the Square is the 1890 steamboat gothic-style Woodstock Opera House. Inside are an art gallery, a restaurant and banquet facility, and the Chester Gould/Dick Tracy Museum—dedicated to Woodstock's most famous citizen and creator of the well-known comic strip. Two repertoire theater companies make their home here, and the operal house hosts the annual Woodstock Mozart Festival and a wide variety of year round musical and theatrical performances. Both structures were designated National Historic Landmarks in 1972. In the neighborhoods surrounding the square, you can take a self-guided walking tour of the fine examples of period homes.

At one time, a drive to Woodstock was synonymous with a drive to the country. Although development approaches from the south and east, Woodstock still sits in a moat of farmland, so you can pretend you're out in the country without having to drive too far.

WHAT TO SEE & DO

Challenger Learning Center Aspiring pilots and astronauts can get a feel for the air at this hands-on learning center. The center's jet flight simulator lets you pilot a Boeing 737 from Chicago's now-defunct Meigs Field to O'Hare. If you bring a group, you can run a two-hour simulation of a space mission at the center's two-room mission control center. The center does not hold regular hours of operation; you must schedule your visit in advance. > 222 Church St., Woodstock, tel. 815/338–7747, www.challengerillinois.org. $50 per ½ hr. By appointment only.

Chester Gould-Dick Tracy Museum Way back in the 1930s, an ambitious young cartoonist hounded the *Chicago Tribune* until its editors finally picked up one of his characters. The resulting strip, Dick Tracy, became a classic. This small museum displays
original drawings by Chester Gould, Tracy's creator, along with interactive exhibits
that enable you to discover you own inner cartoonist. > 101 N. Johnson St., in the Old
Courthouse Arts Center, Woodstock, tel. 815/338–8281, www.chestergould.org. Free.
Thurs.–Sat. 11–5, Sun. 1–5.
Old Court House Arts Center The Old Court House, built in 1857 and vacated in
1972, is now home to an art gallery with revolving exhibits. Past exhibits include a selection of landscapes done by local artists. > 101 N. Johnson St., Woodstock, tel.
815/338–4525. Thurs.–Sat. 11–5, Sun. 1–5.
Woodstock Opera House This restored 1890s opera house on Woodstock Square
hosts concerts, plays, and dance performances. The auditorium, with its horseshoe-
shape balcony, is on the second floor. Reservations are highly recommended, especially for such annual events as the July–August Mozart festival. If you're just passing
through, you can pop in for a quick look at the facility if the staff has the time to show
you around. > 121 Van Buren St., Woodstock, tel. 815/338–5300. Daily 9–5.

Sports

GOLF
Crystal Woods Golf Course The 18 holes of this course are in a relatively flat section
of the county. Weekend rates are $52 including cart rental. > 5915 S. Rte. 47, Wood-
stock, tel. 815/338–3111.
Plum Tree National Golf Course Besides 18 holes traversing rolling terrain, this facility, 8 mi northwest of Woodstock, also has practice ranges. Rates are $65 and include a
cart. > 19511 Lembcke Rd., Harvard, tel. 815/943–7474, www.plumtreegolf.com.

HIKING
Moraine Hills State Park Hiking, fishing, biking, boating, cross-country skiing, and
other activities are available at this park 12 mi southeast of Woodstock. You can rent
rowboats at the park for $18 a day for fishing and boating on Lake Defiance and the
Fox River. > 914 S. River Rd., McHenry, tel. 815/385–1624.

Shopping

Downtown Woodstock shopping comes alive on weekends, in and around Woodstock Square. Antiques, dolls, European foods, gifts, crafts, and country-casual
clothes are the mainstays. Side streets that spoke out from the square are also filled
with specialty shops and are worth exploring. Many stores are closed Monday; during
the off-season, many are also closed Tuesday or Wednesday.

Colonial Antique Mall Apart from the many antiques stores that abound in the
Woodstock area, this mall is among the best of the genre. Dealers cram their booths
with vintage jewelry, china, kitchenware, tools, linens, toys, and clothes. This is also a
good spot to find refinished antique furniture. > 890 Lake Ave., Woodstock, tel.
815/334–8960, www.colonialantiquemall.com. Daily 10–5.
Hebron Eight miles north of Woodstock on Route 47 is the tiny hamlet of Hebron.
The intersection of Routes 47 and 173 is populated by no fewer than six antiques and
collectibles shops, mainly of the *junque* genre.
Richmond Richmond lies 16 mi northeast of Woodstock. Just south of the intersection of Routes 173 and 31 is a cluster of antiques shops selling heirloom-quality silver,
crystal, furniture, restored vintage appliances, books, and other goods.

Stone Meadow Farm In May and October, Annie Grosvenor invites the public to meet local folk artists, artisans, furniture makers, jewelers, and farmers and to browse among their wares set up in her house and garden. In summer, potted flowers, garden accessories, and other warm-weather domestic gear prevail; in autumn, the theme is fall and holiday. You can buy baked goods to take home or for an impromptu picnic on-site. The farm is 4 mi southeast of Woodstock in the rolling hills of Bull Valley. > 2321 Cherry Valley Rd., Woodstock, tel. 815/455–6254.

Save the Date

FEBRUARY
Groundhog Days The celebration ends on February 2, which is the official Groundhog Day, but starts several days before, regardless of whether or not the event spans a weekend. > Tel. 815/338–2436.

MAY
Farmers' Market on the Square Every Saturday morning, local farmers and producers sell their foodstuffs in Woodstock Square. > Tel. 815/338–2436.

JUNE
Dick Tracy Days Band concerts, a drum-and-bugle-corps pageant, and a parade are some of the activities at this festival that takes place for five days near the end of the month in Woodstock Square. The parade is free, but the drum-and-bugle-corps pageant costs $10. > Tel. 815/338–2436.

JULY
Woodstock Folk Festival At this mid-July festival, Woodstock Square is set up with multiple stages, where storytellers hold forth and folk musicians strum. > Tel. 815/338–4245, www.woodstockfolkmusic.com.

JULY–AUGUST
Mozart Festival Symphony performances of works by Mozart and his contemporaries are given at the Woodstock Opera House the last weekend in July and first two weekends of August. > Tel. 815/338–5300.

OCTOBER
Annual Autumn Drive During the third weekend in October, you can visit approximately 16 farms along Garden Valley Road and take part in a variety of activities—fall harvests of pumpkin and squash; and sales of art, antiques, crafts, and food. > Tel. 815/568–8823.

NOVEMBER
Lighting of the Square and Christmas Parade The mayor throws the switch on the decorated square. A day or two later, Santa arrives, as scheduled. > Woodstock, tel. 815/338–2436.

WHERE TO STAY

Days Inn Woodstock You're 1 mi from the square and opera house when you stay at this chain motel. Family attractions and restaurants are nearby. > 990 Lake Ave., Woodstock 60098, tel. 815/338–0629, fax 815/338–0895, www.daysinn.com. 40 rooms, 4 suites. Restaurant, cable TV, indoor pool, gym. AE, D, DC, MC, V. CP. ¢–$
Holiday Inn Express This motel 1 mi south of downtown has a 24-hour coffee and juice bar. Rooms are spacious, and the hotel is convenient to both Woodstock and golf destinations. > 1785 S. Eastwood Dr., Woodstock 60098, tel. 815/334–9600, fax

815/334–9614, www.ichotelsgroup.com. 51 rooms. Cable TV, indoor pool, gym, hot tub, laundry facilities, Internet, no smoking rooms. AE, DC, MC, V. CP. **$**

Town Square Inn Renovated in 2002, this European-style inn is on the second floor of a turn-of-the-20th-century building on the square. Two suites overlook the square, and decor mixes antiques and contemporary furnishings with bright yellow and blue walls. > 112½ Cass St., Woodstock 60098, tel. 815/337–4677, www.townsquareinn.com. 3 rooms, 2 suites. AE, DC, MC, V. BP. **$$–$$$**

WHERE TO EAT

Angelo's Restaurant At this hometown café, neighbors sit in vinyl booths and swap gossip over a bottomless cup of coffee and a light omelet or crisp club sandwich. > 117 Van Buren St., Woodstock, tel. 815/338–0180. Reservations not accepted. No credit cards. **¢–$**

Harvest Moon Cafe Tucked into a Victorian building that overlooks the square, you can watch the goings-on through lace curtains while perusing a menu that includes grilled salmon, pasta, tenderloin, and wild game. > 113 S. Benton St., Woodstock, tel. 815/334–9166. DC, MC, V. Closed Sun. and Mon. No lunch Sat. **$–$$$$**

Huntley Dairy Mart Indulge your craving for a hand-built sundae at this drive-in, 6 mi south of Woodstock on Route 47. Fried food rounds out the menu. > Rte. 47, Huntley, tel. 847/669–5737. No credit cards. Closed in winter. **¢**

Jailhouse Restaurant The slammer theme is played to the hilt here, with meals served in cells of the original city jail. The restaurant dishes up hearty midwestern fare, such as grilled pork chops and steaks. > 101 N. Johnson St., Woodstock, tel. 815/334–9450. AE, MC, V. Closed Mon. **$$–$$$**

Rainault's With decor that's more French country than German, this eatery prepares German-American classics. The chicken schnitzel is terrific; salads are innovative. > 108 Case St., Woodstock, tel. 815/337–7700. AE, DC, MC, V. Closed Wed. **$–$$$**

Sweet William's Tea Room Light lunches and tea classics are served in a parlor with lace curtains and flowery decor. In summer, tea is served on the lawn. Try the quiche or a salad. > 115 N. Johnson St., Woodstock, tel. 815/337–0765. AE, MC, V. Closed Mon. No dinner. **$–$$**

ESSENTIALS

Getting Here

You can drive or take a train to Woodstock. Train service links Chicago's downtown with Woodstock's downtown. Driving is a must if you intend to go antiquing or take in any of the numerous farm stands that sprout up in summer and fall. There is no bus or air service to Woodstock.

BY CAR

To get to Woodstock take I–90 to Route 47 north. Take Route 47 to Route 14 west, which angles northwest. Then turn north on Dean Street to arrive at the square. Woodstock is easy to navigate; everything is oriented to the square. Parking can be tight around the square, but you can find unlimited free public parking on the blocks surrounding the square. Try those first if you are there for a special event. Parking on the square is limited to two hours.

BY TRAIN

The Union Pacific Northwest line, operated by Metra, links Chicago to Wood-stock. Trains depart from Ogilvie Transportation Center at Canal and Madison in the Loop. In Woodstock, the station is one block north of the town square.
TRAIN LINE **Metra** > Tel. 312/322–6777, www.metrarail.com.
TRAIN STATION **Woodstock Station** > 90 Church St., Woodstock, tel. 815/338–4300.

Visitor Information

CONTACTS **Woodstock Chamber of Commerce and Industry** > 136 Cass St., Woodstock 60098, tel. 815/338–2436, fax 815/338–2927, www.woodstockilchamber.com. **Woodstock Fine Arts Association** > Box 225, Woodstock 60098, tel. 815/338–5300.

Lake Geneva

73 mi northwest of Chicago

4

By Joanne Cleaver

GREAT SHOPS, RESTAURANTS, CANDY STORES, and striking Geneva Lake greet you as you enter this popular resort community, settled in 1840 amid rolling hills and a lake. The lake itself was formed 18,000 years ago, when the last of the many glaciers retreated to the north, leaving a moraine of gravel hills.

It was in this setting that Christopher Payne, a pioneer settler from Belvidere, Illinois, established a claim for the water power at the White River outlet in 1836. He built the first log cabin, the site of which is marked by a boulder and a plaque on Center Street just north of the river. Sawmills sprung up and lake shore logs and walnut trees were floated to the mills and cut into lumber, from which the town was built. With a thriving milling business, the town drew immigrant settlers from New England and New York. Most arrived by steamboat or sailboat, via the Erie Canal through the Great Lakes, embarking at Milwaukee or present-day Kenosha. By 1840, the town was comprised of two hotels, two general stores, three churches, and a distillery added to the mills, cabins, and houses.

Wealthy Chicago industrialists and their families first began to come here just after the Civil War. Usually, the wives and children would head north for the summer when the city's heat began to get oppressive; on weekends the businessmen would take the train up from Chicago to join them. Families with such recognizable names as Wrigley (chewing gum), Schwinn (bikes), and Maytag (washing machines) all had estates on the lake, and in some cases still do. Many of the extensive plots, however, were sold and broken up plots during and after the Great Depression. Most of the estates that remain are generally on private roads; the best way to see them is either from a boat cruise or on a public footpath that surrounds all 21 mi of the lake.

Although a lot has changed in Lake Geneva since the Gilded Age, when it earned the name "Newport West" for its many wealthy summer people, the town's main draw remains the same—the lake itself. Technically called Geneva Lake to distinguish itself from the city that surrounds its northeast corner, this spring-fed body of water is the second deepest in Wisconsin—144 feet at its deepest point. Boating, water-skiing, parasailing, sailing, swimming, and fishing all continue to bring people to the lake.

Even if you've exhausted the aquatic possibilities for the moment, there's much more to explore in town. Many worthwhile restaurants, gift stores, galleries, clothing stores, and coffee shops are along and off of Lake Geneva's Main Street (Route 50). Be sure to check out the town's library, a single-story building built by a student of Frank Lloyd Wright. Directly on the lake, both Library Park and Big Foot Beach State Park are a good places to take a rest or to get a snack before setting out for something new.

The town is also know for its notable residents, both past and present. Lake Geneva is home to cartoonists Joe and Jay Martin, writers of the "Mr. Buffo", "Willy'n Ethel," and "Tommy" comics. Sidney Smith, creator of the Andy Gump comic strip, also lived here. The Grand Geneva Resort & Spa was once Hugh Hefner's Playboy Club & Resort. The soap opera "The Young and The Restless" was developed here by its producers/creators William Bell and Lee Phillips while they lived in Lake Geneva.

WHAT TO SEE & DO

Big Foot Beach State Park Named for Chief Big Foot of the Potowatomi tribe, this state park is within the Lake Geneva city limits and has camping, hiking, shaded picnic areas, and a sand beach with 1,900 feet of lake frontage. > 1452 Rte. H, Lake Geneva, tel. 262/248–2528, www.dnr.state.wi.us. $7. 3rd Mon. in May–Nov. 1.

Geneva Lake This 5,000-acre lake provides a plethora of water activities and spectacular shorelines. This area was the site of President Calvin Coolidge's summer White House. > 201 Wrigley Dr., Lake Geneva, tel. 800/345–1020. Free. Daily.

Geneva Lake Cruise Line Narrated boat tours of historic Geneva Lake and Dixieland cruises leave from the Riviera Docks. The boats are also used for one of the most unusual—and daring—mail-delivery services in the nation: carriers leap between docks and moving boats to speed the mail to its rightful recipient. > 812 Wrigley Dr., Lake Geneva, tel. 262/248–6206 or 800/558–5911. $11–$45. May–Oct., daily.

Geneva Lake Shore Path One of the most popular tourist attractions in this area is a 20.6-mi path that winds around the lake. You can see mansions from the path, which is accessible through any public park on the lake. A map, called "Walk, Talk & Gawk" gives directions and points of interest. Shorter walks are also mapped out, including an easy 2-mi route. Maps are available free at the Lake Geneva Convention & Visitors Bureau at 201 Wrigley Drive, across from the pier. > Lake Geneva, tel. 800/345–1020. Free. Daily.

NEARBY

The Fireside About 30 mi northwest of Lake Geneva, the Fireside dinner theater has presented musicals and plays for more than two decades. The restaurant serves steaks, chicken, and pasta in a kitschy environment replete with plastic ferns and tiny streams that trickle among the tables. > Rte. 26, Fort Atkinson, tel. 920/563–9505 or 800/477–9595, www.firesidetheatre.com.

Old World Wisconsin This state historic society museum, 30 mi north of Lake Geneva, is made up of more than 50 authentic farmhouses, barns, and village shops. Originally scattered throughout the state, these buildings were moved here and reassembled on this site. The buildings are grouped into an 1870s crossroads village and ethnic farmsteads with household and farm implements, such as butter churns. Costumed interpreters stir up corn bread, let you dig in the garden for potatoes, and handle horses. The Clausing Barn restaurant revives you with its hearty chowders and sandwiches. > S103 W37890 Rte. 67, Eagle, tel. 262/594–6300, www.wisconsinhistory.org. $13. May–Oct., daily 10–4.

Sports

BOATING

Gordy's Recreation Learn to water-ski here, or rent equipment for skiing and boating. > 320 Lake St., Fontana, tel. 262/275–2163, www.gordysboats.com.

Jerry's Marine Pontoons, WaveRunners, parasailing equipment, and charter cruises are all available at this company's four locations on Lake Geneva, Como Lake, and Delavan Lake. > Tel. 262/275–5222.

Marina Bay Boat Rental At the downtown lakefront, this is as convenient as it gets for renting speedboats, pontoons, WaveRunners, and Jet Skis. > 30 Wrigley Dr., Lake Geneva, tel. 262/248–4477.

Watercraft Rentals of Lake Geneva Here you can rent WaveRunners, speedboats, and pontoons from a marina 1 mi south of Lake Geneva. > N2062 Rte. 120, Lake Geneva, tel. 262/249–9647.

FISHING

Area lakes are rife with large- and smallmouth bass, trout, walleye, and northern pike. Local guides are adept at leading visitors to spots where the catch of their choice abound.

Lake Geneva Fishing Guide Service This service takes small groups out fishing for walleye. > N1704 Elm, Lake Geneva, tel. 262/248–3905, www.lakegenevafishing.com.

Robert's Lake Geneva Guide Service Small groups are equipped with everything they need, from worms to poles, for all species of fish. > Tel. 262/763–2520.

Rushing Waters Fisheries About 25 mi northwest of Lake Geneva, this fish farm harbors rainbow trout. It's hard not to catch one. > N301 Rte. H, Palmyra, tel. 800/378–7088, www.rushingwaters.net.

GOLF

Abbey Springs The parklike grounds here, 10 mi from Lake Geneva, have 18 holes and overlook the south side of Geneva Lake. Weekend fees start at $90 and include cart rental. > Country Club Dr., Fontana, tel. 262/275–6111, www.abbeysprings.com.

Aurora University Golf Course The course emphasizes family outings and golf lessons; weekend fee is $21.50 for the 18-hole course. > Rte. 67 at Lakeshore Dr., Williams Bay, tel. 262/245–9507.

The Brute Stamina is required to make it to the end of this 18-hole course, one of the longest courses in the Midwest. Fee of $135 includes cart rental. > Grand Geneva Resort, 7036 Grand Geneva Way, Lake Geneva, tel. 262/248–8811, www.grandgeneva.com.

Evergreen Golf Club With 27 championship holes, bunkers, and challenging terrain, the course is known for its difficulty. Fees are $35 plus golf rental. > N6246 U.S. 12, Elkhorn, tel. 262/723–5722.

Geneva National This complex consists of three courses comprising 54 holes, a lodge and tavern, and meeting facilities. Fees vary by season, ranging from $60 to $125. > Rte. 50 at Como Lake, Lake Geneva, tel. 262/245–7000, www.genevanationalresort.com.

The Highlands This course is designed in the "Scottish style," where greens are smaller and the terrain mimics that of Scotland. The fee of $125 includes cart rental. > Grand Geneva Resort, 7036 Grand Geneva Way, Lake Geneva, tel. 262/248–8811, www.grandgeneva.com.

Hillmoor Golf Club This venerable club is on the east side of town on a hillside. Fees for the 18 holes range from $39 to $55. > 333 E. Main St., Lake Geneva, tel. 262/248–4570, www.hillmoor.com.

HORSEBACK RIDING

Fantasy Hills Ranch At this ranch, 8 mi west of Lake Geneva, trails traverse hills and fields for equestrians of all ability levels. > 4978 Town Hall Rd., Delavan, tel. 262/728–1773, www.fantasyhillsranch.com.

Lake Country Riding Stable Ponies and carriages are available for the horse-shy. The stable runs trail rides year-round. > 5065 Rte. 50, Lake Geneva, tel. 262/728–6560.

Shopping

Delavan About 10 mi west of Lake Geneva, Delavan is quieter, calmer, and provides a plethora of antiques shops. Tommy Gun's Antique Mall (tel. 262/740–1400) is one of the best of the genre, with high-quality collectibles and furniture spread out over two levels.

Lake Geneva From made-in-front-of-you fudge to classic women's resort wear, you can get it all in Lake Geneva's shop-filled downtown. Shops spread out to the surrounding blocks, so explore thoroughly to scope out all the possibilities. Ice cream, lemonade, and fudge are available on nearly every block, inviting you to settle down on a park bench and indulge in some people-watching.

Route 50 Lining Route 50 near Lake Geneva, farm stands sell everything from lettuce and pumpkins to homemade jams, pickled onions, relish, chutney, honey, and other foodstuffs. Most are open midsummer through mid-October. Berry farms are open seasonally (mid-June for strawberries, mid-July for raspberries); usually you can drop in to pick a few pints or simply buy some baskets of already-picked berries.

Walworth About 15 mi southwest of Lake Geneva on Route 67, the tiny town of Walworth has some excellent antiques and specialty shops. Worth the drive is On the Square Antique Mall, which sells only genuine vintage items and antiques.

Save the Date

JANUARY

Winterfest On the first weekend of the month, downtown fills with food stands, entertainment, a winter carnival, a lighted-torch parade, fireworks, and kids' activities, not to mention the U.S. National Snow Sculpting Competition. > Tel. 262/248–4416.

JULY–AUGUST

Concerts in the Park Every Thursday in Flat Iron Park, local groups perform; jazz bands are a popular draw. > Tel. 262/248–4416.

AUGUST

Art in the Park A juried art show takes over Library Park, on the lakefront. Paintings, drawings, and photography prevail. > Tel. 262/249–7988.

Venetian Festival A carnival, entertainment, food, a lighted-boat parade, and fireworks light up the lakefront on the third weekend of the month. > Tel. 262/248–6646.

DECEMBER

Christmas in the Country Christmas decorations, horse-drawn carriage rides, downhill and cross-country skiing, food, and entertainment are on tap Christmas week at the Grand Geneva Resort. > Tel. 800/558–3417, www.grandgeneva.com.

WHERE TO STAY

Ambassador This single-story hotel is on 10 wooded acres. Its spacious lobby has a large brick fireplace and a stained-glass window. Next door there's a miniature golf course. > 415 Wells St., Lake Geneva 53147, tel. 262/248–3452, fax 262/248–0605. 18 rooms. Some in-room hot tubs, some refrigerators, cable TV, pool, hot tub, sauna, business services; no smoking. AE, D, MC, V. CP. **$**

Bella Vista Suites At this downtown hotel, many of the suites face Geneva Lake and most have balconies. Continental breakfast is delivered in baskets to each room. Built in 1998, the hotel is decorated in light colors. > 335 Wrigley Dr., Lake Geneva 53147, tel. 262/248–2100, www.bellavistasuites.com. 39 suites. Refrigerators, microwaves, kitchens, in-room VCRs, indoor pool, hot tub. AE, D, DC, MC, V. CP. **$$$$**

Best Western Harbor Shores Rooms overlook either Geneva Lake or a parking lot, but its downtown location can't be beat. Many rooms have balconies. > 300 Wrigley Dr., Lake Geneva 53147, tel. 262/248–9181 or 888/746–7371, www.bestwestern.com. 108 rooms. Restaurant, room service, microwaves, refrigerators, cable TV, 2 pools (1 indoor), gym, hot tub, meeting rooms, no-smoking rooms. DC, MC, V. CP. ¢–$$$

Case's Turn of the Century Bed & Breakfast The owner of this Victorian farmhouse accumulated furniture and objets d'art during her first career as an antiques dealer, so the entire house is jammed with china, dolls, and other historic items. Breakfast is served at little café tables on the spacious back deck. The bed-and-breakfast is on the north side of Geneva Lake but does not overlook the lake. > N1599 Hillside Rd., Lake Geneva 53147, tel. 262/248–4989, casesbnb.com. 4 rooms. MC, V. BP. $–$$$

Cove of Lake Geneva Steps from the marina, pier, and beach, and two blocks from Main Street, the Cove houses one- and two-bedroom suites with balconies that overlook its complex or its parking lot. Suites are spacious and decorated with modern furnishings; some suites also have gas fireplaces. The outside pool includes a water play area for young children. > 111 Center St., Lake Geneva 53147, tel. 262/249–9460 or 800/770–7107, fax 262/249–1532, www.cove-lake-geneva.com. 220 suites. Restaurant, kitchenettes, cable TV, in-room VCRs, 2 pools (1 indoor), hot tub. DC, MC, V. $–$$$$

French Country Inn Part of this old-world charmer on the shores of Lake Como (less than a mile from Geneva Lake) was built in Denmark for Chicago's Columbian Exposition in 1893; you can still see the original furnishings and cherrywood throughout the main building. All rooms have lake views. Golf is nearby. Three buildings—one Victorian, two modern—comprise the complex. All rooms face Lake Como. > 4190 West End Rd., Lake Geneva 53147, tel. 262/245–5220, fax 262/245–9060, www.frenchcountryinn.com. 32 rooms. Restaurant, cable TV, pool, beach, business services. MC, V. BP. $$–$$$$

General Boyd's Bed and Breakfast A former farmstead on the northern shore of Geneva Lake, but not overlooking it, this rambling federal house is meticulously furnished with comfortable antiques. Classic timber-pegged barns, 20 varieties of trees, and perennial and wildflower gardens accent the property, which is dominated by native white-oak trees. A spacious living room with a large fieldstone fireplace, a dining room, and a library enrich its interior. > W2915 Rte. BB, Lake Geneva 53147, tel. 262/248–3543 or 888/248–3543, fax 262/248–3362, www.generalboydsbb.com. 4 rooms. No room phones, no room TVs. MC. BP. $

Geneva Inn On the northern shore of Geneva Lake, this inn is well away from the bustling downtown. Rooms are lavishly decorated in a variety of styles from colonial to cabbage-rose Victorian. Some rooms have lake views, and all have balconies. Its Grandview restaurant, which overlooks Geneva Lake, is open to the public for lunch and dinner but only to guests for breakfast. Boat slips are available for rent. > N2009 Rte. 120, Lake Geneva 53147, tel. 262/248–5680, fax 262/248–5685, www.genevainn.com. 37 rooms. Restaurant, cable TV, in-room VCRs, some in-room hot tubs, meeting rooms. AE, D, DC, MC, V. CP. $$$–$$$$

Golden Oaks Set on a hillside above the downtown of Lake Geneva, this circa-1856 Victorian mansion was renovated in 2002. Inside are parlors, solariums, and patios to relax in. Many rooms have elaborate bathrooms and four-poster or curvy iron headboards. Ferns, side tables, and bric-a-brac abound. Breakfast is served in the dining room and in a sunny garden room. > 421 Baker St., Lake Geneva 53147, tel. 262/248–9711, fax 262/248–2996, www.goldenoaksmansion.com. 6 rooms. AE, DC, MC, V. BP. $$–$$$$

Grand Geneva Resort Originally a Playboy resort, the Grand Geneva is considerably more sedate these days. The main hotel has decks and lounge areas overlooking the golf courses. The spa and sports complex, renovated in 2002, has indoor tennis, rock climbing, and spa services, from manicures to hot-rock treatments. The resort is renowned for its challenging golf courses. Timber Ridge is a family-oriented, all-suites hotel with a built-in water park, which includes a three-story enclosed water slide that curves outside the building then back in. If you stay at the Grand Geneva lodge, you can buy all-day passes to the Timber Ridge water park. A shuttle circulates to take you to the facilities. The entire complex is on the eastern outskirts of Lake Geneva. The site also includes a condo complex, whose owners also use the sports facilities and restaurants. > 7036 Grand Geneva Way, Lake Geneva 53147, tel. 262/248–8811, fax 262/249–4763, www.grandgeneva.com. Main lodge: 355 rooms; TimberRidge: 225 suites. 4 restaurants, in-room data ports, cable TV, in-room VCRs, driving range, 2 18-hole golf courses, putting green, 6 outdoor and 4 indoor tennis courts, 3 pools, gym, hot tub, spa, boating, bicycles, cross-country skiing, downhill skiing, bar, children's programs (ages infant–14), playground, business services, airport shuttle. AE, D, DC, MC, V. $$$$

Lake Lawn Lodge The rooms in this sprawling complex on Lake Delavan vary in size, quality, and motif. The resort staff organizes many outings and activities daily, ranging from golf lessons on the resort's own course to swimming in the lake and children's activities. The Lake Lawn Princess, the lodge's own boat, makes one-hour cruises around the lake. Shuttle services can be arranged as needed to get you to Lake Geneva and Delavan for shopping and other amusements. > 2400 E. Geneva St., Delavan 53115, tel. 262/728–7900, fax 262/728–2347, www.lakelawnresort.com. 284 rooms. 2 restaurants, some refrigerators, indoor pool, hair salon, spa, lounge, playground. AE, DC, MC, V. $$$–$$$$

Mill Creek Built in 2001 for family use, these suites have balconies and face either parking lots or a small creek. The hotel is just one block from Main Street in downtown Lake Geneva. > 123 Center St., Lake Geneva 53147, tel. 262/248–6647, fax 262/248–6598, www.millcreekhotel.com. 32 suites. Kitchenettes, some in-room VCRs, indoor pool, exercise equipment, hot tub. AE, DC, MC, V. $–$$

Pederson Victorian Bed & Breakfast This 1880 Victorian has gingerbread trim and is landscaped with wildflowers. The porches and the parlor are peaceful spots to curl up and read a book. The inn is 3 mi from downtown Lake Geneva. > 1782 Rte. 120 N, Lake Geneva 53147, tel. 888/764–9653, fax 262/249–9830, www.pedersonvictorian.com. 4 rooms. No room phones, no room TVs. MC, V. BP. $

T. C. Smith Historic Inn Bed & Breakfast A national Historic Landmark, this 1845 Victorian mansion gives a view of the lake but is also close to downtown. It's furnished with period antiques, museum-worthy paintings, and Oriental carpets. Outside is a water garden, a goldfish pond, and a gazebo. > 865 Main St., Lake Geneva 53147, tel. 262/248–1097 or 800/423–0233, fax 262/248–1672, www.tcsmithinn.com. 8 rooms. Bicycles. AE, D, MC, V. BP. $–$$$$

CAMPING

Big Foot Beach State Park Nearly in the middle of Lake Geneva proper, the park provides a rare opportunity to pitch a tent next to the lake and the downtown at the same time. A vehicle fee of $10 per day is required. > Rte. 120, Lake Geneva 53147, tel. 262/248–2528, www.reserveamerica.com. 102 tent sites. Showers. Reservations essential. MC, V. Closed Nov.–Apr. ¢

WHERE TO EAT

Gilbert's Overlooking the marinas and Geneva Lake from an expanded Victorian mansion, the restaurant specializes in creative uses of herbs. Amish chicken is a signature dish; other favorites include seared salmon with polenta and swordfish with pickles and caviar. > 327 Wrigley Dr., Lake Geneva, tel. 262/248–6680. AE, D, DC, MC, V. No lunch weekdays. **$$–$$$$**

Hogs & Kisses Generous appetizer portions are the norm at this popular local hangout, with lots of mirrors and neon signs. Burgers are the best. > 149 Broad St., Lake Geneva, tel. 262/248–7447. MC, V. **¢–$**

Popeye's on Lake Geneva This lake-view restaurant deck is filled with old ship parts, large maps, and tables topped with treasure maps. The bar is made out of a boat. Try the fried cod with potato pancakes and apple sauce, or the homemade broccoli-cheddar soup. Its Friday-night fish fry is a local institution. > 811 Wrigley Dr., Lake Geneva, tel. 262/248–4381. AE, D, MC, V. **$$**

Red Geranium Crisp-white walls painted with cheery red geraniums and punctuated with big windows make the dining room here seem particularly spacious and comfortable. The menu lists such creatively prepared classics as hickory-smoked boneless pork chops sided with roasted red potatoes, and fresh, barely blackened whitefish crusted with savory herbs. In summer, meals are served on the patio. > Main St. and N. Edwards Blvd., Lake Geneva, tel. 262/248–3637. MC, V. **$$–$$$**

Ristorante Brissago In the Grand Geneva Resort, this white-tablecloth restaurant overlooks the woods and fields of the resort's golf courses. Specialties include stuffed shrimp and orzo, and filet mignon. > Rtes. 50 and 21, Lake Geneva, tel. 262/248–8811. AE, D, DC, MC, V. Closed Mon. No lunch. **$–$$$$**

Scuttlebutt's Famous for its breakfast, which includes Swedish pancakes, the restaurant also is known for its oversize sandwiches, not to mention its sweeping view of Geneva Lake. > 831 Wrigley Dr., Lake Geneva, tel. 262/248–1111. MC, V. **$–$$**

ESSENTIALS

Getting Here

A car is the best option if you want to fully explore Lake Geneva and environs. There is no bus or train service directly to Lake Geneva.

BY CAR

From Chicago, take I–94 North to the Route 50 Kenosha/Lake Geneva West Exit. Drive west about 25 mi. Route 50 is Lake Geneva's main street. Parking in Lake Geneva is a perennial headache. If the actual lake is your top priority, stay in downtown Lake Geneva, where the beach, boat lines, restaurants, and shops are within walking distance. Some outlying hotels and inns run shuttles, regularly or as requested, to downtown Lake Geneva. If this is important to you, inquire about such services before you make your lodging reservations. Parking in the peripheral destinations, such as Delavan, is considerably less congested and is easy to manage.

Visitor Information

CONTACT **Lake Geneva Convention and Visitors Bureau** > 201 Wrigley Dr., Lake Geneva 53147, tel. 800/345–1020, www.lakegenevawi.com.

South Bend

90 mi southeast of Chicago

By Jenn Q. Goddu

5

SOUTH BEND HAS A POPULATION OF MORE THAN 100,000 so it may be a misnomer to call it a "college town," but it is difficult not to make this assessment. When the University of Notre Dame was founded back in 1842, South Bend and its sister city of Mishawaka were little more than trading posts along the St. Joseph River. The relationship between the towns and the university has only helped these two northern Indiana cities to prosper. Everywhere you go in South Bend, you're reminded of the "Fighting Irish." Restaurants, and not just the sports bars, proudly display photographs of past football coaches; stores even name their products after the sports greats or the school itself. Many street names recall legendary coaches or players. You might even spot some garden gnomes decked out in Fighting Irish gear.

But it wasn't the gridiron greats that truly shaped this city; entrepreneurs played a major role in its history. In 1852, the Studebaker brothers established a modest wagon repair and horseshoing shop. Their business ultimately evolved into an automotive giant known for its convertible with a bullet-nose grill before it closed in 1963. In the 1870s, the South Bend Iron Works, later known as the Oliver Chilled Plow Works, was turning out 300 plows a day using a patented process for chilling iron as it was poured. Before the end of the 19th century, its president, J. D. Oliver, had built a 1,300-seat opera house, a hotel, and a huge private mansion, Copshaholm. In the 1920s Vincent Bendix introduced a new company to South Bend, developing a self-starting device for automobiles, and later buying the patents for a four-wheel braking system that is now standard on most cars.

Power for some of these firms came from the East Race of the St. Joseph River. Since the 1960s, this area has been the focal point of a 52-acre development project combining older buildings with striking new structures; the waterway itself has been rehabilitated as a concrete-lined canoeing and kayaking course, complete with artificial rapids. The sleek glass Century Center, designed by architects Philip Johnson and John Burgee, soars above the white water of the old West Race.

Today, though, football reigns supreme. South Bend is home to the College Football Hall of Fame. The 1,250 acres of Notre Dame's campus has a number of historic landmarks commemorating the school's spiritual commitment and sports achievements. The golden dome of the university's Main Building can be seen for miles and is especially striking on a clear night. If you're on the south edge of campus you should also get a good view of the so-called "Touchdown Jesus," which is a mosaic of Christ on the wall of the university library. The head of Christ is 9 feet high and the mosaic is nearly 10 stories tall. Across the road is the smaller, but still beautiful, Saint Mary's College, one of the nation's oldest Catholic colleges for women.

South Bend's sister city, Mishawaka, spreads along the St. Joseph River in the middle of north-central Indiana about 5 mi downstream from South Bend. It is roughly half the size and has a population of about 42,000. It was once thick with the woods that inspired its name, which is thought to be a Potawatomi word for "thick woods rapids," but today it is thicker with big-box retailers. But this is more than just a place for Benders to quench a thirst for consumerism: more than a half dozen city parks line the riverbanks between the two cities. Mishawaka is also the home of the four-wheel-drive military troop and cargo vehicle known as the Hummer. Mishawaka's AM General Corporation was awarded a $1.2 billion contract to build 57,000 of these brawny vehicles in 1987, and today the car is the preferred SUV of some of Hollywood's richest and most famous.

WHAT TO SEE & DO

Bendix Woods Fifteen miles from South Bend, this suburban park is known for the giant hedge of pine trees that spells out "Studebaker" (legible only from the air). According to the *Guinness Book of Records* it is the world's largest living sign. Its 195 acres provides a plethora of wooded trails for hiking, picnic sites, and several playgrounds. > 32132 Rte. 2, New Carlisle, tel. 574/654–3155, www.sjcparks.org/bendix.html. Free. Daily 10 AM–sunset.

Century Center The glass-and-stone structure designed by Philip Johnson and John Burgee, completed in 1977, sits on 11 acres above the East Race of the St. Joseph River, towering over downtown. It is the site of special events, conventions, and meetings. The **South Bend Regional Museum of Art** (tel. 574/235–9102, $3, Tues.–Fri. 11–5, weekends noon–5) displays traveling exhibitions in its 5,000-square-foot gallery as well as a permanent collection of works by 19th- and 20th-century midwestern artists. The College Football Hall of Fame and the Marriott hotel are accessible via a skywalk. > 120 S. St. Joseph St., South Bend, tel. 574/235–9711, fax 574/235–9185, www.centurycenter.org. Free. Daily.

College Football Hall of Fame This interactive downtown museum is filled with pigskin pageantry. You can march with bands, cheer with cheerleaders, salute the mascots, and enjoy tailgating, homecoming, and other football activities. A 360-degree surround-sound theater shows game clips, the Hall of Champions recognizes 800 players, and a time line traces the history of the sport. Out front is a 35-yard artificial-surface football field with markings and a goalpost. > 111 South St., South Bend, tel. 574/235–9999 or 800/440–3263, www.collegefootball.org, fax 574/235–5720. $10. Daily 10–5.

East Race Waterway Built during the early 1900s, this section of the St. Joseph River has been turned into an artificial white-water course. Kayakers, canoeists, and rafters come here to challenge the rapids. Those who prefer staying dry can watch from the 5 mi of paved walkways that line the course. > 301 S. St. Louis Blvd., South Bend, tel. 574/235–9328. Daily.

Healthworks Kids can learn about health issues in this sprawling museum run by the Memorial Health foundation. The interactive exhibits explain pimples (push a button and watch it grow), the dangers of smoking, and the skeletal-muscular system. Also here is a skin-crawl wall and a brain theater, which provides a neat and noisy way of teaching kids about how this nerve center works. > 111 W. Jefferson Blvd., South Bend, tel. 574/287–5437. $5. Weekdays 9–5, Sat. noon–5.

Morris Performing Arts Center Built in 1922 as a vaudeville house, the Morris is a restored landmark theater in the city's downtown. It is home to the Broadway Theatre

League, South Bend Symphony Orchestra, and Southold Dance Theater. > 211 N. Michigan St., South Bend, tel. 574/235–9190, www.morriscenter.org. Free. Daily.

Northern Indiana Center for History The center includes Copshaholm, built in 1895 by J. D. Oliver, president of Oliver Chilled Plow Works. The elegantly furnished home is full of parquet floors, leaded-glass windows, and oak, cherry, and mahogany wood-work, and original furnishings. On the grounds is the Worker's Home Museum, which reflects the life of a working-class family in the 1930s. Other exhibits explore the history of the St. Joseph River valley from prehistoric times to the present, as well as the history of Notre Dame. In the Children's Museum, hands-on activities help in-terest young people in history. > 808 W. Washington St., South Bend, tel. 574/235–9664, www.centerforhistory.org. $6. Tues.–Sat. 10–5, Sun. noon–5.

Potawatomi Park This 50-acre park contains Potawatomi Zoo, which is home to more than 400 animals from five continents. Kids can ride a pony or pet a goat in the zoo farm. Among the park's many splendors are the **Potawatomi Greenhouse and Conservatories** (2105 Mishawaka Ave., 46615, tel. 574/235–9442, $1, weekdays 9–3:30, weekends 11–3:30). Three conservatories are open to the public year-round. A small tropical-bird sanctuary separates two conservatories, adjacent to which lies the desert dome, where cacti and succulents are displayed. Greenhouses, built in the 1920s, host three flower shows each year. > 500 S. Greenlawn, South Bend, tel. 574/235–9800, www.potawatomizoo.org. $4.50. Mid-Mar.–Dec. 1, daily 10–5.

Saint Mary's College Founded in 1844 by four Sisters of the Holy Cross from Le Mans, France, the college now enrolls around 2,000 students in undergraduate liberal-arts programs. The campus includes 275 acres of gardens, fields, woods, and walks along the Saint Joseph River. The college is across the street from Notre Dame. > U.S. 933 (Old U.S. 31/33), South Bend, tel. 574/284–4626, www.saintmarys.edu. Free. Daily.

South Bend Chocolate Factory Take a 20-minute tour of this chocolate factory housed, ironically, in a building where chocolate boxes were once manufactured. A video and exhibit in the lobby explain the development of chocolate. You can sample a chocolate right off the line, and if that whets your appetite for more, the on-site store sells some of the factory's 200 different chocolates. > 3300 W. Sample St., South Bend, tel. 574/233–2577 or 800/301–4961, www.sbchocolate.com. Free. Week-days 8–5, Sat. 8–3.

South Bend Civic Theatre This old redbrick firehouse in the Park Avenue District is home to South Bend's oldest continuously operating community theater. The theater stages such popular programs as *Fiddler on the Roof,* Neil Simon's *Rumors,* and the Pulitzer prize–winning drama *Proof,* as well as programs for children and a series of cutting-edge plays. Seating is raked and the theater is tiny, holding only 77. > 701 Portage Ave., South Bend, tel. 574/234–1112, www.sbct.org.

Studebaker National Museum The Studebaker brothers started out in covered wag-ons but they're best known for their automobiles. This museum tells the story of the now-defunct company via horse-drawn and motorized vehicles, photographs, and other artifacts. See a 1934 Bendix and the 1956 Packard Predictor concept car. > 525 S. Main St., South Bend, tel. 574/235–9714 or 888/391–5600, www.studebakermuseum.org. $5.50. Mon.–Sat. 9–5, Sun. noon–5.

University of Notre Dame The Catholic order of the Congregation of Holy Cross runs this coed, private university of 10,000 students with a 1,250-acre campus. Founded in 1842, it is as well known for its academics as it is for athletics and the legacy of famed football coach Knute Rockne. It offers bachelor's degree programs within the Colleges of Arts and Letters, Business Administration, Science and Engineering, and the School of Architecture. Master's and doctoral programs are available through the Graduate School, and professional studies include the Law School and an MBA program. Guided tours cover a half dozen sights and can be picked up at the Eck Visitors Center. > U.S. 33, South Bend, tel. 574/631–5000 or 574/631–5726, www.nd.edu. Free. Campus open daily; tours weekdays.

The **Basilica of the Sacred Heart** (tel. 574/631–7329, free, weekdays 9–11 and 1–4, Sun. 1–4) was built in 1886 in the shape of a Latin cross; it's ornately adorned with gold and brass as well as 19th-century paintings. The basilica's museum displays many artifacts from the Congregation of Holy Cross and the University's history. Home of Notre Dame's Fighting Irish football team since 1930, the **Notre Dame Stadium** (Juniper Rd. and Courtney La., tel. 574/631–5726, free) seats 80,795. Notre Dame football teams have produced seven Heisman Trophy winners, the most of any university.

There are two domes to the **Joyce Athletic and Convocation Center** (Juniper Rd. and Courtney La., tel. 574/631–5726, free), the home of Fighting Irish basketball, hockey, volleyball, fencing, and swimming, as well as the athletic department's administrative offices and the Sports Heritage Hall. The facility has served as a site for March Madness four times. A focal point of the university is the **Main Building** (Holy Cross Rd. and St. Mary's Rd., free) in the middle of campus. The Golden Dome administrative building, named for its distinctive architectural feature, contains murals depicting the life of Christopher Columbus. The dome is covered in 23-karat gold leaf which is regilded every 20 to 30 years.

The 14-story granite **Notre Dame Hesburgh Library** (Bulla Rd. and Juniper Rd., tel. 574/631–5252, free) holds 2 million volumes and can hold half the student body. The library is named for the legendary Theodore M. Hesburgh, who served as football coach between 1952 and 1987. The south facade of the library displays the "Word of Life" mosaic depicting Christ with his arms outstretched. It is aligned with the football stadium in such a way that it appears as though Christ is signaling "touchdown" and the mosaic is commonly referred to as "Touchdown Jesus." The 69,000-square-foot **Snite Museum of Art** (Juniper Rd., tel. 574/631–5466, free, Tues. and Wed. 10–4, Thurs.–Sat. 10–5, Sun. 1–5) houses an impressive collection of 21,000 art objects that includes Rembrandt etchings, 19th-century French paintings, European photographs, and works by American artists.

MISHAWAKA

Bethel College This evangelical Christian college offers a liberal arts education on a lovely campus nestled amidst giant oaks. The school is not entirely eclipsed by the Irish, its men's basketball team has won several NAIA championships. > 1001 W. McKinley Ave., Mishawaka, tel. 574/259–8511, www.bethel-in.edu.

Hannah Lindahl Children's Museum Exhibits on local history from prehistoric times to the present day are geared toward children. Highlights include a winding street that shows what Mishawaka might have looked in the mid-1800s, Native American artifacts, and a one-room schoolhouse. > 1402 S. Main St., Mishawaka, tel. 574/258–3056, www.hlcm.org. $1. Sept.–May, Tues.–Fri., 9–4; June, Tues.–Thurs. 10–2.

Merrifield Park–Shiojiri Niwa Japanese Gardens Landscape architect Shoji Kanaoka has created a 1-acre haven along the St. Joseph River with gracefully arched bridges over dry waterfalls and streams surrounding a tea house. Kanaoka is the same landscape architect who designed the Japanese Gardens at Walt Disney

Tailgating & Pigskin Passion

NOTRE DAME MAY HAVE ONE OF *the most renowned college football teams in the nation. The university and football have been practically synonymous, ever since coach Knute Rockne first brought national attention to the college as a football powerhouse in the 1920s. The spirit of success was subsequently sustained by seven Heisman Trophy winners and dozens more All-Americans who have competed here. Consequently, its tough to get a ticket for a Fighting Irish game.*

Since 1966 every Irish home game has sold out, with the exception of a Thanksgiving Day matchup with Air Force in 1973. That game was played on the holiday to accommodate national television, but the students weren't on campus that day. In 1997, 21,000 seats were added to the stadium—it's at 80,795 now—but the fans still heavily outnumber the seats. Every one of 11,000 students gets a ticket and faculty and staff also get passes. Since 1966, lotteries have been used to distribute tickets to alumni, but the demand always outnumbers available tickets.

You can get tickets from a broker before the game but expect to pay a premium. Depending on the opponent or the way the season has been going for the Irish, you may be able to buy some seats at the stadium on game day from students. Tailgating thrives in lots all around the stadium, *including the far-flung satellite lots. Although the university has cracked down to curb underage drinking, tailgating is an art in and of itself. Fans for some teams arrive in RVs days before the game, plant their flags, and start feasting and drinking right then and there.*

Once inside the stadium, you can see a sea of green over by the north goalpost. That's all the students—most of them dressed in an emerald green shirt sold at the campus bookstore at the start of each season. When the home team scores a touchdown, students bob up and down in the air as they are hoisted over the heads of their fellow celebrants. It's one of the joys of seeing a game live that doesn't come across when ND games are nationally televised. In 2004, the team is scheduled to play seven home games against Michigan (September 11), Washington (September 25), Purdue (October 2), Stanford (October 9), Boston College (October 23), Brigham Young (November 6), and Pittsburgh (November 13). As long as you can shout "Go Irish!" you'll fit right in.

World's Epcot Center. > 1000 E. Mishawaka Ave., Mishawaka, tel. 574/258–1664. Free. Daily.

Richard Clay Bodine State Fish Hatchery The hatchery releases fish into the St. Joseph River. It produces 225,000 steelhead trout and 350,000 3-inch Chinook salmon annually. You can explore four fish ladders, circular ponds, biofilters, and a wastewater lagoon. > 13200 E. Jefferson, Mishawaka, tel. 574/255–4199. Free. Weekdays 8–3:30.

Tours

Notre Dame Campus Tour Your guide will take you to the Basilica of the Sacred Heart, the Grotto, Hesburgh Library, the school's Main Building (with its distinctive Golden Dome) and the stadium. The free tours are conducted at 11 AM and 3 PM, weekdays throughout the year. In summer additional 9 AM and 1 PM tours are added. > 10 Eck Center, Notre Dame Ave., South Bend, tel. 574/631–5726.

Save the Date

JUNE

Summer in the City Festival This event held annually over a weekend in mid-June brings crafts, ethnic food, rides, entertainment, a car show, and a parade to Howard Park on the east side of South Bend's downtown. > Tel. 877/792–7687.

Summerfest This day in the park includes a walk-run, food, crafts booths, children's rides, games, and a free evening concert. Don't miss the pig race in Mishawaka's Merrifield Park. This festival is held the last weekend in June. > 600 E. 3rd St., Mishawaka, tel. 574/258–1664.

JUNE–AUGUST

Firefly Festival of the Performing Arts A critically acclaimed series of music, dance, and theater is presented under the stars every Saturday evening in summer in St. Patricks County Park on the north side of South Bend. > 111 S. St. Joseph St., South Bend, tel. 877/792–7687.

AUGUST

College Football Hall of Fame Enshrinement Festival The induction of new members into the College Football Hall of Fame is celebrated at the museum in early August with a FanFest that includes an autograph session, a game of flag football played by the new Hall of Famers, and a skills clinic for youngsters. > 111 S. St. Joseph St., South Bend, tel. 574/235–9999, www.collegefootball.org.

AUGUST–SEPTEMBER

Kee-Boon-Mein-Kaa This huckleberry harvest festival is hosted by the Potawatomi Indian Nation. Traditional native dancing is one of the highlights of this annual event held Labor Day weekend at St. Patrick's County Park in South Bend. > Tel. 877/792–7687.

WHERE TO STAY

Airport Days Inn & Suites This three-story concrete hotel, built in 1999, is across the street from the airport. Although the setting is barren, the inn is convenient to the South Bend airport but far enough away from the sounds of airplanes arriving or departing. > 23040 U.S. 20 W, Michigan City 46628, tel. 574/233–3131, fax 574/289–6187, www.daysinn.com. 60 rooms. In-room data ports, some microwaves, some refrigerators, indoor pool, hot tub, exercise equipment, laundry service, laundry facilities, business services. AE, D, DC, MC, V. CP. ¢–$$

Cushing Manor Inn Twelve-foot ceilings, ornate woodwork, and antiques fill this 1822 Second Empire mansion with a mansard roof, arched dormers, and rooms named for such literary lions as Charlotte Brontë, Louisa May Alcott, and Jane Austen. The porch swings are a great place to curl up and read your favorite book. The Tippecanoe restaurant and College Football Hall of Fame are five blocks away. > 508 W. Washington, South Bend 46601, tel. 574/288–1990 or 877/288–1990, fax 574/234–2338, www.cushingmanorinn.com. 5 rooms. In-room data ports, cable TV, business services; no smoking. AE, MC, V. BP. $–$$

Days Inn This motel is close to Notre Dame (1½ mi) and South Bend (2 mi). Many of the rooms overlook the parking lot, but this inn is set further back from the main strip than others in this hotel row, making it more peaceful. > 52757 U.S. 31 N, South Bend 46637, tel. 574/277–0510, fax 574/277–9316, www.daysinn.com. 180 rooms. In-room data ports, cable TV, pool, business services; no pets. AE, D, DC, MC, V. CP. ¢

English Rose Inn, Bed, Breakfast and Antique Shoppe Built in 1892, this Victorian home across the street from Tippecanoe Place has an antiques store on the first floor and rooms upstairs. Breakfast is delivered in a basket to your door, and rooms are filled with old lace and linen and stocked with robes, wine, and candy from a local merchant. > 116 S. Taylor St., South Bend 46601, tel. 574/289–2114 or 877/288–1990, www.englishroseinn.com. 7 rooms. Cable TV, in-room VCRs, shop; no kids under 12. MC, V. BP. ¢–$$

Holiday Inn City Centre This hostelry is downtown, one block from the Century Center. The rooms are on eight floors of the Valley American Bank Building and all have city views. It's the only high-rise building in South Bend's downtown core so you may even get a view of the St. Joseph River. > 213 W. Washington St., 8th–16th flrs., South Bend 46601, tel. 574/232–3941, fax 574/284–3715, www.holiday-inn.com. 176 rooms. Restaurant, room service, cable TV, indoor pool, massage, exercise equipment, bar, laundry service, business services, airport shuttle. AE, D, DC, MC, V. CP. $–$$

Holiday Inn–University Area A Holidome recreation center is the focal point of this motel ½ mi north of Notre Dame. The two-story building has a corporate office park feel to it and the rooms are convenient rather than cozy. > 515 Dixie Hwy., South Bend 46637, tel. 574/272–6600, fax 574/272–5553, www.holiday-inn.com. 229 rooms. Restaurant, picnic area, room service, cable TV, 2 pools (1 indoor), wading pool, exercise equipment, hot tub, bar, laundry facilities, business services, airport shuttle, some pets allowed. AE, D, DC, MC, V. CP. $

Inn at St. Mary's Rooms are large and papered in subdued hues in this hostelry at St. Mary's College campus and adjacent to Notre Dame's campus. Be sure to ask for a room on the Ivy Road side. This will win you a view of the campus instead of the toll road off-ramp. > 1408 N. Ivy Rd., South Bend 46637, tel. 574/232–4000 or 800/947–8627, fax 574/289–0986, www.innatsaintmarys.com. 150 rooms. In-room data ports, some in-room hot tubs, some microwaves, some refrigerators, gym, sauna, shops, bar, laundry service, laundry facilities, business services, airport shuttle. AE, D, DC, MC, V. CP. $–$$$

Knights Inn Two miles from the University of Notre Dame, this inn provides well-appointed ground-floor rooms at bargain prices. These small rooms are best for Notre Dame loyalists who simply must be in town for the football game tailgate parties. The higher your room number, the quieter it is as you get farther above from the main street. > 236 Dixie Way N, South Bend 46637, tel. 574/277–2960 or 800/418–8977, fax 574/277–0203, www.knightsinn.com. 106 rooms. Some in-room hot tubs, some kitchenettes, some cable TV, pool, business services. AE, D, DC, MC, V. CP. ¢–$$

Marriott A skywalk links this nine-story glass-and-steel downtown landmark to Century Center. Contemporary furnishings fill the rooms. Rooms overlook the river or an indoor atrium. > 123 N. St. Joseph St., South Bend 46601, tel. 574/234–2000 or 800/328–7349, fax 574/234–2252, www.marriott.com. 298 rooms. Restaurant, in-room data ports, cable TV, indoor pool, hot tub, exercise equipment, bar, business services. AE, D, DC, MC, V. CP. ¢–$$

Morris Inn of Notre Dame Handsomely appointed guest rooms with wing chairs in quiet lounge areas distinguish this inn in the center of the university's campus. Keep an eye peeled for the crucifix above every door, a reminder that this is a Catholic institution. > Notre Dame Ave., South Bend 46556, tel. 574/631–2000, fax 574/631–2017, www.themorrisinn.com. 92 rooms. Restaurant, picnic area, room service, some refrigerators, cable TV, 18-hole golf course, exercise equipment, bar, business services. AE, D, DC, MC, V. BP. $

Oliver Inn Bed and Breakfast South Bend's largest bed-and-breakfast, this gabled 1886 Victorian home rests on a wooded acre with a carriage house next door. Fireplaces and porches add quiet charm. Check out the dining room's vaulted ceiling or peek into the butler's pantry before heading up to your room, which might have a claw-foot tub or a four-poster bed. Breakfast is served by candlelight. It's ½ mi from Notre Dame Stadium. > 630 W. Washington St., South Bend 46601, tel. 574/232–4545, 888/697–4466 reservations, fax 219/288–9788, www.oliverinn.com. 9 rooms, 7 with bath. Picnic area, cable TV, putting green, business services, some pets allowed; no smoking. AE, D, MC, V. CP. **$–$$**

Queen Anne Inn A wraparound porch fronts this 1893 mansion. The house is filled with Victorian furnishings and crystal chandeliers, and the wooden bookcases in the library were designed by Frank Lloyd Wright. Be sure to check behind your room's mirror; one room has a wall safe hidden behind it. The inn is ½ mi from Notre Dame Stadium. > 420 W. Washington St., South Bend 46601, tel. 574/234–5959, 800/582–2379 reservations, fax 574/234–4324, www.queenanneinn.net. 6 rooms, 1 suite. Business services, airport shuttle; no smoking. AE, D, MC, V. BP. **¢–$**

Residence Inn by Marriott The all-suites hotel is in a quiet area 1 mi from the Notre Dame campus. It is a two-story inn adjacent to the St. Joseph River. Since it caters to travels staying for longer visits, the rooms are on the spacious side. > 716 N. Niles Ave., www.queenanneinn.net 46617, tel. 574/289–5555, fax 574/288–4531, www.marriott.com. 80 suites. Kitchenettes, microwaves, cable TV, pool, hot tub, exercise equipment, playground, laundry facilities, business services, some pets allowed (fee). AE, D, DC, MC, V. CP. **$–$$$**

Signature Inn Notre Dame is 1 mi from this two-story motel. A grand lobby outfitted with sports memorabilia gives way to small and nondescript rooms. If you're a fan of the Irish, check out the gridiron glory mural over the pool. > 215 Dixie Way S, South Bend 46637, tel. 574/277–3211, fax 574/277–3211, www.signature-inns.com. 123 rooms. In-room data ports, cable TV, pool, exercise equipment, hot tub, business services. AE, D, DC, MC, V. CP. **¢–$**

MISHAWAKA

Beiger Mansion Inn This four-story neoclassical limestone building modeled after a home in Newport, Rhode Island, was built as a summer home between 1903 and 1909. Rooms are furnished with Victorian antiques. Breakfast is served in the State Dining Room. A two-night stay is required over a Notre Dame football weekend. > 317 Lincolnway E, Mishawaka 46544, tel. 574/256–0365 or 800/437–0131, fax 574/259–2622, www.beigermansion.com. 6 rooms, 1 suite. Restaurant, cable TV, bar. AE, D, DC, MC, V. BP. **$–$$$**

Carlton Lodge Mishawaka This chaletlike motel resembles a mountain retreat, even though you're in the midst of Mishawaka and about 3 mi from the university. Expect florals, ferns, and blonde wood in your room. > 420 W. University Ave., Mishawaka 46545, tel. 574/277–2520, www.carltonlodge.com. 80 rooms. Cable TV, indoor pool, laundry services, business services. AE, D, DC, MC, V. CP. **$**

Courtyard by Marriott This three-story chain hotel is 3 mi from Notre Dame and 5 mi from the College Football Hall of Fame. The spacious rooms here have sitting areas and a desk at where you actually have enough room to do some work. > 4825 N. Main St., Mishawaka 46545, tel. 574/273–9900 or 800/321–2211, fax 574/272–0143, www.marriott.com. 78 rooms, 3 suites. In-room data ports, some in-room hot tubs, cable TV, indoor pool, laundry service, business services. AE, D, DC, MC, V. **$–$$**

Hampton Inn Notre Dame is 3½ mi from this three-story hostelry, which is also a block from Edison Lakes Corporate Park. This no-frills inn, with its quiet rooms, is well placed if you're planning to hit the big box stores or the mall. > 445 University Dr., Mishawaka 46545, tel. 574/273–2309 or 800/426–7866, fax 574/273–0258, www.hamptoninn.com. 62 rooms. Cable TV, some refrigerators, pool, gym; no pets. AE, D, MC, V. BP. ¢–$

Varsity Clubs of America Suites Hotel All the rooms are suites in this upscale hotel, 3 mi from the university. The hotel also displays rare ND memorabilia artifacts in its lobby and rooms, a few examples of which include uniforms from then and now, a mannequin dressed as a cheerleader, and a floor lamp dressed in a referee's outfit. A big-screen TV in the lobby enables you to catch the game from here if your tickets for the home game fall through. > 3800 N. Main St., Mishawaka 46545, tel. 574/277–0500 or 800/946–4822, www.ilxresorts.com. 62 rooms. Restaurant, in-room data ports, in room hot tubs, kitchenettes, pool, gym, business services. AE, D, DC, MC, V. $$–$$$$

WHERE TO EAT

Bibler's Original Pancake House Apple pancakes and a dozen different omelets are the specialties of this popular breakfast and lunch spot. Adorned in floral print wallpaper and lots of stained glass, the restaurant looks sort of like your grandma's kitchen. > 1430 N. Ironwood Dr., South Bend, tel. 574/232–3220. MC, V. No dinner. ¢–$

Carriage House Crisp white linens dress the tables of this candlelit restaurant in an old brick church in a country setting 15 mi northwest of downtown. You can dine under classic white umbrellas on a patio in fine weather. Entrées such as the beef Wellington, caramelized salmon, or veal piccata are served with house salad or the chef's featured soup. > 24460 Adams Rd., South Bend, tel. 574/272–9220. AE, DC, MC, V. Closed early Jan. and Sun. and Mon. No lunch. $$$–$$$$

Damon's This is one of a national chain of casual restaurants specializing in St. Louis–style ribs and other barbecue favorites. > 52885 U.S. 31 N, South Bend, tel. 574/272–5478. AE, D, DC, MC, V. $–$$$

East Bank Emporium Rich woodwork, touches of brass, and plants decorate this spacious, airy restaurant across the river from downtown South Bend and the Morris Performing Arts Center. The house cuts its own steaks; prime rib is the house specialty. Try the Bourbon Street Pie, a chocolate pecan pie splashed with bourbon. > 121 S. Niles Ave., South Bend, tel. 574/234–9000. AE, D, DC, MC, V. No lunch Sun. $–$$

Eastern Pacific Grille and Bar This trendy seafood and steak restaurant is near the end of the East Race Waterway. You can enjoy a river view while dipping your chips in crab salsa and waiting for your salmon, grouper, or New York strip steak to arrive. > 501 N. Niles Ave., South Bend, tel. 574/233–1300. AE, DC, MC, V. Closed Sun. and Mon. No lunch Sat. $$–$$$$

Heartland & Chicago Steak House Vintage black-and-white photographs of the Windy City and ticket stubs from bygone sporting events cover the walls of this Chicago-theme restaurant. The house specialty steaks are served with peppercorn or blue-cheese sauce. Grilled fish and pasta are also on the menu. The Heartland nightclub is next door. > 222 S. Michigan St., South Bend, tel. 574/234–5200. AE, DC, MC, V. ¢–$$

LaSalle Grill Bright paintings lend sophistication to this stylish restaurant in a vintage building downtown. The kitchen is known for its top sirloin steaks, but you might also find grilled ostrich, Amish chicken, or Indiana duckling on the ethnic-inspired menu that changes seasonally. > 115 W. Colfax, South Bend, tel. 574/288–1155 or 800/382–9323. AE, D, DC, MC, V. Closed Sun. No lunch. $$–$$$$

Sorin's at the Morris Inn When celebrities are in town for football games, they often have a meal in this college restaurant at Notre Dame. An institution in itself, its terraced dining room overlooks the campus. Murals on one wall depict Notre Dame's development through the years. Wood-grilled flavors dominate much of the menu. > Notre Dame Ave., South Bend, tel. 574/631–2000. Reservations essential. AE, D, DC, MC, V. Closed mid-Dec.–early Jan. **$$–$$$**

Sunny Italy Plates of spaghetti or ravioli are the standard at this family-owned Italian restaurant open since 1926. Specialties are the spaghetti in white clam sauce or shrimp ragout; steak, chops, and some seafood round out the menu. > 601 N. Niles Ave., South Bend, tel. 574/232–9620. MC, V. Closed Sun.–Tues. No lunch. **$–$$$**

Tippecanoe Place Tippecanoe Place occupies George M. Studebaker's lavish 40-room mansion, full of intricately carved woodwork and stained glass. The kitchen is known for its oven-roasted filet mignon medallions in whisky-peppercorn sauce. Seafood options are also available. > 620 W. Washington St., South Bend, tel. 574/234–9077. AE, DC, MC, V. No lunch Sat. **$$–$$$**

The Vine You can watch people playing on the College Football Hall of Fame's artificial gridiron from this sleek downtown restaurant. Pasta and pizza are standards on the menu but you can also order seasonal specialties. Eat inside or snag a steel stool and a café table on the sidewalk patio. > 122 S. Michigan St., South Bend, tel. 574/234–9463. AE, MC, V. Closed Sun. **¢–$$**

MISHAWAKA

Beiger Mansion Inn Restaurant In this neoclassical four-story mansion with a Victorian-style dining room, you can try such innovative dishes as chicken with cream sherry–soaked apricots and a sun-dried cranberry muffin; grilled lamb chops marinated in rosemary and anchovies; and mushroom and hazelnut soup. All desserts and breads are homemade. > 317 Lincolnway E, Mishawaka, tel. 574/256–0365 or 800/437–0131. Reservations essential. AE, D, DC, MC, V. Closed Sun. and Mon. No lunch. **$–$$**

Doc Pierce's A downtown landmark accentuated with dark wood and more than 60 Tiffany lamps, this restaurant is known for its four different sirloins and seafood dishes. > 120 N. Main St., Mishawaka, tel. 574/255–7737. AE, D, DC, MC, V. Closed Sun. **¢–$$**

Mishawaka Brewing Company Even the ales are named for Notre Dame sports legends here. Try a Four Horsemen Irish Ale brewed on-site at this microbrewery. The restaurant serves pub grub such as pizza, burgers, and calzones. You don't have to wait for a Friday-night fish fry here; fish-and-chips are served daily. > 3703 N. Main St., Mishawaka, tel. 574/256–9993. AE, D, DC, MC, V. **$–$$**

ESSENTIALS

Getting Here

Only 90 mi east of Chicago, South Bend is easy to get to and the drive is relatively pleasant. Once you get past the steel mills of northwest Indiana, the rural rolling hills on the Indiana Toll Road unfold. Greyhound has regular service to the city and Amtrak caters to commuters with its train schedule. The South Shore Line is slower, but has more frequent trains. The fastest way to get here is by plane from Midway or O'Hare, but the cost may be hard to justify when you consider the short distance.

BY BUS

Greyhound makes three trips daily to South Bend from Chicago. The trip takes 2 hours and 25 minutes. The return trip can take 1 hour and 40 minutes to 2 hours. There are four departures from South Bend for Chicago each day. The round-trip fare is $53.

BUS DEPOT **South Bend Regional Airport** > 4671 Terminal Dr., South Bend 46628, tel. 574/287–6542.

BUS LINE **Greyhound** > Tel. 800/229–9424, www.greyhound.com.

BY CAR

A car is convenient here, since South Bend is so spread out. To get here, you can take I–94 all the way into Indiana, exit at I–65, head north a few miles and get on the Indiana Toll Road (I–80 [I–90]). For $2, you can take the Chicago Skyway (I–90), which will get you here more directly and with less traffic; it meets up with the Indiana Toll Road. Here you pay 50¢ before getting to Portage, where you pick up a ticket, which you'll pay for when you exit the toll road. The most your toll will be for the rest of the trip is $2.20.

Three exits off the toll road will take you to South Bend and Mishawaka. The main route into the city is Exit 77. To get to Notre Dame turn right onto Michigan (Route 933). Make a left at Angela Boulevard, then a left at Notre Dame Avenue. Visitor parking is on the right side of Notre Dame Avenue. To get downtown just follow Michigan Avenue south. Plenty of metered parking is in the city center near the museums. Exit 83 takes you to the east end of Mishawaka. Take Capital Avenue south to Douglas Road. Go west to Main Street (Route 331) and head south. This will take you away from the shopping, through town, and to the St. Joseph River.

BY PLANE

The South Bend Regional Airport (SBN) is served by national and regional carriers. The flight from Chicago is 45–50 minutes. United Express has three flights, from Sunday through Friday, connecting South Bend with O'Hare airport; two additional flights are available on Saturday. ATA Connection flies from South Bend to Chicago's Midway airport seven times daily on weekdays; the schedule is cut back by one or two flights on weekends.

AIRPORT **South Bend Regional Airport** > 4477 Progress Dr., South Bend, tel. 574/282–4590, www.sbnair.com.

CARRIERS **ATA Connection** > Tel. 800/225–2995, www.ata.com. **United Express** > Tel. 800/241–6522, www.ual.com.

BY TRAIN

The South Shore Line connects South Bend, northwestern Indiana, and Chicago with regular service daily. The train departs from Randolph Station and makes more stops than Amtrak does as it travels along the scenic route of Indiana's National Dunes Lakeshore. The trip takes 2 hours and 20 minutes and costs under $20. Amtrak's schedule serves commuters best. It travels to South Bend two times daily at 5:35 PM and 7 PM. The trains returning to the city are at 7:01 AM and 8:43 AM. Round-trip fares are under $40. Both train lines arrive at the west end of the city at the South Bend Airport.

TRAIN LINES **Amtrak** > Tel. 800/872–7245, www.amtrak.com. **South Shore Line** > Tel. 800/356–2079, www.nictd.com.

TRAIN STATION **South Bend Train Station** > 2702 Washington Ave., South Bend, tel. 574/288–2212.

Visitor Information

CONTACTS **Eck Notre Dame Visitors Center** > Notre Dame Ave., 110 Eck Center South Bend 46617, tel. 574/631–5726. **South Bend/Mishawaka Convention and Visitors Bureau** > Commerce Center, 401 E. Colfax Ave., Suite 310 South Bend 46617, tel. 888/811–3875, www.livethelegends.org.

Starved Rock State Park

94 mi southwest of Chicago

6

By Kevin Cunningham

THE SECOND LARGEST OF ILLINOIS'S STATE PARKS, Starved Rock's 18 glacier- and stream-etched canyons, modest waterfalls, and access to the Illinois River make it one of the most popular outdoors destinations in the region. Starved Rock is the centerpiece of an enclave of parkland that includes Buffalo Rock State Park (across the river to the northeast) and the underrated Matthiessen State Park.

Starved Rock State Park is a strip of woodlands running parallel to the river. The rock that gave the park its name rises 140 feet, providing those making the climb an extraordinary view of the surrounding forest and the river. Activities and sports aside, one of the park's great appeals is that it invites you to explore cool and shady forests, shallow caves, and smooth sandstone bluffs. Sure, all of it is relatively easygoing—admittedly, this isn't Yosemite—but the area's contrast to the nearby flat prairie can have a jarring impact. It's a refreshing hint of wilderness, only a few miles from the interstate no less, especially in spring and after storms when the waterfalls are flowing.

The Rock, and the river it overlooks, played an important role in both Native American history and the Age of Exploration. Around AD 1000 local tribes came under the influence of the mound-building civilization centered at Cahokia, near modern-day St. Louis. Mounds, albeit less spectacular than those at Cahokia, have been discovered throughout the Illinois River valley. Some time later the Kaskaskias, a subtribe of the area's dominant Illiniwek, established a village at Old Kaskaskia, across the river from Starved Rock. They supported themselves through agriculture, supplemented by gathering and the bounty of a twice-yearly bison hunt.

In August of 1673, the French explorers Father Jacques Marquette and Louis Jolliet, on their way home from paddling the Mississippi, landed at Old Kaskaskia. Marquette returned two years later to establish a mission. Native tribes flocked to the area to trade with the French, occupying the canyons and the diaries of the awestruck Jesuits sent to convert them. Another explorer, Robert Cavelier de LaSalle, a man of greater ambition and a more military bent, built a fort atop the rock in 1682. He hoped to use it as part of a grand plan to colonize the Mississippi Valley. His successors preferred Peoria, however, and abandoned the fort. Fur traders and natives used it off and on until angry locals burned it down in 1721.

The name Starved Rock came out of the intertribal wars of the 1700s. The story, more fiction than fact, is nonetheless a grim legend. Stories say an Illiniwek murdered the Ottawa chief Pontiac, the leader of the famous rebellion against the British. The Ottawa, along with their allies the Potawatomi, declared war to avenge him. Eventually they laid siege to an Illiniwek group that had taken refuge atop a sandstone butte overlooking the river. Unable to escape, and expecting no quarter from their enemies, the Illiniwek starved to death—hence, Starved Rock.

In 1836, work began on the Illinois and Michigan (I & M) Canal from Lake Michigan to the Illinois River, which in turn fed into the Mississippi. The 12-year building time

allowed the railroads to catch up. Trains soon trumped barges in the lucrative passenger trade. The canal turned to commercial hauling and made a go of it, albeit with
diminishing returns, until 1933, when it was replaced by the Illinois Waterway.

The area's extensive public land means you can find an outlet for just about any of
your outdoor urges. You can camp throughout the area; Matthiessen State Park rents
cross-country skis for its wide, well-groomed trails; you can canoe or fish the Illinois
in many places; hiking trails are shady and maintained; Starved Rock keeps its own
stable for guided horseback rides through Matthiessen; other winter sports include
snowmobiling along the canal and ice-climbing in selected canyons.

Utica is the gateway to Starved Rock. Built as a canal town in the 1830s, it supplied
the limestone used to make the cement that built the lock and dam. Numerous casual restaurants and crafts businesses line Mill Street, making it a good refueling
stop for those who wish to stay close to the parks. Overnighters can choose from
bed-and-breakfasts, a few hotels, and nearby campgrounds.

Ottawa is east of the parks along I-80. Famous as the site of the first Lincoln-
Douglass debate, it prospered from the canal and later evolved into a manufacturing
center. Today, the town uses grant money for renovations, with an emphasis on its
commercial and historical legacy. Accommodations and dining are plentiful. Farther
west along I-39 are LaSalle and Peru. LaSalle was built on mining and related industries, but in the 1940s had a brief heyday as a gambling mecca nicknamed "Little
Reno." Peru's small historic neighborhood fronts a stretch of the Illinois River. Both
towns have restaurants, but the bulk of the lodging is in LaSalle.

WHAT TO SEE & DO

Starved Rock State Park Punctuated with bluffs, canyons, and waterfalls, Starved
Rock has spectacular views of the Illinois River and an abundance of recreational options. Thirteen miles of trails link a series of 18 canyons running alongside the Illinois
River. Well marked and maintained, the trails snake through shady forests. Although
you can set off on a 4- to 5-mi haul from the visitor center or either end of the park,
numerous trailheads let you sneak into some of the best canyons with a short hike.
On the well-traveled routes the going is fairly easy—steady descents, helpful stair-
ways—though be aware of some sheer drops. The interior trails, however, are
rougher and more challenging. Neither should be attempted in poor light. Keep in
mind that beneath the thick forest canopy twilight comes earlier than it does outside.

Waterfalls are at their most vigorous during the spring thaw or after hard rains. Conditions can vary, but falls often last longest at St. Louis, French, and LaSalle canyons.
In fact, if you can't wait, try the small parking lot at the trailhead leading to St. Louis
Canyon (accessible via the park's more southerly entrance from Route 178). No map
is necessary—just follow the trail.

To see the justly celebrated view from atop Starved Rock, climb the gently winding
ramp that starts behind the visitor center. To the east you can see Lover's Leap Overlook, a worthwhile reward for those starting on the interior trails, and the Starved
Rock Lock and Dam. East of Pontiac Canyon the trails more or less hug the river and
become less crowded. If you take the 4.7-mi hike from the visitor center to Illinois
Canyon at the east end, you can see a handful of overlooks for both the views and an
infusion of warm sunlight. The park's east end contains Council Overhang, a vaulting

History Underfoot

AROUND THE STATE PARKS signs tell you it's illegal to remove artifacts from the premises, and for good reason. The entire Starved Rock region has an extensive geological and archaeological history, all because of a singular relationship between water and an unpretentious rock called St. Peter's sandstone.

Around 9000 BC, when a Wisconsinan glacier retreated, it left behind doomed mastodons and odd foreign boulders—known as glacial erratics—that squat in fields throughout the upper Midwest. A lake formed in front of the retreating glacier, and the meltwater from it gushed into the valley of the Illinois River. Erosion eventually exposed the sandstone, and over the next several thousand years streams carved caves and canyons out of it at Starved Rock and Matthiessen parks.

Archaeologists believe Native Americans first camped atop Starved Rock during the Archaic Period and that it was continuously inhabited for at least 5,000 years. It's thought the early inhabitants used the Rock as a perch to watch for herd animals. Digs have yielded artifacts from the Archaic, Woodland, and Mississippian eras, as well as from the period after European contact. The early French explorers built their fort on the sandstone summit as a show of force against marauding Iroquois—and encouragement for local tribes to come and trade. Many who did so sheltered in caves scooped out of the sandstone.

St. Peter's sandstone proved useful in industry, too. Although when looking at the bluffs you may find it hard to imagine glass, St. Peter's sandstone is an excellent raw material for glassmaking. In the early part of the 20th century, glassworks in Ottawa turned sandstone into such products as colored glass for church windows, lamp shades, and Pullman cars. Perhaps most famous was the Peltier Glass Company, manufacturer of marbles. For decades millions of Ottawa nibs and shooters were used on playgrounds coast-to-coast.

shallow cave that's one of the park's more jaw-dropping highlights. Park in the paved lot off Route 71. The Overhang—definitely a can't-miss—is a short walk away. Much-photographed Kaskaskia Canyon is a quarter mile beyond.

Starved Rock has a range of activities including paddleboat rides, canoe rental, fishing (catfish, white bass, sauger, walleye, carp, and crappie), horseback riding, and camping (reservations essential May–October). Even though the bulk of visitors come in summer, Starved Rock keeps the trails open year-round. A lodge, restaurant, visitor center, and snack bar are on the grounds, and a concert theater opened in 2003. The main park entrance is 1 mi south of Utica on Route 178. A secondary entrance is on Route 71, a mile from where it crosses Route 178. The visitor center is roughly in the center of the park. > Box 509, Utica 61373, tel. 815/667–4726 or 815/667–4906, fax 815/667–5353. Free. Park: daily 5:30 AM–10 PM; visitor center: weekdays 9–5, weekends 9–6.

NEAR THE PARK

Buffalo Rock State Park Once an island, this park now sits on a promontory across the river from the eastern end of Starved Rock State Park. According to archaeological finds, Native Americans who once lived here traded with tribes as far away as Florida. Today, it's one of the best nature sites in the area. Buffalo Rock's most spectacular feature is the Effigy Tumuli, a series of five earthen sculptures representing animals native to the Illinois River. Park facilities include picnic areas, horseshoe pits, camping (primitive), and trails. Watch for a pair of dour-looking American bison meandering around their pasture near the baseball diamond. > Dee Bennett Rd. and Rte. 34, Ottawa, tel. 815/433–2220. Free. Daily dawn–dusk.

Donnelley/DePue State Wildlife Area and Complex Spread over two counties and 18 mi west of Starved Rock State Park, this 3,000-acre refuge has nature preserves and hiking and horse trails. You can fish and boat on Lake DePue. Those interested in exploring the wildlife areas should call the park office in advance; the areas devoted to nature preserves have restricted access. > 1001 W. 4th St., DePue, tel. 815/447–2353. Free. Daily dawn–dusk.

I & M Canal State Trail You can hike, bike, and snowmobile on the 61-mi network of trails between Rockdale and LaSalle, which you can access in Buffalo Rock State Park or off Canal Street in Utica, approximately 1 mi north of the west entrance to Starved Rock State Park. No open fires are allowed, and you can camp only in designated areas. > Buffalo Rock State Park, Dee Bennett Rd. and Rte. 34, Ottawa, tel. 815/942–0796. Free. Daily.

Illinois Waterway Visitor Center You can get up-close views of the Illinois River lock and exhibits on Illinois waterways at this center, 2 mi east of Utica and across the river (2 mi by road) from Starved Rock State Park. Most of the pamphlets, brochures, and other information are available here, as are public rest rooms. > 950 N. 27th Rd., Ottawa, tel. 815/667–4054, fax 815/667–4954. Free. Daily 9–5.

LaSalle County Historical Museum Built in 1848 as a general store, the building housing this museum in downtown Utica contains memorabilia from the area; the complex itself includes a historic schoolhouse, barn, and blacksmith shop. On display you can see furnishings from the homes of pioneers and the carriage Abe Lincoln took from Ottawa's train station to his debate with Stephen A. Douglas. It's also a good source for pamphlets and other information on the area. > Canal and Mill Sts., Utica, tel. 815/667–4861, www.lasallecountymuseum.org. $1. Apr.–mid-Dec., Wed.–Fri. 10–4, weekends noon–4; mid-Dec.–Mar., Fri.–Sun. noon–4.

Matthiessen State Park If Starved Rock is too crowded for you, the trails and canyons at this nearby park are an excellent alternative. Named for a prominent industrialist, Matthiessen State Park began as a private 176-acre park—it's now almost 2,000 acres. Matthiessen is actually divided into two parts: the Dells area to the north and the Vermilion River area to the south. For hiking, start in the Dells area, where a short walk to Cascade Falls leads you toward the colorful rocks and wildlife in the shady canyons of the Lower Dells. The 3.2 mi of trails are well marked. Those in the upper areas are fairly easy; but those in the interior require more caution, especially in wet conditions. The odors of pine and honeysuckle mingle in the air and wildflowers bloom throughout the warm-weather months. Animal life includes flying squirrels, woodpeckers, and red-tailed hawks in the trees, and salamanders and toads on the moist canyon floors. A covered picnic area (with nearby phones and rest room facilities), archery range, cross-country ski rental facilities, and a horseback campground are here as well. Kids can romp around on a miniature fort built to honor the French forts of the 17th and 18th centuries. At **Starved Rock Stables** (Rte. 71, 1 mi west of Rte. 178, tel. 815/667–3026, $20 per hr, Wed.–Fri. noon–4, weekends 10–4, no credit cards), one-hour guided trail rides leave for Matthiessen State Park three times a day Wednesday–Friday and four times a day on weekends, weather permitting. Reservations are essential on weekends. The Vermilion River area has the bulk of the parking (even horse parking) and more trails, including trails along the river. > Rte. 178, Utica, tel. 815/667–4868 or 815/667–4906, fax 815/667–5353. Free. Park daily 7 AM–10 PM; visitor center weekdays 9–5, weekends 9–6.

Tours

Fall Color Tour In October the park takes advantage of its spectacular foliage by leading a 3½-hour tour. The admission price of $20 includes lunch in the dining room at the lodge, a trolley tour, and a guided hike. > Tel. 800/868–7625.

Land-n-Water Cruise On Monday in July, August, and the first two weeks of September, this 3½-hour tour in an air-conditioned trolley covers the Starved Rock area and adds a 1-hour ride aboard the *Belle of the Rock,* a paddle-wheel boat that plies the Illinois River. A soup-and-salad-bar lunch at the lodge is included. Admission is $28. > Tel. 800/868–7625.

Starved Rock Trolley Departing from Starved Rock Lodge, these 75-minute scenic tours cover the state park and Utica area. From June to October, two tours are given on Wednesday and Thursday, three tours from Friday to Sunday. Tours are given less often from November to May. Cost is $10. > Tel. 800/868–7625.

Tri-Park Tour On selected summer dates, the ubiquitous green trolley leads compact tour of the highlights of Buffalo Rock, Matthiessen, and Starved Rock state parks. A soup-and-salad-bar lunch at the lodge is included. Cost is $20. > Tel. 800/868–7625.

Save the Date

JANUARY

Bald Eagle Watch On the last weekend in January, the Audubon Society sets up high-powered spotting scopes at the Illinois Waterway Visitor Center for an up-close look as the eagles hunt for fish below Starved Rock Dam. > Tel. 815/667–4356, www.ivaced.org.

Winter Wilderness Weekend Guided hikes take you through Starved Rock State Park to frozen waterfalls and other winter sights. Hikes leave from the visitor center one weekend in mid-month at 9 AM and 1 PM each day. > Tel. 815/667–4906, www.ivaced.org.

FEBRUARY

Cross-Country Ski Weekend The first weekend in February is when you can take a guided cross-country ski trip through Matthiessen and Starved Rock state parks. The excursion leaves from Matthiessen each day at 9 AM and 1 PM. > Tel. 815/667–4906, www.ivaced.org.

MAY

Illinois State Morel Mushroom Hunting Championship On the first Saturday in May, you can join mushroom lovers at the Ruby Peterson Park in Magnolia (25 mi southwest of Peru). From here you are carted off to a secret spot (which changes each year) for a two-hour hunt, after which judging and awards in many categories for the found morels occur back at the park. > Tel. 309/364–3319, www.ivaced.org.

Wildflower Pilgrimage Guided hikes through Starved Rock State Park to view the area's wildflowers depart from the visitor center the first weekend of May at 9 AM and 1 PM each day. > Tel. 815/667–4906, www.ivaced.org.

JUNE

Montreal Canoe Weekend You can take a ride in a 34-foot voyageur canoe that's a replica of one used by the French to explore North America. The four-hour trip starts from Point Shelter at the east end of Starved Rock State Park on the second weekend of the month at 11 AM, both Saturday and Sunday. > Tel. 815/667–4906, www.ivaced.org.

Taste of Illinois Valley Held in Peru's Centennial Park, this popular two-day festival includes food, live music, games, rides, and more. > 1700 West St., Peru 61354, tel. 815/223–7904, www.ivaced.org.

JULY

National Championship Boat Races Powerboats compete for national titles in these races held the last full week of the month on Lake DePue. Evening entertainment, food, music, and a carnival are also on the agenda. > Tel. 815/447–2848, www.ivaced.org.

OCTOBER

Burgoo Festival Locals claim no domestic animals are left in the area after this festival, which pays homage to the pioneers' thick meat stew. The LaSalle County Historical Society cooks up a 150-gallon facsimile to serve on the second Sunday in October, rain or shine. After you fill up on stew, you can wander the village to enjoy the bands, Civil War reenactments, and the wares of more than 250 crafts vendors. > Tel. 815/667–4861, www.ivaced.org.

Fall Colors Weekend Take a guided or unguided hike through, beneath, and around Starved Rock's rainbow of fall foliage. Guided tours leave the visitor center at 9 AM and 1 PM each day on a weekend in mid-October. > Tel. 815/667–4906, www.ivaced.org.

WHERE TO STAY

Starved Rock Lodge and Conference Center This hostelry in the eponymous park is convenient to all its facilities and activities. Four of the deluxe cabin rooms have fireplaces and 14 of the cabins in the woods can be rented year-round. The wood-shingled buildings are on a service road accessible from Route 178, 2½ mi south of downtown Utica, or from Route 71 south of the park. > Rtes. 178 and 71, Utica 61373, tel. 815/667–4211 or 800/868–7625, fax 815/667–4455, www.starvedrocklodge.com. 72 rooms, 22 cabins. Restaurant, café, in-room data ports, cable TV, in-room VCRs, indoor pool, wading pool, hot tub, 2 saunas, hiking, lounge, playground, business services. AE, D, DC, MC, V. **$**

NEAR THE PARK

OTTAWA **Holiday Inn Express** This three-story motel is 11 mi from Starved Rock State Park and within walking distance of restaurants. In addition to its rural location, about 3 mi from Ottawa, and quick access to I–80, the motel has spacious suites and a pool with a woody, lodgelike feel. > 120 W. Stevenson Rd., Ottawa 61350, tel. 815/433–0029 or 800/465–4329, fax 815/433–0382, www.ichotelsgroup.com. 70 rooms, 12 suites. In-room data ports, some microwaves, some refrigerators, cable TV, indoor pool, hot tub, laundry facilities, business services, some pets allowed, no-smoking rooms. AE, D, DC, MC, V. CP. ¢

Marcia's Bed and Breakfast This farmstead off I–80 via Route 71 includes a turn-of-the-20th-century house furnished with antiques and Native American art, a private cottage reflecting the stagecoach era, a horse barn, and other buildings. The innkeeper keeps horses for petting or photos only. Opportunities for scenic canoe trips and biking on the National Heritage Trail are nearby, and come evening you can rest next to a bonfire. > 3003 Rte. 71, Ottawa 61350, tel. 815/434–5217 or 815/488–5217, fax 815/431–2515. 3 rooms, 1 with bath; 1 cottage. Some kitchenettes, some microwaves, some refrigerators, cable TV in some rooms; no smoking. No credit cards. BP. ¢

Ottawa Comfort Inn Starved Rock State Park, Allen Park, and Illini State Park are within 10 mi of this chain hotel, near restaurants and cornfields. > 510 E. Etna Rd., Ottawa 61350, tel. 815/433–9600 or 800/228–5150, fax 815/433–9696, www.comfortinn.com. 53 rooms, 2 suites. In-room data ports, some microwaves, some refrigerators, some in-room hot tubs, cable TV, indoor pool, laundry facilities, business services, no smoking rooms. AE, D, DC, MC, V. CP. ¢

Prairie Rivers Bed and Breakfast This three-story 1890s home combines Queen Anne and New England cottage-style architecture. Its perch on a bluff overlooking the Illinois and Fox rivers gives you views of the waterway from the front porch, a sunroom, and some of the bedrooms. The rooms include the garrett suite with 18-foot ceilings; the Queen Anne room, with a mahogany bed; and a single-occupancy maid's room, with a wrought-iron bed. You can walk down the bluff to Allen Park, where you can fish, canoe, and simply stroll. At the end of the day, three fireplaces help you relax and chase away the nighttime chill. > 121 E. Prospect Ave., Ottawa 61350, tel. 815/434–3226. 4 rooms, 1 suite. No room phones, no room TVs, no smoking. MC, V. BP. ¢–$$

PERU **Comfort Inn** North of I-80, this three-story motel is 6 mi from Lake DePue, and about 10 mi from Starved Rock. Space on all sides guarantees a certain amount of quiet and a view of the horizon for vista-deprived urbanites. > 5240 Trompeter Rd., Peru 61354, tel. 815/223–8585 or 800/228–5150, fax 815/223–9292, www.choicehotels.com. 50 rooms, 1 suite. In-room data ports, some in-room hot tubs, some microwaves, some refrigerators, cable TV, indoor pool, laundry facilities, business services, no smoking rooms. AE, D, DC, MC, V. CP. ¢

Econo Lodge Since this two-story motel rubs up against the parking lot, you rely on the kindness of strangers for quiet, but the rooms get good light and you have easy access to I-80. The hotel is ¼ mi north of Peru and 8 mi from Starved Rock. > 1840 May Rd., Peru 61354, tel. 815/224–2500 or 800/553–2666, fax 815/224–3693, www.econolodge.com. 104 rooms. Restaurant, some in-room data ports, some kitchenettes, some microwaves, some refrigerators, cable TV, indoor pool, exercise equipment, lounge, laundry facilities, business services, some pets allowed (fee), no smoking rooms. AE, D, DC, MC, V. CP. ¢

Super 8 This motel is 8 mi from Starved Rock and Matthiessen state parks and 3 mi north of downtown Peru. Free passes to a nearby health club with a pool, exercise equipment, and tennis courts are available. > 1851 May Rd., Peru 61354, tel. 815/223–1848 or 800/800–8000, fax 815/223–1848, www.super8.com. 60 rooms, 1 suite. Some microwaves, some refrigerators, cable TV, laundry facilities, some pets allowed (fee), business services, no smoking rooms. AE, D, DC, MC, V. CP. ¢

UTICA **Brightwood Inn** Each room in this peaceful inn, within the confines of Matthiessen State Park, is decorated differently, from floral patterns and wicker furniture to dark green interiors and canopied beds. Each room has a queen-size bed and fireplace, and three of the rooms have private balconies. Dinner is served in the dining room Thursday–Sunday. It's 2 mi from Starved Rock State Park. > 2407 N. Rte. 178, Oglesby 61348, tel. 815/667–4600 or 888/667–0600, fax 815/667–4727, www.brightwoodinn.com. 7 rooms, 1 suite. Cable TV, some in-room hot tubs, in-room VCRs; no smoking. AE, D, MC, V. BP. $–$$$$

Lander's House A mile from Starved Rock State Park, this country house has rooms with natural wood furniture and checked quilts in the main house of this converted 1895 barn. Each of the intimate cottages have a fireplace and a private screened-in porch. > 115 E. Church St., Utica 61373, tel. 815/667–5170, fax 815/667–3103, www.landershouse.com. 2 rooms, 4 cottages, 1 suite. Some in-room hot tubs, some minibars, some refrigerators; no room phones, no smoking. MC, V. BP. $$–$$$

CAMPING

Starved Rock State Park Campground South of the canyons, the state park's popular campground has 59 first-come, first-served sites (7 are handicapped accessible) and 74 reserved sites. Each site has electricity and 26 50-amp sites are available. Reserved sites on holiday weekends fill up weeks in advance (months in the case of Labor Day), and in summer first-come sites are usually full by Thursday night for weekends. > Rte. 71, Utica 61373, tel. 815/667–4726. 133 partial hook-ups. Flush toilets, pit toilets, dump station, drinking water, showers, grills, picnic tables, electricity, playground. Reservations essential for weekends. No credit cards. Closed Nov.–Apr. ¢

White Oak Campground Oriented toward families and popular with Boy Scouts and church groups, this woody campground is across the road from Starved Rock State Park's Route 178 entrance. Those wanting authenticity or another merit badge can brave the primitive tent area. > Rte. 178, Utica 61373, tel. 815/667–4758 or 815/433–5489. 200 partial hook-ups. Flush toilets, dump station, drinking water, showers (fee), picnic tables, electricity, general store, swimming (fee). Reservations essential in summer. AE, D, MC, V. Closed Nov.–Apr. ¢

WHERE TO EAT

NEAR THE PARK

LASALLE-PERU **Red Door Inn** Five dining rooms surround an atrium, which includes a real train caboose made into a dining car, at this former saloon dating from the late 19th century. Erté original sculptures and paintings adorn the walls. On the menu are flaming table-side specialties and seafood. > 1701 Water St., LaSalle-Peru, tel. 815/223–2500. AE, D, MC, V. $$–$$$$

Uptown Grill This restaurant has a covered, screened-in patio where you can dine on steaks, seafood, pasta dishes, fajitas, and sandwiches. It's 2 mi south of I–80 in LaSalle. Reservations essential on weekends. > 601 1st St., LaSalle-Peru, tel. 815/224–4545. AE, D, DC, MC, V. $–$$$

UTICA **Cajun Connection** Owner Ron McFarlaine grew up in Louisiana and brought his own recipes north to this casual Cajun restaurant that serves alligator, gumbo, jumbo shrimp, and jambalaya. > 897 E. Rte. 6, Utica, tel. 815/667–9855. MC, V. Closed Mon.–Wed. $–$$

Canal Port Step through the screen door to a homey local joint that serves sandwiches and burgers, but also a diverse list of entrées such as chicken Oscar and grilled salmon. The fried chicken is a local favorite. > 148 Mill St., Utica, tel. 815/667–3010. MC, V. ¢–$$$$

Country Cupboard Though known for its generous ice cream cones and sundaes, this Route 178 eatery also serves burgers and deli sandwiches. Enjoy the bustling parlorlike front room, pull up to a round table in the shady dining area, or stake out one of the seats on the porch. If you stay for dessert, be forewarned: the hot-fudge brownie sundae easily feeds two. > 402 Clarke St., Utica, tel. 815/667–5155. MC, V. ¢–$

Duffy's A long, long bar and an Irish flavor highlight this pub across the street from the LaSalle County Historical Society. The menu includes Irish fare, deli sandwiches, and such midwestern staples as steaks and chops. > Mill and Canal Sts., Utica, tel. 815/667–4324. AE, D, MC, V. ¢–$

Mill Street Market If you're on the go or looking to supply your picnic, this small grocery store has a deli counter in the back. > 130 Mill St., Utica, tel. 815/667–4912. MC, V. ¢

Patti's Pancake House Get flapjacks from scratch and baked goods to take with you at this Utica favorite, attached to a B&B in a converted Victorian house and home to, among other things, a tribe of quirky dolls. > 304 S. Clark, Utica, tel. 815/667–4151. MC, V. No dinner. ¢–$

Skoog's Dark, woody, and homey, this grill with the Swedish flag on the sign serves pub grub, sandwiches, and seafood entrées. > 155 Mill St., Utica, tel. 815/667–5801. MC, V. ¢–$$

ESSENTIALS

Getting Here

A car is your best option for getting to and around the Starved Rock area. Public transportation is nonexistent, and though enthusiastic cyclists will find miles of crushed limestone paths around the I & M Canal, it's still wise to drive. Burlington Trailways (through Greyhound) serves LaSalle-Peru with a single stop at a truck stop outside Peru. Those using the bus will, due to distances, be limited in what they can explore (cyclists being an exception), and will have to seek out rental cars in Ottawa or LaSalle-Peru. Due to the logistics, it's best considered a last option.

BY BUS

One bus runs between Chicago and LaSalle-Peru, usually departing Chicago in the early morning. The fare is around $22 one-way; the trip, depending on traffic getting out of the city, takes about two hours. Bus passengers disembark at the Sapp Brothers Truck Stop just off I–80. From here, you need to take a cab into LaSalle-Peru.

BUS DEPOT **Sapp Brothers Truck Stop** > 3130 May Rd., Peru 61354, tel. 815/224–1065.

BUS LINE **Greyhound** > Tel. 800/231–2222, www.greyhound.com.

BY CAR

From Chicago, Starved Rock State Park is a two-hour trip west on I–80. Exits to the towns and state parks in the Starved Rock area are well marked. If you're going directly to the park, turn off the interstate at Route 178 and drive south 4 mi through Utica. The west entrance to the park is a mile south of town, past the bridge over the Illinois River and across from the White Oaks Campground.

Summer traffic around the entrances can get snarled; narrow roads and huge vehicles make for a bad combination, especially as the weekend nears. Parking in Starved Rock can be a minor annoyance on summer weekends. Several large parking lots are near the lodge and the visitor center. Smaller lots can be found at some of the trailheads. In Utica, you can park on the street or at a lot on Canal Street, half a block from Mill Street.

Visitor Information

CONTACTS **Illinois Valley Area Chamber of Commerce** > 300 Bucklin St. (Box 446), LaSalle 61301, tel. 815/223–0227, www.ivaced.org. **Illinois Waterway Visitors Center** > 950 N. 27th Rd. (Rte. 1), Ottawa 61350, tel. 815/667–4054, fax 815/667–4954. **LaSalle County Historical Society** > Canal and Mill Sts., Utica 61373, tel. 815/667–4861. **Ottawa Visitors Center** > 100 W. Lafayette St., Ottawa 61350, tel. 815/434–2737 or 888/688–2924, www.visit-ottawa-il.com. **Trailheads Visitors Center** > Starved Rock State Park, tel. 815/667–4906.

Milwaukee

95 mi north of Chicago

7

By Joanne Cleaver

ON THE SHORES OF LAKE MICHIGAN, Milwaukee, Wisconsin's largest city, has a small-town spirit because it is more a collection of neighborhoods than a sprawling urban metropolis. First settled by Potowatomi and later by French fur traders in the 18th century, the city boomed with the arrival of German brewers. Today, their legacy is carried on by macro and micro breweries, cultural institutions that continue to thrive, and a diverse manufacturing, service, and shipping economy.

Most people, however, know Milwaukee's lakefront from its enormous, and enormously popular, festival site, which hosts some of the country's biggest beer-and-brats blasts, such as Summerfest. Since the late 1990s, the city has steadily added to the lakefront's year-round amenities. The expansion only makes the lakefront evermore user-friendly. Not only can you go to a lakefront festival in August, but you now can spend a snowy January afternoon having lunch in a glass-walled café just yards from Lake Michigan's crashing waves or strolling through the architectural splendor of its art museum.

In fact, there is no bad season to visit the lakefront. Like Chicago's, it is given over to sweeping public parks; unlike Chicago's, the lakefront is relatively uncrowded. Biking and rollerblading along the lakefront, past the museum campus, and down to the riverfront is easily managed when you don't have to fight through rolling packs of bikers and skaters.

Milwaukee's downtown is 1 mi long, a few blocks wide, and is divided by the Milwaukee River. As you cross the river from the east to the west side, notice that the east-side streets are not directly opposite the west-side streets and that the bridges across the river are built at an angle. This layout dates from the 1840s, when the area east of the river was called Juneautown and the region to the west was known as Kilbourntown. The rival communities had a fierce argument over which would pay for the bridges that connected them; the antagonism was so intense that citizens venturing into rival territory carried white flags. The Great Bridge War was finally settled by the state legislature in 1845, but the streets on either side of the river were never aligned.

Modern steel-and-glass high-rises share downtown space with historic 19th-century buildings. If you walk through, chances are you'll see a building that's on some kind of historic register. Turn-of-the-20th-century ornamentation, lacy grillwork, and elaborate concrete moldings decorate the facades of buildings on almost every block. These architectural salutes literally set the city's brawny history in stone. South of the downtown, an arts district is blooming with warehouses converted to galleries and funky home-decorating and art-supply stores. Although shopping is a bit pedestrian in downtown proper, dedicated browsers can sate their cravings at the excellent specialty stores on the fringes of downtown in the arts district and at the museum stores.

Nightlife here comprises clubs, bars, and a slew of friendly saloons. Downtown, Water Street, beginning at its intersection of Juneau Avenue, holds a large concentration of bars from live music clubs to brewpubs. Milwaukee's theater district is in a two-block downtown area bounded by the Milwaukee River, East Wells Street, North Water Street, and East State Street. Most tickets are sold at box offices. *Milwaukee Magazine* (on newsstands) lists arts and entertainment events. Also check the daily entertainment sections of the *Milwaukee Journal Sentinel.*

The city is also filled with museums, art centers, and an abundance of ethnic restaurants including German, Serbian, and Irish. Since the mid-1990s, Milwaukee's food scene has blossomed. Now, you can get a terrific meal in nearly any cuisine you wish, as the downtown renaissance continues.

WHAT TO SEE & DO

Allen-Bradley Company Clock This clock is a Milwaukee landmark and, according to the *Guinness Book of Records,* "the largest four-faced clock in the world." Great Lakes ships often use the clock as a navigational reference point. > 1201 S. 2nd St.

Betty Brinn Children's Museum Overlooking Lake Michigan and adjacent to the Milwaukee Art Museum, this well-conceived children's museum epitomizes the concept of hands-on learning. Playing on Wisconsin's agricultural economy, this museum lets kids learn the basics of commerce in an exhibit that uses play apples as raw materials for a cider factory. Other perennial favorites are the BodyWorks exhibit, with its amusingly graphic mock-ups of bodily functions; nimble kids can slide through a huge heart to see how the blood flows from one chamber to another. Toddler play spaces are well protected from the general flow of traffic. > 929 E. Wisconsin Ave., tel. 414/390–5437, www.bbcmkids.org. $4. Tues.–Sat. 9–5, Sun. noon–5.

Bradford Beach This long strip of beach along Lake Michigan gets busy in summer, with sunbathers, joggers, swimmers, in-line skaters, skateboarders, and bicyclists. Food booths and vendors are near the center of the strip, within walking distance of any part of the beach. > 2400 N. Lincoln Memorial Dr., tel. 414/645–4095. Free. Daily.

Charles Allis Art Museum Inside a Tudor-style house built in 1911, with stained-glass windows by Louis Comfort Tiffany, this museum houses a stunning international collection of paintings and objets d'art, including works by major 19th- and 20th-century French and American painters. > 1801 N. Prospect Ave., tel. 414/278–8295, www.cavtmuseums.org. $5. Wed. 1–9, Thurs.–Sun. 1–5.

James Lovell Museum of Science, Economics, and Technology Called Discovery World, the museum has more than 140 interactive exhibits on magnets, motors, electricity, health, and computers. It also puts on the "Great Electric Show" and the "Light Wave–Laser Beam Show" on weekends and some weekdays. > Milwaukee Public Museum, 815 N. James Lovell St., tel. 414/765–9966, www.discoveryworld.org. $5.50. Daily 9–5.

Marquette University Founded in 1881, Marquette University provides a Jesuit-based urban education for more than 10,000 students per year. The school's 51 campus buildings are concentrated on the western border of downtown. The St. Joan of Arc chapel is on campus. Marquette is also the home of Jesu Church, a Milwaukee landmark. **Marquette Hall's 48-bell carillon** is near the center of the Marquette University campus. > 1442 W. Wisconsin Ave., tel. 414/288–7250, www.marquette.edu. Free. Mon.–Sat., by appointment only.

Milwaukee Art Museum On the lakefront, the museum houses collections of paintings, drawings, sculpture, photography, and decorative arts. Its permanent collection emphasizes European and American art of the 19th and 20th centuries. In 2001, a soaring, light-filled addition opened, creating a large gallery that hosts major traveling

exhibitions. The museum's lower-level café is a glass-walled promontory that faces
the lake. Here, you can order light lunch or take a mid-afternoon coffee and dessert
break. The addition also includes performance space, so the museum now hosts
dance, installation art, and other performances. > 700 N. Art Museum Dr., tel.
414/224–3200, www.mam.org. $6. Daily 10–5.

Milwaukee County Zoo Inside this enormous park are more than 3,000 wild animals and birds—including endangered species—plus educational programs, narrated tram tours, miniature-train rides, and cross-country skiing trails. Japanese snow
monkeys occupy their own island, and the grizzly bears are reliably entertaining. The
hands-on children's area focuses on dairy animals (this is Wisconsin, after all, the
cheese capital of the country), as well as other critters to pet and hold. > 10001 W.
Bluemound Rd., tel. 414/771–3040, www.milwaukeezoo.org. $9. Daily 9–6.

Milwaukee Public Museum Considered among the best natural history museums in
the country, the museum houses more than 6 million specimens and artifacts. One
hallmark is the "Streets of Old Milwaukee," depicting the city in the 1890s. Cul-de-sacs
showcase domestic settings representing the ethnic groups that have settled Milwaukee, such as Greek, Scandinavian, and German. At the candy shop, you can actually
buy penny candy, stick candy, and other old-fashioned favorites. At the two-story rain
forest, you can explore levels of tropical life from the ground to the treetops. "Third
Planet," complete with full-size dinosaurs, lets visitors walk into the interior of Earth to
learn about its history. Butterflies fly free in their own enclosed habitat, and visitors can
walk among them. Within the museum, the **Humphrey IMAX Dome Theater** (tel.
414/278–2702, $6.75) is run in cooperation with Discovery World. > 800 W. Wells St.,
tel. 414/278–2700, www.mpm.edu. Museum $6.75, IMAX $6.75. Daily 9–5.

Mitchell Park Conservatory The conservatory consists of three 85-foot-high glass
domes that house tropical, arid, and seasonal plants and flowers. Its lilies and poinset-
tias are spectacular at Easter and Christmas. > 524 S. Layton Blvd., tel. 414/649–9800,
www.countyparks.com/horticulture. $4.50. Daily 9–5.

Pabst Mansion Completed in 1892 for the beer baron Captain Frederick Pabst, this is
one of Milwaukee's treasured landmarks. The 37-room Flemish Renaissance–style
mansion, designed by the architectural firm Ferry & Clas, has a tan pressed-brick exterior with carved-stone and terra-cotta ornamentation. Inside, no surface is left un-
decorated. Walls are swathed in elaborately textured and painted coverings, every
window has multiple swags and shades, and stained-glass windows bear sayings (in
German) exhorting servants to work hard. In the adjacent gift shop, pick up the ultimate Milwaukee souvenir: an amber glass beer stein Christmas tree ornament with
glittery foam. > 2000 W. Wisconsin Ave., tel. 414/931–0808, www.pabstmansion.com.
$7. Mon.–Sat. 10–3:30, Sun. noon–3:30.

Pabst Theater Built in 1895 and remodeled in 1976, this Victorian theater downtown
is on the National Register of Historic Places and presents top music and theatrical
entertainment. Of special note is its giant Austrian-crystal chandelier. > 144 E. Wells
St., tel. 414/286–3665, www.pabsttheater.org. Free. Sat. 11:30 AM for public tours; private tours by appointment.

St. Joan of Arc Chapel This small, stone 15th-century chapel with tiny stained-glass
windows was moved from its original site near Lyon, France, in 1964 and recon-
structed here in a courtyard of the university. One of the stones was reputedly kissed
by Joan before she was sent to her death and is discernibly colder than the others.
> Marquette University, 1415 W. Wisconsin Ave., central mall, behind Memorial Li-
brary, tel. 414/288–6873, www.mu.edu. Free. Daily.

St. Josephat's Basilica Built at the turn of the 20th century, this cathedral has a copper dome modeled after the one atop St. Peter's in Rome. Inside is a collection of

relics, statues, and European icons. > 601 W. Lincoln Ave., tel. 414/645–5623. $3. By appointment only.

Third Ward District This neighborhood, listed on the National Register of Historic Places, is close to the Milwaukee River and is made up of a mix of large, often historic buildings (from former warehouses to furniture stores). Many have been restored and now house upscale shops, restaurants, and condos as the area emerges as an arts district. Old-fashioned street lamps illuminate the area, and a small park and a pedestrian mall along Broadway Street strike a verdant note. > Bordered by Broadway, Water, and Erie Sts., and St. Paul Ave.

Villa Terrace Decorative Art Museum Perched on a bluff overlooking its own sweeping lawn and Lake Michigan beyond, this museum is a 1920s era replica of an Italian villa. Although the house is gradually being restored, you can roam its wings and enjoy the view of its Renaissance-style gardens from any of its balconies. > 2220 N. Terrace Ave., tel. 414271–3656. $5. Wed. 1–9, Thurs.–Sun. 1–5.

William F. Eisner Museum of Advertising & Design Advertising is demystified through the museum's exhibits on psychographics, campaign development, and the impact of advertising on popular culture, and vice versa. The museum is in the Third Ward, a few blocks south of downtown proper. > 208 N. Water St., tel. 414/847–3290, www.eisnermuseum.org. $4.50. Wed. and Fri. 11–5, Thurs. 11–6, Sat. noon–5, Sun. 1–5.

Tours

Edelweiss Cruise Dining Enjoy a sightseeing, luncheon, champagne, cocktail, moonlight, or dinner cruise on Lake Michigan, in a European-style, flat-bottom canal boat. Reservations are required. > 1110 Old World 3rd St., tel. 414/272–3625, www.weissgerbers.com/edelweiss/home.asp.

Historic Milwaukee, Inc. This organization conducts walking and bus tours, including a Beer Barons tour (it goes to their historic homes, not the breweries). Durations range from 1½ hours to all afternoon. Reservations are required, and tickets are usually around $20, depending on the type of tour. > 828 N. Broadway, Suite 110, tel. 414/277–7795, www.historicmilwaukee.org.

Iroquois Boat Line Tours From late June to Labor Day, you can take a 90-minute tour down the Milwaukee River, starting downtown on the river's west bank and terminating at Lake Michigan. The tours highlight local history. Boats are double-decker, with canopied tops and below-deck window viewing. Board at the Clybourn Street Bridge. Daily cruises are $8.50. > Tel. 414/294–9450.

River Walk Boat Rentals Cruise the Milwaukee River on the 44-seat *Brew City Queen* or rent canoes to paddle around on your own. Tours are available daily. > 1137 N. Old World 3rd St., tel. 414/283–9999.

Shopping

Using the downtown skywalk system, it's possible to browse in hundreds of stores over several blocks without once setting foot outside. Downtown Milwaukee's major shopping area is Wisconsin Avenue west of the Milwaukee River.

Grand Avenue Mall The city's major downtown retail center spans four city blocks and has 130 specialty shops and kiosks and 17 eateries. Boston Store, a Milwaukee institution, is here as is Brew City Beer Gear, the necessary stop for all things beer. > 275 W. Wisconsin Ave., tel. 414/224–0685, www.grandavenueshops.com.

Historic Third Ward A turn-of-the-20th-century wholesale and manufacturing district listed on the National Register of Historic Places, this arts district is south of down-

Bottoms Up

SAY MILWAUKEE, AND MOST PEOPLE THINK "BEER." Beer built the city, starting with the founding of Miller Brewing Company in 1855. Brewery barons built the mansions and vintage downtown buildings that frame the city's atmosphere. So it's fitting that microbreweries are leading the revival of Milwaukee's downtown. After many of the city's most famous beer labels—Schlitz, Pabst, and Blatz, to name a few—shut down their Milwaukee breweries, a bit of a beer void opened up.

In 1985, a west-coast transplant opened Sprecher Brewing Co., the city's first microbrewery. With Sprecher going strong as a regional brand, the door was opened for a late-20th-century beer blast. Milwaukee pubs proudly serve up lagers, stouts, and other specialty beers made locally by **Lakefront Brewery** (www.lakefrontbrewery.com.), **Leinenkeugel's** (www.leinies.com.), and **Sprecher** (www.sprecherbrewery.com.).

Brewpubs are also now well established in downtown Milwaukee. Among the most popular with local beer aficionados: **Water St. Brewery** (202 N. Water St. www.waterstreetbrewery.com.), **Rock Bottom Brewery** (740 N. Plankinton Ave. www.rockbottom.com.), **Milwaukee Ale House** (233 N. Water St. www.ale-house.com.), and **Stout Bros. Public Ale House** (777 N. Water St. www.stoutbros.com.).

The beer gardens of Summerfest are a terrific place to sample these and other local brews. Nondrinking companions might want to take a taste tour of Sprecher's own special sodas, especially its root beer.

town proper. It's home to a growing number of art-supply stores, galleries, and home-accessories importers.

Save the Date

JUNE
CajunFest A gumbo and jambalaya cook-off, a crawfish-eating contest, music, and entertainment highlight this festival, held at State Fair Park the first week of June. > Tel. 414/476–7303, www.cajunfest.org.
Polish Fest Polish music, food, dancing, and a cultural village make up this festival, held on the third weekend of the month in Henry Maier Festival Park. > Tel. 414/529–2140, www.polishfest.org.

JUNE–JULY
Summerfest The self-styled "World's Largest Music Festival" kicks off the season of fests at Henry Maier Festival Park on the shores of Lake Michigan. It showcases more than 2,500 national, regional, and local acts, and also includes a sports area, a carnival, a kids' play area, face painting, arts, ethnic foods, and vendors. Traditionally the event begins on the last Thursday in June and runs through July 4. > Tel. 414/273–3378 or 800/837–3378, www.summerfest.com.

JULY
Bastille Days French food, a faux Eiffel Tower, French music, and a 5K run called "Storm the Bastille" highlight this festival, held in Cathedral Square and surrounding

streets, just east of the downtown area, on the second weekend of the month. > Tel. 414/271–7400, www.easttown.com.

Festa Italiana Italian food, music, entertainment, and fireworks enrich this festival, held in Henry Maier Festival Park on the third weekend of the month. > Tel. 414/223–2193, www.festaitaliana.com.

German Fest The city's German heritage is celebrated with music, dancing, and food, plus fireworks and a parade draw. Held in Henry Maier Festival Park on the last weekend of the month. > Tel. 414/464–9444, www.germanfest.com.

Great Circus Parade This parade of vintage circus wagons, horses, clowns, elephants, and marching bands winds through downtown Milwaukee in mid-July. > Tel. 608/356–8341, www.circusparade.com.

AUGUST

Irish Fest Milwaukee raises a glass to its Irish brethren with food, music, and dancing. Henry Maier Festival Park hosts this annual event on the third weekend of the month. > Tel. 414/476–3378, www.irishfest.com.

Mexican Fiesta Embrace the city's Mexican spirit at Henry Maier Festival Park on the last weekend of the month. Mexican food, music, and dancing, plus fireworks and a run enrich the experience. > Tel. 414/383–7066.

Wisconsin State Fair A carnival, live entertainment, food booths, arts, crafts, farm animals, kids' activities, and body-building and weight-lifting competitions round out this annual fair, held mid-month at Wisconsin State Fair Park. Don't miss the cream puffs. > Tel. 414/266–7000, www.wistatefair.com.

NOVEMBER

Holiday Folk Fair Peruse authentic crafts from around the world and learn to say "hello" in dozens of languages. Booths at the fair are run by citizens from countries all over the world, and they'll stamp your faux passport at each booth you visit. Munch your way around the globe by sampling the delicious homemade specialties at numerous food stands. The event is held in State Fair Park on the weekend before Thanksgiving. > Tel. 414/225–6225.

WHERE TO STAY

Acanthus Inn Bed & Breakfast Built in the Queen Anne style for a local family at the turn of the 20th century, the inn has retained all the charm and elegance of the period. Surrounded by other large, elegant old homes in the Concordia neighborhood, the inn has its original woodwork and light fixtures, pocket doors, fireplaces, and even a built-in china cabinet with carved cherubs and shells in the dining room. Rooms are decorated in Victorian style. The inn is west of downtown. > 3009 W. Highland Blvd., 53208, tel. 877/468–8740, acanthusinn.prodigybiz.com. 6 rooms, 2 with bath. AE, MC, V. BP. $–$$

Astor Hotel Antiques fill this luxury eight-story hotel, built in 1920, on a bluff above Lake Michigan. The opulent grand lobby, with its stained-glass skylight over the reception area, somewhat overshadow the rooms, which are large and outfitted with antique-reproduction cherrywood furniture and some impressive views of downtown Milwaukee. > 924 E. Juneau Ave., 53202, tel. 414/271–4220 or 800/558–0200, fax 414/271–6370, www.theastorhotel.com. 97 rooms, 30 suites. Restaurant, some kitchenettes, cable TV, concierge, Internet, business services, free parking, no smoking rooms. MC, V. $–$$$

County Clare The guest rooms and pub at this inn are within walking distance of Lake Michigan and downtown, and evoke Ireland, from the architecture to the stained-glass windows and wood-burning fireplace. The pub prepares such Gaelic specialties as Irish stew and shepherd's pie. The cheery rooms have queen-size four-poster beds. Irish music performances are hosted throughout the year. > 1234 N. Astor St., 53202, tel. 414/272–5273, fax 414/290–6300, www.countyclare-inn.com. 30 rooms. Restaurant, in-room data ports, in-room hot tubs, cable TV, business services, free parking. AE, D, DC, MC, V. ¢–$$

Hilton Milwaukee City Center Kids can splash and slide year-round in the hotel's indoor water park. The brick hotel, adjacent to Milwaukee's convention center, was built in 1929 and its lobby is a elegant as ever. Lakefront attractions are a few blocks away. > 509 W. Wisconsin Ave., 53203, tel. 414/271–7250 or 800/445–8667, fax 414/271–1039, www.hilton.com. 730 rooms. 3 restaurants, room service, gym, lounge, shop, laundry services, Internet, business services, meeting rooms. AE, D, DC, MC, V. $–$$$

Holiday Inn Milwaukee City Centre Within blocks of all the restaurants, shopping, and sightseeing opportunities in downtown Milwaukee, this upscale hotel has a modern, glass-enclosed lobby and spare-but-comfortable guest rooms. > 611 W. Wisconsin Ave., 53203, tel. 414/273–2950, fax 414/273–7662, www.holiday-inn.com. 247 rooms. Restaurant, room service, in-room data ports, some microwaves, cable TV, pool, bar, business services, parking (fee). AE, D, DC, MC, V. $$–$$$

Hotel Metro With its aqua and coral color scheme and innovatively designed suites, the Hotel Metro reinterprets the art deco look. A curved wall in each suite shelters the bed from the sitting area. The hotel is three blocks from the lakefront museums. > 411 E. Mason St., 53203, tel. 414/272–1937, fax 414/225–3282, www.hotelmetro.com. 65 suites. Restaurant, in-room data ports, some hot tubs, in-room VCRs, Internet, no smoking rooms. AE, DC, MC, V. $$

Hotel Wisconsin Built in 1913, this 11-story downtown hotel is the second oldest in Milwaukee. The interior includes oak paneling, stained glass, fancy glasswork bearing a badger emblem, and a grandfather clock that is original to the hotel. > 720 N. Old World 3rd St., 53203, tel. 414/271–4900, fax 414/271–9998. 234 rooms. Restaurant, some microwaves, some refrigerators, cable TV, laundry facilities, business services, free parking, some pets allowed, no smoking rooms. AE, D, DC, MC, V. ¢–$$

Hyatt Regency This high-rise hotel has an 18-story open atrium, a revolving rooftop restaurant, and an enclosed walkway to the Grand Avenue Shopping Center. It's about four blocks from the lakefront. > 333 W. Kilbourn Ave., 53203, tel. 414/270–6065 or 800/233–1234, fax 414/276–6338, www.milwaukee.hyatt.com. 484 rooms. 2 restaurants, in-room data ports, cable TV, gym. AE, D, DC, MC, V. $–$$$

Park East This five-story redbrick-and-glass modern building sprawling on the edge of downtown has an elegant, large lobby. You can grab the hotel's complimentary downtown shuttle to get where you want to go without all the hassle of parking. > 916 E. State St., 53202, tel. 414/276–8800 or 800/328–7275, fax 414/765–1919, www.parkeasthotel.com. 159 rooms. Restaurant, in-room data ports, some in-room hot tubs, some microwaves, some refrigerators, cable TV, in-room VCRs, gym, bar, business services. AE, D, DC, MC, V. CP. $–$$$

Pfister Hotel Milwaukee's grandest old hotel dates from 1893. The lobby's long, high barrel-vaulted ceiling puts you in a Victorian frame of mind from the moment you step in. Rooms are decorated with a Victorian flavor and some are odd shapes, reflecting the complications of pouring modern amenities into an old structure, but this only adds to the charm. The Pfister is three blocks east of the lakefront. The penthouse-level bar Blu has a view of the skyline. The Pfister serves an English tea in its fern-shaded dining room most afternoons. > 424 E. Wisconsin Ave., 53202, tel. 414/273–8222 or 800/558–8222, fax 414/273–5025, www.thepfisterhotel.com. 307

rooms. 3 restaurants, room service, in-room data ports, minibars, exercise equipment, concierge, no-smoking rooms. AE, D, DC, MC, V. $$$–$$$$

Wyndham Milwaukee Center In the center of the city's growing theater district by the river and near the Grand Avenue Shopping Center, the Wyndham has an opulent lobby tiled with Italian marble. Guest rooms are contemporary, with mahogany furnishings. The hotel has an excellent pasta bar. > 139 E. Kilbourn Ave., 53202, tel. 414/276–8686 or 800/996–3426, fax 414/276–8007, www.wyndham.com. 220 rooms. Restaurant, laundry services. AE, D, DC, MC, V. $$$–$$$$

WHERE TO EAT

African Hut Who would expect a restaurant with terrific peanut dishes in the heart of Milwaukee's German historic district. Yet, here it is. > 1107 N. Old World 3rd St., tel. 414/765–1110. MC, V. $–$$

Bartolotta's Lake Park Bistro On a bluff overlooking Lake Michigan, this bistro is renowned for its New Orleans–style Sunday brunch. The daily menu includes roast monkfish and Wisconsin trout, with rich and buttery sauces. Mirrors and curtains abound in this formal dining room. > 3133 E. Newberry Blvd., tel. 414/962–6300. AE, D, DC, MC, V. No lunch weekends. $$$–$$$$

Bavarian Inn This chalet on 14 acres displays soccer memorabilia and handmade chandeliers. Along with such classic German fare as sauerbraten and schnitzels, the menu lists such eclectic dishes as wild-game platter and grilled kangaroo. Every Friday, the inn hosts live German music. > 700 Lexington, Glendale, tel. 414/964–0300. AE, D, DC, MC, V. Closed Mon. No lunch Fri. and Sat. $$

Celia Inside the venerable Pfister Hotel, Milwaukee's premier hotel restaurant exudes a formal atmosphere amid modern decor. Recommended dishes are rack of lamb, seared crab cakes, and lobster-and-shrimp bisque. > 424 E. Wisconsin Ave., tel. 414/390–3832. AE, D, DC, MC, V. $$–$$$$

Coquette Café Provincial French bistro fare is served at this café in a large, renovated warehouse in Milwaukee's trendy Third Ward district, just south of downtown. The beer is specially brewed to complement the menu, which is filled with such dishes as roasted mussels and thin-crust Niçoise and Alsatian pizzas. > 316 N. Milwaukee St., tel. 414/291–2655. AE, D, DC, MC, V. $–$$

County Clare This restaurant looks like a traditional Irish pub, with deep-green walls adorned with Gaelic sayings, and a long, ornate bar. The menu includes such dishes as corned beef and cabbage, hearty pub sandwiches, and homemade soups-of-the-day. On Sunday, traditional Irish music is played in the afternoon. > 1234 N. Astor St., tel. 414/272–5273. AE, D, DC, MC, V. $–$$$

Eagan's Impressionist paintings hang on the walls at this chic downtown restaurant. The kitchen serves such delicacies as oysters Rockefeller and lobster. You can dine inside or outside on the patio overlooking popular Water Street. Its well-stocked bar is one of the largest in the state. > 1030 N. Water St., tel. 414/271–6900. Reservations not accepted. AE, D, DC, MC, V. No dinner Sun. $–$$$$

Elsa's on the Park Across from Cathedral Square Park, this chic but casual restaurant has frequently changing art exhibits and serves big, juicy hamburgers and pork-chop sandwiches. > 833 N. Jefferson St., tel. 414/765–0615. AE, MC, V. No lunch weekends. ¢–$$

Giovanni's This bright Sicilian eatery serves large portions of rich Italian food. The menu is varied, with lots of chicken and pasta options, but the real standouts are the veal dishes, such as veal marsala or veal *cotoletta* (a choice cut lightly breaded and sautéed in olive oil, then dusted with Italian seasonings). > 1683 N. Van Buren St., tel. 414/291–5600. AE, D, DC, MC, V. No lunch weekends. **$$$–$$$$**

Grenadier's Imaginative dishes, such as tenderloin of veal with raspberry sauce, that combine French classics with Asian or Indian flavors are served in the elegant dining room and in the handsome, darkly furnished piano bar. > 747 N. Broadway St., tel. 414/276–0747. AE, D, DC, MC, V. Closed Sun. **$$$–$$$$**

Historic Turner Restaurant The spacious, high-ceilinged dining area of this former gymnastics center has original wood floors, high-back booths, and an old-style bar accented with brass. The menu includes pasta dishes, a fish fry, oversize sandwiches, and jumbo nacho platters, as well as homemade soups. > 1034 N. 4th St., tel. 414/276–4844. AE, DC, MC, V. **$–$$**

Izumi's This small, cozy restaurant on the east side of town has a sushi bar and a menu of traditional Japanese fare, such as udon and sukiyaki. > 2178 N. Prospect Ave., tel. 414/271–5278. AE, DC, MC, V. No lunch weekends. **$–$$$**

Karl Ratzsch's Old World Restaurant In German tradition dirndl-skirted waitresses serve schnitzel, roast duckling, and sauerbraten at this family-owned restaurant that's decked out with murals, chandeliers made from antlers, and antique beer steins. Piano music on Friday and Saturday nights adds to the fun. A must-go for first-time visitors to Milwaukee. > 320 E. Mason St., tel. 414/276–2720. AE, D, DC, MC, V. Closed Sun. No lunch. **$$–$$$$**

The King and I Thai paintings and wood carvings set the scene for this restaurant's delicious pad Thai and volcano chicken. Large windows overlook the Milwaukee River. > 823 N. 2nd St., tel. 414/353–6069. AE, D, DC, MC, V. No lunch weekends. **$–$$$**

Mader's It's named after the Mader family, not after a German mama. Diners here get the ultimate old-world experience, from the Hummels that occupy niches in the entryway to the dark-wood paneled walls and all the rich German favorites. Weiner schnitzel, sauerbraten, and spaetzle reign. > 1037 N. Old World 3rd St., tel. 414/271–3377. AE, D, DC, MC, V. **$$–$$$**

Mimma's Cafe This café is northeast of downtown in a clapboard building dating from 1890; inside are columns, and walls sponge-painted in subtle hues. The kitchen prepares recipes from northern Italy to Sicily, including some 50 different pasta dishes. > 1307 E. Brady St., tel. 414/271–7337. AE, D, DC, MC, V. No lunch. **$–$$$**

Mo's Subtitled "A Place For Steaks," this downtown eatery is all about meat. Diners get to choose their steaks from a platter of cuts. Side dishes and desserts are outstanding, too. > 720 N. Plankinton Ave., tel. 414/272–0720. Reservations essential. AE, DC, D, MC, V. **$$$–$$$$**

Old Town Serbian Gourmet House This large, candlelit restaurant south of downtown is full of old-world charm, with linen tablecloths and cityscapes on the walls. The menu lists Serbian specialties—such as *sarma* (stuffed sauerkraut rolls) and beef *burek* (spiced meat wrapped with grape leaves)—as well as American, French, and other ethnic dishes. > 522 W. Lincoln Ave., tel. 414/672–0206. AE, D, DC, MC, V. Closed Mon. No lunch weekends. **$$–$$$$**

Polaris At this elegant candlelit revolving restaurant—on the 22nd floor of the Hyatt Regency hotel—you can see Lake Michigan and nearly all of Milwaukee while you dine. Select from prime rib au jus, filet mignon, Wiener schnitzel, fettuccine with shrimp and spinach, or roast chicken. > 333 W. Kilbourn Ave., tel. 414/270–6130. AE, D, DC, MC, V. No lunch. **$$–$$$$**

Sanford Nationally acclaimed chef Sanford D'Amato serves contemporary American cuisine in this restaurant, which occupies a remodeled grocery store on Milwaukee's east side. Menu choices are organized into courses: 3, 4, 5, or 7, with prix-fixe prices from $45 to $75. Long banquettes make things cozy. > 1547 N. Jackson St., tel. 414/276–9608. AE, D, DC, MC, V. Closed Sun. **$$$$**

Safe House The food's not the big draw here, though oversize salads and jumbo hamburgers satisfy. The real reason to visit is the over-the-top "international spy" theme. False doors, props from spy movies and books, and a mazelike layout provide amusement for those who love whodunits. > 779 N. Front St., tel. 414/271–2007. MC, V. **$–$$**

Saz's This turn-of-the-20th-century brick roadhouse west of downtown is known as a fun nightspot with great food. It's almost always crowded, with a diverse group of customers enjoying ribs and filet mignon in the beer garden. > 5539 W. State St., tel. 414/453–2410. AE, D, MC, V. **$–$$$**

Three Brothers This small, candlelit Serbian restaurant occupies an 1897 Cream City Brick building about 10 minutes south of downtown. Original paintings by Serbian and Yugoslav artists hang on the walls. Specialties include chicken *paprikash* (stewed with paprika), roast goose and duck, boneless leg of lamb stuffed with spinach and cheese, and homemade desserts. > 2414 S. St. Clair St., tel. 414/481–7530. No credit cards. Closed Mon. No lunch. **$–$$**

Watts Tea Room A genteel spot for breakfast, lunch, or tea with scones, this eatery is above George Watts & Sons, Milwaukee's premier store for china, crystal, and silver, on the east side of downtown. Indulge in fresh-squeezed juice and a custard-filled sunshine cake. > 761 N. Jefferson St., tel. 414/290–5720. AE, D, MC, V. Closed Sun. No dinner. **$–$$**

Weissgerber's Third Street Pier This elegant downtown dining room in a six-story riverfront plaza has a view of the Milwaukee River, lots of shiny brass and fresh flowers, and a menu of steak and fresh fish. Desserts such as cherries jubilee and bananas Foster are prepared table-side. Open-air dining is available on a patio overlooking the river. A jazz trio plays Friday nights, and a pianist entertains on Thursday and Saturday. > 1110 N. Old World 3rd St., tel. 414/272–0330. AE, D, DC, MC, V. No lunch. **$$$–$$$$**

ESSENTIALS

Getting Here

Downtown Milwaukee is easily navigated by foot, making cars optional. Parking is plentiful, especially on the weekend, and reasonably priced. If you're planning on visiting destinations outside downtown, a car is essential. The best way to get here from Chicago is straight up I–94.

BY BUS

Greyhound runs buses daily from Chicago to Milwaukee. Schedules, however, constantly change so check the daily schedule before you make your plans. The Milwaukee Country Transit System operates buses to and from the airport and throughout Milwaukee County. Buses circulate through the downtown.

A trolley runs north–south along the lakefront and east–west along Wisconsin Avenue, connecting many of the major downtown destinations. The fare is 50¢. Milwaukee County Transit operates buses to and from the airport. Fare is $1.50; exact change is required.

BUS DEPOT **Greyhound Milwaukee** > 606 N. James Lovell St. 53203, tel. 414/272–2156.

BUS LINES **Greyhound Lines** > Tel. 800/231–2222, www.greyhound.com. **Milwaukee County Transit System** > Tel. 414/344–6711, www.ridemcts.com.

BY CAR

Since parking is plentiful and reasonably priced in downtown Milwaukee and nearby destinations, driving is the most convenient option for visiting here from Chicago. From the Lake County, Illinois, border, allow 90 minutes to get to Milwaukee. Interstate 94 leads to downtown from Chicago and other points south and west. If you are traveling to sites in the wider metropolitan area, you can connect to I–894 from I–94, which bypasses central Milwaukee, and to I–43 from I–94, which takes you to north of downtown toward Green Bay.

Lake Michigan is the city's eastern boundary, which is fronted by Lakeshore Drive. Wisconsin Avenue is the main east–west thoroughfare. The Milwaukee River divides the downtown area between east and west. The East–West Expressway (I–94 [I–794]) is the dividing line between north and south. Streets are numbered in ascending order from the Milwaukee River west well into the suburbs.

BY PLANE

General Mitchell International Airport, 6 mi south of downtown via I–94, is served by 16 domestic and international carriers. It is the largest airport in Wisconsin. Milwaukee authorities try to position it as an alternative to often-crowded O'Hare, so Mitchell sometimes is unexpectedly busy. Taxis between the airport and downtown take about 20 minutes; fares are $22–$25.

CARRIERS **Air Canada** > Tel. 800/247–2262, www.aircanada.com. **AirTran Airways** > Tel. 800/247–8726, www.airtran.com. **America West** > Tel. 800/327–7810, www.americawest.com. **American, American Eagle** > Tel. 800/433–7000, www.aa.com. **ATA** > Tel. 800/435–9282, www.ata.com. **Delta** > Tel. 800/221–1212, www.delta.com. **Midwest Airlines** > Tel. 800/452–2022, www.midwestexpress.com. **Northwest** > Tel. 800/225–2525, www.nwa.com. **United Express** > Tel. 800/864–8331, www.united.com. **US Airways** > Tel. 800/428–4322, www.usairways.com.

AIRPORT **General Mitchell International Airport** > 5300 S. Howell Ave., tel. 414/747–5300, www.mitchellairport.com.

BY TRAIN

The Milwaukee train station is on the west side of downtown. It is within walking distance of the conference center and adjacent hotels, and a short cab ride from hotels and destinations on the east side of downtown and along the lakefront.

TRAIN LINE **Amtrak** > Tel. 800/872–7245, www.amtrak.com.

TRAIN STATION **Milwaukee Train Station** > 433 W. St. Paul Ave., tel. 414/271–0840.

Visitor Information

INFORMATION **Greater Milwaukee Convention and Visitors Bureau** > 5101 W. Wisconsin Ave., Suite 425, 53203-2501, tel. 800/554–1448, www.milwaukee.org.

Rock River Valley

100 mi west of Chicago

8

By Rick Marzec

A WEEKEND TRIP TO THE ROCK RIVER VALLEY really elucidates the term "road trip." It's not a trip where you drive to one destination, stay for a couple of days, and drive home. This is a trip that affords you the opportunity to relax, roll down the windows, and enjoy the country scenery as you take in the area's historic sites and splendid state parks.

The towns of the valley are quick and easy to get to and less than two hours from Chicago. Once you're there, you may find the drives between sites, most of which are no more than a 10- or 20-minute jaunt from each other, pleasant. Except for downtown Dixon, congestion in this area doesn't really exist, in part because the area has not become overly developed like so many other weekend destinations.

Some parts of the landscape remain as they did back in the 1700s and early 1800s. when the Potawatomi and the Winnebago Indian tribes lived and roamed the area. Here, they paddled their canoes and established villages along the banks of the Rock River. In 1828, a French Indian named Joseph Ogee built a cabin and established a ferry service along the river.

Two years later, John Dixon purchased Ogee's claim and settled on the spot with his family. When an uprising with the Indians led to the Black Hawk Wars, the ferry was turned into Fort Dixon, which later became Dixon. Today you can see not only signs and statues honoring both John Dixon and Abe Lincoln, the latter of whom served in the militia here in 1832, but also sites honoring another president: Ronald Reagan. It's here in Dixon where Reagan grew up, and travelers come from around the nation to tour his boyhood home.

A little farther upstream, at a C-shape bend in the river, is the tiny hamlet of Grand Detour, where pioneers from Vermont first settled in the early 1800s. One of those pioneers was John Deere.

North of Grand Detour is the town of Oregon, one of the hidden gems of the state, where homes set amid lush trees on rolling hills create a tranquil setting. From here the river snakes its way toward the Mississippi through forests and bluffs. Many state parks enshrine this beauty; all you need is a pair of hiking boots and a camera to fully enjoy and remember it.

East of Dixon, as you move into the flatter farmland, are the small towns of Amboy and Franklin Grove. Mere specks on the map, these places are where you can discover the sense of community and volunteerism found in small-town America. In Amboy you can see where residents banded together and creatively saved a city park from a destructive storm by transforming fallen trees into a remarkable collection of wooden sculptures. In Franklin Grove, volunteers have recreated a 19th-century prairie village from old, abandoned buildings found scattered around the countryside.

Another speck on the map, just west of DeKalb, is Rochelle. Few Chicagoans may have heard of this tiny town, yet to the world's train enthusiasts it's a major capital. With some 100 trains rumbling past each day, more than 60,000 people from around the globe come here because of its premier location for train spotting.

Geologically speaking, DeKalb may not be considered part of the Rock River valley, but because it's roughly two-thirds of the way between Chicago and the valley, it's a perfect point to start or end your exploration of the Rock River valley. DeKalb is named for the French general, Baron John DeKalb, who served under George Washington during the Revolutionary War. It was in the town of DeKalb where Joseph Glidden invented barbed wire in 1874, and the success of barbed wire gave the town its nickname of "Barb City." As home to the nation's first farm bureau, DeKalb also has had a long tradition as a center for agriculture. It's safe to say that everyone who has ever looked out their window while driving through Midwest farmlands has seen the famous winged-corn signs that read "DeKalb," from the giant DeKalb Genetics that is based here. Today, DeKalb is known as the home to Northern Illinois University. With 25,000 students, it's the state's second-largest school. There are museums and other historic sites worthy of exploring in this city.

WHAT TO SEE & DO

DEKALB
DeKalb Public Library This grand art deco building was constructed in 1931 from funds donated by barbed wire magnate Jacob Haish. The facade is Indiana Bedford limestone, and interior details include art deco marble, carvings, and mouldings.
> 309 Oak St., DeKalb, tel. 815/756–9568, www.dkpl.org. Free. Mon.–Thurs. 9–9, Fri. 9–6, Sat. 9–5, Sun. 1–4 (Sept.–May only).
Egyptian Theater On the National Register of Historic Places, this 1929 Egyptian–art deco structure's design was influenced by the then-recent discovery of King Tut's Tomb. It is still used today for movies and live performances. Tours are given by appointment only, and can last between 45 minutes and 1½ hours, depending on how many levels of the theater you wish to see. > 135 N. 2nd St., DeKalb, tel. 815/758–1215. $5. Sept.–July, daily.
Ellwood House Museum This dwelling, built by barbed wire millionaire Isaac Ellwood in 1879, now houses exhibits of much of its original furnishings along with other period artifacts and information about the history of the area. > 509 N. 1st St., DeKalb, tel. 815/756–4609, www.ellwoodhouse.org. $6. Tours Mar.–mid-Dec., Tues.–Fri. at 1 and 3, weekends at 1, 2, and 3.
Harley-Davidson Museum You can almost feel the wind in your face as you view the more than 65 antique and modern motorcycles on display here, along with memorabilia and vintage clothing dating back to the 1920s. Items include old parts, accessories, and other cycle features. The museum's collection also includes one of the first two low-riders manufactured by Harley. > 969 Peace Rd., DeKalb, tel. 815/756–4558. Free. Weekdays 9–5, Sat. 9–3.
Heritage Square Gallery At this gallery, you can see the changing face of DeKalb's downtown, from 1860 through the present, through hundreds of photographs. > 105 N. 1st St., DeKalb, tel. 815/756–1445. Free. Weekdays 9–5.
Northern Illinois University DeKalb's institution is the main campus of this university and includes seven degree-granting colleges and a law school, in which combined there are 22,000 students. Famous alumni from the drama school includes

Joan Allen (Tony and Oscar winner) and Steve Harris (best known as Eugene on *The Practice*). Tours are given weekdays at 1:30 PM and Saturday at noon. A tour includes a walk to Altgeld Hall, an administration building that resembles a 14th-century Edwardian castle, and Martin Luther King Jr. Memorial Commons, a plaza for student gatherings, which has a three-story memorial sculpture dedicated to Dr. King's principles. > 1425 W. Lincoln Hwy., DeKalb, tel. 815/753–1535, www.niu.edu. Free. Daily.
Rochelle Railroad Park One of just a few such train-spotting parks in the country, this park sits at the crossing of two sets of double tracks used by major rail lines. Roughly 100 trains per day pass this junction. Because the park is open 24 hours, some railroad fans literally spend all night watching trains go by. A gift shop on the grounds sells anything train-related you can imagine, including the latest railroad enthusiast magazines and audio CDs of train sounds. > 124 N. 9th St., 20 mi west of DeKalb, off Rte. 38, Rochelle, tel. 815/562–8107, rochellerailroadpark.tripod.com. Free. Park: daily; gift shop: Wed.–Sun. 9–5.
Standard Oil Filling Station Built in 1918, this was Rochelle's first gasoline filling station. Though no longer in use, the restored station includes its original canopy over the pumps and 1918 equipment. Inside are displays of antique Standard Oil memorabilia. > 500 Lincoln Ave., 20 mi west of DeKalb, off Rte. 38, Rochelle, tel. 815/562–7031. Free. Wed.–Sun.

DIXON
Amboy City Park A disastrous storm struck this park in June 1999, and severely damaged many of the large trees. The town of Amboy rallied together and came up with the idea of making carvings out of these trees. What stands now is unique park filled with nearly two dozen wooden sculptures that include a 7-foot-tall Indian Chief, a baseball umpire, and a variety of animals. > E. Main St., 11 mi east of Dixon on Rte. 52, Amboy, tel. 815/857–3814. Free. Daily.
Amboy Illinois Central Depot Museum Built in 1876, this depot houses hundreds of historic items that fill its 19 rooms. Rooms have different themes throughout, so not everything contained within is related to the railroad. The Fireman Room contains old firefighting equipment, and the Army Room contains items soldiers used during the world wars. Listed on the National Register of Historic Places, the depot retains many of its original features including 12-foot ceilings, 10-foot-high windows, and 2-inch-thick hardwood floors. > 50 N. East Ave., 11 mi east of Dixon on Rte. 52, Amboy, tel. 815/857–4700. Free. May–Sept., Wed., Thurs., and Sun. 1–4, Fri. and Sat. 10–4.
Blackhawk Chocolate Trail Through the Blackhawk Waterways Convention and Visitors Bureau in Polo, you can obtain self-guided tours for the four-county region—Carroll, Ogle, Lee, and White Side counties—focusing on restaurants and stores where you can find special chocolate treats—fudge, sundaes, and variations on Death by Chocolate. > 201 N. Franklin St., 13 mi northeast of Dixon on U.S. 52, Polo, tel. 800/678–2108. Free. Daily.
Chaplin Creek Historic Village A re-created 19th-century midwestern village, this "work in progress" is continually adding new buildings to the site by salvaging those found from around the state. You can tour buildings such as a blacksmith shop and a country school. > 1715 Whitney Rd., 9 mi east of Dixon on Rte. 38, Franklin Grove, tel. 815/456–2382, www.franklingroveil.org/clncrk.htm. Free (donations accepted). Mid-Apr.–mid-Oct., Sat. 10–4, Sun. noon–5, or by appointment.
Dillon Home Museum Built in 1858, this home provides an excellent opportunity to view examples of Italianate architecture. The Dillon family purchased the home in 1882, and the artifacts and antique furnishings displayed were originally used by the

From Prairies to Farmland

**THE SMALL TOWN OF GRAND DE-
TOUR, ILLINOIS, IS THE BIRTH-
PLACE** of one of the greatest agricultural
revolutions in history. What happened here
in the Rock River valley not only impacted
Illinois but also reached around the world.

Born in 1804, John Deere grew up in Vermont learning the blacksmith trade. By the
mid-1820s he worked as a journeymen
blacksmith and earned a reputation for his
high quality and service. But Vermont's
business conditions deteriorated in the
1830s, causing Deere to think about his future. He became curious about the tales
told of opportunity available in the "New
West." (Back then Illinois was considered
part of the West.) Pioneers were returning
to Vermont and talking about a new town
named Grand Detour. They tried to per-
suade their neighbors to relocate their businesses and join them with the hopes of
creating a thriving community. Deere bit
at the chance.

In 1836, with a small bundle of tools and
little money, Deere ventured west alone.
He left his wife and children behind until
he could build a homestead. As good luck
would have it, Grand Detour was so des-
perate for a blacksmith that within just
two days of his arrival he built a forge and
was open for business.

At first, Deere shod horses and made
equipment for farmers and local businesses. But soon he heard concerns among
his fellow pioneers about how cast-iron
plows they brought from the East were no
match for the rich, sticky soil of this new
prairie land. After every few steps farmers
were forced to stop and scrape off soil that
clung to their plow, take a few more steps,
and repeat the process. The problem was
so bad that some farmers considered moving back East.

Deere realized there must be a solution.
After testing different designs, he discovered that if the plow's shape was modified
and the steel was highly polished, then the
soil would fall (or scour) off. Creating the

first such plow from the remains of a broken saw blade, Deere introduced the "self-
polishing" steel plow to the public in 1837.
Word quickly spread among farmers
throughout the Midwest about this mirac-
ulous new plow that could turn the soil
over and leave a path of neat furrows. Or-
ders came pouring in. Deere quickly converted his small blacksmith shop into a
plow factory. It wasn't long before the
great plains of Illinois and surrounding
states would begin their great transforma-
tion—endless miles of prairie could now be
turned into farmland, step by step, furrow
by furrow.

Deere stayed in Grand Detour until 1848,
when he moved his factory to Moline to
take advantage of the Mississippi River's
waterpower and shipping capabilities.
Today, the company John Deere founded in
1837 remains in Moline and continues to
be the world's largest manufacturer of
farm equipment.

family. A carriage house at the back of the grounds displays exhibits on local history, including photos and old clippings. You can see a vintage locomotive and caboose toward the back of the grounds. > 1005 E. 3rd St., 16 mi west on I–88, Sterling, tel. 815/622–6202. $2. Tues., Thurs., and Sat. 10–noon and 1–4, Sun. 1–5.

Franklin Creek Grist Mill You have to follow the winding country road to get to this re-creation of a four-story 1847 gristmill, built by community volunteers. It uses a 4-ton waterwheel to power pulleys and gears to turn a millstone, creating a hauntingly serene chimelike sound throughout the building. You can explore the building yourself or take a free 15-minute guided tour. Bags of cornmeal, freshly grounded on-site, are available for purchase. > 1893 Twist Rd., 9 mi east of Dixon on Rte. 38, Franklin Grove, tel. 815/456–2718. Free. Apr.–Oct., Sat. 10–4, Sun noon–4.

Franklin Creek State Natural Area Franklin Creek snakes its way through hardwood forests, bedrock outcroppings, and variety of flora and fauna at this 664-acre park, 1 mi northwest of the village of Franklin Grove. Hiking trails and picnic areas traverse the park. You can also see plenty of horses on the 6 mi of designated equestrian trails. In winter, 4 mi of these trails are open for snowmobiling and the other 2 mi are designated for cross-country skiing. The nature area is down the road from the Franklin Creek Grist Mill. > 1872 Twist Rd., 9 mi east of Dixon on Rte. 38, Franklin Grove, tel. 815/456–2878. Free. Daily.

John Deere Historic Site At this site, John Deere forged a new self-scouring steel plow that revolutionized the world of agriculture in the 1830s. Deere's original blacksmith shop was discovered by a team of University of Illinois archaeologists in 1962, and the historic site was built around it. An 1830s homestead and archeological exhibits are also part of the site. > 8393 S. Main St., 6 mi northeast of Dixon on Rte. 2, Grand Detour, tel. 815/652–4551, www.deere.com. $3. Apr.–Oct., daily 9–5.

Lincoln Highway National Headquarters This restored pre–Civil War building was built by Abe Lincoln's cousin, Henry Isaac Lincoln, in 1860. It now serves as the headquarters for the Lincoln Highway Association, a group devoted to preserving and promoting America's first transcontinental highway. Displayed here is everything from old signposts to postcards to books written about the 3,000-mi highway. LHA director Lynn Asp is on-site and happy to regale with stories of the history of the building, the highway, and the Franklin Grove area. > 136 N. Elm St., 9 mi east of Dixon on Rte. 38, Franklin Grove, tel. 815/456–3030. Free. Mon.–Sat. 10–4, Sun. noon–4.

Lincoln Statue Park A statue of Abraham Lincoln, who served in the 1832 Black Hawk War, is the focal point of this park. The park is also home to the Old Settlers' Memorial Log Cabin, which contains antiques and articles that belonged to the region's early settlers. Tours are available. > 115 Lincoln Statue Dr., Dixon, tel. 815/288–7204. Free. Park: daily; cabin: Memorial Day–Labor Day, weekends 1:30–4:30.

Nachusa Grasslands These 1,500 rolling acres provide a peaceful place to hike or bird-watch. With more than 500 native plants, more than 100 bird species, and a variety of butterflies, you can almost always see something new. Although it's open year-round, April through October are the best months for blooms. > 8772 S. Lowden Rd., 9 mi east of Dixon on Rte. 38, Franklin Grove. 815/456–2340. www.franklingroveil.org. Free. Daily.

Ronald Reagan's Birthplace Here, you can visit the apartment where former president Ronald Reagan was born. It has been restored and redecorated to reflect the early 1900s. Adjoining the building is a gift shop and museum with displays of period photos, postcards, and letters from the Reagan family. > 111 S. Main St., 25 mi southwest of Dixon, Tampico, tel. 815/438–2130. Free (donations accepted). Apr.–Dec., Mon.–Sat. 10–4, Sun. 1–4.

Ronald Reagan's Boyhood Home From 1920 to 1923, the boy who grew up to become the 40th president of the United States lived in this house. The house was restored in the early 1980s based on President Reagan's own recollections. Free guided tours are conducted, and a gift shop and informative video presentation are in the house next door. > 816 S. Hennepin St., Dixon, tel. 815/288–5176. Free (donations accepted). Apr.–Nov., Mon–Sat. 10–4, Sun. 1–4; Feb. and Mar., Sat. 10–4, Sun. 1–4.

OREGON

Castle Rock State Park Sandstone rock formations provide views of the Rock River in this park, 3 mi south of downtown Oregon. A nature preserve, 6 mi of hiking trails, picnic sites, and fishing make this an idyllic destination for outdoor enthusiasts. Brochures and maps can be picked up at the park office at the entrance. > 1365 W. Castle Rd., Oregon, tel. 815/732–7329. Free. Daily sunrise–sunset.

Conover Square Twenty local businesses, including 13 specialty shops, are housed under one roof in this converted piano factory. You can find shops selling handmade luxury soaps, designer clothing, and jewelry, and visit a working pottery studio. > 201 N. 3rd St., Oregon, tel. 815/732–3950. Daily 10–5.

Lowden-Miller State Forest You can explore 2,225-acre forest 3 mi south of Oregon on the Rock River via the many miles of hiking and cross-country skiing trails. You can pick up maps and brochures from information boxes near the parking lots. > Lowden and Nashua Rds., Oregon, tel. 815/732–7329. Free. Daily.

Lowden State Park Less than 2 mi from downtown Oregon, perched atop bluffs overlooking the Rock River, this park has 4 mi of hiking trails, fishing, and camping. The park has no visitor center, but maps and brochures are available near parking lot areas. The park is also home to the **"Black Hawk" Statue.** Designed by artist Lorado Taft, this 50-foot-tall creation is believed to be the second-largest concrete monolith statue in the world. Dedicated to the character of the American Indian, this giant work of art depicts an Indian gazing down the Rock River with arms folded. Informative panels on its construction are at its base, where you can also see a panoramic view of the surrounding Oregon area. > 1411 N. River Rd., Oregon, tel. 815/732–6828. Free, camping $11 per night. Daily.

Ogle County Historical Society Museum Historical artifacts of Oregon and Ogle County that tell how people lived in the late 1800s are displayed in the historic Ruby Nash home. Built in 1878, the midwestern prairie-style home displays period clothing, furniture, a pianoforte used at the 1842 inauguration of Illinois governor Thomas Ford, and the original kitchen with cast-iron stove. > 111 N. 6th St., Oregon, tel. 815/732–6876. Free. May–early Oct., Thurs. 9–11, Sun. 1–4.

Oregon Public Library Art Gallery Several oil paintings and sculptures by early-20th-century artists from the Eagle's Nest, a local art colony, are displayed at this library and gallery. > 300 Jefferson St., Oregon, tel. 815/732–2724. Free. Mon.–Thurs. 9–8, Fri. and Sat. 9–4.

Pride of Oregon A 15-mi, two-hour ride on this paddleboat takes you on the Rock River to see the cliffs, forests, and towns that line its banks. The boat departs twice daily from Maxson Riverside Restaurant. Lunch, dinner, or buffet cruises are available. > 1469 Illinois St. (Rte. 2), Oregon, tel. 815/732–6761 or 800/468–4222, www.maxsonrestaurant.com. $12 sightseeing, $24 lunch, $30 dinner, $26 Sun. buffet. Apr.–mid-Nov., Mon.–Sat. 11 AM and 6:30 PM; Sun. 11 AM and 2:30 PM.

Soldiers' Monument A 1916 war memorial by sculptor Lorado Taft sits in Courthouse Square. It was erected to honor the contributions made by men of Ogle County during the Civil War. > 4th and Washington Sts., Oregon, tel. 815/732–1100. Free. Daily.

T.J.'s Canoes Two-hour, four-hour, and overnight canoe trips down the Rock River are provided by this outfitter. All trips are self-guided and include a shuttle service to bring you and your rental canoe back to your car. Reservations are suggested for groups of five or more. > 305 S. 1st St., Oregon, tel. 815/732–4516, www.tjscanoerental.com. Canoe rental: $27 2 hrs, $45 4 hrs, $50 overnight. Apr.–Nov.

White Pines Forest State Park This 385-acre park, 5 mi south of Mount Morris, includes the nation's southernmost stand of white pine. Conifers, which have long, silky needles, were once common in the area, but they have mostly disappeared. The area is teeming with deer and smaller mammals, such as chipmunks and raccoons. You can hike on limestone bluffs, and cross-country ski on trails in winter. A visitor center and restaurant are near the center of the park. > 6712 W. Pines Rd., 8 mi west of Oregon, Mount Morris, tel. 815/946–3717 park information. Free. Daily 8–sunset.

Save the Date

JUNE

Baron DeKalb Day To celebrate this German-American Revolutionary War hero, this day's events throughout town include museum tours, Revolutionary War reenactments, and a vintage bathing-suit show. The "Baron" himself makes surprise appearances. Usually held in late June. > DeKalb, tel. 815/748–7788, www.cityofdekalb.com.

JUNE–AUGUST

StageCoach Players Community Theater The StageCoach Players stage a variety of performances throughout summer, including musicals. > 1516 Barber Green Rd., DeKalb, tel. 815/758–1940, www.stagecoachers.com.

JULY

Petunia Festival Games, carnival rides, and live entertainment, including a midwestern drum-and-bugle competition, highlight this weeklong festival held around the Fourth of July. > Dixon, tel. 815/284–3361.

AUGUST

Amboy Depot Days This four-day festival, held the weekend before Labor Day, hosts a carnival, crafters, and live entertainment. It also includes one of the largest car shows in northern Illinois, with more than 500 antique cars and trucks. > Amboy, tel. 815/857–3814.

Corn Fest You can indulge in the shopping, eating, and drinking provided by the many vendors and local businesses at this festival. A carnival, music, and other live entertainment enrich the experience. It all takes place downtown during three days the last weekend of the month. > DeKalb, tel. 815/748–2676, www.cornfest.com.

Two-Cylinder Show Every other year, two-cylinder fanatics flock to Detour for this three-day show, where more than 80 fully restored tractors, maintained by two-cylinder clubs, are exhibited. This event usually takes place the first weekend in August, on odd-numbered years. > 8393 S. Main St., Grand Detour, tel. 815/652–4551.

SEPTEMBER

Grand Detour Arts Festival Artists from throughout the Midwest display their work at this festival, usually held in the middle of September at the John Deere Historic site. > 8393 S. Main St., Grand Detour, tel. 815/652–4551.

Scarecrow Festival Festivities scattered throughout town comprise this mid-September festival. Events include a pig roast and music along the Rock River on Friday and Saturday nights and daytime activities for kids, such as pumpkin painting, a pet parade, and a soapbox derby. Saturday's highlight is the scarecrow-decorating competition. > Dixon, tel. 815/288–2308.

OCTOBER

Autumn on Parade During the first weekend in October, you can join the revelry in the streets of downtown Oregon, where strolling madrigal and country singers, jugglers, and a parade roll by. A vintage-car and motorcycle show, a petting zoo, pony rides, a pig scramble, a tug-o'-war spanning the river, and a reenactment of life at the turn of the 20th century add to the fun. > Oregon, tel. 815/732–2100.

White Pines Ranch Family Weekend Normally only for youth groups, the 200-acre White Pines Dude Ranch opens itself up for a three-day family-focused weekend. The timing coincides with Oregon's Autumn on Parade during the first weekend of October. The $100 per person fee includes lodging, horseback riding, and meals (from Friday supper through Sunday brunch). Reservations are essential. > 3581 Pines Rd., Oregon, tel. 815/732–7923, www.whitepinesranch.com.

WHERE TO STAY

DEKALB

Baymont Inns & Suites Near Northern Illinois University and close to downtown, this inn is within walking distance of several national chain restaurants. Rooms are decorated in dark and solid colors. > 1314 W. Lincoln Hwy., DeKalb 60115, tel. 815/748–4800, fax 815/756–5047, www.baymontinns.com. 53 rooms. Cable TV, indoor pool, gym, laundry facilities. AE, D, DC, MC, V. CP. ¢–$

Best Western DeKalb Inn & Suites Rooms have a country flair at this two-story motel, 3 mi from downtown DeKalb. You're right next to NIU's stadium, which means all campus facilities are down the road; restaurants are within walking distance. > 1212 W. Lincoln Hwy., DeKalb 60115, tel. 815/758–8661 or 800/528–1234, fax 815/758–0001, www.bestwestern.com. 95 rooms. Some kitchenettes, cable TV, pool, gym, laundry facilities, laundry service, business services, some pets allowed. AE, D, DC, MC, V. CP. ¢–$$

Comfort Inn & Suites At the junction of Routes 251 and 38, these accommodations are 16 mi west of DeKalb. Built in 2002, this eight-story hotel includes hot-tub suites with glass-block enclosed spas. > 1133 N. 7th St., Rochelle 61068, tel. 815/562–5551 or 800/228–5150, fax 815/562–3911, www.rochelle.net/~comfortinn. 93 rooms, 27 suites. Restaurant, in-room data ports, some microwaves, cable TV, indoor-outdoor pool, health club, hot tub, bar, laundry facilities, laundry service, business services. AE, D, DC, MC, V. CP. ¢

Harbor Inn The "no frills" policy at this motel keeps the prices down, and you are 3 mi from downtown in a busy area, with strip-mall shopping and a large bookstore nearby. Rooms are decorated modestly with modern furnishings. > 2675 Sycamore Rd., DeKalb 60115, tel. 815/756–3552, fax 815/756–8257. 46 rooms, 3 suites. Some microwaves, some refrigerators, cable TV, pool. AE, D, DC, MC, V. ¢

Super 8 Just off I-88, this two-story motel is near the NIU campus and downtown DeKalb. Rooms have contemporary furnishings, and spa suites are available. > 800 W. Fairview Dr., DeKalb 60115, tel. 815/748–4688 or 800/800–8000, fax 815/748–4688, www.super8.com. 44 rooms. Cable TV, indoor pool, hot tub, laundry facilities. AE, D, DC, MC, V. CP. ¢

DIXON

Best Western Reagan Hotel A few miles outside downtown Dixon, this redbrick lodge is set amid the rolling hills of the Rock River valley. Rooms are larger than the average chain hotel room, and furnishings are dated but comfortable. > 443 Rte. 2, Dixon

61021, tel. 815/284–1890 or 800/528–1234, fax 815/284–1174, www.bestwestern.com. 91 rooms. Restaurant, in-room data ports, cable TV, some in-room VCRs, pool, exercise equipment, hot tub, bar, business services, some pets allowed (fee). AE, D, DC, MC, V. CP. ¢–$

Comfort Inn Though surrounded by cornfields, this motel and its rooms are thoroughly modern, and for those interested in the former actor and president Ronald Reagan, you can stay in a suite with his name. The hotel is off I–88 and 2 mi south of downtown Dixon. > 136 Plaza Dr., Dixon 61021, tel. 815/284–0500, fax 815/284–0509, www.comfortsuites.com. 41 rooms, 7 suites. In-room data ports, some in-room hot tubs, some microwaves, some refrigerators, cable TV, indoor pool, gym, business services. AE, D, DC, MC, V. CP. ¢

Crawford House Inn Inside this Italianate house are 12 spacious rooms to roam. Built in 1869, and owned by one of Dixon's founders, Joseph Crawford, this mansion opened as a bed-and-breakfast in 1998. Either a king or queen feather bed and Victorian furnishings fill each room. The inn is within walking distance of Ronald Reagan's home. > 204 E. 3rd St., Dixon 61021, tel. 815/288–3351, www.crawfordhouseinn.com. 3 rooms without bath. D, MC, V. BP. ¢–$

Hillendale Bed and Breakfast You can choose among themed rooms, such as the Aloha and the Australian Outback, in this 1890s Tudor mansion in Morrison, about 25 mi west of Dixon. Rooms, some of which have fireplaces, are furnished with antiques and mementos from the owners' world travels. > 600 W. Lincolnway, Morrison 61270, tel. 815/772–3454, fax 815/772–7023, www.hillend.com. 10 rooms. Cable TV, some in-room VCRs, gym, cross-country skiing; no smoking. AE, D, DC, MC, V. BP. ¢–$$

OREGON

Chateau Lodge This lodge is 1 mi north of downtown Oregon and near White Pines Forest, Castle Rock, and Lowden state parks. Though it sits near the highway and rooms are modern, it's an economical and convenient place to spend the evening. > 1326 Rte. 2, Oregon 61061, tel. 815/732–6195. 12 rooms. Refrigerators, cable TV. D, MC, V. ¢

Colonial Rose Inn This 1855 brick Italianate mansion sits on 2½ acres with perennial gardens. A baby grand piano rests in the front parlor, and wicker furniture fills the porch. Elegant wallpaper, original oil paintings, and a pleasant mix of Oriental rugs and hardwood floors enrich the home. The inn is two blocks from John Deere Historic Site. > 8230 S. Green St., Grand Detour 61021, tel. 815/652–4422, www.colonialroseinn.com. 4 rooms. MC, V. BP. $

Paddle Wheel Inn The suites here have balconies with panoramic vistas. Rooms are modestly decorated with country patterns and pine furniture. One mile north of downtown Oregon, the inn sits on the banks of the Rock River across from Lowden State Park. > 1457 N. Illinois Rte. 2, Oregon 61061, tel. 815/732–4540 or 800/468–4222, fax 815/732–3404, www.paddlewheelinn.com. 39 rooms. In-room data ports, some in-room hot tubs, cable TV, some in-room VCRs, gym, sauna. AE, D, DC, MC, V. CP. $

Patchwork Inn This two-story inn with front porches on both levels was built in 1835 as a brick Greek-revival home. Abraham Lincoln ate and slept here, and you can stay in the same room, with a fireplace and period furnishings. Braided rugs and handmade quilts adorn the rooms; the parlor is Victorian. The inn is a block from downtown, at the intersection of Routes 64 and 2. > 122 N. 3rd St., Oregon 61061, tel. 815/732–4113, fax 815/732–6557. 10 rooms. In-room hot tubs, cable TV. D, MC, V. CP. ¢–$

Pinehill Bed and Breakfast This 1874 Italianate country villa with front porch and period furnishings is a chocolate-lover's delight. Fresh fudge is baked daily for afternoon tea, and the library is stocked with chocolate history and recipe books. > 400 Mix St., Oregon 61061, tel. 815/732–2067 or 800/851–1131, www.pinehillbb.com. 4 rooms, 3 with bath. MC, V. **$–$$$**

White Pines Inn Rustic cabins and a restaurant nestle in the middle of 385 acres of forest in White Pines State Park, 8 mi from Oregon. The cabins were constructed in the 1930s by the Civilian Conservation Corps. They have gas fireplaces, and three cabins have four adjoining units. No cooking is allowed in or around cabins. Reservations are essential. > 6712 W. Pines Rd., Mount Morris 61054, tel. 815/946–3817, fax 815/946–3006, www.whitepinesinn.com. 25 cabins. Restaurant, cable TV, some in-room VCRs, fishing, hiking, volleyball, playground. D, MC, V. **¢**

CAMPING

Green River Oaks Resort Activities abound here, including a lake for fishing, a tennis court, 18-hole minigolf, volleyball, and a softball field. Eleven RV trailers are available for rent. > 1442 Sleepy Hollow Rd., Amboy 61310, tel. 815/857–2815. 225 sites, full and partial hook-ups, 100 tent sites. Flush toilets, dump station, laundry facilities, shower, grills, picnic tables, general store, 2 pools. Reservations essential. MC, V. Closed mid.-Oct.–late Apr. **¢**

Mendota Hills Camping Resort With 130 acres, three fishing holes, and a lake for swimming, you have plenty of room to hit a golf ball, go for a hayrack ride, paddle a boat, or catch a fish. > 642 U.S. Rte. 52, Amboy 61310, tel. 815/849–5930. 20 full hook-ups, 80 partial hook-ups. Flush and portable toilets, dump station, shower, picnic tables, general store, playground. MC, V. Closed mid-Oct.–mid-Apr. **¢**

River Road Camping and Marina This 30-acre site accommodates both campers and tents. On the Rock River, the campground also has a canoe rental and a boat launch. > 3922 River Rd., Oregon 61061, tel. 815/234–5383, www.gocampingamerica.com. 150 full hook-ups, 200 tent sites. Flush and portable toilets, dump station, drinking water, showers, grills, picnic tables, electricity, general store, pool. V. Closed Dec.–Mar. **¢**

WHERE TO EAT

DEKALB

Hillside Restaurant This homey dining room filled with antiques has a seasonally changing menu but regularly hosts a Bohemian night on Wednesday, Italian nights on Thursday and Sunday, and brunch on Sunday. > 121 N. 2nd St., DeKalb, tel. 815/756–4749. AE, D, MC, V. Closed Tues. **$–$$**

Rosita's Pottery and Aztec imagery create an old-Mexico environment, where in addition to the customary burritos and tacos, you can choose less common fare such as Mexican steak grilled with green peppers, and fried Mexican sausage with scrambled eggs. > 642 E. Lincoln Hwy., DeKalb, tel. 815/756–1201. AE, D, MC, V. **$**

Thai Pavilion Dishes to try in this Thai eatery near the Northern Illinois University campus are the pad Thai, fried red snapper, and hot-and-sour soup. > 131 E. Lincoln Hwy., DeKalb, tel. 815/756–6445. MC, V. Closed Sun. **¢–$**

DIXON

Colonial Rose Inn Restaurant This restaurant in an 1850s inn is known for its filet mignon, fresh fish, and hickory-smoked pork chops, as well as its antique bar. > 8230 S. Green St., Grand Detour, tel. 815/652–4422. MC, V. Closed Sun.–Tues. No lunch. **$$–$$$$**

Galena Steak House Steak is the specialty here, but chicken and fish are also served in this wood-paneled restaurant, a local favorite. > 1101 N. Galena, Dixon, tel. 815/285–1625. AE, D, MC, V. $–$$

Rivers Edge Inn Chicken strips and ribs are the favorites in this dining room surrounded by large windows, through which you have a view of the Rock River. > 2303 W. 1st St., Dixon, tel. 815/288–7396. AE, MC, V. No lunch. $–$$

OREGON

Jay's Drive In A throwback to the true drive-ins of 1950s and 1960s, Jay's lets you eat without leaving the car. Just find an empty spot, order via intercom, and your burger, fries, and malt will be brought to your car on a tray that's hung on your window. Tables are also available in the indoor dining area. > 107 Washington St., Oregon, tel. 815/732–2396. No credit cards. ¢

La Vigna Seafood, steaks, pasta, and veal dishes get a Northern Italian spin at this trattoria. Several dining rooms help create an intimate, yet casual dining experience. > 2190 S. Daysville Rd., Oregon, tel. 815/732–4413 or 800/806–4982. AE, D, DC, MC, V. Closed Mon. No lunch. $–$$

Maxson Riverside Restaurant Dine on veal marsala, chicken piccata, pasta, or prime rib at this spot overlooking the Rock River. Large windows frame panoramic views of tree-filled hills across the river. This is also the departure point for the *Pride of Oregon* paddle-wheel tours and dinner cruises. > 1469 Rte. 2 N, Oregon, tel. 815/732–6761 or 800/468–4222. AE, D, DC, MC, V. Closed Mon. No lunch. $$

The Roadhouse A rustic yet elegant dining room and cocktail bar is filled with antiques and the largest known collection of miniature wagons. If you crave a hearty steak or BBQ ribs, this is the place to go. But legend has it there may be a ghost watching you dine. > 807 S. 7th St., Oregon, tel. 815/732–2300 or 888/290–0076. MC, V. Closed Mon.–Wed. No lunch. ¢–$$

ESSENTIALS

Getting Here

Driving to and from the Rock River valley area is your best, and really your only, option. There is no rail or commuter air service, and the only available bus service is between Chicago and DeKalb, which primarily serves the NIU college student and not the weekend traveler. You will need a car to visit most sites, and few sites are within walking distance of each other.

BY CAR

The easiest route between Chicago and the Rock River valley is via I–88. This is a toll road, and tolls cost 40¢ near the city and 95¢ as you head west. If you leave during the evening rush hour, you most likely will encounter bumper-to-bumper traffic from downtown Chicago to as far as the Aurora area. Once past Aurora, the drive is fairly uncongested. During non–rush hour times, the drive takes about two hours between downtown Chicago and the Route 26 exit at Dixon.

To hit all the towns and sites in between the Rock River valley area and DeKalb, take Route 38 instead of I–88. A recommended route is to take I–88 to Dixon or Rock Falls, see the sites there, then follow Route 38 East to stop at the attractions as you move your way back toward Chicago. Taking this route allows you to visit roadside stands with farm-grown produce. Once you pass DeKalb, you can always hop back onto the tollway and head home.

Visitor Information

CONTACTS **Blackhawk Waterways Convention and Visitors Bureau** > 201 N. Franklin Ave., Polo 61064, tel. 800/678–2108, fax 815/946–2277, www.blackhawkwaterwayscvb.org. **DeKalb Area Chamber of Commerce** > 164 E. Lincoln Hwy., DeKalb 60115, tel. 815/756–6306, fax 815/756–5164, www.dekalb.org. **Dixon Area Chamber of Commerce** > 101 W. 2nd St., Suite 210, Dixon 61021, tel. 815/284–3361, www.dixonillinoischamber.com. **Oregon Chamber of Commerce** > 124½ N. 4th St., Oregon 61061, tel. 815/732–2100, www.oregonil.com.

Amish Country

115 mi east of Chicago

9

By Jenn Q. Goddu

AMISH COUNTRY, off the 75-mi corridor from South Bend southeast to Fort Wayne, is rife with odd juxtapositions. The abundance of recreational vehicle manufacturers in Elkhart or nearby in Goshen or Middlebury is found alongside establishments in which Amish artisans are crafting fine furniture using methods that have been passed down from generation to generation. You might at first think you've gone in the wrong direction as you drive towards the historic Amish farm buildings, auction houses, and family-style restaurants in Nappanee. Modern living has encroached on the Amish domain, and northern Indiana's largest Amish living-history settlement is opposite a car sales lot; an open-air market of arts, crafts, antiques, and collectibles is down a road past a row of industrial parks.

And yet time can seem to stand still on the back roads here. Fresh-faced children, boys wearing straw hats, and girls in bonnets pile in horse-drawn black-box buggies clip-clopping along dusty country roads. You may even see some of the teenagers, ready for the independence of traveling alone, pedaling down the main streets on unadorned, dated bicycles. Plain white farmhouses are surrounded by fields that are still plowed the old-fashioned way, by a pair of sturdy draft horses. Many of the farms operate even today without the benefit of modern conveniences such as electricity, gas, or telephones.

Like a flashback to the early 20th century, simplicity is a way of life for more than 4,000 Amish in northern Indiana, which is one of the largest Amish settlements in the United States. The Amish first settled in Indiana in the mid-1800s. Their faith dates back to the late 17th century, when Jakob Amman and a small group split from the Swiss Mennonites. Named after their leader Amman, the Amish started settling in the United States in the 1720s. They were first drawn to Lancaster County, Pennsylvania, because of the state's religious tolerance. The Amish are farmers for the most part, and over the years they have continued to migrate westward in search of fertile land. Their lives are rooted in a conservative Christian faith and literal interpretations of the Bible.

Indiana's Amish Country has embraced the essence of the Amish lifestyle with dozens of homey bed-and-breakfast inns, home-style restaurants in big barnlike buildings, general stores and bakeries at crossroads communities, and charming small towns filled with shops selling crafts, gifts, and antiques. Even hitching posts front of some of the fast-food joints. Collectors and casual browsers come to Amish Country seeking the perfect handcrafted quilt, solid wood dining room table, or homespun gift. Some brave the brisk bidding at an auction or strolling an open-air flea market—Shipshewana's weekday market is one of the largest in the country. While driving through the region, keep an eye out for signs touting cottage industries such as Amish homes that have set up shop to sell candles, beeswax, fresh flowers, or pies.

A number of towns, all within 35 mi of each other, dot the winding and rolling hills here. Elkhart is the gateway to Amish Country. It is bustling with modernity and its

downtown sits by its namesake river. A looping tour of the region will take in Nappanee, where busy Amish farms and furniture shops are nestled among the commercialism and convenience that occupy the non-Amish (called English by the Amish).
Fourteen miles northeast of Nappanee, heading into the real back-roads part of
Amish Country, is Elkhart County's seat of Goshen. Founded in 1895 by the Mennonites, Goshen covers less than 10 square mi. "Maple City," as Goshen calls itself, is
filled with tree-lined streets and gracious older homes. Nine miles farther northeast is
Middlebury. Once the mail-order gardening capital of the world, this rural town retains a lush and diverse park system and simple charm despite the presence of many
RV manufacturers. At the farthest point from Chicago, 7 mi farther east of Middlebury, is Shipshewana with its more than 90 specialty shops featuring every imagina-
ble type of handicraft. This village, tucked away on the buggy-filled secondary roads,
is worth the drive.

WHAT TO SEE & DO

ELKHART

Midwest Museum of American Art The museum, which occupies a restored bank
building downtown, displays sculpture, photography, paintings, and prints dating
from the mid-1800s to the present. The collection includes works by Alexander
Calder, Norman Rockwell, and Grandma Moses. > 429 S. Main St., Elkhart, tel.
574/293–6660. $3, free Sun. Tues.–Fri. 11–5, weekends 1–4.

National New York Central Railroad Museum Two 1915 rail coaches, a scale model
of a steam locomotive, films, and thousands of period photographs tell the history of
the railroad in Elkhart. You can step into the cab of a diesel locomotive, build a railroad track, or blow the whistle of a steam locomotive. Also scattered across the
grounds are several other locomotives and train cars. > 721 S. Main St., Elkhart, tel.
574/294–3001, www.nycrrmuseum.org. $3. Tues.–Sat. 10–4, Sun. noon–4.

Ruthmere Museum A. R. Beardsley, of Miles Laboratories, built this beaux arts–style
home in 1908 and fitted out his grand mansion in opulent style with intricately
painted ceilings and a marble wraparound veranda. Today, velvet and silk window
coverings and upholstery evoke the overall mood along with original Tiffany lamps
and a collection of fine art. It's near the center of Elkhart on the banks of the St.
Joseph River and is listed on the National Register of Historic Places. > 302 E. Beardsley Ave., Elkhart, tel. 574/264–0330 or 888/287–7696, www.ruthmere.com. $6.
Guided tours only: Tues.–Sat. at 10, 11, 1, 2, and 3; Sun. at 2 and 3.

RV/MH Hall of Fame & Museum In a 15,000-square-foot display area, this museum
houses historical recreational vehicle units, as well as photos and memorabilia dating
back to the 1920s. The Hall of Fame recognizes more than 150 people who have influenced the development of the industry. > 810 Benham Ave., Elkhart, tel. 574/293–2344
or 800/378–8694, www.rv-mh-hall-of-fame.org. $3. June–Aug., weekdays 9–4, Sat. 10–3.

"Time Was" Museum Exhibits focusing on Elkhart's commercial life are housed in
two apartments above a circa-1899 retail building. The collection includes vintage
photographs of all of Elkhart's downtown buildings, archived newspapers reaching
back to 1856, school yearbooks, city directories, and local industrial publications. A
postcard collection has more than 1,000 cards depicting Elkhart and the surrounding
area through the years. > 125-A N. Main St., Elkhart, tel. 574/293–6005. Free.
Mon.–Sat. 10–2.

Woodlawn Nature Center This small museum of natural history on 10 acres of woodland trails has exhibits about native plants and animals. It's on the north edge of

Generations of Craftsmanship

IF THE CLOSEST YOU'VE COME TO BEING HANDY WITH A HAMMER is pounding some nails into a wall to hold up a picture, you may be impressed by the fine craftsmanship on display in Amish Country. Carpentry has been a hobby and industry for the Mennonite and Amish for hundreds of years. Many of today's woodworkers are third- and fourth-generation artisans who have learned to construct furniture, cabinets, clocks, or collectibles from their ancestors.

A good way to introduce yourself to these artisans of northern Indiana is to pick up the "Furniture Crafters Tour" booklet from the Elkhart County visitor center. The booklet comes with an audio tour as well as introduces you, over a 90-mi loop journey, to Amish culture and 10 different artisans working in Middlebury, Shipshewana, Goshen, Nappanee, and Elkhart. You can also drive the back roads on your own and visit the many furniture shops open to the public throughout the area.

Although many of the artisans here share a set of beliefs and a simpler way of life, their craftsmanship reflects many styles. For instance, en route to Shipshewana from Middlebury is B&L Woodcrafts, which specializes in outdoor furniture such as picnic tables, chairs, small bridges, and bird feeders. In Shipshewana, Wana Cabinets does much more than its name suggests.

The 4,000-square-foot showroom displays a full line of furniture custom-made in cherry, hickory, maple, and oak. Stop for a visit at Riegsecker's Marketplace, also in "Shipshe" (as the locals call it). Mel Riegsecker got his start making model wood horses and now his outfit is one of the largest furniture makers in the area. Nappanee is nationally known for kitchen cabinetry, but differences are found from showroom to showroom. Borkholder Country Furniture uses tongue-and-groove construction in its large line of cabinet designs and furniture pieces, and Ayr Cabinets is a custom-design shop that only makes cabinets to order.

Besides noting the diversity of style and approach to the art of woodworking, take the time to look at the actual way in which each piece is put together. Furniture making is an art of design and of construction for the Amish. There has to be a reason, after all, that these artisans aren't content with the beautiful heirloom pieces that have been passed down to them. They've discovered the certain satisfaction that comes from creating their own masterpieces.

Elkhart. > 604 Woodlawn Ave., Elkhart, tel. 574/264–0525. $1. Mar.–Oct., Tues.–Sat. 11:30–4:30; Nov.–Feb., Tues.–Fri. 1:30–4:30, Sat. 11:30–4:30.

GOSHEN

Bonneyville Mill Since the 1830s, the dark-red Bonneyville Mill has been grinding grain, making it the state's oldest continuously operating gristmill. A shady park surrounds the mill and pond. Watch the mill in operation, then purchase a sack of fresh-ground cornmeal or rye, buckwheat, or wheat flour. > Rte. 131, 10 mi north of Goshen, Bristol, tel. 574/535–6458. Free. May–Oct., daily 10–5.

Goshen College The Mennonite Church owns and operates this four-year liberal arts college, which has received national attention for the value of the education for the tuition price. Most (70%) students spend 14 weeks in a developing nation, learning and volunteering. About 1,000 students are enrolled in 30 majors including education, nursing, social work, art, music, and business. Both its annual Frisbee football tournament and annual Groundhog Day festival draw quite a crowd. > 1700 S. Main St., Goshen, tel. 219/535–7000, www.goshen.edu. Free. Daily.

Goshen Historical Society Museum This small museum devoted to the city's history is in one of Goshen's original stores downtown. The exhibits focus on the entrepreneurs who made Goshen what it is today. Advertising, old ledgers, and products manufactured and sold in Goshen are on display in this historic storefront. > 312 S. Main St., Goshen, tel. 574/975–0033. Free. Sat. 10–1.

Maple City Greenway This network of bicycle and pedestrian pathways and hiking trails winds through the heart of Goshen. Parts of the 13 ½-mi follow the hydraulic canal that once powered the city's industry. Access points include Shanklin Park (411 W. Plymouth Ave.), Goshen Middle School (1216 S. Indiana Ave.), or Bethany Christian School (2904 S. Main St.). > Goshen, tel. 574/534–2901. Free. Dawn–11 PM.

Mennonite Historical Library The Harold and Wilma Good Library houses the independent Mennonite library on the third floor, which has an extensive collection of genealogical, theological, and historical material on the Mennonite Church (which is related to the Amish faith). The Good Library's art gallery occupies the lower level of the building. > 1700 S. Main St., Goshen, tel. 574/535–7418. Free. Weekdays 8–5.

The Mill Race Market Center This farmer's market sells a plethora of locally produced foods and handcrafted items. > 212 W. Washington St., Goshen, tel. 574/533–4747 or 877/456–2753. Free. Tue. 3–7, Sat. 8–1.

Old Bag Factory Twenty shops and workshops of artists and craftspeople fill this 1896 redbrick building, on the northwest end of town, which was once a paper-bag factory. You can watch artists such as a potter or sculptor at work, then browse the shops. > 1100 Chicago Ave., Goshen, tel. 574/534–2502, www.oldbagfactory.com. Free. Weekdays 9–5, Sat. 9–4.

Ox Bow Park On the Elkhart River, the 223-acre park has an observation tower, nature and running trails, an open-air chapel, an archery range, an 18-hole golf course, and picnic shelters. In winter the trails are groomed for cross-country skiing and there are two sledding hills. > Rte. 45, 1 mi north of Goshen, Dunlap, tel. 574/535–6458. $2.50 per vehicle Apr.–Oct., free Nov.–Mar. Daily.

MIDDLEBURY

Deutsch Kase Haus Amish cheese makers demonstrate a tradition of more than two centuries in this cheese factory and gift shop. All the cheese is produced from the milk of hand-milked cows on Amish farms. Cheese is normally made daily on weekdays but it's a good idea to phone ahead. > Rte. 250, 3 mi east of Middlebury, Middlebury, tel. 574/825–9511. Free. Mon.–Sat.

Krider Gardens These 2 ½ acres of walk-through gardens hark back to Middlebury's heyday as a mail-order gardening center. The ponds, English Tea House, and giant toadstool were created for a horticultural exhibit in the 1934 Chicago World's Fair. > Rte. 8, 2 mi northwest of Middlebury, Middlebury, tel. 574/825–1499. Free. Daily.

NAPPANEE

Amish Acres This 18-building 80-acre farm complex gives an overview of Amish life. You can take horse-drawn buggy rides around the grounds and walking tours through the original house, the main house, and barn outbuildings. You can see a blacksmith shop, maple-sugar camp, icehouse, mint still, and broom shop. The documentaries *The Genesis of the Amish*, *The Exodus of the Amish*, and the children's film *Bonnets & Britches* are shown at the greeting barn. A huge barnlike restaurant serves a hearty home-style meal, and professional actors at the Round Barn Theatre present musical theater including the lively Broadway comedy about Amish love and life, *Plain and Fancy*. Stores on the grounds include a meat and cheese shop, soda shop, fudge shop, bakery, and garden shop. > 1600 W. Market St., Nappanee, tel. 547/773–4188 or 800/800–4942, www.amishacres.com. $9.95, includes tours and films. Mar.–Dec., daily 10–5.

Bird's Eye View Museum In 1961, DeVon Rose began building accurate miniature scale models—five times smaller than a dollhouse—of Wakarusa's business district, an Amish farm, and Indiana landmarks. Rose's materials include toothpicks, candy wrappers, Popsicle sticks, wooden grape boxes, cardboard, and shrink-wrap. > 325 S. Elkhart St., 4 mi north of Nappanee, Wakarusa, tel. 574/862–2367. Free. Weekdays 8–5, Sat. 8–noon.

Borkholder Dutch Village Freemon Borkholder, who started Borkholder American Vintage Furniture, converted old chicken houses into a 70,000-square-foot marketplace in 1987 complete with a flea market, arts-and-crafts and antiques malls, a restaurant, an events center, and village shops. Auctions are held at 8 AM on Tuesday. Special events include doll shows, gun shows, and holiday celebrations. > 71945 Rte. 101, Nappanee, tel. 574/773–2828, www.borkholder.com. Free. May–Oct., Mon.–Sat. 9–5; Nov.–Apr., Mon.–Sat. 10–5.

Historic Architecture Walk of Nappanee Many architectural styles are on display in Nappanee's downtown district. Take a leisurely walk over seven blocks and see Queen Anne mansions, arts-and-crafts–and prairie-school–style homes as well as "the House the Depression Built," a Tudor-revival home constructed of many recycled elements. > 451 N. Main St., Nappanee, tel. 574/773–7812. Free.

SHIPSHEWANA

Menno-Hof Experience history in a hands-on environment at this Mennonite-Amish visitor center. Interactive multimedia exhibits help you learn about the Mennonite and Amish way of life. The barn structure was erected using rough-sawn oak beams fastened together with only knee braces and wood pegs. > 510 S. Van Buren St., Shipshewana, tel. 260/768–4117, www.mennohof.org. $5. Mon.–Sat. 10–5.

Riegsecker Marketplace What started out as a single small home workshop has become a full marketplace today with a craft barn, toy store, furniture and collectibles shop, and restaurant. You can still see the craftsmen working on the oak and cherry furniture on a guided tour of the woodworking shop. Buggy and carriage rides through the streets of Shipshewana are available and the Blue Gate Theater presents family entertainment. > 105 E. Middlebury St., Shipshewana, tel. 260/768–4725, www.riegsecker.com. Free. Daily; tours May–Oct., at 10 and 1.

Shipshewana Auction & Flea Market In warm-weather months, this quiet community hosts the Midwest's largest open-air flea market with more than 1,000 vendors sprawled out on 50 acres, just blocks south of Shipshewana's business district. Among the stalls are sunglasses, knickknacks, kitchen utensils, fresh produce, handmade wood furniture or crafts, garden decorations, books, candy, and kettle corn. Livestock and horse auctions are held on Wednesday and Friday year-round. > Rte. 5 S, Shipshewana, tel. 260/768–4129, www.tradingplaceamerica.com. Free. May–Oct., Tues. 7–5, Wed. 7–3. Auctions: Wed. 8 AM–8 PM; Fri. 9 AM–mid-afternoon.

Tours

Buggy Lane Tours Take a horse-and-buggy tour of the town of Shipshewana, the surrounding farmland, or the Amish Country area. Tours are 15 minutes, 30 minutes, and 60 minutes in length. The full-length tour takes in an Amish dairy farm, and all

4:30 PM tours include watching cows get milked by hand. Rates are $5–$20. Tours are available on Tuesday, Wednesday, Friday, and Saturday. > Rte. 5 across from flea market, Shipshewana, tel. 888/442–8449, www.buggylinetours.com.

Down the Road Tours View Amish Country from the comfort of your own car with a personal guide. As you drive the area's back roads you'll hear about Amish culture, custom, and lifestyle. The tour stops at a cheese factory, buggy factory, farms, and gardens. The customized tours, led by a non-Amish Elkhart native, are half- or full-day. The cost is $85 or $150. > 51231 Shady La., Elkhart, tel. 574/266–0048.

Save the Date

MARCH

Wakarusa Maple Syrup Festival Tour a maple-syrup camp in Wakarusa, then feast on pancakes smothered in real maple syrup during this festival held the third weekend in March. There's also a parade, games, and an antiques and crafts fair. > Tel. 574/862–2714.

MAY

The **Great Race Sports Festival** Some 28 competitive events are held on one day in Elkhart. These include swimming, paddling, bicycling, basketball, and 5K and 10K walks and runs. Contests are held in and around Elkhart on the third weekend of May. > Tel. 574/296–5890, www.thegreatrace.net.

JUNE

Elkhart Jazz Festival This premier jazz event celebrates the town's heritage as the Band Instrument Capital, with 150 internationally known jazz musicians performing everything from bebop to big band and smooth jazz in venues around town. The festivities are held for three days over the third weekend in June. > Tel. 800/597–7627, www.elkhartjazzfestival.com.

Festival of the Wild Rose Moon A living-history village is re-created on Loveway Grounds in Middlebury on the first weekend in June with period artisans and entertainment, Native American dancers, and foodstuffs. > Tel. 800/262–8161.

JULY

Elkhart County 4-H Fair One of the nation's largest county fairs provides family fun and gets Goshen hopping with its 4-H exhibits, demonstrations, top-name grandstand entertainment, a giant midway, and food. The fair runs for eight days in mid-July. > Tel. 574/533–3247, www.4hfair.org.

AUGUST

Amish Acres Arts and Crafts Festival Some 350 artists show up for this four-day event in Nappanee to market their handcrafted wares. There's also live entertainment at this festival held the second weekend of August at the historic Amish Acres farm complex. > Tel. 574/773–7812.

Elkhart Air Show See wing-walking, aerobatics, and military plane flybys. Fireworks and ground displays add to the excitement in the skies over the Elkhart airport on the second weekend in August. > Tel. 574/293–1531, www.elkhartairshow.com.

Summer Festival Held the second weekend in August, this festival in the center of Middlebury salutes summer with a parade, concert, dancing, games, and garden tractor pull. > Tel. 574/825–1499.

SEPTEMBER

Apple Festival The third week of the month brings many an apple-themed event to Nappanee's Depot Plaza, including a beauty and talent contest for kids (resulting in the crowning of the "Apple Dumpling"), as well as an apple-peeling contest. Each year a 6-foot-diameter apple pie is baked, and is then sold by the slice. A parade, antiques show, and tractor pull add to the festivities. > Tel. 574/773–7812.

Michiana Mennonite Relief Sale This auction and sale of handmade quilts and antiques is held the fourth Saturday of September at Goshen's Elkhart County Fairgrounds. Proceeds benefit worldwide relief efforts. > Tel. 574/533–3247, www.4hfair.org.

OCTOBER

Amish Country Harvest Festival The first full weekend in October, on the grounds of Das Dutchman Essenhaus in Middlebury, crafters, musicians, quilters, and antiques and food vendors meet to sell their wares. There are also a quilt raffle, kids' activities, and entertainment. > Tel. 574/825–1499.

WHERE TO STAY

ELKHART

Best Western This three-story modern hotel is one block north of I–80/90 at Exit 92 (Elkhart) and is found among a strip of restaurants. > 3326 Cassopolis St. (Rte. 19), Elkhart 46514, tel. 572/262–8761 or 800/611–8262, fax 574/266–8984, bestwestern.com. 60 rooms. In-room data ports, some kitchenettes, some whirlpool tubs, cable TV, indoor pool, gym, business services. AE, D, DC, MC, V. CP. ¢–$

Elkhart Super 8 Motel This two-story motel was built in 1986 and has been updated. It's ¼ mi from I–80/90, Exit 92 (Elkhart). Its convenient to the commercial district on the north side of town. > 345 Windsor Ave., Elkhart 46514, tel. 574/264–4457 or 800/800–8000, fax 574/264–4457, www.super8.com. 62 rooms. Some microwaves, some refrigerators, cable TV, free parking, some pets allowed. AE, D, DC, MC, V. CP. ¢–$

Hampton Inn Elkhart Museums are 4 mi from this Hampton Inn, which opened in 1997. The motel is off I–80 (I–90), Exit 92 (Elkhart) on the north side of Elkhart. The hotel is within walking distance of many chain restaurants and nearby to area shopping. > 215 N. Point Blvd., Elkhart 46514, tel. 574/264–2525 or 800/426–7866, fax 574/264–9164, www.hamptoninn.com. 118 rooms. Cable TV, indoor pool, exercise equipment, hot tub, business services. AE, D, DC, MC, V. CP. ¢–$$

Ramada Inn At I–80 (I–90), Exit 92 (Elkhart), this two-story hotel, built in 1974, has a stylish atrium with brown-tile floor, dark wood, and plants. This is the city's largest hotel, and since it's away from the road, its spacious rooms are quiet. > 3011 Belvedere Rd., Elkhart 46514, tel. 574/262–1581, fax 574/262–1590, www.ramadainnelkhart.com. 145 rooms. Restaurant, room service, in-room data ports, some refrigerators, cable TV, putting green, 2 pools (1 indoor), gym, hot tub, sauna, bar, playground, laundry facilities, business services. AE, D, DC, MC, V. ¢–$$

Signature Inn This modern two-story hotel built in 1987 on the north edge of town caters mainly to business travelers. Spacious rooms are off an interior corridor. > 3010 Brittany Ct., Elkhart 46514, tel. 574/264–7222 or 800/822–5252, www.signatureinns.com. 125 rooms. In-room data ports, microwaves, refrigerators, cable TV, outdoor pool, business services. AE, D, DC, MC, V. CP. ¢–$

GOSHEN

Checkerberry Inn American and country-French antiques and bright furnishings create an aura of comfort at this three-story farmhouse-style inn on 100 acres in the heart of Amish Country. This elegant hostelry has the state's only professional croquet course. The restaurant serves dinners amid candlelight, fine wines, and inventive American cuisine. > 62644 Rte. 37, Goshen 46528, tel. 574/642–4445, www.checkerberryinn.com. 14 rooms. Restaurant, putting green, tennis court, pool, business services; no smoking. AE, MC, V. CP. **$$–$$$$**

Courtyard by Marriott Warm oak furniture, a fieldstone fireplace in the lounge, and shades of green and mauve fill the interior at this two-story hotel. It is 1 mi from the Elkhart County Fairgrounds. > 1930 Lincolnway E, Goshen 46526, tel. 574/534–3133 or 800/321–2211, fax 574/534–6929, www.courtyard.com. 91 rooms. Restaurant, in-room data ports, some in-room hot tubs, cable TV, indoor-outdoor pool, exercise equipment, gym, laundry facilities. AE, D, DC, MC, V. CP. **¢–$**

Goshen Ramada Inn and Conference Center In this hotel in the south end of Goshen, contemporary oak furnishings accented with shades of blue and mauve adorn the rooms. Many rooms have a view of the hotel's Fundome, which houses an Olympic-size pool and spa complex. > 1375 Lincolnway E, Goshen 46526, tel. 574/533–9551 or 888/246–7436, fax 574/533–2840, www.ramadagoshen.com. 207 rooms. Restaurant, room service, cable TV, indoor pool, exercise equipment, gym, sauna, bar, laundry facilities, business services. AE, D, DC, MC, V. CP. **¢–$**

Holiday Inn Express Between Shipshewana and Amish Acres this three-story hotel, built in 1997, is in the heart of Amish country. Bright rooms have full size, queen, or king beds. > 2309 Lincolnway E, Goshen 46526, tel. 574/533–0200, fax 574/533–1528, www.basshotels.com. 74 rooms. Some in-room spas, some in-room hot tubs, some kitchenettes, cable TV, indoor pool, hot tub, exercise equipment, business services. AE, D, DC, MC, V. CP. **$**

Prairie Manor Bed and Breakfast A two-story inn set on 12 acres of lawn and surrounded by shade trees, flower gardens, and woods, Prairie Manor was built in the 1920s. Details include arched doorways, wainscoting, and a wood-paneled library with window seats. The living room was designed after the owner's favorite painting in New York City's Metropolitan Museum of Art, an English baronial hall with a huge fireplace. Room have four-poster beds and rocking chairs. > 66398 U.S. 33, 1 mi south of Goshen, Goshen 46526, tel. 574/642–4761 or 800/791–3952, fax 574/642–4762, www.prairiemanor.com. 4 rooms. D, MC, V. BP. **¢–$**

Spring View Bed & Breakfast When you stay in this 1995 home on 48 acres, the Amish neighbors will take you on a buggy ride. Breakfast is served in the sunroom, overlooking the spring-fed pond. All rooms have dark or light wood furniture and king-size beds covered in brightly patterned homemade quilts. > 63189 Rte. 31, Goshen 46526, tel. 574/642–3997, fax 574/642–2697, www.springview.com. 5 rooms. In-room data ports, in-room hot tubs, cable TV, in-room VCRs, boating, fishing, bicycles; no smoking. AE, D, MC, V. BP. **¢**

Stagecoach Inn Bed and Breakfast It is believed that the stagecoach stopped here while traveling along the Lincoln Trail between Fort Wayne and South Bend. This 1863 home is filled with Victorian furnishings, antiques, and quilts, including a king-size canopy bed in the Wells Fargo room and a queen canopied bed in the Prairie room. In the back of the house is a patio, swing, gazebo, garden, and fountain. > 66063 U.S. 33, Goshen 46526, tel. 574/642–5005 or 877/219–5005, fax 574/642–4376, www.the-stagecoach-inn.com. 4 rooms, 1 with bath. Cable TV, no smoking. D, MC, V. BP. **¢**

MIDDLEBURY

Essenhaus Country Inn Built in 1986 to resemble a white Amish farmhouse, this inn is filled with handmade Amish furnishings and crafts, and rooms have floral wallpaper and simple, sturdy Amish furniture and quilts. Quilt squares decorate the walls. One mile southwest of Middlebury, the inn is steps away from the Essenhaus restaurant and shops. > 240 U.S. 20, Middlebury 46540, tel. 574/825–9471 or 800/455–9471, www.essenhaus.com. 33 rooms. Restaurant, some in-room hot tubs, gift shop. AE, D, MC, V. BP. **$–$$$**

Patchwork Quilt Country Inn An authentic Amish buggy is parked out front and a rustic red barn sits out back of this country inn on 18 acres of woods and gardens. Nine of the inn's rooms are in the 1875 historic inn and the rest are in the owner's house. Each has a private bath and the beds are covered with handmade Amish quilts. > 11748 Rte. 2, Middlebury 46540, tel. 574/825–2417, www.patchworkquiltinn.com. 14 rooms. Restaurant, some in-room hot tubs, some kitchenettes, gym, gift shop. D, MC, V. BP. **$–$$**

That Pretty Place Bed & Breakfast Secluded on 37 acres in the woods, this inn overlooks a private pond. The common area has a fireplace. Themed rooms include the Victorian Rose room, Ivy room, Brass and Crystal room, Woodland Rose room, and a honeymoon suite with heart-shape tub and canopy bed; several rooms overlook the garden. > 11748 Rte. 2, Middlebury 46540, tel. 574/825–3021 or 800/418–9487, www.thatprettyplace.com. 5 rooms. No smoking, no kids under 12. D, MC, V. BP. **$–$$**

Varns Guest House Relax on the front porch and watch the buggies go by from the porch of this modest two-story 1898 home. The inn is handsomely furnished with traditional furniture, patterned wallpaper and fabrics, some antiques, and family mementos. > 205 S. Main St., Middlebury 46540, tel. 574/825–9666. 5 rooms. No room TVs, no smoking. MC, V. BP. **$**

NAPPANEE

Christian S. Stahly Olde Buffalo Inn Bed and Breakfast This Amish farmhouse, built in 1840, predates the establishment of Nappanee itself. A white picket fence surrounds the 2½-acre lot, which also includes a barn, redbrick paths, and a windmill. You are welcome to stroll, tickle the ivories of the grand piano, or play a game of chess in the common area. Victorian items and antique beds furnish the rooms. The inn overlooks a golf course six blocks from downtown. > 1061 Parkwood Dr., Nappanee 46550, tel. 574/773–2223 or 888/773–2223, fax 574/773–4275, www.olde-buffalo-b-b.com. 7 rooms. Cable TV in some rooms, bicycles. D, MC, V. BP. **¢–$**

Homespun Country Inn Sit on the porch swing of this Victorian home to watch the traffic—car, bike, and buggy—heading in and out of downtown Nappanee, a block away. The rooms are furnished with antiques and knickknacks the owners have gathered over years of collecting. > 302 N. Main St., Nappanee 46550, tel. 574/773–2034 or 800/311–2996, www.homespuninn.com. 5 rooms. In-room VCRs. D, MC, V. BP. **¢**

Inn at Amish Acres On the grounds of the Amish Acres complex, this building is styled after the area's white Amish barns. Patterned quilts and handcrafted oak furniture fill the rooms, and rocking chairs decorate the porches overlooking the perennial garden–ringed outdoor pool. > 1234 W. Market St., Nappanee 46550, tel. 574/773–2011 or 800/800–4942, fax 574/773–2078, www.amishacres.com. 64 rooms, 16 suites. Some microwaves, some refrigerators, cable TV, pool, business services, airport shuttle. D, DC, MC, V. BP. **¢–$**

Nappanee Inn Part of the Amish Acres farmstead complex ½ mi away, this dark red building is styled after the area's Amish barns. Brightly colored quilts cover guestroom beds, and oak furniture adds a homey touch. The two-story inn sits amid corn and wheat fields and next door to an Amish harness shop. > 2004 W. Market St., Nappanee 46550, tel. 574/773–5999 or 800/800–4942, fax 574/773–5988, www.amishacres.com. 66 rooms. Restaurant, cable TV, pool, business services. Closed Nov.–Apr. D, DC, MC, V. BP. **¢–$**

Victorian Guest House With its purple-and-green color scheme, this impressive tur-reted Queen Anne mansion is immediately identifiable on Route 6. The house was built in 1887 for Frank Coppes, who manufactured freestanding kitchen cabinets known as Nappanee Dutch Kitchenettes and was a stickler for craftsmanship. When it came to building his wife's dream mansion, he pulled out all stops, outfitting it with etched glass, cross-cut oak, and stained glass—all of which remains today, set off to good ad-vantage by antique furnishings. Some of the rooms have private balconies. Eat break-fast at the 11-foot original dining room table. The guest house is two blocks east of the downtown junction at U.S. 6 and Route 19. > 302 E. Market St., Nappanee 46550, tel. 574/773–4383 or 877/773–4383, fax 574/773–4275, www.victorianb-b.com. 6 rooms. Cable TV. MC, V. BP. ¢–$

SHIPSHEWANA

Amish Log Cabin Lodging Private cabins, each built by local Amish artisans, are nes-tled among the woods on this campground near Shipshewana. The private cabins have handcrafted furniture, private baths, and a front porch with swing. You can also stay in one of the camping cabins, which have a more functional furnishings (including bunk beds) but do not have private baths. > 5970 N. Rte. 5, at Rte. 120, Shipshewana 46565, tel. 260/768–7770, www.amish.org. 15 cabins. MC, V. Closed Nov.–Mar. BP. ¢–$

Der Ruhe Blatz Motel The motel's name means "The Rest Place," and after a day shopping at the flea market ½ mi away you might need it. Solid oak furniture fills each room in this comfortable country-style motel. > 1195 S. Van Buren St., at Rte. 5 S, Shipshewana 46565, tel. 206/768–7750, www.derruheblatzmotel.com. 30 rooms. Cable TV, shop. D, MC, V. CP. ¢–$

Farmstead Inn The styling of this inn is inspired by the white Amish farmhouses that dot the surrounding countryside. A basketball court and recreation facilities are in the adjoining Red Barn building. The inn is across from the famous Shipshewana Auc-tion & Flea Market and a two-block walk from 70 shops in the tiny downtown area. Bright and spacious rooms have wood furniture and patterned bedding. > 370 S. Van Buren St., at Rte. 5 S, Shipshewana 46565, tel. 260/768–4595, fax 260/768–7319, www.tradingplaceamerica.com. 85 rooms. Indoor pool, wading pool, exercise equip-ment, basketball; no smoking. AE, D, MC, V. CP. ¢–$

Morton Street Bed & Breakfast The rooms here are found in three homes, all built in the 1880s, in the center of town. Walk to the flea market or Shipshewana's shops after spending the night in a room decorated with a Victorian or country-house flair. > 140 Morton St., Shipshewana 46565, tel. 260/768–4391 or 800/447–6475, shipshe-wanalodging.com. 8 rooms. Cable TV. AE, D, DC, MC, V. BP. ¢–$$

WHERE TO EAT

ELKHART

Bill's Bar-B-Que Elkhart's oldest barbecue restaurant serves ribs and chicken smoth-ered in sauce, as well as fish specials. You can dine in, carry out, or drive through in this casual eatery in a former Taco Bell building. > 1706 Cassopolis St., Elkhart, tel. 574/266–9285. MC, V. $–$$

Bulldog Restaurant and Lounge Expect Notre Dame, Green Bay Packers, or Chicago Cubs games to be on the television in this bar filled with sports memora-bilia. Steak, fish, salads, and sandwiches fill out the menu. Thursday brings live piano, and Saturday it's karaoke. > 3763 E. Jackson Blvd., Elkhart, tel. 574/294–6000. AE, D, DC, MC, V. ¢–$$

Calabria Since 1995, this family-run restaurant has served up southern Italian fare. House specialties are the Italian baked chicken, spaghetti *calabrese,* and veal marsala. Pizza and seafood join pasta on the menu. A map of Italy, which highlights Calabria, hangs by the front door and bright paintings help evoke the town's spirit. > 21813 Rte. 120, Elkhart, tel. 574/294–6994. MC, V. Closed Sun. and Mon. $–$$

Matterhorn This elegant restaurant on the north side of town has a dark-blue carpet and brass light fixtures, a wood-beamed vaulted ceiling, and stained glass. Salmon, walleye, and steaks highlight the menu. On the first Friday of each month, the restaurant hosts a seafood buffet. > 2041 Cassopolis St., Elkhart, tel. 574/262–1509 or 800/404–2714. AE, D, DC, MC, V. No lunch Sat. $$–$$$

GOSHEN

Brick House Steak and Seafood Restaurant Dine on steak, seafood, chops, or duck served in a restored historic home circa 1870. Wood upholstered chairs and period wallpaper lend this restaurant's dining room a relaxed intimacy. The specialty is prime rib. > 16820 Rte. 38, Goshen, tel. 574/537–1171. AE, D, MC, V. Closed Sun. No lunch Sat. $$–$$$$

Citrus, an American Bistro Surrounded by rural Amish countryside, this bistro in the Checkerberry Inn presents a careful blend of country and luxury. The dining room is intimate and candlelighted, with just a few tables, and the kitchen attracts attention for its seasonal menu of locally raised food. Try the citrus-infused salmon or beef tenderloin complemented by a port or cognac. The dining room is semiformal with American antiques and bright paintings. > 62644 Rte. 37, Goshen, tel. 574/642–0191. Reservations essential. AE, MC, V. Closed Sun., Mon., and Jan. $$–$$$

Crackers At the Ramada Inn, Crackers hosts prime rib specials on Friday and Saturday nights. Like a smaller-scale and toned down Applebee's or TGIF's, this restaurant's regular menu includes New York strip steak, ham, chicken-fried steak, shrimp tempura, pasta, chicken Alfredo, and burgers. > 1375 Lincolnway E, Goshen, tel. 574/533–9551 or 888/246–7435. No dinner Sun. AE, D, DC, MC, V. $–$$

South Side Soda Shop Diner This diner, a few blocks away from Goshen College, is a popular spot for hoagies, sandwiches, salads, fountain drinks, and homemade pie. Slide into a red leather booth and enjoy friendly service and food served at prices students can afford. > 1122 S. Main St., Goshen, tel. 574/534–3790. No credit cards. Closed Sun. and Mon. ¢–$

Town Haus Family Restaurant You can dine casually here, with fare from the buffet or menu. Salisbury steak, ribs, chicken, macaroni and cheese, mashed potatoes, and a salad bar make up the buffet. The menu lists burgers, sandwiches, baked fish, shrimp, and more. There's a buffet at breakfast. > 1105 W. Pike St., Goshen, tel. 574/534–1004. Reservations not accepted. MC, V. ¢–$

MIDDLEBURY

Das Dutchman Essenhaus This Amish family restaurant is a local institution for its all-you-can-eat chicken, roast beef, baked steak, or ham family-style meals, served with all the fixin's. If you order à la carte, consider the beef and noodles or creamed chicken and biscuits. Be prepared, the portions are generous. > 240 U.S. 20, Middlebury, tel. 574/825–9471 or 800/455–9471. D, MC, V. Closed Sun. ¢–$$

Patchwork Quilt Country Inn Step up to this inn's buffet with salads, soups, vegetables, and three hot entrées or order one of the plate dinners such as buttermilk pecan chicken or baked ham. Ask for a table by the fireplace if you dine here during the cold months. > 11748 Rte. 2, Middlebury, tel. 574/825–2417. D, MC, V. Closed Sun. and Mon. No lunch. $

NAPPANEE

Country Table A 40-foot-long buffet is the star at this antiques-filled family restaurant on the east side of town. Country cooking reigns including pastas, chicken dishes, real mashed potatoes, and all manner of hot and cold desserts. > 1401 E. Market St., Nappanee, tel. 574/773–2201. AE, D, MC, V. No dinner Sun. ¢–$

Restaurant Barn at Amish Acres In this bright red, turn-of-the-20th-century barn in Amish Acres farm-museum, you sit at antique tables with hand-hewn beams overhead to chow down on an all-you-can-eat Threshers Dinner, which includes two meats from a choice of roast beef, turkey, ham, and chicken, and such side items as beef and noodles; the cider-baked ham and stone hearth–baked bread are famous. > 1600 W. Market St., Nappanee, tel. 574/773–4188 or 800/800–4942. D, DC, MC, V. Closed Jan. and Feb. $$

SHIPSHEWANA

Blue Gate Restaurant The Amish Country Sampler is one of the most popular items on the menu here. It includes chicken, ham, roast beef, mashed potatoes, gravy, homemade bread, sides, and salad. Soups, salads, and sandwiches round out the menu. You can eat family-style or order from the menu. > 105 E. Middlebury St., Shipshewana, tel. 260/768–4725. D, MC, V. Closed Sun. $

Wana Cup Restaurant The homemade pies and ice cream might get you in the door, but this is also a good place for home-style food served fast. Sandwiches, burgers, and pizza are the menu mainstays. The specialty is a pizzaburger. On Thursday, Mexican specialties such as tostadas, tacos, or a beef-and-bean burrito are served. > Rte. 5, Shipshewana, tel. 260/768–4923. D, MC, V. Closed Sun. ¢

ESSENTIALS

Getting Here

Part of the pleasure of driving here is sharing the winding back roads with the black horse-drawn buggies driven by the Amish. You can take the train or bus but the schedules are geared to commuters or those on long journeys, which makes the hours of arrival unworkable—4 AM is an odd time for a tourist to arrive for the weekend, even if some of the Amish farmers are early risers.

BY BUS

Two different bus lines will take you to Elkhart but to get as far as Shipshewana you'd need to take Lakefront Trailways, which sells its tickets in the Greyhound depot. Lakefront Trailways' near-four-hour trip to Shipshewana is a red-eye departing Chicago at 12:01 AM. The round-trip fare is $61. This is the same bus you'd take to get to Elkhart only you'd pay $9 less. Greyhound arrives in Elkhart four times a day and the trip can run from 2 hours and 25 minutes to 3 hours, depending on the time of day. The round-trip fare is $53.
BUS DEPOT **Greyhound** > 26084 County Rd. 6, Elkhart, tel. 574/262–4406. *BUS LINES* **Greyhound** > Tel. 800/231–2222, www.greyhound.com. **Lakefront Trailways** > Tel. 800/638–6338, lakefrontlines.com.

BY CAR

Easily the most convenient way to travel to Amish Country is by car. Take the toll road, I–80 (I–90), as far as Elkhart at Exit 92. From here, you have different scenic options. You can follow Route 19 some 20 mi south to Nappanee, via Wakarusa. Go east on Route 6 to get to Amish Acres and Borkholder Dutch Village. Another option is to veer off Route 19 when it becomes Elkhart's Main Street. This will lead into U.S. 33, which is a direct route to Goshen. To get quickly to Goshen, without the Elkhart detour, stay on I–80 (I–90) until Exit 101. Or if Shipshewana is the primary destination, speed along the interstate to Exit 107 and then take Route 13 South to Middlebury. Shipshewana is to the east on Route 20. Plenty of numbered county roads bisect the area, making it easy to explore the back roads and find the way back to a main highway. Particularly scenic routes include Route 119, which heads north from Nappanee to Goshen, or Route 22 from Goshen to Middlebury.

Pass buggies with caution. Don't try to pass a buggy on a hill or curve. Don't pull up to close behind a buggy at an intersection as horses can back up unexpectedly. Watch for reflective markings on buggies when traveling at night. Give more time to brake than you think you need. Even the fastest horse is probably no match for your car. Don't use your horn, horses can be easily frightened.

BY TRAIN

Amtrak can get you as far as Elkhart, but it only schedules one trip a day to and from an unmanned station. There is no automated ticket booth so purchase a round-trip ticket for $48 in Chicago before getting on the 5:35 PM train arriving in Elkhart at 7:24 PM. The return trip departs at 8:22 AM and arrives in Chicago at 11 AM.

TRAIN LINE **Amtrak** > Tel. 800/872–7245, www.amtrak.com.
TRAIN STATION **Elkhart Train Station** > 131 Tyler Ave., Elkhart.

Visitor Information

CONTACTS **Amish Country/Elkhart County Convention & Visitors Bureau** > 219 Caravan Dr., Elkhart 46514, tel. 574/262–8161 or 800/262–8161, www.amishcountry.org. **Goshen Chamber of Commerce** > 232 S. Main St., 46526, tel. 219/533–2102 or 800/307–4204, www.goshen.org. **LaGrange |County Convention & Visitors Bureau** > 440½ S. Van Buren St., Rte. 5 S, Shipshewana 46565, tel. 574/768–4008 or 800/254–8090, www.backroads.org. **Middlebury Chamber** > 418 N. Main St., Middlebury 46540, tel. 574/825–1499, www.middlebury-in.com. **Nappanee Chamber of Commerce** > 451 N. Main St., 46550, tel. 574/773–7812, www.nappanee.org.

South Haven & Saugatuck/Douglas

120 mi northeast of Chicago

10

By Jennifer Vanasco

SOUTHWESTERN MICHIGAN IS THE MIDWEST'S VERSION OF CAPE COD —and the cities that epitomize that laid-back beach resort feeling are Saugatuck, Douglas, and South Haven. Blueberries hang heavily on bushes in August. Brilliantly colored leaves light up fall. Winter brings quiet, snow-covered trails and twinkling Christmas lights, and spring heralds the first local festivals of summer.

Set along the state's fruit belt, these towns have beaches with arching dunes and sugary sand, plus well-preserved downtowns and quiet residential streets. More than 900 boats are anchored in their shared harbor and almost 40 bed-and-breakfasts open their doors to visitors. The towns are an outdoor haven, surrounded by state and county parks that welcome sunbathers, kayakers, hikers, fishers, bikers, bird-watchers, and other outdoorsy types.

Saugatuck and Douglas are sometimes slurred together as if they are one city— Saugatuck/Douglas. They share a tourists' bureau, B&B directories, 19th-century architecture, and city transportation, but their downtowns, about a mile apart, are very different. Saugatuck welcomes visitors with a sign accented by a large artist's palette, signifying its status as an artist colony. Its vibrant downtown is nestled in a curve of the Kalamazoo River and includes about 30 galleries and dozens of gift shops, cafés, and restaurants. In summer, parking is impossible, but walking along the tree-shaded streets is a pleasure. Downtown Douglas, just south of Saugatuck, is much smaller— about two blocks—but many regulars prefer its less-touristy antiques stores and excellent dining.

Both towns were settled by lumber interests in the mid-1800s (it was Michigan pine shipped from Saugatuck that helped rebuild Chicago after the Great Fire of 1871), but by the early 1900s Chicagoans were already escaping the city heat by spending summers on Saugatuck and Douglas shores. In the 1930s, those Chicagoans included gangster Al Capone.

In 1910 a group of Chicago artists established a summer painting school at Saugatuck's Ox-Bow Lagoon. Ox-Bow, now run by the School of the Art Institute, continues to train artists today and is considered one of the nation's premiere art schools. This arts legacy still draws artists, artisans, and art lovers to the area, and its liberal bent makes it a haven for gay and lesbian travelers.

Beachfront and blueberries are what draw visitors to South Haven, which stretches across both sides of the Black River to Lake Michigan. It's a getaway with a true small-town feel, where a local is likely to engage you in conversation, stores shut down in the early evening, and the business district's movie theater offers free popcorn on Thursday if you bring your own bag. A patchwork of farms lies just outside of town, offering pick-your-own blueberries, peaches, grapes, apples, and cherries.

Like Saugatuck and Douglas, South Haven was once a bustling port for the 19th-century steamships from Chicago that imported summer vacationers and exported fruit and lumber to Chicago and Milwaukee. Ten million feet of lumber were cut in local sawmills and more than 50 wooden ships were built here in the late 1800s; you can still walk out on the long concrete-and-steel pier where locals and tourists would gather to watch them come in.

There was a lull in the town's popularity in the 1970s and 1980s, which drove many of the lodgings away, but South Haven is making a comeback. More cafés and restaurants are opening and more stores are catering to tourism. The population more than doubles in summer, thanks to South Haven's miles of pristine, curving beaches. Visitors can walk from the mainly Victorian business district to South Beach along the quiet harbor, stopping for ice cream along the way.

WHAT TO SEE & DO

SAUGATUCK/DOUGLAS

Blue Coast Artist Studios Eight artists, joined in a loose collaboration with studios stretching from Saugatuck to South Haven, have agreed to open their studios to anyone who might drop by on summer weekends. Their work ranges from hand-thrown ceramics to glass sculpture to landscape painting. > www.bluecoastartists.com. Free. May–Oct., Fri.–Sun. 11–5.

Fenn Valley Vineyards and Wine Cellar Self-guided tours tell you about the wine-making process and take you to the cellars at this small, family-owned winery, which sits in the rolling hills of southwestern Michigan. Guide-led tours in early fall take you into the vineyards. A picnic area is the perfect spot for a tasting. > 6130 122nd Ave., Fenn Valley, tel. 269/561–2396, www.fennvalley.com. Free, $5 for vineyard tours. Mon.–Sat. 11–5, Sun. 1–5. Free cellar tours May and June, Sat. at 2; July and Aug., Sat. at 2, Fri. at 4. Vineyard tours Sept. and Oct., weekends at 2:30.

***Keewatin* Marine Museum** The SS *Kewatin* is the only ship in the world with the same interior and machinery as the doomed *Titanic*. This restored 1907 passenger steamer once plied the Great Lakes for the Canadian Pacific Railroad. Today, it serves as a marine museum with everything from the ornate cabins and furnishings to the meticulously kept engine room on view. Guided tours take you through selected rooms on the ship. > 225 Union St., Saugatuck, tel. 269/857–2464. $8. Memorial Day–Labor Day, daily 10–5; last tour at 4:30.

Oval Beach The "singing sand" squeaks and groans beneath your feet at this beach, which is often ranked among the top beaches in the world. Walk or swim along the graceful shoreline, take in the sunset, or climb the 282 steps of Mount Baldhead, the towering dune known as Baldy. Don't worry, there are benches along the way. > West end of Perryman Rd., Saugatuck, tel. 269/857–2603. Memorial Day–Labor Day, weekdays 9–6 $5; weekends 9–6 $8; free all other times. Daily.

Ox-Bow Chicago's School of the Art Institute runs this intensive summer art school. It was the seed for Saugatuck's artist community when a small group started it in 1910. Now, artists of all levels can register in advance for the two-week courses. Those who just appreciate art come to the Friday-night open studios, held weekly in summer. You can take a studio tour, attend a gallery opening, watch a demonstration on painting or glassblowing, or buy the work of up-and-coming artists at ridiculously low prices. > 3435 Rupprecht Way, at the end of Park St., Saugatuck, tel. 269/857–5811, www.ox-bow.org. Free. June–Aug.

Saugatuck Chain Ferry Glide slowly across the Kalamazoo River between the road to Oval Beach and downtown on this hand-cranked chain ferry, built in 1857 and the only one left in North America. > Water St. at Wicks Park, Saugatuck, tel. 269/857–2603. $1. Memorial Day–Labor Day, daily 9–9.

Saugatuck-Douglas Museum Housed in a former pump house on the west side of the Kalamazoo River, this museum displays annual exhibits on local history. A library contains over 200 oral histories of residents and former residents. > 735 Park St., Saugatuck, tel. 269/857–7900. Free. Memorial Day–Labor Day, daily noon–4; Sept. and Oct., weekends noon–4.

Saugatuck Dune Rides Your driver will no doubt yell "I lost the brakes," but it's all in a day's fun on these 35-minute rides over the breathtaking Saugatuck dunes. > 6495 Blue Star Hwy., $\frac{1}{2}$ mi west of I–196, Exit 41, Saugatuck, tel. 269/857–2253, www.saugatuckduneride.com. $13.50. May–mid-Sept., Mon.-Sat. 10–5:30, Sun. noon–5:30; mid-Sept.–mid-Oct., weekends only noon–5.

Saugatuck Dunes State Park This secluded park, $3\frac{1}{2}$ mi north of Saugatuck, in-cludes $2\frac{1}{2}$ mi of Lake Michigan beach and 13 mi of hiking trails. Swimming is permit-ted at the beach, but you have to hike $2\frac{1}{2}$ mi from the parking lot to get there. The beach has picnic tables and rest rooms. > West end of 138th St., Saugatuck, tel. 269/637–2788. $4 per car. Daily dawn–dusk.

Tabor Hill Winery & Restaurant Lake Michigan's wine country is one of the finest in the world, sometimes compared to those in Italy and France. The Tabor Hill Win-ery, which produces such varietals as chardonnay, Riesling, merlot, and cabernet franc, is the oldest in Michigan. The vineyard and winery, in the rolling hills of Berrien County, was renovated in 2003. The fronts of the beautiful carved oaken casks have been cut from the barrels and moved to a meeting room for public view-ing. > 185 Mount Tabor Rd., Buchanan, tel. 800/283–3363, www.taborhill.com. Free. Wine tours: Memorial Day–Labor Day, daily noon–4:30; wine tasting: Memorial Day–Labor Day, Mon. and Tues. 10–5, Wed.-Sat. 10–10, Sun. noon–9; Sept.–May, Sun.–Thurs. 10–5, Fri. and Sat. 10–9.

SOUTH HAVEN

Blueberry Store Everything blueberry is sold at this shop, run by the Michigan Blueberry Growers Association, from coffee, jams, and syrups to the fresh or frozen berries themselves. > 525 Phoenix St., South Haven, tel. 800/889–3324, www.thebueberrystore.com. Closed Mon. and Tues. Sept.–Dec.

DeGrandchamp's Blueberrry Farm, Inc. Twenty-five varieties of blueberries are just waiting for you to pluck them and throw them into a bucket you hang around your neck. There's also a market if you'd rather have someone else do the work. > 15575 77th St., South Haven, tel. 888/483–7431, www.degrandchamps.com. July–Sept., daily 8–6.

Gingerman Raceway Primarily a test track for clubs and companies, this raceway also holds some racing events that are open to the public. If you've always wanted to do a few laps, check the schedule and call the raceway. Some clubs let visitors zoom around the 1.88-mi track for a nominal fee, often less than $10. > 61414 Phoenix Rd., South Haven, tel. 269/637–3915, www.gingermanraceway.com.

Kal-Haven Trail State Park This former railroad bed, stretching between South Haven and Kalamazoo, is now a 34-mi well-groomed trail for hiking, biking, and cross-country skiing. The popular trail travels over ravines and across gentle hills, often stopping in the small farming communities along the way. > Bailey St. and E. Wells St. off Blue Star Hwy, South Haven, tel. 269/637–2788. Free. Daily dawn–dusk.

Liberty Hyde Bailey Birth Site Museum The former home of botanist and horticul-turist Dr. Liberty Hyde Bailey now contains family-related memorabilia and such farmstead artifacts as kitchen equipment. One of the earliest houses in South Haven,

Ghost Town Beneath the Sands

ONCE UPON A TIME, SAUGATUCK *had a twin sister city named Singapore. In 1836, East Coast investors sent Oshea Wilder to choose some land for a sawmill. He bought 200 timber-rich acres at the foot of the Kalamazoo River and founded Singapore, now one of Michigan's most famous ghost towns. Wilder hoped that the new town would rival Chicago and Milwaukee as a port. It certainly outshone Saugatuck, its neighbor to the south. At its peak, the town had a population of 150 and several general stores.*

Singapore began with a sawmill and a bank—but the founding fathers had an idea. Why not have the bank print its own money as a way to build the economy? Unfortunately, the U.S. government eventually caught on, but not until the bank had issued about $50,000. The bank was closed in 1842.

The pivotal year for Singapore was 1871, when dry conditions caused fires to sweep the Midwest—Chicago and Holland, Michigan, both burned, and people needed lumber to rebuild. Soon, Singapore's sawmill went into overdrive, working around the clock and bringing the town prosperity. Woodcutters chopped down every tree they found, including the pines rooting the dunes in place. But within four years, the wood supply was depleted. The three mills closed, and were consequently

taken down board by board and shipped out to other ports. Singapore residents packed their bags, and some moved their entire houses. Twelve homes, in fact, were moved across the frozen Kalamazoo to Saugatuck and one still stands on Butler Street today.

Slowly, the sands of the dune that stood between Singapore and Lake Michigan settled into the buildings that stayed behind. A persistent legend says that one fisherman refused to move, even when the sands filled the first floor of his house, forcing him to enter and exit by a second-story window. But finally he, too, left. By 1899, the only sign of Singapore was the peaked roof of his cottage.

Today nothing is left of Singapore, though some residents say a pole pokes up through the dunes and occasionally a brick or piece of pottery will work itself up through the sand. All that remains are some photographs and the story.

it is a National Historic Site. > 903 S. Bailey Ave., South Haven, tel. 269/637–3251. Free. Thurs.–Mon. 1–5.

Michigan Maritime Museum Michigan has more recreational boats and freshwater coastline than any other state. This maritime museum, one of the state's largest, brings to life the stories of the people who built and sailed boats on Michigan's Great Lakes and waterways. Displays include accounts from passenger steamers that once crossed Lake Michigan, a working light from a former Michigan lighthouse, maps, artifacts, marine art, and a U.S. Coast Guard exhibit. > 260 Dyckman Ave., South Haven, tel. 269/637–8078, fax 269/637–1594, www.michiganmaritimemuseum.org. $2.50. May–Oct., Mon.–Sat. 10–5, Sun. noon–5; Nov.–Apr., Mon. 10–5, Wed.–Sat. 10–5, Sun. noon–5.

North Beach Local teenagers consider this the cool beach; it's about 1½ mi west of downtown. Concessions, a playground, picnic tables, and lifeguards are available in summer. > West end of Lakeshore Dr., South Haven, tel. 269/637–0700, www.southhavenmi.com/content/parksandbeaches.htm. $5. Daily dawn–11 PM.

South Beach This popular, family-oriented beach is three blocks from downtown. The 800-foot steel-and-concrete pier ends at a cherry-red lighthouse and includes a railing in case the wind is rough. In winter, ice formations coat the pier with strange, mystical shapes. Concessions, picnic tables, a playground, a shady dining pavilion, and lifeguards are available in summer. > West end of Water St., South Haven, tel. 269/637–0700, www.southhavenmi.com/content/parksandbeaches.htm. $5. Daily dawn–11 PM.

South Haven Center for the Arts Rotating exhibits from local artists and artistic communities are the highlight of this small arts center, which focuses on sculpture, painting, and drawing. Housed in a former 1906 library, the center hosts occasional concerts and poetry readings. > 600 Phoenix St., South Haven, tel. 269/637–1041, www.southhavenarts.org. Free. Tues.–Thurs. 10–5, Fri. 10–4, weekends 1–4.

Van Buren State Park High sand dunes and almost 1 mi of Lake Michigan frontage are the keystones of this 407-acre park. It has a 6-mi connector trail to the Kal-Haven Trail State Park, a rails-to-trails route between Kalamazoo and South Haven that is a favorite of cyclists and cross-country skiers. Picnic areas, a playground, sand dunes, swimming, and camping also are available. > 23960 Ruggles Rd., South Haven, tel. 269/637–2788 or 800/447–2757, www.michigan.gov/dnr. $4 per car, per day. Daily 8 AM–10 PM.

Tours

Harborduck Adventures Harborduck conducts an amusing 45-minute to one-hour narrated tour of Saugatuck and Douglas over both water and land in their refurbished World War II boat-truck. Not only do they comment on local history, but they regale you with stories about local characters. The legends and stories may or may not be true, but it's the quickest way to get an overview of both towns. You can join the tour in either Saugatuck or Douglas. Tours, which cost $15, are conducted every day, weather permitting. > Center St., Douglas, tel. 269/857–3825, www.harborduckadventures.com.

Saugatuck Walking Tour Guided one-hour tours by volunteers from the historical society showcase the business district's history, architecture, and legendary people. Tours are at 2 PM Wednesday, Friday, and Saturday from June to the second weekend of September. Tours leave from the information booth at Butler and Culver streets, across from the town hall. > Saugatuck, tel. 269/857–7900, www.saugatuck.com.

Star of Saugatuck You embark on a 90-minute narrated tour on this 150-passenger stern-wheeler, which lazily travels the Kalamazoo River to Lake Michigan. Spectacular Lake Michigan sunsets are the highlight of the last cruise of the day. Cruises are conducted daily, from Memorial Day through Labor Day, at 11 AM, 1 PM, 3, 5, and 8. The cost is $13. > 716 Water St., Saugatuck, tel. 269/857–4261, www.saugatuckboatcruises.com.

Sports

BIKING

Biking through South Haven and Saugatuck area is glorious. In summer, sailboats glide on Lake Michigan; in fall, trees display their brightest colors. The Kal-Haven Trail is a particularly popular ride, but shorter, unnamed (and unmapped) trails abound. There's only one rental spot in Saugatuck/Douglas, though many B&Bs provide bicycles to their guests.

Kal-Haven Trail State Park For 34 mi, this asphalt trail—once a former railroad bed—stretches between South Haven and Kalamazoo. There are plenty of places to stop for refreshment and interesting trail features, such as bridges and wetlands, along the way. > Bailey St. and E. Wells St. off Blue Star Hwy., South Haven, tel. 269/637–2788. Free. Daily dawn–dusk.

Van Buren State Trail Park A multiuse dirt and gravel trail provides a more challenging ride than the Kal-Haven at this park. > Exit 13 off I–96, South Haven, tel. 269/637–2788, www.michigandnr.com.

RENTALS **Big Lake Outfitters,** > 640 Water St., Saugatuck, tel. 269/857–4762, www.biglakeoutfitters.com. **Outpost Sports,** > 114 Dyckman, South Haven, tel. 269/637–5555, www.outpostsports.com. **Rock 'n' Road Cycles,** > 315 Broadway, South Haven, tel. 269/639–0003, www.rocknroadcycle.com.

HIKING

Traveling over the dunes is a privilege reserved for hikers in most cases; bikes damage their fragile ecosystems. Dune walking can be surprisingly rigorous, but there are more gentle hikes in the area as well. The Allegan State Forest and the Kal-Haven Trail also make for good hiking.

Allegan State Forest Fifty thousand scenic acres make this the premiere outdoor playground in the state. Twenty miles of trails cross ponds, the Kalamazoo River, and wetlands, and traverse forest that remains much as it did as when it was first explored. The forest is 26 mi southeast of Saugatuck and 36 mi northeast of South Haven. > 4590 118th Ave. (Rte. 3), Allegan, tel. 616/673–2430.

Kal-Haven Trail State Park This 34-mi paved trail provides both short and long hiking and walking opportunities. There are plenty of places to stop for refreshment and interesting trail features, such as bridges and wetlands, along the way. Watch out for bikers, they zoom by fast. > Bailey St. and E. Wells St. off Blue Star Hwy., Saugatuck, tel. 269/637–2788. Free. Daily dawn–dusk.

Saugatuck Dunes State Park Scenic vistas overlooking Lake Michigan are the reward for those hiking on this secluded park's 13 mi of trails. The park is 3½ mi north of Saugatuck. > West end of 138th St., Saugatuck, tel. 269/637–2788. $4 per car. Daily dawn–dusk.

Save the Date

FEBRUARY

Ice Breaker Ice sculptors carve big blocks of ice all over town in this annual competition on the second full weekend in February. A chili cook-off helps keep things warm. > Tel. 269/637–2141, www.bythebigbluewater.com.

APRIL–SEPTEMBER

Allegan Antiques Market More than 400 exhibitors from around the country sell their goods on the last Sunday of each summer month at the Allegan County fairgrounds. > Tel. 616/453–8780, www.alleganantiques.com.

JUNE

HarborFest Dragon-boat races, music, lighthouse tours, and an antiques fair are some of the attractions of this family-focused event celebrating the end of the long winter in South Haven. HarborFest is held the first weekend of June. > Tel. 269/857–8851.

Waterfront Film Festival One of the top festivals in the country, this film festival, held the second weekend in June, includes talks by top names in the independent and mainstream film industry. > Tel. 269/857–8351, www.waterfrontfilm.com.

AUGUST

National Blueberry Festival The area's berries take center stage during this four-day bash on the Lake Michigan shore, the second week of the month. South Haven, the country's blueberry capital, salutes its top industry with blueberry treats, a sand-sculpting contest, beach volleyball, parades, a fish boil, and other fun. > Tel. 269/637–5171, www.blueberryfestival.com.

SEPTEMBER

Saugatuck/Douglas Heritage Festival On the third weekend in September, a celebration of local history takes over both towns, with house tours, a Native American drumming ceremony, a vintage baseball game, and bonfires lit along the Kalamazoo River. > Tel. 269/857–7900, www.saugatuck.com/arts/artofbeing_frame.htm.

Taste of Saugatuck The city's best restaurants gather for a Labor Day weekend street festival on Water Street. Food booths, open-air entertainment, and more are on tap. > Tel. 269/857–1701.

OCTOBER

Annual Goose Festival This town-wide celebration in nearby Fennville, held the second weekend in October, honors the Canada goose. Arts and crafts, free entertainment, a parade, and a wildlife art show enrich the experience. > Tel. 269/561–5550.

Gallery Stroll Participating galleries in downtown Saugatuck and nearby Douglas open their doors on the first weekend of the month to packs of roving art enthusiasts, with music by local performers and refreshments. > Tel. 269/857–1557.

WHERE TO STAY

SAUGATUCK/DOUGLAS

Bay Side Inn Inside a renovated 1927 boathouse in downtown along the Kalamazoo River, this inn has rooms with contemporary furniture and private balconies facing the city or water. Four rooms are efficiencies with fireplaces. Breakfast is served on a patio overlooking the river. > 618 Water St., Saugatuck 49453, tel. 269/857–4321 or 800/548–1870, fax 269/857–1870, www.baysideinn.com. 5 rooms, 5 suites. Cable TV, in-room VCRs, hot tub; no smoking. AE, D, MC, V. **$$–$$$**

BeachWay Resort and Hotel Most of the pink-awninged rooms have views of the river at this hotel near Oval Beach. The 1906 hotel was renovated in 1996 because it was sinking into a sand dune. Now it has contemporary furnishings, the bottom of the pool is painted with sharks, and a series of decks overlook the river. Downtown is across the river. A chain ferry can take you across or you can take the Blue Star Highway through Douglas to cross over the bridge, about a 5-mi journey. Sleek, intimate efficiency apartments on the river are also available. > 106 Perryman St., Saugatuck 49453, tel. 268/857–3331, fax 269/857–3912, www.beachwayresort.com. 10 rooms, 7 suites. Cable TV, in-room VCRs, pool, some free parking; no smoking. AE, D, DC, MC, V. Closed Nov.–May. **¢–$$$**

Belvedere Inn This 1913 stone mansion sits on 5 acres of landscaped grounds and gardens. Hardwood floors, armoires, and four-poster beds fill the rooms, all of which have views of the grounds. > 3656 63rd St., Saugatuck 49453, tel. 269/857–5777 or 877/858–5777, fax 269/857–7557, www.thebelvedereinn.com. 10 rooms. Restaurant, pond; no kids under 12, no smoking. AE, D, MC, V. BP. **$$$**

Holiday Inn Express Saugatuck Some of the larger rooms here have king-size beds, fireplaces, and views of the woods. One mile from I-196, Exit 41, this two-floor hotel is next to a golf course and ½ mi from Saugatuck Dune Rides. > 3457 Blue Star Hwy., Saugatuck 49453, tel. 269/857–7178, fax 269/857–7169. 52 rooms. In-room data ports, refrigerators, in-room hot tubs, cable TV, indoor pool, gym, laundry service, business services. AE, D, DC, MC, V. CP. **$$–$$$**

Kirby House Lavish breakfasts are served in an oak-paneled dining room and prepared by one of the owners of this elegant Victorian B&B. The house is a short walk from downtown Douglas and about ½ mi to downtown Saugatuck. Rooms are thoughtfully cozy, furnished with Victorian antiques—one room has a daybed, another a claw-foot tub. Throw blankets are tossed over chairs and shaving cream is in the bathrooms. Three guest rooms have fireplaces; one has a small balcony overlooking the woodsy backyard. Trees surround a deck with pool and hot tub. > 294 W. Center St., Douglas 49406, tel. 800/521–6473, www.kirbyhouse.com. 8 rooms, 6 with bath. Pool, hot tub, free parking; no room phones, no kids under 12, no smoking. MC, V. BP. **$–$$$**

Lake Shore Resort At this family-owned motel 3 mi south of Saugatuck you can hike nature trails in a wooded area or borrow a bicycle or kayak. If you prefer, you can stroll or sun on the resort's private beach or relax in a chaise longue on one of the decks. > 2885 Lake Shore Dr., Saugatuck 49453, tel. 616/857–7121, fax 616/857–4656, www.lakeshoreresortsaugatuck.com. 30 rooms. Cable TV, refrigerators, outdoor pool, beach. MC, V. Closed Nov.–May. **$$–$$$**

Maplewood Hotel Upscale traditional touches, including many antiques, adorn this three-story Greek-revival hotel in downtown. A large common room has a player piano and television. Breakfast is served daily in the elegant dining room or on the glass-enclosed porch. > 428 Butler St., Saugatuck 49453, tel. 800/650–9790, fax 269/857–1773, www.maplewoodhotel.com. 15 rooms. Cable TV, pool; no smoking. AE, MC, V. CP. **$$–$$$**

Park House The Greek-revival–style house that's this hostelry's main building was built in 1857 and is the oldest house in Saugatuck. Pine floors and stenciled walls give the place a distinctly New England appearance. Some room have fireplaces. The more secluded cottages have full kitchens and private hot tubs. One of them overlooks the Kalamazoo River. > 888 Holland St., Saugatuck 49453, tel. 269/857–4535 or 800/321–4535, fax 616/857–1065, www.parkhouseinn.com. 8 rooms, 3 suites, 4 cottages. Picnic area, business services; no phones in some rooms, no TV in some rooms. AE, D, MC, V. BP. **$–$$$**

Rosemont Inn Bed & Breakfast Gas fireplaces, antiques, and country-style accents adorn the rooms of this early-1900s romantic Victorian retreat. A long veranda and gazebo allow you to relax and take in the Lake Michigan views. In the back you can walk out to the landscaped waterfall garden. In winter, most rooms have water views—in summer, you must peer through the trees. > 83 Lake Shore Dr., Saugatuck 49453, tel. 616/857–2637 or 800/721–2637. 14 rooms. In-room data ports, cable TV, pool, hot tub, sauna, beach, business services; no kids, no smoking. AE, D, MC, V. BP. **$$$$**

Shangrai-La You can stroll through the landscaped grounds of this single-story motel built in the mid-1950s. Though it's in a wooded country area, it's only 3 mi from area restaurants and shopping. > 6190 Blue Star Hwy., (U.S. 2 A), Saugatuck 49453, tel. 269/857–1453 or 800/877–1453, fax 616/857–5905, www.saugatuck.com/sbonline/shangraila. 20 rooms. Picnic area, in-room VCRs with movies, outdoor pool. AE, D, MC, V. **¢–$$**

Sherwood Forest The rooms in this red, Victorian-style B&B built in the early 1900s have exotic themes—one has a hand-painted mural of trees. The cottage has a full kitchen, a gas fireplace, and a deck with grill. The beach is only a half block away, and don't miss the pool during the warm months. At the bottom is a mural of a sunken ship surrounded by a rainbow of tropical fish. The innkeepers occasionally stage Monopoly tournaments. > 938 Center St., Saugatuck 49453, tel. 616/857–1246 or 800/838–1246, fax 616/857–1996, www.sherwoodforestbandb.com. 3 rooms, 2 suites, 1 cottage. Picnic area, in-room VCRs with movies, pool, hot tub, bicycles; no room phones, no TV in some rooms, no smoking. D, MC, V. BP. **$–$$**

Twin Gables Country Inn A long front porch catches your eye when you see this B&B overlooking Kalamazoo Lake, five blocks south of downtown. Inside is a spacious common room with large wood-burning fireplaces and a reading area. Additionally, the inn has 2 beautifully landscaped acres for strolling and a pond. > 900 Lake St., Saugatuck 49453, tel. 269/857–4346 or 800/231–2185, fax 269/857–1092. 11 rooms, 3 suites. Picnic area, pool, hot tub, business services, airport shuttle; no room phones, no TVs in some rooms, no kids under 12. AE, D, DC, MC, V. BP. **$–$$$**

Wickwood Country Inn Cookbook author Julee Rosso-Miller (*The Silver Palate*) and her husband, Bill, have bedecked the common areas of their B&B with their favorite appointments, such as French and English antiques, Oriental rugs, overstuffed chairs, flowers, and original art and sculptures. Rooms in the two-story house, built in 1925, are eclectically furnished, each decorated thematically. Lavish breakfasts— brunch on weekends—are served in the Garden Room. You'll also get to sample Julee's scrumptious snacks and hors d'oeuvres. > 510 Butler St., Saugatuck 49453, tel. 269/857–1465 or 800/385–1174, fax 269/857–1552, www.wickwoodinn.com. 11 rooms. Library, business services; no room phones, no room TVs. MC, V. BP. **$$$–$$$$**

SOUTH HAVEN

A Country Place Bed & Breakfast Nestled in a former fruit orchard, this early-20th-century Greek revival 2 mi north of downtown is shaded and tranquil. Lake Michigan beach access is across the street. Rooms are decorated in a floral country style and look out into the trees. On sunny days, breakfast is served on the back deck or the screened-in gazebo, and freshly baked pastries are available for a late-night snack. Cottages have microwaves, charcoal grills, and screened porches. > 79 North Shore Dr., South Haven 49090, tel. 269/637–5523. 5 rooms, 2 cottages. TVs in some rooms; no kids under 12, no smoking. D, MC, V. BP. **$–$$**

Holiday Inn Express Hotel & Suites This chain property, 1 mi east of downtown is right against the highway. Rooms have jewel-colored carpets and bedspreads and feel spacious; the ones at the ends of the building are quietest. > 1741 Phoenix St., South Haven 49090, tel. 269/637–8800 or 800/465–4329, fax 269/637–8810, www.holidayinn-express.com. 42 rooms, 20 suites. Indoor pool, gym, business services, laundry service. AE, D, DC, MC, V. CP. **$–$$$**

Carriage House at the Harbor Lushly appointed, this Victorian mansion overlooks Black River Marina from its perch on the hill. Wallpapered rooms have lacy curtains, patterned wing chairs, Amish antiques, and windows that catch the harbor breezes. The breakfast and evening hors d'oeuvres are served on a long, glassed-in breakfast room overlooking the water. Some rooms have fireplaces, and some have decks. > 118 Woodman St., South Haven 49090, tel. 269/639–2161, www.carriagehouseharbor.com. 11 rooms. Some in-room hot tubs, cable TV, in-room VCRs, business services, meeting rooms; no room phones, no kids under 18, no smoking. AE, MC, V. BP. **$$$–$$$$**

Hotel Nichols Since 1885, this brick property has served as a hotel or boarding-house; today, it's one of only two downtown lodgings. It retains its original tin ceiling; the floorboards creak gently underfoot, and the dark-wood doors are opened by skeleton keys. Some rooms have partial views of Black River harbor, others face South Haven's main commercial street. Stuffed animals sit on shelves and in chairs among other knickknacks and plenty of books. The wood-paneled apartments have sleeper sofas, tables, plenty of magazines, and a warm, lived-in feel. > 201 Center St., South Haven 49090, tel. 269/637–8725, www.hotelnichols.com. 14 rooms (6 share baths), 1 suite, 2 apartments. Cable TV, bicycles; no smoking. MC, V. CP. **¢–$$$**

Inn at HawksHead This elegant white 1930s lodge is on the Black River, 5 mi west of town. Some rooms have a fireplace, and some have a handsome window seat where you can look out over the golf course, the river, or the woods. A Continental breakfast is brought to your room. The restaurant serves lunch and dinner in a large dining room with lots of windows and a fireplace. > 523 Hawknest Dr., South Haven 49090, tel. 269/639–2146, fax 616/637–2324, www.hawksheadlinks.com. 9 rooms. Restaurant, bar, driving range, 18-hole golf course, putting green. AE, D, MC, V. Nov.–Feb. CP. $–$$$

Lake Bluff Inn & Suites Sitting on a dune overlooking Lake Michigan, this three-story property has many rooms facing the water. The property, 2 mi from downtown, is close to beaches and area attractions. Contemporary furnishings and floral arm-chairs in the long, narrow rooms frame wide views. Luxury suites have kitchenettes and/or fireplaces. > 76648 11th Ave., South Haven 49090, tel. 269/637–8531 or 800/686–1305, fax 269/637–8532, www.lakebluffinnandsuites.com. 23 rooms, 29 suites. Picnic area, some hot tubs, kitchenettes, recreation room, billiards, Ping-Pong, outdoor pool, wading pool, sauna, business services. AE, D, DC, MC, V. ¢–$$$$

Old Harbor Inn Most of the bright, generously sized rooms in the four separate buildings of this inn have balconies overlooking the Black River harbor; others have a view of the cheerful wood-paneled buildings of the Harbor Village shopping area. Its prime downtown location means shops, restaurants, and the beach are steps away. Boldly colored rooms have contemporary furnishings and nautical appointments. The master suite has a hot tub and fireplace. > 515 Williams St., South Haven 49090, tel. 269/637–8480 or 800/433–9210, fax 269/637–9496, www.oldharborinn.com. 38 rooms, 6 suites. Grill, microwaves, cable TV, indoor pool, hot tub, bar, laundry facili-ties, meeting rooms, no smoking rooms. AE, D, DC, MC, V. CP. $$–$$$$

Will O'Glenn Country Inn This 1920s farmhouse is on 17 groomed acres, 10 mi north of town. Cozy sitting areas are near wood-burning fires. Decorated in deep pinks and greens, rooms have floral touches and views of the well-kept property. Some guest rooms have a canopy bed and a fireplace. The lush gardens have more than 200 tulip and daffodil bulbs. Six horse stalls accommodate equestrian-loving guests who bring their friend along. The Manor House apartment has three bedrooms, 1½ baths, and a full kitchen. > 1286 64th St., South Haven 49408, tel. 269/227–3045 or 888/237–3009, www.willoglenncountryinn.com. 5 rooms, 1 apartment. Some in-room hot tubs, cross-country skiing, some pets allowed. MC, V. $–$$$

Yelton Manor A mansion originally built in 1890 is home to this Victorian B&B fur-nished with antiques and reproductions. A second building next door, called the Manor Guest House, accommodates those who want a more private stay. Both over-look Lake Michigan and both are within walking distance of shops, parks, and restau-rants. Some rooms have jetted tubs and views of the garden. The Manor holds an extensive collection books for you to read and plenty of spots to read them, including double swings in the garden and nooks in the house. > 140 N. Shore Dr., South Haven 49090, tel. 269/637–5220, fax 269/637–4957, www.yeltonmanor.com. 15 rooms, 5 suites. Cable TV; no room phones, no kids under 8, no smoking. AE, MC, V. BP. $$–$$$$

WHERE TO EAT

SAUGATUCK/DOUGLAS

Belvedere Restaurant Hardwood floors, chandeliers, and fireplaces embellish three dining rooms in this 1913 mansion. Begin your dinner with sautéed Brie with al-monds and honey, then choose roast duck, pork chops, filet mignon, or ravioli stuffed with duck, pecan, and ricotta as your entrée. > 3656 63rd St., Saugatuck, tel. 269/857–5777 or 877/858–5777, fax 269/857–7557. MC, V. Closed Sun.–Tues. June–Labor Day and Sun.–Wed. Labor Day–May. **$$–$$$**

Blue Moon Bar and Grille Tasty, inventive cuisine such as the grilled salmon paella and pan-seared ruby trout is served in a chic dining room in this eatery on the outskirts of Douglas. Long banquettes with jewel-covered pillows line burnt-umber walls. Tables are separated by walls adorned with large, illuminated slides. > 310 Blue Star Hwy., Douglas, tel. 269/857–8686. AE, D, MC, V,. **$$**

Chequers This pub-restaurant in downtown Saugatuck has dark paneling and British sporting paraphernalia on the walls. Dishes include fish-and-chips, the ploughman's platter with a selection of cheeses accompanied by bread and English pickle relishes, and classic shepherd's pie. Not surprisingly, the bar stocks the area's largest selection of British brews. > 220 Culver St., Saugatuck, tel. 269/857–1868. Reservations not accepted. AE, DC, MC, V. **$–$$$**

Crane's Pie Pantry Restaurant Homemade pies with fruit picked fresh from the backyard orchard draw people from all over southwestern Michigan to this Fennville café. Everything is homemade—which is why there are no soft drinks, only ice tea and fresh cider. Have a sandwich or just a thick slice of just-baked bread with honey. > 450 Washington Sq., Fennville, tel. 269/561–2297. D, MC, V. Closed Mon., Nov.–Dec. No dinner. **¢**

Everyday People Cafe Considered by some to be the best eatery in the area, this restaurant turns fresh ingredients into gastronomic wizardry, especially their peppercrusted ahi tuna and porterhouse leg of lamb. The art deco surroundings exude casual elegance. > 11 Center St., Douglas, tel. 269/857–4240. AE, D, MC, V. Closed Wed. **$$$–$$$$**

Ida Red's Cottage Cafe Within this little red house they serve an extravagant breakfast. Omelets are the specialty, but come for the homemade muffins, fresh squeezed orange juice, and tasty griddle cakes. Sandwiches and pasta are also available. > 645 Water St., Saugatuck, no phone. Reservations not accepted. No credit cards. Closed Mon.–Wed. No dinner. **¢**

Loaf and Mug Grab a few tasty sandwiches for an impromptu picnic on the beach or sit a spell in one of two charming dining areas, one inside and one out. Soups and pastas are served in round homemade bread bowls. The specialties are the ribbon sandwich, which layers egg and tuna salad sandwiches on top of each other, and the whitefish Reuben. The garden patio seats up to 70. > 236 Culver St., Saugatuck, tel. 616/857–3793. AE, D, MC, V. No dinner Sun.–Thurs. **$$–$$$**

Restaurant Toulouse Enjoy a bit of sunny Provence in western Michigan. Named after artist Henri Toulouse-Lautrec, the restaurant takes its inspiration from both his work and homeland. Whitewashed walls lined with art and cozy tables for two in front of a roaring fireplace make it a romantic favorite. Menu staples include wild mushrooms duxelles with saffron cream sauce and a casserole of beef, lamb, pork, duck, and white beans. There's a patio, where you can enjoy your meal under umbrellas in summer. > 248 Culver St., Saugatuck, tel. 269/857–1561. AE, D, MC, V. Closed Tues. Jan. and Feb., Mon.–Wed. **$$–$$$$**

SOUTH HAVEN

Captain Lou's Bar and Grill Fried perch is the specialty at this outdoor spot on the harbor and next to the drawbridge. High wooden tables hold college students and retirees; on the weekends, there's live music. > 278 Dyckman, South Haven, No phone. Reservations not accepted. No credit cards. Oct. 15–May 15. **$**

Clementine's Formerly a bank, this early 20th-century building still has exposed brick walls, teller windows, and safes. Vintage photographs depicting Great Lakes shipping and the ornately carved bar salvaged from a long-gone steamship give it a nautical flair as well. Menu choices include prime rib with grilled mushrooms, onions, and roasted red peppers as well as sandwiches and salads. The handmade onion rings arrive on a wooden pole. > 500 Phoenix St., South Haven, tel. 616/637–4755. AE, D, MC, V. **$–$$**

Idler **Riverboat–Magnolia Grille** The riverboat home of this eatery was built as a private steamer at the turn of the 20th century. It's docked beside the Old Harbor Inn on the Black River. The staterooms, with dark-wood paneling and views of the harbor, now are dining rooms. The menu emphasizes fresh seafood, thick cuts of beef, and Cajun-inspired dishes, but also includes sandwiches for lighter appetites. > 515 Williams St., South Haven, tel. 269/637–8435. AE, D, DC, MC, V. Closed Oct.–mid-Apr. **$$$$**

Phoenix Street Cafe and Deli Creative lunch fare made with top ingredients is the staple of this cheery yellow café. Hamburgers, vegetarian sandwiches, salads, and homemade soups fill out the menu. > 524 Phoenix St., South Haven, tel. 269/637–3600. Reservations not accepted. AE, D, MC, V. No dinner. **¢–$**

Tello's Champagne Room and Trattoria This elegant, welcoming restaurant 2 mi north of town has white linen and lamp lights—and brown paper and crayons for kids. Old-style Italian scenes and photos of jazz and blues singers cover the walls. One of the specialties is blackened seafood pasta, a linguine dish with sautéed crab, shrimp, leeks, garlic, and pancetta blackened with squid ink and topped with fresh basil and smoked salmon. Desserts include homemade cannoli, tiramisu, and cheesecake. > 1701 N. Shore Dr., South Haven, tel. 269/639–9898. D, MC, V. **$–$$$**

Three Pelicans No table is without a view in the upstairs dining room of this local favorite—even though it seats 250. The large picture windows frame the water; the tables frame old nautical maps. Half the seating is outside. Dishes include lobster, perch, and shrimp. > 38 N. Shore Dr., South Haven, tel. 269/637–5123. AE, D, DC, MC, V. Closed Nov.–May. **$$$–$$$$**

ESSENTIALS

Getting Here

Cars provide the best means of transportation to and around Saugatuck/Douglas and South Haven, even though summer parking in downtown Saugatuck is a headache. Planes, trains, and buses are all possible, but the extra time and expense probably isn't worth it. If you don't have a vehicle, think about renting a car and keeping it at your lodging while you ramble through downtown Saugatuck. Then use it to explore the small towns and farms dotting the countryside—there's just nothing like a Sunday-afternoon drive in southwestern Michigan, especially in fall.

BY BUS

Greyhound stops in South Haven—it's about a 3½-hour ride and costs about $60—but not in Saugatuck or Douglas. If you are just going to Saugatuck/Douglas, the Amtrak station in Holland is closer. A cab ride from there to downtown will cost about $20.

Interurban runs an on-demand service between and within Saugatuck and Douglas from Memorial Day to Labor Day; a ride is $1.

BUS DEPOTS **Amtrak Station** > 171 Lincoln Ave., Holland, tel. 616/396–8664, www.greyhound.com. **South Haven Bus Station** > 1210 Phoenix Rd., South Haven, tel. 269/637–2944, www.greyhound.com.
BUS LINE **Interurban** > Tel. 269/857–1418.

BY CAR

From Chicago, take I–90 (the Skyway) until it merges again with I–94 in Indiana (you can take I–94 the whole way and skip the tolls, but the Skyway is quicker). Once you're in Michigan, take I–196 North to U.S. 31, which will bring you into South Haven. The trip takes about 2½ hours. Saugatuck and Douglas are about 20 mi farther north on U.S. 31. Southwestern Michigan roads are sleepy, even in summer, except for in Saugatuck and Douglas, where the traffic rivals Chicago on July and August weekends. If you're visiting then, look for lodging with parking that's available to guests and walk into town or take the Interurban.

BY PLANE

Flying to southwest Michigan isn't really necessary. Car travel is a breeze and the train will get you there for less. But if you must, Gerald R. Ford International Airport is about 60 mi northeast of South Haven, and Kalamazoo/Battle Creek International Airport is about 30 mi southeast.
AIRPORTS **Gerald R. Ford International Airport** > 5500 44th St. SE, Grand Rapids, tel. 616/233–6000, www.grr.com. **Kalamazoo/Battle Creek International Airport** > 5235 Portage Rd., Kalamazoo, tel. 269/388–3668, www.kalcounty.com/airport.htm.
CARRIERS **American Eagle** > Tel. 800/433–7300, www.aa.com. **ATA Connection,** > Tel. 800/435–9282, www.ata.com. **United Airlines,** > Tel. 800/864–8331, www.ual.com.

BY TRAIN

The closest Amtrak depot is in Holland, about 30 mi from South Haven and 12 mi from Saugatuck/Douglas. Service is regular, a train a day, but it is often delayed.
TRAIN LINE **Amtrak** > Tel. 800/872–7245, www.amtrak.com.
TRAIN STATION **Amtrak Station** > 171 Lincoln Ave., Holland, tel. 800/872–7245, www.amtrak.com.

Visitor Information

CONTACTS **South Haven Lakeshore Convention and Visitors Bureau** > 415 Phoenix St., South Haven 49090, tel. 269/637–5252 or 800/764–2836, www.southhaven.org or www.bythebigbluewater.com. **Saugatuck-Douglas Convention and Visitors Bureau** > Douglas 49406, tel. 269/857–1701, www.saugatuck.com.

Champaign & Urbana

135 mi south of Chicago

11

By Joanne Cleaver

THE UNIVERSITY OF ILLINOIS SPRAWLS ACROSS these central Illinois twin cities. With a combined population of a little more than 100,000, both Champaign and Urbana's spiritual and cultural center revolves around this nucleus of 36,000 students. The university straddles the town line, with the tiny downtown of Urbana at the northeast corner of the campus and the larger Champaign downtown about a mile to the northwest. Urbana is the older of the two; it was settled in 1822 and became the Champaign County seat in 1833. Champaign began its existence as West Urbana, but when Urbana tried to annex the town, voters turned down the plan and incorporated as Champaign in 1860. Both cities have museums and outdoor attractions, including downtown areas that are well worth a visit.

Culture abounds at the UIUC campus and has spread to the rest of the metropolitan area. The Krannert Center for Performing Arts presents as many as 350 performances each year, from classical music, ballet, opera, and theater to jazz, folk, and world music, modern dance, contemporary theater, and family events. In fall, college football fans flock to the city to see the Fighting Illini, one of the Midwest's most prestigious and competitive teams. The intensely loyal fan base descends on Memorial Stadium each home game to see its Big 10 team battle one of its opponents.

The cities, because of the work done at the university, have also become home to a number of high-tech and computer-based industries. Parks and green spaces are also an integral part of both communities. In 1907, the Urbana Park District formed in 1907 and has grown to 22 parks; Champaign has more than 30. Downtown Urbana hosts the Urbana Sweetcorn Festival, which brings thousands to Main Street to share in the best that traditional, small-town America has to offer. From May through November, Urbana's Market at the Square houses nearly 100 vendors selling everything from homegrown produce and plants to homemade baked goods and handcrafted works of art. In June and July, Champaign hosts the Taste of Champaign-Urbana, which celebrates food made at local restaurants, and the weeklong Champaign County Fair.

Champaign-Urbana is a town with hidden beauty. Its relaxed college-town pace provides a cultural respite from the big city. A worthwhile destination in its own right is the Heartland Spa in Gilman, about 45 minutes north.

WHAT TO SEE & DO

Curtis Orchard At this family-run activity orchard, you can pick apples, watch goats trot on an overhead bridge, jump in a haystack, and pick out that perfect Halloween pumpkin. > 3902 S. Duncan Rd., Champaign, tel. 217/359–5565, www.curtisorchard.com. Free. Aug.–Dec.

Krannert Center for the Performing Arts Catch up-and-coming university student stars here, as well as famous performers and groups, such as the Chicago

Symphony Orchestra. > 500 S. Goodwin Ave., Urbana, tel. 800/527–2849, www.krannertcenter.com.

Lake of the Woods County Park This park near Mahomet, 10 mi west of Champaign, encompasses 900 acres. You can wander the sand-bottomed lake in a paddleboat, lounge on the beach, golf, and hike. Inside the Early American Museum here, small galleries showcase artifacts typical of frontier life, such as lamps and quilts, but the real action is on the lower level, where kids can play in a replica of a Native American camp, pretend to shoe a horse, and role-play daily chores from pioneer life, among other hands-on displays. > I–74, Exit 174, Mahomet, tel. 217/586–3360 park, 217/586–2612 museum, 217/586–2183 golf course, www.earlyamericanmuseum.org. Free. Daily.

Orpheum Children's Science Museum Kids can test the basic principles of science at this hands-on museum. As though evolution hadn't come up with enough odd-looking critters, one exhibit here allows kids to create their own dinosaur from plastic parts of various species. The water exhibit has running streams, waterfalls, and lots of ways to get wet making bridges and dams. Most of the exhibits explore physics. > 356 N. Neil St., Champaign, tel. 217/352–5895, www.m-crossroads.org/orpheum. $3. Wed.–Sun. 1–5.

University of Illinois The 1,400-acre campus of the university sprawls into both Champaign and Urbana. Its 36,000-student body makes it the state's largest university, and the school's library houses an impressive 8 million volumes. This is where the Internet for the masses was invented in the form of Mosaic, the first human-friendly web browser. The campus buildings are punctuated with wide lawns and groves of trees. The stadium on the south edge of the campus is the home of the Illinois Illini football team. On the Champaign side, the **Krannert Art Museum** (500 E. Peabody Dr., Champaign, tel. 217/333–1861, free, Tues. and Thurs.–Sat. 10–5, Wed. 10–8, Sun. 2–5) exhibits European and Asian art, photography, ceramics, and glassware. The nondescript exterior belies a spacious network of galleries that make up the second-largest art museum in the state. > 919 W. Illinois St., Urbana, tel. 217/333–0824, www.uiuc.edu. Free. Daily.

William M. Staerkel Planetarium Educational astronomy shows are presented at this planetarium. A matinee show is added in summer. > 2400 W. Bradley Ave., Champaign, tel. 217/351–2200. $3. Fri. and Sat. 7 PM–9:30.

NEARBY

Hardy's Reindeer Ranch Even adults can get disoriented in the 6-acre corn maze, 10 mi north of Champaign, that the Hardys cut into their fields each summer. That's part of the fun, as is visiting the reindeer in late fall and cutting your own Christmas tree. > 1356 Rte. 2900 N, off I–57, Exit 136, Rantoul, tel. 217/893–3407, www.reindeerranch.com. $5. July–Oct., Mon.–Sat., 10–8; Nov. and Dec., Mon.–Sat. 10–7.

Octave Chanute Aerospace Museum Aviation blew into central Illinois on the tailwind of World War I and hit a cruising altitude from World War II through the 1980s at this former Air Force hangar, now converted into a rambling museum. Staffed by military retirees who delight in telling tales of past exploits, the museum serves more than old planes, uniforms, and engines. Read about the harrowing account of the paratrooper who was turned into a human yo-yo when his chute got hung up on the plane, and see the cheeky "date application" form that amusement-starved recruits used to woo local girls. > 1011 Pacesetter Dr., Rantoul, tel. 217/893–1613, www.AeroMuseum.org. $7. Mon.–Sat. 10–5, Sun. noon–5.

Sports

GOLF

Brookhill Golf Course Fees are $20 for weekdays, $23 for weekends, at this 18-hole course, 10 mi north of Champaign. Take I–57 to Exit 250. > N. Maplewood Dr., Rantoul, tel. 217/893–1200.

Hartwell C. Howard Memorial Golf Course This 18-hole course, 7 mi west of Champaign, with a 9-hole course and a practice range, is a local favorite. Fees are $35, which includes a cart. > Lake of the Woods County Park, Mahomet, tel. 217/586–2183, www.ccfpd.org.

Orange and Blue Golf Courses Used by the university for practice and competition, each of these 18-hole courses, 2 mi south of Champaign, provides a challenging array of water and sand features. Fees are $13 to $21. > 1800 Hartwell Dr., Savoy, tel. 217/359–5613.

Stone Creek Golf Club On the grounds here, you can golf on both an 18-hole and 9-hole course. Fees are $35. > Stone Creek Blvd., Savoy, tel. 217/367–3000, www.stonecreekgolfclub.com.

Willow Pond Golf Course Air Force officers used to play at this base course with 18 holes. Fees are $14 weekday, $18 weekends. > 1126 Country Club La., Rantoul, tel. 217/893–9000.

Save the Date

JUNE

Taste of Champaign–Urbana Samplings of food made by local restaurants are served in Champaign's West Side Park on Church Street at this summer food fair, where arts and crafts are sold as well. > Tel. 217/398–2550.

JULY

Champaign County Fair Blue-ribbon vegetables and animals compete with midway rides and games for your attention at this weeklong county fair, held in mid-July at the county fairgrounds. > Coler and Fairview Sts., Urbana, tel. 217/367–8461.

AUGUST

Sweet Corn Festival At this summer festival, held in late August, you can wander Urbana's Main Street, sampling hot buttered sweet corn and other treats from food vendors, while listening to live music. There's also a sidewalk sale of arts and crafts. > Tel. 217/384–6304.

SEPTEMBER–DECEMBER

Illini Football Season Intensely loyal fans from all over the Midwest's most prestigious league, the Big Ten, descend on each other's cities in full war paint to cheer on their teams. U of I colors are navy and orange. Home games are played at Memorial Stadium. > 200 E. Florida Ave., Champaign, tel. 217/333–3470, www.fightingillini.ocsn.com.

WHERE TO STAY

The Chancellor One of the largest hotels in Champaign, the hotel is two blocks from the university's athletic complexes. Rooms have lots of light and are decorated with contemporary furnishings. > 1302 E. John St., Champaign 61820, tel. 217/352–7891, fax 217/352–8108. 224 rooms. Restaurant, some microwaves, some refrigerators, cable TV, 2 pools (1 indoor), exercise equipment, gym, hot tub, airport shuttle, no-smoking rooms. AE, DC, MC, V. CP. $

Comfort Inn These accommodations are 3 mi north of the University of Illinois campus. The hotel is in a fast-growing, busy shopping area. > 305 W. Marketview Dr., Champaign 61821, tel. 217/352–4055 Ext. 329, fax 217/352–4055, www.hotelchoicece.com. 66 rooms. Some microwaves, some refrigerators, cable TV, indoor pool, hot tub, business services, some pets allowed. AE, D, DC, MC, V. CP. ¢–$

Courtyard by Marriott Off I–74 at the Neil Street North exit, this hotel is 1 mi from shopping and 4 mi from the University of Illinois. Rooms have contemporary furnishings. > 1811 Moreland Blvd., Champaign 61820, tel. 217/355–0411, fax 217/355–0411, www.marriott.com. 75 rooms, 3 suites. Restaurant, in-room data ports, some microwaves, refrigerators, cable TV, some in-room VCRs, indoor pool, gym, hot tub, bar, laundry facilities, laundry service, business services. AE, D, DC, MC, V. CP. $

Eastland Suites This hostelry in Urbana is a 10-minute drive from the University of Illinois. Although the room decor could use an update, this hotel easily accommodates large groups. > 1907 N. Cunningham Ave., Urbana 61802, tel. 217/367–8331, fax 217/384–3370, www.eastlandsuitesurbana.com. 52 rooms, 74 suites. Microwaves, some refrigerators, cable TV, some in-room VCRs, indoor pool, exercise equipment, bar, business services, airport shuttle, some pets allowed. AE, D, DC, MC, V. CP. ¢–$$

Hawthorn Suites This all-suites hotel is near both downtown and the University of Illinois, and one block west of the city park. Suites comprise two small rooms and are popular with those visiting the university. > 101 Trade Center Dr., Champaign 61820, tel. 217/398–3400, fax 217/398–6147, www.hawthorn.com. 199 suites. In-room data ports, microwaves, some refrigerators, cable TV, some in-room VCRs, indoor pool, exercise equipment, hot tub, laundry facilities, business services, airport shuttle. AE, D, DC, MC, V. CP. $–$$

Historic Lincoln Hotel Tudor gone wild describes the decor at this quirky hotel, built in 1924, at the western edge of the U of I campus. Its lobby walls are upholstered in embroidered crewelwork, and heavy, dark-wood furniture dominates throughout. Most beds in most rooms have at least a half canopy; four suites have gas fireplaces. > 209 S. Broadway Ave., Urbana 61801, tel. 217/384–8800, fax 217/384–9001, www.historiclincolnhotel.com. 126 rooms, 4 suites. Restaurant, cable TV, indoor pool, lounge, no smoking rooms. MC, V. ¢–$$

La Quinta Across the street from the Market Place mall, which has a food court in the shopping area, this modern motel is within 2 mi of more than 20 restaurants and 6 mi from Willard Airport. > 1900 Center Dr., Champaign 61820, tel. 217/356–4000, fax 217/352–7783, www.laquinta.com. 122 rooms. In-room data ports, cable TV, pool, laundry facilities, some pets allowed. AE, D, MC, V. CP. ¢

Lindley House On northwest border of the U of I campus, this Victorian house invites you to settle down on the wide front porch for a leisurely cup of tea. A blend of antique and contemporary furnishings fills each room, some of which have four-poster beds. > 312 W. Green St., Urbana 61801, tel. 217/384–4800, www.lindley.cc. 5 rooms. MC, V. BP. $–$$

Park Inn Large rooms with unassuming modern decor populate this hotel, in a quiet spot near a busy intersection on the east side of town. Ask for a room with a fireplace. > 2408 N. Cunningham Ave., Urbana 61801, tel. 217/344–8000, fax 217/344–0013. 133 rooms, 4 suites. Refrigerators, no smoking rooms. MC, V. ¢

Red Roof Inn A mile north of downtown Champaign, this motel is 3 mi from the University of Illinois, and within 2 mi of more than 20 restaurants in a suburban commercial district. > 212 W. Anthony Dr., Champaign 61820, tel. 217/352–0101, fax 217/352–1891, www.redroof.com. 112 rooms. Cable TV, business services, some pets allowed. AE, D, DC, MC, V. ¢

NEARBY

Heartland Spa Indulge yourself at this spa getaway, amid a rolling lawn and pockets of privacy. The overgrown farmhouse, connected via underground tunnel to a spacious exercise barn, has several lounges for hanging out with friends new and old. You can take "aquacise" classes in the heated pool; soak in the hot tub; get a massage, sea-weed wrap, manicure, or pedicure; and work with a trainer to develop an exercise plan you can carry on back at home. Room decor is country flavored with lots of grapevine wreaths and pine furniture; the staff, friendly. Groups often reserve blocks of rooms long in advance, so plan accordingly. The hamlet of Gilman, which is 40 mi north of Champaign, provides no amusements, so if you want to escape for shopping, a movie, or a rich dessert, you'll have to head south to Champaign/Urbana. The spa requires a minimum weekend stay. > 1237 E. 1600 North Rd., Gilman 60938, tel. 800/545–4853, www.heartlandspa.com. 16 rooms. Dining room, tennis courts, 2 pools (1 indoor), ex-ercise equipment, gym, hot tub, sauna, cross-country skiing. MC, V. FAP. $$$$

CAMPING

Harry L. Swartz Campground Operated by the Champaign County Forest Preserve District at the Middle Fork River Forest Preserve, this campground is shaded by na-tive Illinois trees, such as hickories and hackberries. Nearby is the Middle Fork River, which has swimming, fishing, boat rentals, hiking, and playgrounds. The preserve is also home to a 130-acre waterfowl management area, where birds nest. > 3433 Count Rd. 2700 E, 34 mi northeast of Champaign, Penfield 61862, tel. 217/595–5432 superin-tendent, 217/595–5692 campground, www.ccfpd.org. 65 full hook-ups. Flush toilets, showers, playground. No credit cards. ¢

Prairie Pines Campground Prairie Pines is operated by the village of Rantoul. A former military housing site, the campground is set among tall trees and has roomy sites. > Chandler and Talon Sts., Rantoul 61866, tel. 217/893–0461, www.village.rantoul.il.us. 100 full hook-ups. Laundry facilities, showers, playground. Reservations essential. MC, V. ¢

WHERE TO EAT

Alexander's Steak House After you choose your steaks, you grill them on one of the huge indoor braziers at this steak house. Picnic tables add to its rustic setting. > 202 W. Anthony Dr., Champaign, tel. 217/359–1789. MC, V. $$–$$$$

Basmati Curries, masalas, and tikkas are on the menu at this family-style eatery. > 302 S. 1st St., Champaign, tel. 217/351–8877. MC, V. $

Biaggi's Ristorante Italiano Mediterranean palazzo decor provide a warm setting for one of the area's most dressy restaurants. This is a favorite for celebrations. The grilled seafood is excellent, pizza can be ordered as an appetizer or entrée, and the lasagna is a local favorite. > 2235 S. Neil St., Champaign, tel. 217/356–4300. Reserva-tions essential. MC, V. $$–$$$$

Courier Cafe Tucked into a turn-of-the-20th-century building on the north fringe of downtown Urbana, this popular eatery has a huge breakfast menu as well as sand-wiches. Omelets are a standout. > 111 N. Race St., Urbana, tel. 217/328–1811. Reserva-tions not accepted. No credit cards. $–$$

Great Impasta Among the pasta dishes of northern Italy here, lasagna is a favorite but homemade soups and breads are also worth trying. The restaurant's stucco walls evoke the spirit of Tuscany. > 114 W. Church St., Champaign, tel. 217/359–7377. AE, D, DC, MC, V. $–$$

Kennedy's Best known for its fresh seafood and game, Kennedy's also serves steak and pasta. Tall windows afford views of the adjacent country-club grounds and balance the dark wood. > 2560 S. Stone Creek Blvd., Urbana, tel. 217/384–8111. AE, D, DC, MC, V. No lunch Sun. **$$–$$$$**

Legends Neon, beer signs, and TV screens abound at this wildly popular sports bar, known for its pizza and oversize salads. Bar stools and tables make up the room. > 522 E. Green St., Champaign, tel. 217/355–7674. MC, V. **¢–$**

Ned Kelly's With plenty of knickknacks to evoke the Australian outback, this informal place serves steak, rotisserie chicken, prime rib, and pasta. > 1601 N. Cunningham Ave., Urbana, tel. 217/344–8201. AE, D, DC, MC, V. **$$**

Silvercreek Exposed brick accents the neo-western theme at this restaurant, where a selection of tapaslike appetizers highlights one of the more imaginative menus in the area. The restaurant's signature dish is "33 pasta," which has three different kinds of mushrooms in a sauce made with three different kinds of cheese. > 402 N. Race St., Urbana, tel. 217/328–3402. MC, V. **$–$$$**

Timpone's The pasta, pizza, fish, and game dishes here are Tuscan, and the ornate floors and arches are like those you might see in Florence. > 710 S. Goodwin Ave., Urbana, tel. 217/344–7619. MC, V. Closed Sun. No lunch Sat. **$$–$$$$**

ESSENTIALS

Getting Here

By far the easiest way to get around Champaign/Urbana is by car. Your main reference point is intersection of I–74 and I–57, which is the northwest corner of Champaign. Route 45 is the main drag through the University of Illinois campus; it tracks with Neil Street in Champaign, turns east along Springfield Avenue through the campus, and then heads north in Urbana. Driving by car also enables you to visit sites outside of the Champagne/Urbana area. Traveling via bus or Amtrak to Champaign/Urbana is strictly for campus-only visits, which might be less hassle than trying to legally park on campus.

BY BUS

Greyhound runs six buses each day between Chicago and Champaign. The Illinois Terminal, in downtown Champaign, serves both Greyhound and Amtrak. You can catch both taxis and the local Champaign/Urbana Mass Transit buses here.

BUS DEPOT **Illinois Terminal** > 45 E. University Ave., Champaign, tel. 217/384–3577.

BUS LINES **Champaign/Urbana Mass Transit** > Tel. 217/384–8188, www.cumtd.com. **Greyhound Bus Service** > Tel. 217/352–4150, www.greyhound.com.

BY CAR

The two-hour drive from Chicago to Champaign/Urbana travels across the fields of central Illinois. Conditions can be treacherous in winter, when winds whip and freezing rain and snow accumulate on the roads. Champaign/Urbana can get congested on university event weekends. Parking is scarce and expensive around the university. Overall, though, traffic flows quickly through the area and all destinations outside of the university area have plenty of free parking.

BY PLANE

Tiny, but efficient, Willard Airport is open from 5 AM to midnight daily. Flights from and to Willard arrive and originate only at Chicago's O'Hare International Airport. No flights are scheduled between Chicago's Midway Airport and Willard.

AIRPORT **Willard Airport** > Rte. 45 and Monticello Rd., Savoy, tel. 217/244–8600, www.willardairport.com.

CARRIERS **American Airlines & American Connection** > Tel. 800/433–7300, www.americanairlines.com. **Northwest Airlines** > Tel. 800/225–2525, www.nwa.com.

BY TRAIN

Amtrak makes three round-trips daily between Champaign/Urbana and Chicago. The journey usually takes no more than three hours but almost always is at least an hour late. Most trains have at least one handicapped accessible car.

TRAIN LINE **Amtrak** > Tel. 800/872–7245, www.amtrak.com.

TRAIN STATIONS **Illinois Station** > 45 E. Union Ave., Champaign, tel. 217/384–3577. **Union Station** > 225 S. Canal, Chicago, tel. 312/655–2101.

Visitor Information

CONTACT **Champaign-Urbana Convention and Visitors Bureau** > 1817 S. Neil St., Suite 201, Champaign 61820, tel. 217/351–4133 or 800/369–6151, www.champaigncounty.org.

Grand Haven & Holland

146 mi northeast of Chicago

12

By Jennifer Vanasco

HOLLAND AND GRAND HAVEN, THOUGH ONLY 20 MI APART, couldn't be more different. Holland is known for its "Dutch Touch." Tulips bloom along the streets in spring, and the staff at Dutch attractions wear klompen, or wooden shoes. Although it has a beach on Lake Michigan and on the smaller Lake Macatawa, the waterfront isn't the center of community life. Its northern neighbor Grand Haven, however, revolves around the water. The city's downtown is perpendicular to the Grand River and sits just 2½ mi from a flat, sandy beach on Lake Michigan.

Holland was settled in 1847 by Dutch immigrants seeking to escape religious perse-cution. Southwestern Michigan's climate, which was similar to their native Holland, proved an ideal home. It didn't take long for the industrious Dutch to build their community, and signs of their presence are everywhere. To successfully engage in commerce, residents took up picks and shovels and dug a channel to connect their own Lake Macatawa to Lake Michigan. Even the brick sidewalks have a bit of Dutch magic—they're heated, so that the finicky Holland residents always have a place to walk that's free from slush and snow.

Today, Holland has one of the best-maintained small-town main streets in the Mid-west. Bronze sculptures honoring such moral values as fidelity and love dot down-town, and more than 200 shops and restaurants thrive in their Victorian-era buildings. During the annual Tulip Time festival, which brings a half million visitors from around the world, merchants get together to scrub the sidewalks and store-fronts. On the outskirts of town are tulip farms, amusement parks, and other attrac-tions, which highlight Dutch culture and evoke a taste of life in the old country. The town also celebrates its more recent Latino heritage at the local history museum and during Tulipanes, the annual Latino film-and-arts festival. Holland has one of the highest concentrations of Hispanics in the state, thanks in part to the Heinz pickle plant just west of downtown, which has brought new labor into the community. On warm summer days, the smell of pickles adds a tang to the air.

Nearby Grand Haven has one of the Great Lakes' most protected harbors, which means that the busy port, with its four marinas, is still one of the focal points for resi-dents and tourists alike. A boardwalk provides a pleasant stroll from downtown to the lakeside Grand Haven State Park. One of Michigan's largest fleets of fishing charters plies the waters for salmon and trout. A Coast Guard festival in August honors the men and women who watch over Grand Haven's two lighthouses, and every summer day "the world's largest musical fountain" presents dancing streams of water and light that shimmer to music.

Grand Haven was founded by the French trappers who came to the area in the 1630s and traded with the Ottawa tribe. John Jacob Astor established his fur-empire founda-tion here, with 20 trading posts including the Grand Haven hub. Astor and his col-leagues were followed by the lumber barons of the 1800s, who shipped Michigan's pine forests down the Grand River and into Lake Michigan, later to be sold around the country. Grand Haven alone was once home to 18 lumber mills.

Today, Grand Haven's downtown is coming to life with a resurgence of new gift shops and restaurants. Beyond the center of town, Grand Haven is surrounded by 14 state and county parks—and 14 city and township parks—which provide miles and miles of biking and hiking trails, as well as access to Lake Michigan's sparkling waters and towering dunes. According to local geologists, it's also one of the few areas where there is "singing sand"—sand made up of tiny particles that "whistle" when you walk on it.

WHAT TO SEE & DO

GRAND HAVEN

Grand Haven State Park Popular Grand Haven State Park lies along Lake Michigan, with ½ mi of sandy beach. Swimming, picnicking, fishing, camping, and a playground bring a constant flow of visitors in summer, about 1 million a year. A boardwalk leads to downtown, following the Grand River. In winter, you can walk into the closed park. > 1001 Harbor, Grand Haven, tel. 616/847–1309, www.michigan.gov/dnr. $4 per car, per day. Apr.–Nov., daily.

Harbor Trolleys Routes through Grand Haven, Ferrysburg, and Spring Lake take you to city attractions and state parks. Chinook Pier, at Jackson and Harbor streets, is the best place to jump on the trolley. Buy your ticket with cash from the driver. > Grand Haven, tel. 616/842–3200. $1. Labor Day–Memorial Day, daily 10–5; Memorial–Labor Day, Sun.–Fri, 6 AM–5:30, Sat. 9–3:30.

Municipal Marina A trolley stop and a mix of stores and restaurants with outside seating are at this busy marina. > 101 N. Harbor Grand Haven, tel. 616/847–3478. Free. Daily. The *Harbor Steamer* excursion boat has narrated 1- and 1½-hour sightseeing cruises of the waterfront via Grand River and Spring Lake on a 90-person paddle-wheel replica. Evening cruises with live music are also available. Reservations are recommended. > 301 N. Harbor, Grand Haven, tel. 616/842–8950, www.harborsteamer.com. $8–$10. Memorial Day–Labor Day, daily 1–10.

Musical Fountain The world's largest musical fountain displays synchronized concerts combining light, music, and streams of water beginning at dusk in summer. Audiences gather to watch and listen on the waterfront bleachers or lay out a blanket in the park. Most nights, the music is big band or classical standards, but on Sunday, it's gospel. > Washington Ave. and Harbor Dr., Grand Haven, tel. 616/842–2550, www.grandhaven.com/fountain. Free. Memorial Day–Labor Day, daily at 10 PM.

Pere Marquette 1223 Locomotive This nonoperative 1941 steam locomotive is one of only two remaining from the old Pere Marquette line, which ran from Buffalo, New York, to Chicago. Volunteers maintain it and give occasional tours on Tuesday evenings and at the ice cream social in late August. Call to schedule a visit. > Harbor Ave. and Chinook Peer, Grand Haven, tel. 616/842–0700, www.grandhaven.com. Free. By appointment.

Tri-Cities Museum Spring Lake, Ferrysburg, and Grand Haven are the three cities whose histories are told at this small museum housed in an 1870 train depot. Guided tours and exhibits explain the importance of Lake Michigan and Grand Haven to the growth of such industries as fur trade, fishing, lumbering, and tourism. Nautical exhibits and a Victorian-period diorama with a parlor and dining room enrich the experience. > 1 N. Harbor Dr., Grand Haven, tel. 616/842–0700,

Big Red

THE MOST PHOTOGRAPHED LIGHTHOUSE IN MICHIGAN, *Big Red is a beloved local landmark, guarding the Holland canal between Lake Macatawa and Lake Michigan. Big Red is only one of Michigan's 116 lighthouses, but it's the most famous. Indeed, it has inspired a mass-produced lamp, the name of a toy bear, and a jigsaw puzzle. For locals, though, it signifies the Dutch settlers' struggle to dredge the harbor and canal that ensured their survival.*

In the early 1900s, a steel tower held the light that guided boats safely into the harbor. It could be seen for 13 mi, but it was useless in the fog. So in 1907, the three-story Queen Anne–style Harbor House was built to house a steam-operated fog signal. The light was automated in 1932—you can try out the original light in the Holland Museum downtown—and four years later, the freestanding steel structure was removed and a two-level tower was added between the Harbor House gables.

At first, the lighthouse was an unassuming pale yellow. But in 1956, a new requirement stated that navigational aids on the right side of any harbor entrance must be red. So the Coast Guard sandblasted the lighthouse and repainted it a glowing scarlet. Now the color seems to enhance the lake sunsets, which no doubt helped save Big Red when the Coast Guard decided in 1970 that it was no longer necessary and too expensive to maintain. A group of citizens banded together to form the Holland Harbor Lighthouse Historical Association and raise funds to keep it in repair.

There are two ways to see Big Red (which, be warned, is actually surprisingly small). The best view is from across the channel. You can park at Holland State Park, on Ottawa Beach Road, and walk along the boardwalk to the north pier. Big Red stands solidly on the opposite pier and is dazzling against the water and sky. You can also get up close by driving to the end of South Shore Drive and asking at the private guardhouse for directions and a map.

www.grandhaven.com/museum. Memorial Day–Labor Day, Tues.–Fri. 10–9:30, weekends noon–9:30; Labor Day–Memorial Day, Tues.–Fri. 10–9:30, weekends noon–4.

HOLLAND

Cappon House The Victorian-era Cappon House was once the residence of the town's first mayor. Its interior includes detailed woodwork and hardware and a variety of original furnishings that belonged to the Cappon family. > 228 W. 9th St., Holland, tel. 616/392–9084 or 888/200–9123, www.hollandmuseum.org. $3, includes Settlers House. Late May–late Oct., Wed.–Sat. 1–4; late Oct.–late May, Fri. and Sat. 1–4.

Dutch Village Go back to a 19th-century Netherlandish town at this 10-acre theme-park-like "village," 2 mi from Holland. Besides a working windmill, the village has canals, gardens, *klompens*, or wooden shoe dancers, a carousel, a petting zoo, and old-fashioned swing rides. It also has a museum of Dutch culture, a gift shop, and a café serving Dutch specialties. > U.S. 31 and James St., Holland, tel. 616/396–1475, www.dutchvillage.com. $8. Mid-Apr.–mid-Oct., weekdays 9–5, weekends 9–6.

Holland Museum Housed in a 1914 classical-revival building, the museum contains well-curated exhibits on local history and the area's Dutch heritage. The extensive Dutch decorative arts collection includes pewter, furniture, and classic delft blue-and-white pottery. A minicarousel, an intricate clock, and glass representations of Dutch churches are holdovers from the 1934 New York World's Fair. The Volendam Room is an 18th-century Dutch fisherman's cottage imported from the Netherlands. > 31 W.

10th St., Holland, tel. 616/392–9084 or 888/200–9123, www.hollandmuseum.org. $3. Mon., Wed., Fri., Sat. 10–5, Thurs. 10–8, Sun. 2–5.

Holland State Park With 143 acres that include a bathhouse, a long broad beach, sand volleyball courts, and 311 modern campsites, this is one of the Lower Peninsula's most popular and accessible (it's 10 mi west from downtown Holland) parks. You can rent Jet Skis and boats or arrange a parasailing trip nearby. Take River Street north to Douglas. Go west on Douglas, which turns into Ottawa Beach Road. > 2215 Ottawa Beach Rd., Holland, tel. 616/399–9390 or 800/447–2757, www.michigan.gov/dnr. $4 per car, per day. Apr.–Nov., daily 8 AM–10 PM; Dec.–Mar., daily dawn–dusk.

Hope College Founded by the Dutch Reformed Church in America in 1866, this private liberal arts college is known for its music, dance, and theater programs. Tours are available, and a popular theater program in season includes musicals such as *Guys & Dolls* and serious, classic plays such as *The Caine Mutiny*. > 69 E. 10th St., Holland, tel. 616/395–7890, fax 616/395–7000, www.hope.edu. Free. Daily.

Settlers House Within this 1867 white clapboard house are exhibits on how the early working-class Dutch settlers lived, from the wallpaper they purchased to the buttons, broken bottles, and doll heads they threw out the back door. > 190 W. 9th St., Holland, tel. 616/392–9084 or 888/200–9123, www.hollandmuseum.org. $3, includes Cappon House. Late May–late Oct., Wed.–Sat. 1–4; late Oct.–late May, Fri. and Sat. 1–4.

Veldheer Tulip Farm Four million tulips blossom here each spring in row after colorful row—and all 200 varieties of bulbs are for sale. The summer gardens include peonies, daylilies, iris, and other perennials. Windmills, drawbridges, and canals add local charm to the 80-acre demonstration gardens. Housed inside the building next to the tulip farm, the **Delftware and De Klomp Wooden Shoe Factory** is the only factory outside the Netherlands where earthenware is hand-painted and fired using delft blue glaze. In the next room, traditional wooden shoes are machine-carved in all sizes, from doll-size to giant. View and talk to both sets of artisans for free through windows at the back of a large gift shop. > 12755 Quincy St., Holland, tel. 616/399–1900, www.veldheer.com. $5. Jan.–Apr, weekdays 9–5; May–Dec., weekdays 8–6, weekends 9–5.

Windmill Island Holland's Dutch heritage is celebrated on this 36-acre, city-owned island with gardens, canals, dikes, and tulips. The huge DeZwaan windmill is a Netherlands import built in 1780 and still producing fine graham flour. Diversions include grazing Fresian cows, an antique carousel, and candle-making demonstrations. > 7th Ave. and Lincoln St., Holland, tel. 616/355–1030, fax 616/355–1035, www.ci.holland.mi.us/windmill. $6. Apr.–Oct. Mon.–Sat. 9–6, Sun. 11:30–6.

Sports

BIKING

Western Michigan's gentle hills and lakefront paths make for relaxing rides for both the novice and seasoned rider. Ottawa County has over 100 mi of bike paths—including 20 mi along the lake.

Lakeshore Connector Path These 20 mi of well-kept, paved paths along Lake Michigan, connecting Holland to Grand Haven, wander through beachfront parks and downtown Grand Haven. The Holland trailhead is in Holland State Park. The Grand Haven trailhead is at the corner of Robbins Road and Lake Shore Drive. > Grand Haven, tel. 616/738–4810 or 888/731–1001 Ext. 4810.

Musketawa Trail The "Mighty Musketawa" is the longest paved recreational path in Michigan, 26 mi long. Bikers, hikers, rollerbladers, and cross-country skiers wend their way through farmland and wetlands as they travel from Muskegon to Marne. The Muskegon end, called the Broadway trailhead, is 15 mi north of Grand Haven. From

Grand Haven, take U.S. 31 East to Sherman Boulevard. Go east on Sherman to Broadway, then turn left on Broadway. The trailhead is on the left 1 mi up. > Muskegon, tel. 616/738–4810 or 888/731–1001 Ext. 4810, www.musketawatrail.org.

Winstrom Park A 1-mi path in this pocket park on the north side of Lake Macatawa is across the street from the lake and south of the marshes. The park also serves as an excellent staging area for the Lakeshore Connector Path. It's 1 mi from Holland State Park and parking is free. > Perry St. and 160th Ave., Holland, tel. 616/394–0000, www.holland.org.

BIKE RENTALS **Beachside Bike Rental,** > 2011 Ottawa Beach Rd., Holland, tel. 616/399–9230. **Cross Country Cycle,** > 137 N. River Ave., Holland, tel. 616/396–7491, www.crosscountrycycle.com. **Rock 'n' Road,** > 300 N. 7th St., Grand Haven, tel. 616/846–2800, www.rocknroadcycle.com.

HIKING

Places to hike are plentiful in the Holland and Grand Haven area, including some paths—mostly along the lakeshore dunes—that are off-limits to bikers. The dunes, even when covered with protective boardwalks, make for a surprisingly rigorous climb; other parks are scenic, with wetland and forest.

DeGraff Nature Center You can see foxes, skunks, and more than 100 species of birds along the gentle, hard-packed walking trails here that wind through marsh and woodland. A visitor center showcases local wildlife and dried-plant exhibits. > 600 Graafschap Rd., Holland, tel. 616/355–1057.

P. J. Hoffmaster State Park The sand dunes here, 5 mi north of Grand Haven, tower above Lake Michigan; you can climb the 193 steps for the view or hike over 10 mi of dune trail. From downtown Grand Haven, take U.S. 31 North and exit at Pontaluna. A left at the end of the exit ramp puts you on Lake Harbor Road. The road ends at the park. > 6585 Lake Harbor Rd., Muskegon, tel. 231/798–3711.

Pigeon Creek Park Once a pine plantation, this county park 15 mi north of Holland has 10 mi of forested trails winding through its 282 acres. > 12524 Stanton St., West Olive, tel. 616/738–4810 or 888/731–1001 Ext. 4810.

Save the Date

JANUARY

WinterFest A citywide celebration of the season in Grand Haven held the last weekend in January includes arts, music, and theater events; family activities; a kids' area; and lots of chilly fun, including a cardboard toboggan race and the Polar Ice Cap Golf Tournament. > Tel. 800/303–4097, www.grandhavenchamber.org.

MAY

Great Lakes Stunt Kite Festival One of the nation's largest kite festivals has sport-kite pilots as well as family high-fliers. Seminars and demonstrations are popular with families. Held the second weekend in May at Grand Haven State Park. > Tel. 616/846–7501, www.grandhavenchamber.org.

Tulip Time Festival One of Michigan's best-known festivals blooms during the first week of May in Holland. Millions of colorful tulips, big-name entertainment, street scrubbing, *klompen* dancers, parades, fireworks, and much more enrich the experience. > Tel. 616/396–4221 or 800/822–2770, www.tuliptime.org.

JUNE

Feast of the Strawberry Moon Step back into the days when French fur traders lived side by side with Native Americans during this weekend reenactment of 18th-century life during the third weekend of June. Merchants ply their wares on Harbor Island, while blacksmiths, basket weavers, and river pirates go about their trades. > Grand Haven, tel. 616/842–0700, www.grandhaven.com/museum/fotsm.htm.

JULY–AUGUST
National Coast Guard Festival The U.S. Coast Guard celebrates its birthday in Grand Haven, with western Michigan's largest parade, a community picnic, arts and crafts, a main-street carnival, a drum-and-bugle competition, and a fireworks festival. The festival runs from the last weekend in July to the first weekend in August. > Tel. 888/207–2434, www.ghcgfest.org.

OCTOBER
Goose Festival The fall migration of the stately Canada goose is marked with parades, an art fair, and food and music at this event in downtown Fennville, 6 mi south of Holland. It is held the second weekend in October. > Tel. 616/561–6660, www.holland.org.

Tulipanes Thirty percent of Holland's population is Hispanic and this arts-and-film festival, held the first weekend of October, celebrates the city's Latino culture with movies, art exhibits, music, and lectures. > Tel. 616/748–1970, www.tlaff.org.

DECEMBER
Dutch WinterFest Sinterklass, the Dutch Santa Claus, appears on his white horse and children parade through the streets with paper lanterns during this two-week-long celebration of the holiday season in Holland. There's also an ice-sculpting competition, concerts, and a European-style outdoor Christmas market. The fun begins the day after Thanksgiving and runs through the first two weeks of December. > Tel. 616/394–0000 or 800/506–1299, www.holland.org.

WHERE TO STAY

GRAND HAVEN
Best Western Beacon This chain hotel, in a commercial area near beaches and shopping, is within ½ mi of downtown. Two-story and three-story buildings house rooms with modern furnishings. The rooms in the courtyard building are the quietest and you can relax in the chairs on the lawn outside. The rooms in the main building open up onto the indoor pool and can be noisy, especially when children are playing. > 1525 S. Beacon Blvd., Grand Haven 49417, tel. 616/842–4720 or 800/780–7234, www.bestwesternmichigan.com. 107 rooms. Picnic area, some in-room hot tubs, refrigerators, cable TV, indoor pool, airport shuttle. AE, D, DC, MC, V. **$–$$**

Boyden House Bed & Breakfast Wicker chairs rest on the wide front porch of this 1874 sumptuous bed-and-breakfast, set on a quiet residential street. Inside, the house is richly decorated with antiques and fresh flowers. A curving wooden staircase leads to the rooms; out back, attached to the house, are the suites. A deck overlooks a goldfish pond and a massage room downstairs invites you to loosen up those tense muscles. > 310 S. 5th St., Grand Haven 49417, tel. 616/846–3538, www.boydenhouse.com. 7 rooms, 2 suites. In-room VCRs; no room phones, no smoking. AE, D, MC, V. BP. **$–$$**

Days Inn Modern furnishings fill the small rooms of this two-story motel in a commercial area 1 mi south of town. During the week, the inn caters to business travelers; on weekends, families fill the rooms. Cross-country and downhill skiing are a mile away. > 1500 S. Beacon Blvd., Grand Haven 49417, tel. 616/842–1999 or 800/388–7829, fax 616/842–3892, www.daysinn.com. 100 rooms. Restaurant, room service, cable TV, indoor pool, hot tub, bar, laundry facilities, business services. AE, D, DC, MC, V. **$**

Fountain Inn This hotel is 2 mi outside of downtown and a short walk from the beach. Surrounded by trees, the two floors have small rooms with contemporary furnishings. It's not fancy, but it's the least expensive option in a town that has few hotel rooms. > 1010 S. Beacon Blvd., U.S. 31, Grand Haven 49417, tel. 616/846–1800 or 800/745–8660, fax 616/847–9287. 47 rooms. Picnic area, cable TV. AE, D, MC, V. CP. ¢–$

Harbor House Inn Built in 1987, this farmhouse-style B&B overlooks the downtown waterfront. Victorian furnishings and antique-looking wide wood plank floors fill its three floors. Breakfast includes homemade caramels and cinnamon-raisin bread. > 114 S. Harbor Dr., Grand Haven 49417, tel. 616/846–0610 or 800/841–0610, fax 616/846–0530, www.harborhousegh.com. 17 rooms. In-room VCRs, hot tub, business services; no smoking. AE, MC, V. BP. $$–$$$$

Lakeshore Bed & Breakfast A sterling collection of U.S. president artifacts line the walls and display cases of this contemporary B&B in a 1935 estate. You can see a lock of Washington's hair, Harry Truman's Bible, and a golf ball used by JFK. The Presidential Suite's floor-to-ceiling windows gaze out over the lawn and 275 feet of private Lake Michigan beach. All three suites have fireplaces and are decorated with a mix of antique and contemporary furnishings. The intimacy of this small B&B and its location on a quiet residential street will make you feel like a guest in someone's home. A full breakfast is served on White House china. > 11001 Lakeshore Dr., Grand Haven 49460, tel. 616/844–2697 or 800/342–6736. 3 suites. Cable TV, beach, free parking; no smoking. AE, MC, V. BP. $$$–$$$$

Looking Glass Inn An electric trolley takes you up the steep hill where the Looking Glass perches across the street from the beaches of Grand Haven State Park. Rooms are decorated in wicker and white painted wood, and have a beach-house feel. Two rooms have lake views, but you can also take in vistas from the large wooden deck. > 1100 S. Harbor Dr., Grand Haven 49417, tel. 616/842–7150 or 800/951–6427. 5 rooms. Some in-room hot tubs, beach; no smoking. AE, MC, V. BP. $$

HOLLAND

Bonnie's Parsonage 1908 This inn was built in 1908 as a church parsonage. The dark oak woodwork gleams and leaded-glass windows let in lots of light. In winter, hot spiced cider is served in front of the fire; in summer, lemonade is a treat on the screened porch. Holland's first B&B, it sits amid an upscale residential neighborhood, a few blocks away from Hope College. The bright rooms are elegantly decorated with antiques. > 6 E. 24th St., Holland 49423, tel. 616/396–1316. 4 rooms. No room phones, no room TVs. No credit cards. BP. $–$$

Centennial Inn Centennial Park is across the street from this 1889 brick-and-fieldstone house on a large corner lot. Some rooms have vaulted ceilings and some have fireplaces. Dutch and American antiques add warmth to the sunny rooms. Unwind on the big patio in back or on the front porch. The inn is within walking distance of downtown. > 8 E. 12th St., Holland 49423, tel. 616/355–0998, www.yesmichigan.com/centennial. 8 rooms. Some in-room hot tubs, library; no room phones, no kids under 16, no smoking. MC, V. BP. $–$$

Comfort Inn Just 3 mi from downtown Holland, this motel also is a 20-minute drive from Saugatuck beach. The inn caters to families on weekends and business travelers during the week. Chain restaurants are within walking distance. > 422 E. 32nd St., Holland 49423, tel. 616/392–1000, fax 616/392–1421, www.comfortinn.com. 71 rooms. Microwaves in some rooms, refrigerators in some rooms, some in-room hot tubs, cable TV, outdoor pool. CP. AE, D, DC, MC, V. $–$$

Country Inn by Carlson The lobby's hardwood floors, Delft tile-lined fireplace, and a large wicker-filled porch reflect the name of this motel on the north side of town. Shopping and dining are within a few blocks. Cookies and milk are served nightly. The maple hutches and iron bed frames give the rooms a country feel. > 12260 James St., Holland 49424, tel. 616/396–6677 or 800/456–4000, fax 616/396–1197, www.countryinns.com. 116 rooms. Cable TV, in-room data ports, indoor pool, business services. CP. AE, D, DC, MC, V. **$**

Dutch Colonial Inn A white clapboard house built in the 1930s is home to this B&B. Antiques furnish the rooms, and a garden, patio, and a porch with rocking chairs enhance the warm, country ambience. A large, sunny common room upstairs has plenty of seating. Three rooms have double whirlpool tubs and two have fireplaces. The inn is less than 2 mi from downtown, and a short drive from the area's beaches and Hope College. > 560 Central Ave., Holland 49423, tel. 616/396–3664, fax 616/396–0461. 5 rooms. Picnic area, in-room data ports, some in-room hot tubs, cable TV, in-room VCRs; no smoking. AE, D, MC, V. BP. **$–$$**

Fairfield Inn by Marriott Just off U.S. 31 on the north side of Holland, this three-story motor inn is within walking distance of malls and restaurants and less than 2 mi from downtown. Families stay mainly on the weekends; the hotel fills with business travelers during the week. > 2854 Westshore Dr., Holland 49424, tel. 616/786–9700, fax 616/786–9700, www.fairfieldinn.com. 64 rooms. Cable TV, indoor pool, hot tub, business services. AE, D, DC, MC, V. CP. **$**

Haworth Inn and Conference Center The Haworth has simple, modern hotel rooms, which resemble what you'd find in a chain hotel. The draw is location. It's the only lodging property in downtown Holland. Owned by Hope College, the inn provides you with access to the school's facilities, including the library, the racquetball courts, and the Olympic-size pool. > 225 College Ave., Holland 49423, tel. 616/395–7200 or 800/903–9142, fax 616/395–7151, www.haworthinn.com. 50 rooms. Cable TV, gym. AE, D, MC, V. CP. **$**

Holiday Inn A lobby filled with bright, Caribbean-style colors and paintings invites you in to this four-story chain hotel, 1 mi from downtown Holland. Some rooms have balconies overlooking the indoor domed pool and spa area, others have outside entrances. The pool is shaped like the state of Michigan—a red star points out "you are here." > 650 E. 24th St., Holland 49423, tel. 616/394–0111, fax 616/394–4832, www.holiday-innhldmi.com. 168 rooms. Restaurant, 2 bars, some refrigerators, room service, cable TV, indoor pool, hot tub, sauna, exercise equipment, laundry facilities, business services, airport shuttle. AE, D, MC, V. **$$**

Shaded Oaks Bed and Breakfast The guest rooms at this Cape Cod–style house on Lake Macatawa are actually suites with separate sitting areas. Splashes of white, from the white fireplace and bed curtains in one to the coffee and tea area in the other, accentuate the wine-color furnishings in each suite. You can take breakfast or afternoon coffee on the deck and enjoy the views of water and wooded grounds. > 444 Oak St., Holland 49424, tel. 616/399–4194, fax 616/393–0823, www.shadedoaks.com. 2 rooms. Cable TV, in-room VCRs with movies; no room phones. MC, V. BP. **$$–$$$$**

WHERE TO EAT

GRAND HAVEN

Arboreal Inn Two dining rooms, one relaxed and one formal with chandeliers, and an eat-in bar distinguish this cottagelike restaurant decorated in an early-American style.

The menu ranges from filet mignon to Alaskan king crab and shrimp scampi. > 18191 174th Ave., Spring Lake, tel. 616/842–3800. AE, D, MC, V. Closed Sun. No lunch. $$–$$$$

Dee-Lite Bar and Grill The weekend Bloody Mary bar alone is worth coming to this 1950s-style diner housed next to an abandoned movie theater. Or, if you'd prefer, have a burger accompanied by something from Dee-Lite's venerable martini bar. Their pancakes and sandwiches are pretty good, too. > 24 Washington St., Grand Haven, tel. 616/844–5055. AE, MC, V. ¢–$$$

K2 Dozens of fresh ingredients—from anchovies to almonds to asparagus—can be added to the wood-fired pizzas created here. The casual second-floor dining room shares a building with two other restaurants and is the most laid-back of the three. Four pool tables and video game machines are yours to enjoy while you eat what locals call the best pizza in town. > 2 Washington St., Grand Haven, tel. 616/846–3299. AE, MC, V. $–$$

Kirby Grill Spinach artichoke ravioli is on the menu here, as is polenta-crusted walleye and lobster bruschetta This is innovative cuisine served in a casual ambience—the brick walls are covered with the scrawls of locals who've been here before. Microbrewed beers and smiles from the friendly waitstaff spice up the experience. > 2 Washington St., Grand Haven, tel. 616/846–3299. AE, MC, V. $–$$

Poncho's Simple Mexican food stars at this colorful downtown restaurant, where strings of colored lights and an occasional piñata hang from the ceiling. Sandwiches and burgers round out the menu. > 22 S. Harbor Dr., Grand Haven, tel. 616/842–5555. AE, D, MC, V. ¢–$$

The Rosebud This Victorian-looking restaurant with stained glass and its original 1874 pressed-tin ceiling serves pasta, pizza, and freshly cut steaks. High wooden booths provide intimacy in the narrow room. Bands play almost every night, from rock to folk to jazz. > 100 Washington St., Grand Haven, tel. 616/846–7788. AE, D, DC, MC, V. Closed Labor Day–Memorial Day, Sun. ¢–$$

Snug Harbor The picture windows overlooking the harbor and the expansive deck make this a local favorite. Try the grilled swordfish steaks or blue-crab ravioli; soups are freshly made daily. > 311 S. Harbor Dr., Grand Haven, tel. 616/846–8400. AE, MC, V. ¢–$$

HOLLAND

Alpenrose Extensive woodwork, including hand-carved chairs, enhances the German-Austrian look in this restaurant's several dining rooms. Entrées include traditional German dishes such as sauerbraten, chicken shortcake, and schnitzel, and classic American seafood, lamb, and duck. When the weather cooperates, you can dine on the patio. > 4 E. 8th St., Holland, tel. 616/393–2111. AE, D, MC, V. Closed Mon. No dinner Jan.–Apr. $$–$$$$

8th Street Grille Memorabilia and photographs celebrating downtown Holland fill this eatery that seats 250. The fish-and-chips and soup bar are the big draws here, but the extensive menu also includes fresh whitefish, steaks, quesadillas, and sandwiches. > 20 W. 8th St., Holland, tel. 616/392–5888. AE, MC, V. Closed Sun. $–$$

New Holland Brewing Company Restaurant and Pub Sandwiches are the specialty at this microbrewery; one burger is even marinated in a homemade beer sauce. Eight to 10 seasonal beers are always on draft, all New Holland's own, but try the house-made root beer for a real kick. Each of the dining rooms has a different design, including the narrow, chic front room anchored by the curving metal bar; a family-friendly loft upstairs; an area in the front with a few couches pressed against a window for the dating crowd; and a concrete-floor pool and video game room. > 66 E. 8th St., Holland, tel. 616/355–6422, fax 616/393–0027. AE, D, MC, V. Closed Sun. ¢–$$

Pereddies Wooden floors, the owner's photos of Italy, and white tablecloths add to the old-world charm of this restaurant, bakery, deli, and gift store. Pizza, chicken cacciatore, and other standard Italian fare fill the menu. Reservations are essential for Friday and Saturday. > 447 Washington Sq., Holland, tel. 616/394–3061. AE, DC, MC, V. Closed Sun. $$–$$$

Pigeon Lake Lodge If you're arriving by boat, you can tie up to this casual restaurant's dock, though the restaurant itself doesn't overlook the water. The mounted local game—including deer and fish—give this place a hunting lodge feel, though the wooden beams and cream walls add airiness. The whitefish is a local favorite, but the perch or prime rib is also worth a try. > 7175 Lake Shore Dr., West Olive, tel. 616/399–6161. AE, D, MC, V. Closed Sun. and Mon. $$–$$$

Piper Huge picture windows overlook Lake Macatawa and docking facilities at this casual restaurant, long known as the Sandpiper. Lake Superior walleye is its specialty, but don't overlook the wood-fired pizzas and creative pastas. You can dine inside on one of the three tiers, all with lake views, or, weather permitting, sit outside overlooking the water. Reservations are essential on Friday and Saturday. > 2225 S. Shore Dr., 5 mi west of Holland, Macatawa, tel. 616/335–5866. AE, D, MC, V. Closed Sun. and Mon. Sept.–Apr. No lunch. $$–$$$

Remember When Cafe Good diner food makes a comeback at this roadside café between downtown Holland and the beach. The house specialty is the olive burger, a roughly chopped green olive dressing served over a perfectly fried burger, augmented with crispy french fries. > Holland, tel. 616/335–8422. No credit cards. No dinner. ¢

Till Midnight Fresh ostrich (from a nearby farm) and panfried fresh trout occasionally surface on the eclectic menu in this small, art deco establishment, which also includes homemade pastas, pizzas, and more than 40 wines by the glass. Other attractions include a pâté of the day, vegetarian entrées, a bakery on the premises, and sidewalk dining. > 208 College Ave., Holland, tel. 616/392–6883. AE, D, MC, V. Closed Sun. $$$–$$$$

ESSENTIALS

Getting Here

Cars are are the easiest way to travel to and around Grand Haven and Holland. Planes, trains, and buses are all possible, but the extra time and expense probably isn't worth it; it's cheaper to rent a car in Chicago and drive.

BY BUS

Greyhound serves both Grand Haven and Holland, though in Holland the station is closed on weekends. The trip takes approximately seven hours from Chicago, depending on the schedule. Two buses a day come from Chicago, one that arrives in the late afternoon and one that arrives around midnight. In Grand Haven, the on-demand city bus, called Harbor Transit, will take you where you want to go for $1. The buses don't run on a regular schedule, so call for a pickup. In Holland, call the Macatawa Area Express (MAX) at least 24 hours in advance to schedule a pick up to take you downtown. The cost is $2. You can also take Greyhound between the two cities.

BUS DEPOTS **Amtrak Station** > 171 Lincoln Ave., Holland, tel. 616/396–8664, www.greyhound.com. **Greyhound Grand Haven Bus Depot** > 440 N. Ferry St., Grand Haven, tel. 616/842–2720, www.greyhound.com.
BUS LINES **Greyhound Lines** > Tel. 800/231–2222, www.greyhound.com.
Macatawa Area Express > Tel. 616/355–1010,
www.ci.holland.mi.us/manager/max.

BY CAR

From Chicago, take I–90 (the Skyway) until it merges again with I–94 in Indiana (you can take I–94 the whole way and skip the tolls, but the Skyway is quicker). Once you're in Michigan, take I–196 North to U.S. 31, which will bring you into Holland. Grand Haven is 18 mi farther north on U.S. 31. Once you get out of the Chicago metro area, traffic should flow quickly—expect to drive at least the speed limit, which in Michigan is 65 mph. Getting to Holland should take about three hours, much less if you travel on Sunday or in the late evening. Both Grand Haven and Holland are small, and a car will enable you to explore the nearby surrounding communities and the pastoral countryside. Both towns have plenty of downtown parking. Expect heavy traffic during festival weekends, such as Tulip Time.

BY PLANE

Flying to southwest Michigan isn't really necessary. Car travel is a breeze and the train will get you there for less. But if you must, Gerald R. Ford International Airport is about 30 mi east of Holland and is home to three carriers serving Chicago. If you fly to Muskegon, about 15 mi north of Grand Haven and 35 mi north of Holland, you'll be routed through Detroit. From either, you will need to take a taxi or rent a car to get downtown Grand Haven or Holland.
AIRPORTS **Gerald R. Ford International Airport** > 5500 44th St. SE, Grand Rapids, tel. 616/233–6000, www.grr.com. **Muskegon County Airport** > 99 Sinclair Dr., Muskegon, tel. 231/798–4596, www.muskegonairport.com.
CARRIERS **American Eagle** > Tel. 800/433–7300, www.aa.com. **ATA Connection,** > Tel. 800/435–9282, www.ata.com. **Northwest Airlines** > Tel. 231/733–3107, www.nwa.com. **United Airlines** > Tel. 800/864–8331, www.ual.com.

BY TRAIN

Amtrak runs one train a day from Chicago to Holland. It takes about four hours, when it's running on time. A bus or a cab will take you to Grand Haven.
TRAIN LINE **Amtrak** > Tel. 800/872–7245, www.amtrak.com.
TRAIN STATION **Amtrak Station** > 171 Lincoln Ave., Holland, tel. 800/872–7245, www.amtrak.com.

Visitor Information

CONTACTS **Grand Haven/Spring Lake Area Visitors Bureau** > 1 S. Harbor Dr., Grand Haven 49417, tel. 616/842–4910 or 800/303–4092, www.grandhavenchamber.org. **Holland Area Chamber of Commerce** > 76 E. 8th St., Holland 49423, tel. 616/392–2389, fax 616/392–7379, www.hollandchamber.org. **Holland Area Convention and Visitors Bureau** > 76 E. 8th St., Holland 49423, tel. 800/506–1299, www.holland.org.

Around Sheboygan County

145 mi north of Chicago

13

By Jenn Q. Goddu

THE AREA IN AND AROUND SHEBOYGAN COUNTY provides a spectrum of activities for the weekender, from relaxing on a beach and catching your own fish for dinner to spending a Saturday perusing dusty antiques stores. The farthest point on a looping tour of Elkhart Lake, Sheboygan, Port Washington, and Cedarburg is 60 mi north of Milwaukee so it's easy to explore the area at a relatively leisurely pace.

The lure of the lake is strong in Sheboygan. The city's name can be traced to Native American words all relating to water, and it is the water that continues to draw visitors away from the condos and city streets of Chicago.

Lake Michigan is merely a pleasant backdrop to life in the Windy City, but up here it is a source of pride. This attractive shoreline city's attachment to its maritime heritage is evidenced by a revitalized row of old, weathered fish shanties (which seem true in spirit compared to the gaudy commercialism of Chicago's Navy Pier).

Sure, the city has culture with its theater and art galleries, and culinary claims to fame (brat fries are a long-standing Sheboygan tradition), but it is the fishing, sailing, sunbathing, and sand-castle building that captivates the weekend visitor. There's a sense of getting away to a place where the sound of waves hitting the shores is truly appreciated. It's relaxing and you're always somehow reminded of just how much the riverfront and lakefront location has meant to the continued prosperity of this city, first chartered in Wisconsin in 1853.

A prime location on the shores of Lake Michigan also makes Port Washington a place to get out and stretch your legs for a few hours as you make your way around this area on I–43. The downtown consists of a few blocks of retail shops, restaurants, and galleries. A tiny tourist office across from the harbor will supply you with a self-guided tour map that explains the historic import of the otherwise unassuming buildings. Settled in 1835, this small community has one of the first man-made harbors dug in North America. It remains a magnet for anglers and water-sports enthusiasts, or simply those looking for a tasty and fresh seafood dinner.

Elkhart Lake, 20 mi northwest of Sheboygan, may only be 286 acres (making it a mere puddle in comparison to Lake Michigan) but the clear blue waters in this community have been drawing city-weary travelers to the shores of its namesake lake for more than 130 years. The railroad provided the first easy access to this charming historic resort community. Today some of the same sweepingly impressive hotels that once counted gangsters and gamblers among their guests are still open for business. The tree-lined streets, Victorian architecture, eclectic shops, and varied eating stops give this village added appeal. When you're planning your trip, though, be sure to find out first if it's a road-racing weekend. You may not hear the roar of the engines 4 mi away but the sheer volume of visitors to the area may crimp the idyllic feel of your escape from Chicago.

When you visit cozy Cedarburg, the closest of these destinations to the Windy City, you journey back in time more than 150 years. Many buildings made of cream brick and blue-gray Niagara limestone (provided from a local quarry) are still standing from the days when German and Irish immigrants settled this riverfront town. It's part of the reason this city has the nickname, "the city with the stone face." But don't worry, the locals don't have the disposition that moniker might suggest—they're quick to greet visitors with a smile. Downtown Washington Avenue is listed in the National Register of Historic Places. This main strip's nine blocks are almost entirely devoted to antiques shops, galleries, craft stores, confectioneries, and restaurants. As you drive in you can see many attractive Victorian homes, and spanning Cedar Creek just north of town is the state's last remaining original covered bridge.

WHAT TO SEE & DO

CEDARBURG

Cedar Creek Settlement The Wittenberg Woolen Mill, built in 1864, and adjacent buildings on the corner of Washington Avenue and Bridge Road comprise the Cedar Creek Settlement. It houses more than 25 restaurants, antiques stores, gift shops, and artists' studios. The rushing waters of Cedar Creek powered the looms and knitting machines used to convert heavy Wisconsin wool into yarns, blankets, and even the white socks worn by the Chicago White Sox in the 19th century. The **Cedar Creek Winery** (tel. 262/377–8020 or 800/827–8020, Mon.–Sat. 10–5, Sun. 11–5) occupies the lower floors of a 130-year-old woolen-mill building in Cedarburg's historic section downtown. Wine tours and tastings are available. The mill's stone cellars have proved an ideal location for barrel-aging chardonnay, cabernet sauvignon, syrah, or the winery's Cedar Creek Vidal. > N70 W6340 Bridge Rd., Cedarburg, tel. 866/626–7005, www.cedarcreeksettlement.com. Free. Mon.–Thurs. and Sat. 10–5, Fri. 10–8, Sun. 11–5.

Cedarburg Cultural Center In the heart of Cedarburg's downtown historic district, this center houses both permanent and changing exhibits focusing on the area's heritage, history, and contemporary culture. > W62 N546 Washington Ave., Cedarburg, tel. 262/375–3676. Donations accepted. Tues.–Sat 10–5, Sun. 1–5.

Covered Bridge Park Just 2½ mi north of town on Covered Bridge Road, this park features Wisconsin's last original covered bridge, which was built over Cedar Creek in 1846 and remained in service until 1962. Today the bridge is open to foot traffic and there's a picnic area next to the water. > Covered Bridge Rd., Cedarburg, tel. 262/377–9620 or 800/237–2874. Free. Daily.

Historic Downtown Cedarburg Designated a National Historic District, this ½-mi stretch a block up from the Cedar Creek is filled with restored 1850s buildings now serving as cafés, taverns, and shops purveying gifts and antiques. > Washington Ave. between Spring and Sheboygan Sts., Cedarburg, tel. 262/377–9620. Free. Daily.

InterUrban Trail This 30-mi recreational trail follows the route of a railway that ran between Milwaukee and Sheboygan from 1907 to 1948. Activities permitted are hiking, walking, running, biking, rollerblading, and skiing. Several small gaps in the trail exist. A trailhead is at the Interurban Trail Bridge, one block east of Washington Avenue on Turner Road. > Cedarburg, tel. 262/377–9620, www.interurbantrail.us. Free. Daily.

Kuhefuss House This two-story, stone house is one of the oldest homes in historic Cedarburg. Once a month and for special holiday events the 1849 home is open to the public for interpretive tours led by volunteers dressed in period costumes. The home was restored in 1989 and you can tour the sitting room, parlor, sewing room, bedrooms, and garden. > W63 N627 Washington Ave., Cedarburg, tel. 262/375–3676. Donations accepted.

Paul J. Yank's Brewery Works Fine Arts Complex An 1843 brewery has housed sculptor Paul J. Yank's working studio and the Ozaukee Art Center since 1973. Works of other artisans are exhibited as well. Exhibits change every six weeks. > W62 N718 Riveredge Dr., Cedarburg, tel. 262/377–8230. Donations accepted. Wed.–Sun. 1–4.

ELKHART LAKE

Broughton-Sheboygan County Marsh Park and Wildlife Area This 13,000-acre area 1 mi northwest of town is open for hunting, fishing, and wildlife observation. A 30-acre in the marsh has campgrounds, picnic areas, a restaurant, and canoe, and boat rentals. You can also access the Sheboygan County snowmobile trail system here. > W7039 Rte. SR, Elkhart Lake, tel. 920/876–2535. Free. Daily.

Crystal Lake This lake 2 mi south of town harbors largemouth bass, crappie, bluegill, and yellow perch. The lake is the most heavily used lake for fishing and boating in the Elkhart Lake area; however, motorboating is not permitted on Sunday. > Rte. C, Elkhart Lake, tel. 920/876–2922. Free. Daily.

Elkhart Lake The lake that gives this village its name is home to such fish species as musky, walleye, northern pike, largemouth bass, bluegill, and yellow perch. A public boat landing, beach, picnic shelters, and volleyball courts are also here. > Rte. P, Elkhart Lake, tel. 920/876–2922. Free. Daily.

Elkhart Lake Depot Museum Inside a former railroad station, the museum traces community history with original depot furnishings, photos, and memorabilia. Built in 1904, the building is on the National Register of Historic Places. > Rhine and Lake Sts., Elkhart Lake, tel. 920/876–2922. Donations accepted. Memorial Day–Labor Day, weekdays 10–6, Sat. 7–3; Labor Day–Sept. 30, weekdays 10–6, Sat. 8–1.

Henschel's Museum of Indian History This museum, on an archaeological-dig site, houses artifacts dating from 8000 BC and a collection of Indian copper and pottery. > N8661 Holstein Rd., Elkhart Lake, tel. 920/876–3193. $4. Memorial Day–Labor Day, Tues.–Sat. 1–5; May, Sept., and Oct., by appointment only.

Little Elkhart Lake A small lake, 2 mi south of town, Little Elkhart may be surrounded by homes but it's also a popular fishing spot. The waters hold primarily largemouth bass, bluegill, and yellow perch. The lake has a boat launch and small beach. > Rte. 67, Elkhart Lake, tel. 920/876–2922. Free. Daily.

Pioneer Corner Museum This museum houses historic room displays, tools, toys, and a collection of more than 15,000 buttons, much of it from German immigrants who founded New Holstein in 1848. > 2103 Main St., New Holstein. $1. Memorial Day–Labor Day, Sun. 1–4; Labor Day–Memorial Day, by appointment only.

Timm House This Victorian painted lady 15 mi north of Elkhart Lake in New Holstein is furnished with original and period pieces and provides a glimpse of small-town life before the turn of the 20th century. The exterior colors of this home, which is listed on the National Register of Historic Places, reflect the original paint scheme. > 1600 Wisconsin Ave., New Holstein, tel. 920/898–5766. $1. Memorial Day–Labor Day, Sun. 1–4; Labor Day–Memorial Day, by appointment only.

Wade House & Wesley Jung Carriage Museum Guides in 1850s attire give tours of the buildings included in this living-history museum in Greenbush, about 15 mi west of Elkhart Lake. Wade House is a three-story, 1850s Greek-revival stagecoach inn. The carriage museum has 100 horse-drawn vehicles and carriages, and horse-drawn wagon rides are available. You can also watch a demonstration of a water-powered sawmill or stop by the blacksmith's. > W7747 Plank Rd., Greenbush, tel. 920/526–3271, www.wisconsinhistory.org/sites/wade. $10. Mid-May–mid-June, Wed.–Sun. 9–5; mid-June–mid-Oct., daily 9–5.

PORT WASHINGTON
Eghart House Leopold Eghart, a local probate judge, lived in this Victorian cottage, built in 1872. The gabled home stayed in the Eghart family until 1969. Then a group of locals saved the house from becoming a parking lot and restored it as a museum. Some of the period furnishings are original to the home. > 316 Grand Ave., Port Washington, tel. 262/284–2897 or 262/284–2875. $1. June–Aug., Sun. 1–4.
InterUrban Trail This 30-mi recreational trail crosses Ozaukee County from north to south passing through eight different communities, including Port Washington. The trailhead here is at the Pebble House. > 126 E. Grand Ave., Port Washington, tel. 414/284–0900, www.interurbantrail.us. Free. Daily.
Light Station Museum This 1860 lighthouse, north of downtown on a bluff 106 feet above Lake Michigan, provides information on Port Washington's local and maritime history. An ongoing restoration of the Port Washington Light Station began in 2000. > 311 E. Johnson St., Port Washington, tel. 262/284–0900. Donations accepted. Memorial Day–Labor Day, Sun. 1–4.
Pebble House Blacksmith Edward Dodge and his wife spent many a night sorting out smooth stones of varying colors to create the striped pattern on the walls of this 1848 house. It's now home to the Port Washington Chamber of Commerce. Stop in here to pick up your a tour map for a self-guided Historic City Center Tour or Old Town Port Tour. > 126 E. Grand Ave., Port Washington, tel. 414/284–0900. Free. May–Oct., daily 10–4; Nov.–Apr., weekdays 10–4.
Pioneer Village The village, 10 mi northwest of Port Washington, has a collection of 20 log, stone, and frame buildings from the mid- to late 19th century. Each building is furnished with artifacts capturing the lives of early pioneer settlers. > 4880 Rte. I, Saukville, tel. 262/284–0900. $4. Memorial Day–2nd Sun. in Oct., weekends noon–5.
Rotary Park On a man-made peninsula jutting out into Port Washington's harbor, which can now hold 220 small boats, is this small park. Several informational displays detail commercial fishing methods used in the area and depict the marina then and now. Also here is the Fisherman's Memorial, a monument to those lost to the Lake. Look east and you can see the city's distinctive 1934 art deco lighthouse. > Port Washington. Daily.
St. Mary's Catholic Church Climb the 85 steps up the hill at the north end of Franklin Street to get a good view of downtown and the marina from the grounds of this Gothic-revival-style Church. > 430 Johnson St., Port Washington, tel. 262/284–5771. Free. Daily.

SHEBOYGAN
Above & Beyond Children's Museum This interactive kids' museum has dozens of hands-on exhibits in its 5,000 square feet of space. Kids can make body impressions on a giant pin screen, compose music, climb to the treehouse, or discover how an air current makes a Ping-Pong ball float. > 902 N. 8th St., Sheboygan, tel. 920/458–4263, www.abkids.org. $3.50. Tues.–Sat. 9:30–5, Sun. 1–5; June–Aug. also Mon. 9:30–5.
John Michael Kohler Arts Center A former family mansion, built in the Italian-villa style, is at the center of this light-filled complex that plays a key role in the rejuvenated downtown scene. A visual- and performing-arts complex devoted to contemporary American art, it also encompasses a turn-of-the-20th-century carriage house and

a historic library. Plays and musical events are staged here along with an annual out-door festival. > 608 New York Ave. (Rte. 23), Sheboygan, tel. 920/458–6144. Free. Mon., Wed., and Fri. 10–5, Tues. and Thurs. 10–8, weekends 10–4.

Kohler-Andrae State Park Just south of town is this 1,000-acre park on a mile-long stretch of Lake Michigan beach backdropped by sand dunes. You can fish, beach-comb, swim, camp, and hike 3½ mi of all-purpose woods and dune trails. The Sanderling Nature Center has nature exhibits and interpretive programs. The park is east of I–43, off Exit 120. > 1520 Old Park Rd., Sheboygan, tel. 920/451–4080, www.dnr.state.wi.us. $7. Daily.

Lakeland College Founded by German immigrants in 1862 and run as a religious in-stitution, it became a liberal-arts school in 1956 and was renamed Lakeland College. Some 850 students attend school at this 700-acre campus, which includes a fine-arts gallery, a nature area, and a museum. The campus is 7 mi west of Sheboygan. Take I–43 to Route 42, north to Route A. > W3718 South Dr., Rte. M, Plymouth, tel. 920/565–2111, www.lakeland.edu. Free. Daily.

Old Plank Road Trail This 17-mi county recreation trail is half paved and half turfed and runs from Sheboygan to Greenbush, passing Kohler, Sheboygan Falls, and Ply-mouth. It's great for rollerblading, horseback riding, hiking, biking, and snowmobil-ing. In Greenbush the trail connects with the Ice Age National Trail. > 4015 Erie Ave. (Sheboygan trailhead), Sheboygan, tel. 920/459–3060. Free. Daily.

Sheboygan County Historical Museum Exhibits in this museum complex on the western edge of town showcase Sheboygan County history. You can visit the 1852 Judge David Taylor home, an 1864 log house, an 1867 cheese factory, and an 1890s barn. Exhibits include Indian history, ice harvesting, local sports, early agriculture, and maritime trades. > 3110 Erie Ave., Sheboygan, tel. 920/458–1103. $3. Apr.–Oct., Tues.–Sat. 10–5, Sun. 1–5.

Waelderhaus The daughter of the Kohler Company founder built this house in 1931 in memory of her father. This "house in the woods" is a replica of the 1850 Kohler home in Vorarlberg, Austria. Its intricate carvings, woodcuts, and iron and pewter work were designed and executed by Austrian sculptor-architect Kaspar Albrecht. The house sits on a high bluff, 3 mi west of Sheboygan, overlooking the Sheboygan River. > W. Riverside Dr., Kohler, tel. 920/452–4079. Free. Daily tours at 2, 3, and 4.

Wreck of the *Lottie Cooper* This white oak schooner built in 1876 was recovered and reassembled in 1992, and subsequently placed in Deland Park, near Lake Michi-gan in downtown Sheboygan. You can walk through its hold and see the craftsman-ship in the 89-foot center section, which is all that remains of the three-masted schooner that capsized in gale-force winds in the Sheboygan harbor in 1894. Both guided and self-guided tours are available. > 882 Broughton Dr., Sheboygan, tel. 920/458–2974. Daily.

Tours

Fall Color Driving Tour Approximately 25 mi of the Kettle Moraine Scenic Drive run through western Sheboygan County. For a stunning display of fall color follow County Routes A and S or drive around Crystal Lake. Peak color is seen generally mid-Sep-tember through mid-October. Route map brochures are available from the Plymouth Chamber of Commerce. > 386 S. Main St. Sheboygan, tel. 920/823–0079.

Landmark Tours This escorted sightseeing tour takes in historic Cedarburg and its surrounding countryside. You can visit stone homes, a mill, and an outbuilding built in the 1840s in nearby Hamilton. The tour continues to Covered Bridge Park before heading to the Cedar Creek Settlement and downtown Cedarburg. Custom and group tours are available for $21.95 per person. Call ahead to arrange a tour. > Cedarburg, tel. 262/375–1426.

Sports

PORT WASHINGTON

FISHING Full-day, half-day, and evening charters are available from Port Washington if you're on the lookout for king or coho salmon, or rainbow, brown, or lake trout. To dock your own boat contact the Port Washington Marina (106 N. Lake St. Port Washington, tel. 262/284–6606).

Renegade Sportfishing Charters The *Renegade* is a 36-foot Pacemaker Sportfisherman, helmed by a captain with 25 years experience fishing Lake Michigan. Chinook salmon, brown trout, rainbow trout, and lake trout can keep you and your group of up to six busy on tours ranging in length from 3 to 10 hours. > Port Washington, tel. 262/377–4560 or 800/343–0089.

Seahawk Fishing Charters Since 1985, the *Seahawk* has been trolling Lake Michigan for salmon and trout. The 34-foot *Sea Ray* is available for twilight, half-day, or two-day charters for up to six people. > 1538 Scott Rd., Port Washington, tel. 262/284–4693.

SHEBOYGAN

FISHING Trout and salmon are yours to hook and net in the waters off Sheboygan. Catch your "big one" on half-day, or full-day fishing or cruising charter or set your own boat afloat from a launch at the 8th Street Bridge or the major launch area at the lakefront. The Sheboygan River is also popular for fly-fishing, particularly in fall and spring. The Sheboygan County Convention and Visitors Bureau publishes a Fishing Facts brochure each year.

Dumper Dan's Sportfishing Charters Groups of one to six people can climb aboard one of Dumper Dan's three 28-foot Baha Cruiser sportfishing boats. You can troll Lake Michigan for trout and salmon aboard Sheboygan's only multiboat charter fishing fleet. > 4022 N. 51st St., Sheboygan, tel. 920/457–2940.

Sorry Charlie Sport Fishing Service Captain Randy Even guarantees the charter trips aboard his 31-foot Uniflite will be successful. The trip is free if he can't steer you to some of Lake Michigan salmon or trout. > 4226 S. 13th St., Sheboygan, tel. 920/452–9964, www.u-charters.com.

Shopping

Kohler Design Center This dramatic three-level space is a premier showroom for plumbing products manufacturer Kohler Company. You can get kitchen, bath, and home-furnishing ideas from the more than 25 rooms, all designed to reflect home-renovation and spa trends. A museum and gallery present exhibits depicting the evolution of the company, the village of Kohler, and original pieces of ceramic, cast-iron, and brass art. While you're here, take a free tour of Kohler's huge manufacturing facility. You can get an overview of the manufacturing of vitreous china and enameled cast-iron plumbing products. The tour, conducted Monday through Friday, starts at 8:30 AM and takes 2½ hours. No kids under 14 are permitted on the tour. > 101 Upper Rd., Kohler, tel. 920/457–3699, www.kohler.com.

Save the Date

FEBRUARY

Schnee Days The village is bustling with winter fun from a chili cook-off to snow sculptures, winter golf, and downhill bowling during this annual festival held the first weekend of February. > Elkhart Lake, tel. 877/355–4278.

Winter Festival This downtown festival held the first weekend of the month in the historic district includes a chili contest, a parade, snow golf, ice carving, sled-dog racing, and the Mill Pond Bed Race, in which costumed participants race over the ice carrying decorated beds. > Cedarburg, tel. 262/377–9620 or 800/237–2874.

JUNE

Stone and Century House Tour On this driving tour, held the first weekend in June, you can visit 19th-century houses in Ozaukee and Washington counties. Many of the homes contain antiques, art, and collectibles. > Cedarburg, tel. 800/237–2874.

Strawberry Festival The locally produced favorite is served in shortcake, sundaes, and slushes at this downtown festival held the last weekend in June. A craft show, an art show, and even a pet fashion show add to the fun. > Cedarburg, tel. 262/377–9620 or 800/237–2874.

JULY

Ducktona 500 Three thousand plastic ducks race for prizes down the Sheboygan River in nearby Sheboygan Falls on the first weekend of July. Other events include an antique car show, music, and aqua-bike races. > Sheboygan, tel. 920/467–6206.

Great Cardboard Boat Regatta People-powered cardboard boats race along a 200-yard course on the riverfront off Rotary Park, at Pennsylvania and Broughton drives, every July 4. The Titanic Award—for the most dramatic sinking—is among the awards. > Sheboygan, tel. 920/458–6144.

Outdoor Arts Festival Approximately 140 artists display their work at this juried art fair on the grounds of the John Michael Kohler Arts Center, at New York Avenue and 6th Street, on the third weekend in July. > Sheboygan, tel. 920/458–6144.

Ozaukee County Fair This traditional county fair held the first week of August at the county fairgrounds includes livestock, a carnival, contests, exhibits, food, and music. > Cedarburg, tel. 262/377–9620 or 800/237–2874.

Port Fish Day The world's largest one-day outdoor fish fry takes place downtown on the lakefront on the third Saturday in July. A parade kicks off the festivities, which include live music. > Port Washington, tel. 800/719–4881.

AUGUST

Downtown Night Local restaurants serve food outside accompanied by live music on the village square one evening in mid-month. > Elkhart Lake, tel. 920/876–2922.

Lion's Fest & Fish Derby Anglers from all over the country come to Port Washington to compete in this big prize fishing derby. Food, music, and other entertainment add to the weekend festivities, held the first weekend of August. > Port Washington, tel. 800/719–4881.

Road America Racing Champ Car World Series Top auto racers attack the turns and straights of Road America's 4-mi course in this Championship Auto Racing Teams weekend, held at the end of August. > Elkhart Lake, tel. 920/892–4576.

SEPTEMBER

Sheboygan County Fair Traditional ribbon judging competitions, more than 16,000 exhibits, food, grandstand shows, and entertainment come to Plymouth Fairgrounds Park, 7 mi south of Elkhart Lake. > Elkhart Lake, tel. 920/458–8004.

Wine and Harvest Festival This annual wine festival in downtown Cedarburg attracts between 30,000 and 40,000 people and includes grape stomping, a grape-seed spitting contest, a farmers' market, a scarecrow contest, apple bobbing, music, food samples, and craft shows. It's held the third weekend of the month. > Cedarburg, tel. 262/377–9620 or 800/237–2874.

WHERE TO STAY

CEDARBURG

Stagecoach Inn This large stone inn filled with antiques was a stagecoach stop before the Civil War and is now on the National Register of Historic Places. Rooms are individually decorated with such touches as rich wood furniture, brass beds, antique writing desks, exposed stone walls, or a skylight. Two of the suites in the restored 1853 building have fireplaces. > W61 N520 Washington Ave., Cedarburg 53012, tel. 262/375–0208 or 888/375–0208, fax 262/375–6170, www.stagecoach-inn-wi.com. 6 rooms, 6 suites. In-room hot tubs, cable TV in some rooms, bar, business services; no kids under 10, no smoking. AE, D, DC, MC, V. CP. **$–$$**

Washington House Inn Period pieces fill this 1886 Victorian Cream City brick building in the center of Cedarburg's historic district. Gardens are behind the building and fireplaces are in the common gathering room. The inn also operates the **Schroeder Guest House,** a luxury suite in a converted historic home. > W62 N573 Washington Ave., Cedarburg 53012, tel. 262/375–3550 or 800/554–4717, fax 262/375–9422, www.washingtonhouseinn.com. 34 rooms. In-room hot tubs, cable TV, in-room VCRs, sauna, business services. AE, D, DC, MC, V. CP. **$–$$$$**

ELKHART LAKE

Osthoff Resort This resort has 500 feet of sandy shoreline for swimming and boating. The hotel has a stone fireplace and brass chandelier in the lobby and light, bright suites with large windows, understated furnishings, and cream carpeting. > 101 Osthoff Ave., Elkhart Lake 53020, tel. 920/876–3366 or 800/876–3399. 145 suites. Restaurant, cable TV, in-room VCRs, 2 tennis courts, indoor-outdoor pool, exercise equipment, sauna, beach, boating, bicycles, basketball, volleyball. AE, D, DC, MC, V. **$$–$$$$**

Siebkens Resort The rooms in this family-owned turn-of-the-20th-century resort are furnished in Victorian style. It is across the street from the Elkhart Lake. > 248 S. Lake St., Elkhart Lake 53020, tel. 920/876–2600 or 888/876–2600. 50 rooms. Cable TV, beach, bar. MC, V. **¢–$$**

Victorian Village on Elkhart Lake An authentic Victorian main building anchors this Victorian-style complex of nine buildings, which includes accommodations from suites and condos to town houses on the lakeshore. Floral wallpaper and bedding enrich the wicker or honey-color wood furniture in the rooms. > 279 S. Lake St., Elkhart Lake 53020, tel. 920/876–3323, fax 920/876–3484, www.vicvill.com. 80 rooms. Restaurant, dining room, in-room data ports, cable TV, some in-room VCRs, miniature golf, 2 pools, beach, dock, boating, hiking, bar, business services. AE, D, MC, V. **$$–$$$$**

PORT WASHINGTON

Best Western Harborside Motor Inn Two blocks from the marina in downtown Port Washington, this brick hotel anchors the town's main strip of stores. Some of the rooms, decorated with cherry-red wood and brass lamps, have views of the marina. > 135 E. Grand Ave., Port Washington 53074, tel. 262/284–9461 or 800/528–1234, fax 262/284–3169, www.bestwestern.com. 96 rooms. Some in-room hot tubs, cable TV, pool, exercise room, hot tub, sauna, dock, bar, business services, free parking, some pets allowed. AE, D, DC, MC, V. **$–$$**

Port Washington Inn When this house was built in 1903 the chandeliers were equipped to operate with electricity or gas. The house retains its stained-glass and leaded-glass windows and hardwood floors, and each room is decorated with antiques. Four blocks from Lake Michigan, the inn is on one of the highest points in town and the suite has a view of the lighthouse and harbor. > 308 W. Washington St., Port Washington 53074, tel. 262/284–5583 or 877/794–1903, www.port-washington-inn.com. 3 rooms, 1 suite. Cable TV; no kids under 12, no smoking. AE, MC, V. BP. $–$$

SHEBOYGAN

American Club Built in 1918 to house immigrant workers at the Kohler company, this Tudor-style residence reopened as a luxury resort in 1981. Elegance emanates from the grand lobby and comfortable sitting areas, complete with plush furniture, hand-crafted woodwork, and chandeliers. Rooms are filled with luxurious 18th-century-style furniture. The adjacent carriage house, also built in 1918, houses more rooms and the Kohler Water Spa. The resort, about 5 mi west of Sheboygan in Kohler, is set on 500 acres of rolling hills and meadows, some of which is part of a wildlife preserve. > 419 Highland Dr., Kohler 53044, tel. 920/457–8000 or 800/344–2838, fax 920/457–0299, www.americanclub.com. Main house: 223 rooms, 13 suites; carriage house: 43 rooms, 9 suites. 3 restaurants, room service, in-room data ports, in-room hot tubs, minibars, some refrigerators, cable TV, in-room VCRs, 4 18-hole golf courses, 6 indoor and 6 outdoor tennis courts, pool, gym, hot tub, spa, bicycles, hiking, horseback riding, bar, shops, business services. AE, D, DC, MC, V. $$$$

Baymont Inn Just 1 mi west of town, this brick two-story hotel is painted white with green shutters and is near restaurants and shopping malls. Rooms are furnished with honey-color wood furniture, floral comforters, and framed prints on the walls. > 2932 Kohler Memorial Dr., Sheboygan 53081, tel. 920/457–2321 or 877/229–6668, fax 920/457–0827, www.baymontinn.com. 96 rooms. Cable TV, business services, some pets allowed. AE, D, DC, MC, V. CP. ¢–$$

Brownstone Inn This stately mansion built just after the turn of the 20th century combines the history of a 1907 inn with modern comforts. Canopy or sleigh beds, fireplaces, and detailed ceilings and elegant staircases evoke the era. > 1227 N. 7th St., Sheboygan 53081, tel. 920/451–0644 or 877/279–6786, fax 920/457–3426, www.brownstoneinn.com. 7 rooms. Cable TV, spa, billiards, business services; no smoking. D, MC, V. CP. $–$$$$

English Manor Bed & Breakfast This 1908 four-story English Tudor is listed on the state's Register of Historic Places. Guest rooms all have private baths and sitting areas, and each has different amenities, such as hot tubs and fireplaces. Other aesthetic touches include original bathroom fixtures, oak built-ins, beamed ceilings, hardwood floors, and a billiards room and pub in the lower level. Afternoon tea and wine and cheese are served daily. > 6332 Michigan Ave., Sheboygan 53081, tel. 920/208–1952 or 800/557–5277, fax 920/208–3792, www.english-manor.com. 5 rooms. Cable TV, exercise equipment. AE, D, MC, V. BP. $–$$$

Harbor Winds Hotel At the base of the Sheboygan Riverfront Boardwalk, this hotel's two stories blend in color-wise with the weathered fish shanties. But it's all modern decor inside these unassuming hotel rooms. > 905 S. 8th St., Sheboygan 53081, tel. 920/452–9000, fax 920/452–0093, www.pridehospitality.com. 28 rooms. Cable TV, business services. AE, D, DC, MC, V. CP. ¢–$

Lake View Mansion Overlooking Lake Michigan, this 1912 redbrick Georgian mansion has 11 fireplaces, built-in buffets, bookcases, hand-carved woodwork, and hardwood floors. You can roam the entire first floor of this house, which includes a library, large foyer, living room, dining room, and sunroom. Complimentary beverages are available all day. > 303 St. Clair Ave., Sheboygan 53081, tel. 920/457–5253, www.lakeviewmansion.com. 5 rooms. Some in-room hot tubs, cable TV; no room phones. AE, D, MC, V. BP. **$$–$$$$**

Rochester Inn Rooms in this former general store and post office, built in 1848, have four-poster beds and Queen Anne furniture. The inn is 3 mi west of Sheboygan. > 504 Water St., Sheboygan Falls 53085, tel. 920/467–3123 or 800/421–4667, www.rochesterinn.com. 1 room, 5 suites. In-room hot tubs, some microwaves, cable TV, in-room VCRs, cross-country skiing; no smoking. AE, MC, V. BP. **$–$$$**

Riverview Spa Suites On the Sheboygan Riverfront Boardwalk, this hotel houses suites filled with contemporary furnishings. Oversize leather furniture fills the common lounge area. > 841 Riverfront Dr., Sheboygan 53081, tel. 920/451–9576, fax 920/803–0351. 3 suites. Cable TV, kitchenettes, hot tub, business services. D, MC, V. CP. **$$–$$$**

WHERE TO EAT

CEDARBURG

Chocolate Factory Fresh subs and croissant sandwiches make this downtown restaurant a great lunch spot. Housed inside a restored historic building, it's filled with wooden booths and old photos. Be sure to leave room for Blommer's Homemade Wisconsin Ice Cream sundae. > W62 N577 Washington Ave., Cedarburg, tel. 262/377–8877. DC, MC, V. **¢–$**

Cream and Crepe Cafe This country-quaint café is in the Woolen Mill, overlooking Cedar Creek. Crepes are entrées or dessert here but you can also order soups, sandwiches, and salads. > N70 W6340 Bridge Rd., Cedarburg, tel. 262/377–0900. AE, DC, MC, V. **¢–$**

Galioto's Vintage Grille Just south of Covered Bridge Park is this up-scale casual restaurant serving American steak, chops, seafood, and chicken with Italian flair. The dining room evokes the spirit of Tuscany. > 1221 Wauwatosa Rd., Cedarburg, tel. 262/377–8085. AE, DC, MC, V. Closed Mon. **$–$$$**

Klug's Creekside Inn After 14 years as the chef of Barth's at the Bridge, Bruce Klug and his wife Kris (a former bartender and hostess) are now the owners of this steak-and-seafood supper club on the banks of Cedar Creek. They have added a German influence to the menu, but Thursday is still prime-rib night and Friday is a fish fry. > N58 W6194 Columbia Rd., Cedarburg, tel. 262/377–0660. AE, MC, V. Closed Mon. **$–$$$$**

Settlers Inn You can order grilled sandwiches, salads, or low-fat and vegetarian food items in a smoke-free dining room in this late-18th-century building in historic downtown Cedarburg. The authentic decor includes the original bar, icebox, and tin ceiling. You can also visit the deli next door for sandwiches and soups and sit at the tables along Washington Avenue. > W63 N657 Washington Ave., Cedarburg, tel. 262/377–4466. AE, MC, V. **¢–$**

ELKHART LAKE

Dillinger's Dine alfresco lakeside or fireside in this restaurant in Victorian Village. Try a daily special made with fish caught in the lake you are looking out at or enjoy steak or a vegetarian entrée. > 279 S. Lake St., Elkhart Lake, tel. 920/876–3645. AE, D, DC, MC, V. Closed Mon. No lunch in winter. **$–$$$**

Lake Street Cafe A vibrant bar and an outdoor patio contribute to this stylish café. Serving California bistro–style fare and wood-fired pizzas, it also serves a variety of draft beers and has extensive list of wines and vodkas. > 21 S. Lake St., Elkhart Lake, tel. 920/876–2142. D, DC, MC, V. Closed Sun.; Mon for lunch. **$$–$$$$**

Otto's Restaurant This restaurant on the lake level of the Osthoff Resort serves American and Continental cuisine. Expect a choice of seafood, meats, and pastas. Across the back of this intimate and elegant dining room is a wall of windows overlooking Elkhart Lake. > 101 Osthoff Ave., Elkhart Lake, tel. 920/876–5857. AE, D, DC, MC, V. $$$–$$$$

Thyme Savours Housed in the village's first train station, this delicatessen specializes in fresh "from scratch" soups, salads, sandwiches, and baked goods. European-style breads such as sourdough and Portuguese white bread are baked daily. Salads and baked goods are sold by the pound. > 44 Gottfried, Elkhart Lake, tel. 920/876–3655. AE, MC, V. Closed Sun. in winter. ¢

PORT WASHINGTON

Another Thyme Health food is served in this former hardware store, which is adjacent to a natural-food store. Menu items include vegetarian dishes, soups, salads, salmon, and healthful cookies and brownies. Organic products are used when possible. > 308 N. Franklin St., Port Washington, tel. 262/284–5754. D, MC, V. Closed Sun. No dinner. ¢

Dockside Deli Enjoy the harbor view while eating breakfast, lunch, or a sweet snack in this sleek café. The menu has sandwiches deli-style or grilled, soup or salad, and six hot or cold breakfast options. Box lunches are available. > 222 E. Main St., Port Washington, tel. 262/284–9440. D, MC, V. Closed Sun. No dinner. ¢

Newport Shores This casual restaurant overlooks Lake Michigan and has a 97-foot-long, horseshoe-shape bar. Steak, sandwiches, fish, and prime rib are the menu mainstays. Leave room for the chocolate silk pie or the blueberry sour-cream pie. > 407 E. Jackson St., Port Washington, tel. 262/284–6838. AE, D, DC, MC, V. Closed Mon. No lunch Tues.–Thurs. $–$$$

Pasta Shoppe The black-and-white family photos are one clue this is a family-friendly restaurant, but the crayons on the table and the paper tablecloths seal the deal. Established in 1973, this is a casual spot for pasta and pizza. > 323 N. Franklin St., Port Washington, tel. 262/284–9311. MC, V. No lunch.

Smith Brothers Fish Shanty You don't have to wait for a Friday fish fry at this downtown restaurant where "every day is fry day." The menu here includes fish, burgers, sandwiches, and beers brewed on the premises. Large windows provide a view of the Port Washington marina and Lake Michigan. You can also dine alfresco on the deck. > 100 N. Franklin St., Port Washington, tel. 262/284–5592. D, DC, MC, V. $–$$$$

Wilson House Restaurant Seafood and Sicilian pasta dishes join filet mignon and rack of lamb on the menu at this casual restaurant in the old Union House Hotel, an 1850 building a couple of blocks away from the marina. > 200 N. Franklin St., Port Washington, tel. 262/284–6669 or 866/593–7277. AE, D, MC, V. Closed Mon. No lunch weekends. $–$$$$

SHEBOYGAN

Brisco County Wood Grill A wall of windows gives you a great view of the Sheboygan River as you chow down on rotisserie chicken, sandwiches, fajitas, or stir-fries. The specialty is Black Angus beef cooked over charcoal. > 593 Riverfront Dr., Sheboygan, tel. 920/803–6915. AE, D, MC, V. ¢–$$$

City Streets Riverside This former warehouse in a small shopping district overlooking Sheboygan's historic Fish Shanty Village dates from 1895 and now serves steaks, fresh pastas, seafood, prime rib, and crab legs. > 712 Riverfront Dr., Sheboygan, tel. 920/457–9050. AE, DC, MC, V. Closed Sun. No lunch Sat. $–$$$

Brat-titude in Sheboygan

BRATWURST IS MORE THAN A MERE SAVORY SAUSAGE in the city of Sheboygan. Brats have become their own art form from the preparation to the serving and, the very best part, the eating.

Brats (pronounced broughts) are not native to Sheboygan. City stalwarts may tout this as the "Bratwurst Capital of the World," but when pressed, even they have to admit brats are a German innovation. It was German immigrants settling in the area in the early- to mid-19th century whose longing for a taste of home gave birth to the brat. In the homeland the sausages were made with veal or beef but in Wisconsin pork was more popular and to this day remains the most popular ingredient in brats.

Each brat booster may have their own recipe (and not everyone is willing to share it), but generally it's ground meat and spices ground together and stuffed into a casing. One essential thing to be aware of is that brats are neither boiled nor grilled: they are fried. It's really only a difference in terminology as the brat is fried on a grill over a charcoal fire. But if you want to fit in with the local Sheboyganites it helps to have the proper lingo down.

A brat is meant to be cooked slowly over low heat and turned often so that it cooks evenly. Brats are sometimes simmered in beer, butter, and onions after they are cooked. Other places will put the brat right in the roll for you to smother it with mustard, ketchup, pickles, onions, or maybe (in a nod to the European heritage of this culinary masterpiece) sauerkraut.

It's not hard to find a brat in Sheboygan. The visitor center has a list of restaurants happy to fry some up for you. Or you can visit one of the local meat markets so that you can take some home and perfect the preparation and consumption on your home turf. This is also a good way to avoid the argument over brat dominance and who really deserves that "Brat Capital" moniker.

Il Ritrovo Wood-fired pizza is the specialty at this more casual younger sibling to Trattoria Stefano across the street. You can sit at small tables or in one of the family-size booths, which are designed for an old-fashioned Italian family with Mama, Papa, and eight more sitting down for the meal. A market selling Italian foods and specialty items and a wine bar are in the next room. > 515 S. 8th St., Sheboygan, tel. 920/803–7516. AE, DC, MC, V. Closed Sun. ¢–$

The Immigrant Each of the six small dining rooms at this upscale restaurant inside the American Club, 5 mi west of Sheboygan, are named and decorated in honor of a different European country. Wherever you are seated, you can dine on such dishes as rack of lamb, braised rabbit leg, and seared yellowfin tuna. > American Club, 444 Highland Dr., Kohler, tel. 920/457–8000. Jacket required. AE, D, DC, MC, V. Closed Sun. No lunch. $$$$

Jumes This neon pink downtown diner has an old-style neon sign outside that still says "air-conditioned." This family restaurant has been open since 1928 serving breakfast all day, burgers, shakes, and daily specials. > 504 N. 8th St., Sheboygan, tel. 920/452–4914. AE, DC, MC, V. ¢–$

Mucky Duck Shanty The nautical theme is pervasive in this boardwalk shanty restaurant with outdoor seating in season. Seafood, steaks, and sandwiches make up the bulk of the menu but hearty homemade soups, pasta, and salads are also available. > 701 Riverfront Dr., Sheboygan, tel. 920/457–5577. AE, MC, V. Closed Sun. $–$$

Richard's Linen tablecloths and fresh flowers add polish to this 1840s former stagecoach inn, 5 mi west of Sheboygan in the small town of Sheboygan Falls. The kitchen turns out such dishes as prime rib, pasta primavera, and crab legs, as well as oysters Rockefeller. > 501 Monroe St., Sheboygan Falls, tel. 920/467–6401. D, DC, MC, V. Closed Mon. No lunch. $–$$$$

Trattoria Stefano Pasta dishes and grilled meats with an Italian flavor are served at this informal Italian dinner spot downtown. The building once housed a library and newspaper press but a large mural on the wall over the bar evokes a Mediterranean feel. > 522 S. 8th St., Sheboygan, tel. 920/803–7516. AE, DC, MC, V. Closed Sun. No lunch. $–$$$$

ESSENTIALS

Getting Here

The easiest way to weekend in this part of Wisconsin is in your own car. You can take a train or bus as far as Milwaukee but then you're traveling on a county bus to get around and much of your time may be spent waiting for connections and making frequent stops in towns and village bus depots along the way to your destination.

BY BUS

There is no one bus that will take you to all these destinations. You can take a bus north from Chicago to Milwaukee and then have to transfer to another route from there. Greyhound operates over a dozen daily buses between Chicago and Milwaukee, including late-night and early-morning service. From Milwaukee you can get a Greyhound bus to Sheboygan. Departures from Milwaukee are three times daily (8:50 AM, 2:20 PM, and 7 PM); buses return to Milwaukee three times daily (5:10 AM, 12:40 PM, or 5:45 PM). Fare is $28.25–$31.25 round-trip. You can also take the Ozaukee County Express, also known as Milwaukee County Transit System Route 143, which provides service to Cedarburg and Port Washington and other Ozaukee County locations. Keep in mind that this is a commuter line so it could be packed on a Friday.

BUS DEPOTS **Milwaukee Bus Depot** > 606 N. James Lovell, Milwaukee, tel. 414/272–2156. **Sheboygan Bus Depot** > 822 Pennsylvania Ave., Sheboygan, tel. 920/803–1832.

BUS LINES **Greyhound** > Tel. 800/231–2222, www.greyhound.com. **Ozaukee County Transit** > Tel. 414/344–6711.

BY CAR

The best way to explore these destinations over a weekend is by car. Interstate 94 connects to I-43 in Milwaukee, which will take you to Cedarburg, Port Washington, Sheboygan, and Elkhart Lake.

To get to Cedarburg, get off at the Cedarburg exit (County C). Drive 3 mi west to Washington Avenue, Cedarburg's main street. Parking is free for two hours on Washington Avenue, or follow the signs as you come in to a free lot just one block east of the main strip off either Western Road, Center Street, or Turner Road. To leave Cedarburg, you can return to I–43 the same way you came in or via Route 60 at the north end of town, which is particularly convenient if you decide to visit the Covered Bridge Park on your way out. If you want to take a scenic route directly to Port Washington, take Route 60 to Route 32 and drive north through the Milwaukee River community of Grafton until you reach Port Washington's Grand Avenue.

To get to Port Washington, get off at Route 32, 6 mi north of the Cedarburg exit, and head east into Port Washington. Street parking is available throughout downtown and metered parking lot is at the harbor at the end of Grand Avenue.

Sheboygan is another 31 mi north on I–43. Exit 126 puts you on Route 23, which is the most direct route into the city. Metered parking is everywhere downtown, and at the marina there is a public parking lot. Route 23 is also the road you take to the village of Kohler to the west.

Elkhart Lake is 15 mi northwest of Sheboygan. Follow Route 23 West 8 mi to Plymouth and then take Route 67 North to Rhine Street (also identified as Route J). Take a left on Rhine or J to get into downtown Elkhart Lake.

BY TRAIN

From Chicago, there are six daily departures of Amtrak's *Hiawatha* for the 90-minute trip north to Milwaukee. From there, you will have to take a bus or rent a car to any of the destinations in the Sheboygan area.

TRAIN LINE **Amtrak** > Tel. 414/271–0840 or 800/872–7245, www.amtrak.com.

Visitor Information

CONTACTS **Cedarburg Chamber and Visitor Center** > Washington Ave. and Spring St., Box 104, Cedarburg 53102, tel. 800/237–2874, www.cedarburg.org. **Elkhart Lake Chamber of Commerce** > 41 E. Rhine St., Elkhart Lake 53020, tel. 920/876–2922 or 877/355–4278, www.elkhartlake.com. **Port Washington Tourism Council** > 126 E. Grand Ave., Box 153, Port Washington 53074, tel. 262/284–0900, www.portwashingtonchamber.com. **Sheboygan County Convention and Visitors Bureau** > 712 Riverfront Dr., Suite 101, Sheboygan 53081, tel. 800/457–9497, www.sheboygan.com.

Madison

148 mi northwest of Chicago

14

By Joanne Cleaver

BIG-CITY CULTURE MIXES WITH SMALL-TOWN CHARM in Wisconsin's capital. It was founded in 1829, when James Duane Doty, a territorial judge and land speculator, traveled through the isthmus and liked it so much he bought 1,200 acres for $1,500 and plotted a town grid. In 1836 he persuaded the territorial legislature to designate his paper city as the site of the new capital.

Madison is an isthmus—a narrow piece of land running between two larger sections. To the northwest of the strip is Lake Mendota; to the southwest is Lake Monona. It's a town dominated by two major institutions—the state capitol and the University of Wisconsin–Madison. The sometimes hazy and sometimes overly idealistic qualities of both organizations have no doubt been the main reason that some have described the city of 200,000 as "twenty-five square miles surrounded by reality" (keep an eye out for the T-shirt). It's also due in large part due to these groups that Madison consistently ranks high in Money magazine's annual survey of the best places in which to live in the United States.

Downtown Madison's major streets all project out from the beaux-arts-style Capitol, a massive, granite-clad building built in 1917. On Wednesday and Saturday mornings, from May to October, its square hosts the Dane County Farmers' Market, where you can buy not only plenty of fruits and vegetables but also cheese curds, honey, and other Wisconsin-produced foods and crafts. And if you happen to be in town during Christmas, be sure to sneak a peek at the state's Christmas tree. Usually taken from the massive forests up north and often decorated by school childrenís ornaments, is makes for a moving sight and an impressive photo.Across the street from the square, near the corner where Carroll and Mifflin streets intersect and State Street begins, is Shakespeare's Books, an outstanding bookstore. As you explore downtown, you'll come across many more, both new and used. The number of such stores surpasses those in many much larger cities; perhaps it's not so surprising that a place with so many working in academia and government has the second-highest per capita rate of book-buying in the nation.

State Street, closed to car traffic, lies in a straight line between the Capitol and the University of Wisconsin's Bascom Hall, its main administrative building. Students can often be found in great numbers shopping or browsing on busy State Street, which extends westward from the corner of Capitol Square. The small boutiques of this pedestrian zone alternate between vintage clothing, New-Age gifts, music stores, and coffee shops. As you near campus, you'll see fewer fancy restaurants and clothing boutiques and more CD stores, falafel joints, and bars. At 211 State Street is the current Civic Center, undergoing a massive renovation due to be finished at the end of 2005. Funded primarily by a $100 million gift from Jerome Frautschi, a local printer, the Overture Center will be a complex of multiple stages, galleries, and theatres.

The neighborhoods immediately to the southwest and northeast of downtown are jammed with spectacular examples of classic midwestern architecture. In the Mansion

Hill historic district and the Third Lake Ridge district, you can see overbearing Victorians and understated Prairie School houses. Mansion Hill is on the wooded hill along the shores of Lake Mendota, between Gorham, Gilman, Henry, and Butler streets. Nearby is the Third Lake Ridge district, on the northern shore of Lake Monona; it runs between Spaight and Rutledge streets along the lakeside to Williamson Street, and between South Blount and South Few streets.

The area also has a number of Frank Lloyd Wright buildings, though some are private homes and not open to the public. The university, state government, and manufacturing provide much of Madison's economic base.

WHAT TO SEE & DO

Henry Vilas Zoo Hundreds of birds and animals from all over the world are on display here in reproduction habitats. Most of the zoo's denizens are for observing only, but there is a small petting zoo with smaller, more kid-friendly critters such as baby goats and sheep. If you're fond of scaly creatures, pay a visit to the herpetarium, which is home to dozens of reptiles. The zoo is southwest of the University of Wisconsin–Madison campus, in Vilas Park on Lake Wingra. > 7092 S. Randall Ave., Madison, tel. 608/266–4732, www.vilaszoo.org. Free. Daily 9:30–5.

Madison Art Center Inside the Civic Center, the center hosts concerts and plays year-round. Visual arts exhibits are ongoing and free to the public. > 211 State St., Madison, tel. 608/258–4141, www.madcivic.org.

Madison Children's Museum Geared for children ages eight and under, the museum presents rotating exhibits on international cultures and nature in a hands-on format. Kids can learn where milk comes from by "milking" a cow. > 100 State St., Madison, tel. 608/256–6445, www.madisonchildrensmuseum.org. $4. Tues.–Sat. 9–4, Sun. noon–4.

Monona Terrace Community and Convention Center This structure on the shore of Lake Monona, near the State Capitol, is Madison's newest downtown showpiece. Designed by Frank Lloyd Wright in 1938, and finally completed in 1997, the center has a rooftop garden, a café, a sports hall of fame, and a memorial to singer Otis Redding, who died in a plane crash nearby. > 1 John Nolen Dr., Madison, tel. 608/261–4000, www.mononaterrace.com. Free.

Olbrich Botanical Garden Olbrich's 14 acres on the north side of Lake Monona include rose, herb, rock, and perennial gardens. A 50-foot-high pyramidal glass conservatory houses tropical plants and flowers. Its indoor habitats are home to tender tropicals, which are tall enough to brush the glass skylights. Outside, you can stroll among the roses or climb the multilevel rock garden. Across a small bridge is the shiny gold Thai Pavilion, an open-sided structure with a peaked roof. Built in 2001, its red lacquered and gilt pillars are a symbol of cross-cultural friendship. The garden's café serves lunch. > 3330 Atwood Ave., Madison, tel. 608/246–4550, www.olbrich.org. Free. Mon.–Sat. 1–4, Sun. 1–5.

State Capitol Designed in the style of the Capitol building in Washington, D.C., the State Capitol is downtown on the highest point on the isthmus. The building dominates the skyline for miles and is flooded with light at night. Public tours are conducted daily. **Capitol Square,** at the center of downtown, has 12 streets radiating outward and connects to the university's campus by State Street, a mile-long tree-lined shopping district of imports shops, ethnic restaurants, and artisans' galleries. > 2 E. Main St., Madison, tel. 608/266–0382. Free. Daily.

State Historical Museum Permanent and changing exhibits on Wisconsin history, from prehistoric Native American cultures to contemporary social issues fill this museum. One highlight is an extensive collection of historic children's clothing, donated by Pleasant Rowland, the Madison resident who founded the American Girls line of books and dolls. > 30 N. Carroll St., Madison, tel. 608/264–6555, www.wisconsinhistory.org. $2. Tues.–Sat. 9–4.

University of Wisconsin–Madison Considered one of the most beautiful campuses in the country, this university on Lake Mendota less than a mile west of the State Capitol is world famous for excellence in academics and sports. Well over 30,000 undergraduate and graduate students call the UW home, and follow courses of study in academic schools of nursing, journalism, business, law, and biochemistry. A variety of tours are available, but they must be booked in advance. Built in 1917, the double-deck **Camp Randall Stadium and Fieldhouse** (1440 Monroe St., tel. 608/262–7425, free) is home to the Badgers, the University of Wisconsin's football team. The site ranks among the nation's largest school-owned stadiums. It includes a study area for student-athletes, training and weight rooms, and a display of football memorabilia. Tours are by appointment. The University of Wisconsin's 85-foot, 56-bell **Carillon Tower** (1160 Observatory Dr., tel. 608/265–9500, free) overlooking Lake Mendota was a gift from the classes of 1917–1926. A concert is held in front of the tower every Sunday afternoon in warmer months. The **Elvehjem Museum of Art** (800 University Ave., tel. 608/263–2246, free), a fine study resource for University of Wisconsin students, contains a permanent collection of fine art, ranging from Renaissance oil paintings to modernist sculpture. Chamber-music concerts are given on Sunday.

Memorial Library (728 State St., tel. 608/262–3193, free) is the University of Wisconsin's main library. Built in 1950, it houses 5.4 million volumes, including the university research library, a rare-book collection, and university archives. Scenic **Observatory and Willow Drives** (716 Langdon St.) cover about 3 mi and enable you to see two different areas of the University of Wisconsin campus. Observatory Drive starts at Park Street, near the entrance to Memorial Union, and provides a view of the lake and the campus grounds. Willow Drive, which is lined with weeping willow trees, starts at the west end of Observatory Drive and takes you down roads along the lower level of the campus, by the lake. Constructed in 1878, the historic **Washburn Observatory** (1401 Observatory Dr., tel. 608/265–9500, free) was the first major private gift to the University of Wisconsin. Away from downtown, the **University Arboretum** (1207 Seminole Hwy., tel. 608/263–7888, free) has more than 1,200 acres of natural plant and animal communities, such as prairie and forest landscapes, and horticultural collections of upper Midwest specimens. > 500 Lincoln Dr., Madison, tel. 608/265–9500. Campus tours free; other tours vary in admission. Daily.

Wisconsin Veterans Museum Dioramas depicting important military battles and exhibits from the Civil War to the present honor all state veterans. Full-size aircraft, scale models of 19th- and 20th-century ships, and military artifacts are also on display. The submarine periscope protruding through a gallery roof provides a novel view of downtown on Capitol Square. > 30 W. Mifflin St., Madison, tel. 608/267–1799. Free. Oct.–Mar., Mon.–Sat. 9–4:30; Apr.–Sept., Mon.–Sat. 9–4:30, Sun. noon–4.

NEARBY

Lake Kegonsa State Park On the northeast corner of Lake Kegonsa, 20 mi south of Madison, this park provides sailing, boating, swimming, fishing, and waterskiing opportunities, as well as family camping, hiking, summer interpretive programs, and

Cheeseheads & Proud Of It

JUST AS THE GREEN-AND-GOLD GREEN BAY PACKERS UNIFORM is standard attire for the team's players at a football game, a "cheesehead" is standard attire for Packer fans and those who want to boast of being from Wisconsin. These hats, made in the shape of a wedge of cheese, originated when an out-of-stater tried to insult Wisconsinite Chris Becker by calling him a cheesehead. Becker took some foam, cut it into the shape of a hunk of Swiss cheese, burned holes into it, colored it yellow, and plopped it on his head. The hat was an instant success. Locals picked up on the idea and Becker went into business by creating the firm Foamation Inc., in the Milwaukee suburb of St. Francis.

Today you can find cheesehead earrings, pins, ties, baseball hats, soap on a rope, and Christmas ornaments; there is also a cheesehead cowboy hat, a cheesehead football autographed by Packer Reggie White, and even a cheesehead firefighter helmet made for Wisconsin's professional firefighters for fund-raising purposes.

Becker says cheesehead hats have become synonymous with Wisconsin, and are being purchased worldwide. Cheesehead hat owners include comedian Tim Allen and entertainer Reba McEntire. Becker says Jay Leno received one from the late comedian Chris Farley (a Madison native), and that a cheesehead hat is said to have saved the life of a man who is now one of his employees. When the small plane the man was in plummeted toward the ground, the man put the foam hat in front of him to cushion his landing. According to representatives of the FAA, doing so saved his life.

cross-country skiing. > 2405 Door Creek Rd., Stoughton, tel. 608/873–9695, www.dnr.state.wi.us. Daily; campground May–Oct.

New Glarus Founded in 1845 by Swiss settlers from the canton of Glarus, New Glarus has made the most of its ethnic heritage. Many of its buildings reflect the stereotypical half-timber mountain look, replete with balconies and planters overflowing in summer with flowers. The small downtown has numerous shops that sell locally produced cheese, antiques, quilt supplies, collectibles, imported clothes, and gifts. The village celebrates several annual festivals related to Swiss national culture. The **Swiss Historical Village** (612 7th Ave., tel. 608/527–2317, www.swisshistoricalvillage.com, $6, June–Oct.) contains original buildings and reconstructions from early New Glarus and traces Swiss immigration to America. > New Glarus Chamber of Commerce, 16 5th Ave., New Glarus, tel. 608/527–2095, www.swisstown.com.

Tours

Betty Lou Cruises A 51-foot, 49-passenger motor yacht leaves from the Mariner's Inn restaurant for lunch, dinner, moonlight, and fall foliage–appreciation cruises on Lake Mendota. Reservations are required. > 5360 Westport Rd., Madison, tel. 608/246–3136, www.bettyloucruises.com. $25–$45. Tours by appointment only.

SHOPPING

Dane County Farmers' Market Vendors sell cheese, fish, meat, and baked goods Wednesdays at Capitol Square and Fridays on Capitol Street, just to the east. The market is open from May through October. > Madison, tel. 920/563–5037. Free. May–Oct., Wed. and Sat. 9–5.

State Street Hemp-fiber clothing, imports from all over, books new and used, coffee, and organic everything are sold in shops along State Street, which connects Capitol Square with the University campus. > Madison.

Williamson Street Stretching northeast from Capitol Square, the Williamson Street/East Washington Avenue area is a funky neighborhood that's happily scruffy even as organic groceries and art house–coffee shops proliferate. It makes for an interesting stroll and is a good place to take a break on a bike tour of Madison's neighborhoods. > Madison.

Save the Date

JUNE

Heidi Festival A play and other performances celebrate the life of the fictional mountain girl at this festival, held the second weekend of June. > New Glarus, tel. 800/527–6838, www.swisstown.com.

JULY

Art Fair on the Square Some 100,000 people come to this juried show on the second weekend of the month to view works by local and national artists at this Capitol Square annual. There's also ongoing entertainment. > Tel. 800/257–0158.

Dane County Fair A carnival, food, entertainment, arts, crafts, and a livestock competition take place at the Alliance Energy Center in mid-month. > Tel. 608/223–4054.

AUGUST

Madison Blues Festival Olin Park swings with performances of local and regional groups, during the last weekend of August. > Tel. 608/836–0020.

Taste of Madison Local restaurants sell their specialties in outdoor stands in Capitol Square at the end of the month. > Tel. 608/850–4900.

WHERE TO STAY

Annie's Garden Bed & Breakfast Only one suite is available here, but what a suite it is. Inside are two bedrooms, a library with fireplace, a double hot tub, and a view of a garden. The bed-and-breakfast is one block from Lake Mendota. > 2117 Sheridan Dr., Madison 53704, tel. 608/244–2224. 1 suite. No kids under 10. AE, MC, V. BP. **$$$**

Arbor House Fittingly, this small inn, which styles itself as environmentally friendly, is across the street from the UW arboretum in a neighborhood west of downtown. Some rooms are in the modern annex and some in the 100-year-old stone farmhouse. Rooms in the antique wing are flavored with country decor; rooms in the modern wing are in a neo-Shaker style. Lake Wingra is only three blocks away. > 3402 Monroe St., Madison 53711, tel. 608/238–2981, fax 608/238–1175, www.arbor-house.com. 8 rooms. Some in-room hot tubs, cable TV. AE, MC, V. BP. **$–$$$$**

Baymont Inn On the western border of Madison, this two-story modern inn has a cozy lobby with a seating area and spacious rooms. > 81092 Excelsior Dr., Madison 53717, tel. 608/831–7711, fax 608/831–1942, www.baymontinn.com. 129 rooms. Some refrigerators, cable TV, pool, exercise equipment, hot tub, bar, laundry facilities, business services, airport shuttle, some pets allowed. AE, D, DC, MC, V. CP. **$**

Best Western Inn on the Park A large, modern nine-story, brick-and-glass-skinned hotel on Capitol Square has views of the Capitol, Lake Mendota, and Lake Monona from the rooms. > 22 S. Carroll St., Madison 53703, tel. 608/257–8811 or 800/279–8811, fax 608/257–5995, www.bestwestern.com. 213 rooms. Restaurants, in-room data ports, cable TV, pool, exercise equipment, hot tub, business services, airport shuttle. AE, D, DC, MC, V. CP. **$–$$**

Best Western West Towne Suites This modest motel has an unexpectedly elaborate lobby with vaulted ceilings, artwork, large plants, and a crystal chandelier. > 650 Grand Canyon Dr., Madison 53703, tel. 800/847–7919, fax 608/833–5614. 101 suites. Some in-room data ports, some microwaves, refrigerators, cable TV, exercise equipment, laundry facilities, business services, some pets allowed. AE, D, DC, MC, V. BP. **¢–$**

Cameo Rose Victorian Country Inn Surrounded by 120 acres of hills, this Victorian inn has a wraparound porch. One room has a fireplace; another has a hot tub. Rooms have Victorian accents, with cast-iron headboards and cabbage-rose prints. > 1090 Severson Rd., Madison 53508, tel. 608/424–6340, www.cameorose.com. 5 rooms. Some in-room hot tubs, some in-room VCRs. MC, V. BP. **$–$$**

Collins House A lumber baron's former home that is now on the National Register of Historic Places, this Prairie School–style house is six blocks east of the Capitol. Breakfast is served on an expansive sunporch that overlooks Lake Mendota. > 704 E. Gorham St., Madison 53703, tel. 608/255–4230, fax 608/255–0830, www.collinshouse.com. 5 rooms. Some in-room hot tubs, microwaves; no smoking. D, MC, V. BP. **$–$$$**

The Edgewater This nine-story, blond-brick hotel was built in 1949 right downtown on the edge of Lake Monona. Most rooms have a view of the lake, and some have a view of the Capitol. Crystal chandeliers and polished oak embellish the lobby. State Street's shops and restaurants are only four blocks away, and you can relax on the hotel's private pier in fine weather. > 666 Wisconsin Ave., Madison 53703, tel. 608/256–9071, fax 608/256–0910, www.theedgewater.com. 109 rooms. Restaurant, room service, some microwaves, cable TV, bar, business services, airport shuttle, some pets allowed. AE, DC, MC, V. **$–$$$$**

Fairfield Inn by Marriott Rooms are plain and clean; the hotel is on the eastern border of Madison, relatively convenient to parks and outdoor activities. > 4765 Hayes Rd., Madison 53704, tel. 608/249–5300 or 800/228–2800, fax 608/240–9335, www.fairfieldinn.com. 135 rooms. Cable TV, pool, gym, business services. AE, D, DC, MC, V. BP. **¢–$**

Hilton Madison Monona Terrace Adjacent to the Monona Terrace Convention Center and a few blocks from Capitol Square, the hotel has beautiful views of either Lake Monona or the State Capitol. > 9 E. Wilson St., Madison 53703, tel. 608/255–5100, www.hiltonmadison.com. 240 rooms. Restaurant, room service, in-room data ports, cable TV, pool, gym, Internet. AE, D, DC, MC, V. **$–$$$**

Holiday Inn–Madison East On the eastern edge of Madison, the hotel is spacious and convenient to the airport. > 3841 E. Washington Ave., Madison 53704, tel. 608/244–2481, fax 608/244–0383, www.holiday-inn.com. 197 rooms. Restaurant, cable TV, pool, gym, hot tub, bar, business services, airport shuttle. AE, D, DC, MC, V. BP. **$–$$**

Howard Johnson Plaza Hotel On the edge of the University of Wisconsin campus, the hotel is convenient to downtown sites but also in the thick of student life. Decorated in clean, modern style, the rooms are generous for a chain hotel. > 525 W. Johnson St., Madison 53703, tel. 608/251–5511, fax 608/251–4824, www.hojo.com. 163 rooms. Restaurant, cable TV, pool, gym, hot tub, bar. AE, D, DC, MC, V. **$–$$$**

Madison Concourse Hotel This 13-story light-brick hotel just north of Capitol Square is filled with large windows and has an elegant lobby with marble and plants. Rooms are decorated in a colonial style. The Governor's Club is on the top three floors of the hotel and offers the best views, as well as appetizers and cocktails. > 1 W. Dayton St., Madison 53703, tel. 608/257–6000 or 800/356–8293, fax 608/257–5280, www.concoursehotel.com. 360 rooms. 2 restaurants, some in-room hot tubs, some microwaves, cable TV, pool, exercise equipment, hot tub, bar, business services, airport shuttle. AE, D, DC, MC, V. CP. **$–$$**

Madison Inn Renovated in 2003, the hotel is essentially on the campus and just a couple of blocks from downtown. Mahogany furniture with Victorian accents enriches the rooms of this boutique-style hotel. > 601 Langdon St., Madison 53703, tel. 608/257–4391 or 800/589–6285, fax 608/257–2832, www.themadisoninn.com. 63 rooms, 10 suites. Restaurant, bar. AE, D, DC, MC, V. CP. **¢–$**

Mansion Hill Inn This 1858 Italianate mansion four blocks from the Capitol has a four-story spiral staircase and individually decorated rooms, among them the Turkish Nook (with a sultan's bed and steam shower) and the Oriental Suite (with a separate sitting room, a skylight, and double whirlpool). Breakfast is served in the rooms. > 424 N. Pinckney St., Madison 53703, tel. 608/255–3999 or 800/798–9070, fax 608/255–2217, www.mansionhillinn.com. 11 rooms. In-room data ports, some in-room hot tubs, minibars, cable TV, some in-room VCRs, business services; no kids under 12, no smoking. AE, MC, V. CP. **$$–$$$$**

Sheraton Madison Hotel Across from the Dane County Expo Center and near the State Capitol and campus is this Sheraton with modern, comfortable rooms. Make reservations well in advance. > 706 John Nolen Dr., Madison 53713, tel. 608/251–2300 or 800/325–3535, fax 608/251–1189, www.sheraton.com. 237 rooms. 2 restaurants, pool, gym. AE, D, DC, MC V. **$–$$$$**

Woodfield Suites This modern, four-story redbrick hotel is about 10 mi from the downtown area and the university campus, in a largely commercial suburban division surrounded by popular chain restaurants and mini-malls. Complimentary cocktails are served every evening. Kids can have fun with the indoor play equipment and pinball machines. Four restaurants are within a mile. > 5217 Terrace Dr., Madison 53718, tel. 800/338–0008, fax 608/245–1644, www.woodfieldswuites.com. 120 suites. In-room data ports, refrigerators, cable TV, some in-room VCRs, 2 pools, gym, hot tub, laundry service, business services, airport shuttle, some pets allowed. AE, D, DC, MC, V. CP. **$–$$**

WHERE TO EAT

Admiralty This elegant restaurant downtown in the Edgewater hotel, with a view of Lake Mendota, serves one of the best Sunday brunches in Madison. Regular menu favorites include beef Wellington and shrimp Provençale. Open-air dining is on a secluded patio, and you can see live entertainment on Friday and Saturday nights. > 666 Wisconsin Ave., Madison, tel. 608/256–9071. AE, DC, MC, V. **$$$$**

Bluephies This hip little joint is in a redbrick strip mall near the Edgewood campus. Dinner entrées to consider include a grilled Portobello mushroom sandwich, topped with sautéed onions and melted mozzarella, served on an organic wheat bun and sided with sun-dried tomatoes, artichoke hearts, and black olives, or possibly the cornmeal-crusted catfish or jerk chicken Gorgonzola. > 2701 Monroe St., Madison, tel. 608/231–3663. AE, D, DC, MC, V. **¢–$$$**

Cafe Continental One of the few Capitol Square–area restaurants that's open on Sundays, the café does pasta and fish right. Desserts—especially those involving chocolate—are top notch and the coffee is strong. The café's small tables are crowded into its corridor-like space. > 108 King St., Madison, tel. 608/251–4880. D, MC, V. **$$–$$$$**

Chocolate Coyote Before you order a scoop of chocolate coyote ice cream, get a tester: it's seasoned with pepper and cinnamon. You can also get more conventional flavors, such as vanilla, at this wildly popular ice cream stand. > 341 State St., Madison, tel. 608/255–4237. No credit cards. ¢

Damon's the Place for Ribs Large platters of ribs and four big-screen TVs featuring sporting events vie for the "most popular" title at this casual restaurant. You can eat at a large bar or at nearby tables. > 8150 Excelsior Dr., Madison, tel. 608/836–6466. AE, D, MC, V. ¢–$$

Ella's Deli Mechanical toys move across the ceiling, a bear drinks water, and kids and adults alike can take a spin on the outdoor carousel. Sandwiches and sundaes are popular, but don't attempt to tackle Ella's famous ice-cream-and-hot-fudge-over-grilled-poundcake sundae without some help. > 2902 Washington Ave., Madison, tel. 608/241–5291. Reservations not accepted. MC, V. ¢–$

Essen Haus This downtown restaurant with Old-World charm displays some 3,000 beer steins and serves such classic fare as Wiener schnitzel and sauerbraten. > 514 E. Wilson St., Madison, tel. 608/255–4674. MC, V. Closed Mon. No lunch. $–$$$

Granita In a historic building dating from 1913, this place is like an old-style Sicilian home with its pictures from Italy. For dinner, you can choose from a variety of classic northern Italian dishes such as pasta primavera and chicken marsala. > 111 S. Hamilton Ave., Madison, tel. 608/251–9500. AE, DC, MC, V. Closed Sun. No lunch. $$–$$$$

L'Étoile In this Capitol Square restaurant adorned with French impressionist paintings, the menu changes seasonally, and the chef uses primarily local ingredients. Try the mushroom and hickory-nut strudel (the nuts are indigenous to the area, the mushrooms are in season, and the strudel is served with vegetables from local farmers' markets). The Market Cafe is adjacent and serves fresh French pastries (try the chocolate croissants), sandwiches, and coffee. > 25 N. Pinckney St., Madison, tel. 608/251–0500. Reservations essential. D, DC, MC, V. Closed Sun. No lunch. $$$–$$$$

Marigold Kitchen Eggs every which way are the menu highlight here, though muffins can't be underestimated. The café is a hangout for local intellectuals. > 118 S. Pinckney St., Madison, tel. 608/661–5559. MC, V. Closed Sun. No dinner. ¢–$

Mariner's Inn Locally caught fish are the highlight on the menu here, which is appropriate, considering the restaurant overlooks Lake Mendota and has an outdoor dining room. > 5339 Lighthouse Bay Dr., Madison, tel. 608/246–3120. Reservations essential. MC, V. No lunch. $$–$$$$

Nau-Ti-Gal In summer, at this nautically themed restaurant in an old tavern, you can dine 30 feet from the Yahara River, which feeds into the northern tip of Lake Mendota. Seating outdoors is on the expansive wraparound deck, and indoors at cozy tables just big enough for small groups of friends. Fresh fish is on the menu every day, but you can also feast on Key West chicken stuffed with seafood, or even a shark steak. > 5360 Westport Rd., Madison, tel. 608/246–3131. MC, V. $$–$$$

Pasta per Tutti Fresh pasta and seafood and homemade breads and desserts make this contemporary Italian restaurant near the theater district a local favorite. > 2009 Atwood Ave., Madison, tel. 608/242–1800. MC, V. No lunch. $–$$$

Quivey's Grove Antiques fill this restaurant in an 1855 mansion and its stables 15 mi from Madison. One of the two dining rooms is formal, with white tablecloths, the other is casual and rustic. Duck, lamb, and quail are all top-notch. > 6261 Nesbitt Rd., Fitchburg, tel. 608/273–4900. AE, D, MC, V. $$–$$$

Radical Rye You can fill out your own order slip for huge sandwiches loaded with fresh-sliced deli meats and vegetables, and have them smothered with toppings of your choosing. There's also always vegetarian chili and a soup of the day. Big windows looking out onto State Street are great for people-watching. > 231 State St., Madison, tel. 608/256–1200. AE, MC, V. ¢–$

White Horse Inn Sunday brunch is a favorite here, and the inn is famous for its chicken Mafalda (grilled chicken, sausage, leeks, and pasta in a cream sauce). Floor-to-ceiling windows bring in lots of light, and let you look at the street life playing out a few feet away. > 202 N. Henry St., Madison, tel. 608/255–9933. AE, DC, MC, V. No lunch. $$–$$$

NEARBY

Deininger's In a renovated Victorian house on a hill above the downtown, this restaurant whips up tasty apple pancakes, French beef stew, and chicken schnitzel. > 119 5th Ave., New Glarus, tel. 608/527–2012. MC, V. Closed Wed. $$–$$$
Glarner Stube Inside this dark-wood-paneled pub, you can dig into schnitzel and plates of meatballs the size of tennis balls. > 518 1st St., New Glarus, tel. 608/527–2216. MC, V. $–$$

ESSENTIALS

Getting Here

Considering that Madison's great appeal is its outdoor life, it's a tad ironic that the best way to get here is by car, especially if you are lugging outdoor gear such as bikes or strollers. If you travel light and hike around the lakes or take in special events, the bus is the way to go. Flying is only worth it if you are already en route to or from somewhere else. There is no passenger rail service to Madison.

BY BUS
With a heavy student population, Madison is well served by bus services. Greyhound operates three daily runs to Madison; the one-way trip takes about 4½ hours. Badger Bus runs between Milwaukee and Chicago. Van Galder Coach runs between O'Hare and Chicago train stations to Madison. Madison Metro is the local bus system.
BUS DEPOT **Madison Bus Depot** > 2 S. Bedford, Madison, tel. 608/255–6771, www.badgerbus.com.
BUS LINES **Badger Bus** > Tel. 608/255–6771, www.badgerbus.com. **Greyhound Lines** > Tel. 800/231–2222, www.greyhound.com. **Madison Metro** > Tel. 608/266–4466, www.ci.madison.wi.us/metro. **Van Galder Coach** > Tel. 800/747–0994, www.vangalderbus.com.

BY CAR
To get to Madison from Chicago, you can take I–94 north to Milwaukee then west to Madison or I–90 West from Chicago. Driving to Madison is a good way to go, especially if you are hauling bikes or strollers with you. A car is necessary if you plan to visit Capitol Square sites and sites around the city. However, it is imperative to get a detailed city map well in advance so that you can choose a hotel that will be close to your most important destinations.

Driving in Madison can be challenging. Streets and their numbering system all stem from Capitol Square, which has multiple six-corner intersections emanating from the points of the square. Many streets are one-way, and that one-way often reverses from block to block. Be prepared to circle Capitol Square several times before you are able to identify the street you need in time to turn. The few signs that are there are small and poorly placed.

Driving in the neighborhoods that spread out from both sides of Capitol Square is equally challenging. Streets are forced into many curves and dead-ends thanks to the lakes and isthmus. If you intend to stay on the outskirts and drive in to Capitol Square, plan extra time and bring money for garage parking. If you intend to stay in the downtown and drive to points outside the city or on its outskirts, allow extra travel time to get from point A to point B. Street parking in the Capitol Square area is scarce and limited to two hours at best. Be prepared to pay $10 or more for garage parking.

BY PLANE

Madison is served by the Dane County Regional Airport, which is on the northeast border of the metropolitan area. The airport is near hotels on the eastern border of the city and about a half-hour drive to Capitol Square.

AIRPORT **Dane County Regional Airport** > 4000 International La., Madison, tel. 608/246–3391, www.msnairport.com.

CARRIERS **American Eagle** > Tel. 800/433–7000, www.aa.com. **Comair (the Delta Connection)** > Tel. 800/221–1212, www.delta.com. **Midwest Airlines, Midwest Connect** > Tel. 800/452–2022, www.midwestexpress.com. **Northwest** > Tel. 800/225–2525, www.nwa.com. **United Express** > Tel. 800/864–8331, www.united.com.

Visitor Information

TOURIST INFORMATION **Greater Madison Convention and Visitors Bureau** > 615 E. Washington Ave., Madison 53703, tel. 608/255–2537 or 800/373–6376, fax 608/258–4950, www.visitmadison.com.

Galena

160 mi northwest of Chicago

15

By Linda Packer

IT WASN'T TOO LONG AGO THAT GALENA'S MAIN STREET consisted of candy and ice cream stores, and antique stores selling silver-coated clip-on earrings or wooden ducks. But it's grown up since then, and now has specialty stores selling estate jewelry, French imports from Provence, handmade stained glass, and quirky one-of-a-kind decor items. It has a broad main street, an elegant French restaurant near the town's favorite pizza place, and a sprawling country estate and historic mansion competing with the town's 60-plus bed-and-breakfasts.

But the mainstays of this little town on the Mississippi River are still the elements of a truly away-from-it-all weekend. The dull flatlands of midwestern Illinois on I–90 segue into Route 20's rolling hills and winding roads. Cows and horses dot the verdant countryside, and ramps for Wendy's and Holiday Inn are replaced with signs for Kelly's Apple Farm and the Old Fort in Elizabeth, built in 1832 to protect the townspeople from Indian warriors.

Galena is tiny, with a population of just over 3,600, and is populated with residents who warmly welcome visitors. When you ask directions they will walk you halfway there. When you ask for a recommendation for dinner, they will call for a reservation. When you'd like a B&B recommendation, they'll give you three or four, describing each room in detail, each breakfast by aroma, each innkeeper by name.

Galena is known as "The Town That Time Forgot." Lead mining took off here in the 1820s, and Galena had a near-monopoly on the shipping of ore down the Mississippi. By 1832 as many as 20 ships per day were docking at the town's port. Steamboat captains and others who lived in town brought home ideas they'd seen in other parts of the country and used them to build large, impressive homes. The town experienced an architectural renaissance in the 1860s when a series of fires destroyed many wooden buildings and consequently provided opportunities for architects to build new structures in the Italianate, Romanesque-revival, high-Victorian–revival, and Queen Anne styles. This renaissance would become a critical factor in Galena's later resurgence in the years after 1854, when the railroad was built and bypassed Galena entirely, causing an economic downfall from which the town never recovered. With no money to renovate or even paint, Galena was lost in time, a near-perfect specimen of a mid-19th-century small river town.

In the 1960s, Galena was rediscovered by artists and historians enamored with its many different redbrick buildings and cobbled paths. They moved in and began to spruce things up. And spruce they did; 85% of the town is now on the Historic Register. Today, a visually stunning canvas unfolds: hilly views overlook sunsets on the Galena River; a level downtown area, perfect for walking; and the cozy touch of winter includes old-fashioned street lamps to light your way and hot chocolate and cookies in front of the fire at your B&B. As you walk the streets, historical sites are at every turn. This was once the home of Ulysses S. Grant, commander of the Union Army in the Civil War and the 18th president of the United States.

Over the past few years, historical preservation and quality of life for both residents and visitors have become priorities. In preparation for a huge 2004 celebration of the 150th anniversary of the completion of the railway from Dubuque to Chicago, the town made more of its 19th-century buildings handicapped accessible. More parks are available for picnicking and playing, and a paved path along the riverfront was set up as a self-guided historic walking tour. The area also provides good biking, cross-country skiing, fishing, walking, and camping opportunities.

At the corner of Park Avenue and Bouthillier Street, the Galena Convention and Visitors Bureau has maps, pamphlets, and information on Galena as well as the tiny towns that surround it, where modern life has similarly bypassed.

WHAT TO SEE & DO

Belvedere Mansion and Gardens J. Russell Jones, a steamboat magnate and ambassador to Belgium, built this Italianate mansion in 1857. Throughout the years, the various owners have peppered the mansion with delightful surprises. Not only has the mansion amassed a collection of Victorian antiques, but it has picked up a random selection of unrelated but fascinating items, including glittering pieces from Liberace's estate and the famous green drapes from *Gone With the Wind*. > 1008 Park Ave., Galena, tel. 815/777-0747. $10. May–Oct., Sun.–Fri. 11–4, Sat. 11–5.

Chestnut Mountain Resort Night skiing on lighted trails is just one of the delights of this resort, just 8 mi southeast of Galena. You can take the 17 mi of trails on foot or by mountain bike in summer and by skis or snowshoes in winter. The resort also has a 120-room inn (see Where to Stay). > 8700 W. Chestnut Rd., Galena, tel. 815/777-1320 or 800/397-1320, fax 815/777-1068, www.chestnutmtn.com. Call for rates.

Dowling House Galena pottery, made by Galena artisans in the early 1800s, and lead-mining artifacts from Galena's 1820s lead-mining boom fill Illinois's first stone structure. The original owners, lead miners themselves, built the structure in 1826 as a trading post. Tours are given every half hour. > 220 Diagonal St., Galena, tel. 815/777-1250. $7. May–Oct., Sun–Fri. 11–4, Sat. 11–5.

Galena Cellars Winery You can taste and purchase more than 25 varieties of wine, plus locally produced cheese and sausage, at this local treasure. Tours include a "sensory program" that explains the wine-tasting experience. > 4746 N. Ford Rd., Galena, tel. 815/777-3330, www.galenacellars.com. $3. Memorial Day–Oct., Fri.–Sun. 11–8.

Galena/Jo Daviess County History Museum A 15-minute video, "Galena: Steamboat Capital of the Old Northwest," provides an interesting orientation to the town, making this an excellent place to start your visit. The video transports you to a time when Galena was at its peak of wealth from mining and provides narration of the steamboat industry's role in the town's growth. Permanent exhibits include artifacts and information from the town's Civil War history. Display cases house period dolls, toys, clothing, and household artifacts. > 211 S. Bench St., Galena, tel. 815/777-9129, www.galenahistorymuseum.org. $4. Mon., Wed., Fri. 10–5; Sat. 10–6; Tues., Thurs., Sun. 11–5.

Grace Episcopal Church Colorful stained-glass windows and a hand-carved pulpit are breathtaking to see at this 1848 Gothic-revival church. > Hill and Prospect Sts., Galena, tel. 815/777-2590. Free. Weekdays 9–noon or by appointment.

Lin Mar Gardens Ponds, waterfalls, and flowers providing bursts of radiant color make up this 3½-acre garden, nestled into a hillside atop natural limestone outcroppings overlooking the city of Galena. Plantings include hostas, viburnums, conifers, daylilies, annuals, and perennials. Don't miss the small mine replica and sunken garden in the ruins of one of the first African-American churches in Illinois. > 504 S. Prospect, Galena, tel. 815/777–1177, www.galena.org/gardens.cfm. $4. June–Sept., daily 10–4; guided tours by appointment.

Old Market House State Historic Site This 1846 Greek-revival building, which you can tour, was the hub of civic and commercial life in 19th-century Galena. Produce and wares were sold on the ground floor, the city council met upstairs, and the basement was the jail. > 123 N. Commerce St., Galena, tel. 815/777–3310. Free, $2 donation suggested. Thurs.–Mon. 9–noon and 1–5.

Ulysses S. Grant Home Built in 1860 in the Italianate bracketed style, this home was presented with much trumpet blowing and flag waving to Grant in 1865 by a group of Galena Republicans in honor of his service to the Union. The Grant family lived there until Grant's victory in the 1868 presidential election and used much of the furnishings currently in the house. The rest of the home has been restored to its post–Civil War appearance. > 500 Bouthillier St., Galena, tel. 815/777–3310, www.granthome.com. $3 suggested donation. Wed.–Sun. 9–5.

Vinegar Hill Lead Mine and Museum At this 19th-century preserved underground mine, the only one open for tours, a guide takes you down into the mine and acquaints you with early mining methods and regales with stories about the miners. The museum displays lead ore samples, primitive mining tools, and early artifacts indigenous to the area. > 8885 N. Three Pines Rd., Galena, tel. 815/777–0855. $5. June–Aug., daily 9–4:30; May, Sept., Oct., weekends 9–4:30.

NEARBY

Dyersville, IA Dyersville is the *Field of Dreams* movie site, and the baseball diamond carved from the cornfield is still there, waiting for you to step up to the plate. Dyersville also has a doll museum and wood-carving museum. > Rte. 20, 40 mi west of Galena.

Hanover Mallards outnumber people 200 to 1 in this little village southeast of Galena, nestled in the Apple River valley among the rolling hills of northwest Illinois. The Crescent Falls Dam was built here in 1829, and contributed much to the village's growth. > Rte. 20, southeast of Galena.

Mississippi Palisades State Park In this park outside Savanna, 28 mi south of Galena, you can bird-watch and hike the trails—parts of which are challenging— where you can see unusual rock formations and spectacular views of the Mississippi River. > 16327A Rte. 84, Savanna, tel. 815/273–2731. Free. Daily.

Stockton The historic village of Stockton dates from February 17, 1827. Many of its earliest buildings remain in its historic downtown, including the schoolhouse, woolen mill, and the Ladies Union Cemetery crypt. Stockton is also the place where, in 1919, the Kraft brothers formed J. L. Kraft and Company. The original structure, however, no longer remains. > Rte. 20, 30 mi east of Galena.

Whistling Wings Hatchery At this hatchery, more than 200,000 mallards per year are hatched; a viewing window lets you see the baby ducks in incubators. The world's largest mallard duck hatchery, it supplies hundreds of thousands of ducks to wildlife refuges and research facilities, as well as to restaurants, throughout the world. > 113 Washington St., Hanover, tel. 815/591–3512.

Tours

Brill's Trolley Tours Making Galena history fun is what this tour is about. The interactive, joke- and anecdote-filled hour covers 40 Galena sites and tells who did what

Ghosts, Past & Present

IN 1842, WHILE GALENA WAS STILL AT THE PEAK OF ITS PROSPERITY from shipping ore down the Mississippi, it had its first ghost sighting. Two women living together in a city apartment began to tell of ghostly reddish lights on the wall of their kitchen at night. They were in such fear for their lives, they moved out. Was it a ghost, or merely shadows from cracks in their stove? No one was quite sure.

Nor were they sure 40 years later, when people saw apparitions on the road between Galena and Dubuque. A girl working in a nearby farmhouse became so distraught she refused to work there anymore. That was enough incentive for a group of townspeople to explore the sightings. Just past the farmhouse, they froze as a man approached them, appearing to float in the air, his feet seeming to appear one minute and disappear the next. As the group moved closer, he floated across the field into a ravine and disappeared.

Since then, stories of ghost sightings in Galena continue, some passed down through the generations, others kept alive through newspaper clippings; others, however, are more recent.

On a cold January afternoon in 1991, two employees of the Galena Historical Museum were sitting in an office doing paperwork when they heard the front door open. Almost simultaneously, they heard another sound—the clumping of someone walking from the second floor down to the first. One of the employees went to see what was happening, but saw no one. He checked the bathrooms, went into the basement, and then walked upstairs. Nothing. Thinking perhaps something had fallen in an exhibit area, he walked from exhibit to exhibit; nothing was out of place. They never discovered what it was that had made the sound.

Four months later, the same employee stayed late to lock up the museum. As he walked down from the second floor, he heard footsteps on the stairs beside him.

He stopped, looked around, and saw no one. He resumed his walk down the steps, and the footsteps followed him. When they both reached the bottom of the stairs, the employee threw some grit on the floor. Soon he heard what sounded like a rubber-soled shoe making a half-circle on the grit. The employee waited. The room became silent. After several minutes of silence, the employee left, never discovering what had followed him.

No one has yet able to determine the cause of this and other mysterious happenings here. When pressed, Galena historian Daryl Watson simply says, "Some things you can't explain—and maybe you shouldn't."

to whom and where. Tours are given every hour. If the group votes "yes," the bus will also stop for the 15-minute tour of Grant's home. > America's Olde Fashioned Ice Cream Parlor, 102 N. Main St., Galena, tel. 815/777–3121.

Galena Trolley Tours Beautiful panoramas from the bluffs add to the enjoyment of these tours, which travel to historical Galena sites. You can choose from either a one-hour or a two-hour narrated tour. The longer tour includes stops at the Ulysses S. Grant home and the Lin Mar Gardens, which are draped with waterfalls and set among ponds and a sunken garden. Tours depart every hour, from 10 to 5 daily. > 314 S. Main St., Galena, tel. 815/777–1248.

Sports

HIKING & BACKPACKING

Apple River Canyon State Park More cliffs and canyons, in addition to camping, fishing, and five 1-mi-long hiking trails, are found here. > 8763 E. Canyon Rd., north of Rte. 20 between Stockton and Warren, tel. 815/745–3302, www.dnr.state.il.us.

Mississippi Palisades State Park This park along the Mississippi River, about 30 mi south of Galena, has hiking trails with river views and nature preserves with accessible lookouts. > 16327A Rte. 84 N, Savanna, tel. 815/273–2731, www.dnr.state.il.us.

Save the Date

APRIL

Festival of Quilts Vendors and quilters alike come from all over the country to spend four days in early April devoted to the art and technique of quilt making. The festival includes lectures, exhibits, classes in techniques, workshops, and lots of informal discussions. > Tel. 815/777–9050.

President Grant's Birthday Celebration The whole town participates in the birthday celebration of Galena's favorite son with period events. Longtime residents conduct walking tours, others teach period dance classes and provide 19th-century entertainment. Recreated military encampments, costumed residents walking through towns, and a grand ball enrich the experience. > Tel. 815/777–9129.

JUNE

Annual Old Market Days–Skills from the Hills On a weekend in mid-June, Galena turns out for a turn-of-the-20th-century, open-air market in the Old Market House Square. Women in period costumes sell produce, breads, pastries, flowers, and crafts. Different types of early-20th-century skills are demonstrated. > Tel. 815/858–3392.

Grand Excursion Celebration June 2004 marks the 150th anniversary of the completion of the railroad running the length of the Mississippi River. The event will be celebrated with the recreation of the 1854 flotilla that carried former President Fillmore and other dignitaries down the river, stopping at ports and partaking in local activities. On June 28, Galena will recreate its famous picnic in Grant Park, complete with upscale box lunches and original 1854 menu. The day will also include a tour of the town's B&B gardens, and instruction in historic dances. > Tel. 815/777–9050.

June Tour of Historic Homes Residents of Galena literally open their doors the second weekend of June, when you can tour several of the architecturally and historically significant homes in the area. > Tel. 815/777–9129.

Stagecoach Trail Festival The towns of Apple River, Scales Mound, Lena, Warren, and Nora celebrate their Native American and pioneer heritage through many types of remembrances of life along the stagecoach trail in this region. It takes place the second weekend of the month. > Tel. 800/747–9377.

JULY
Galena Arts Festival You can admire and purchase the paintings submitted in this juried art show in Grant City Park on the last weekend of the month. > Tel. 815/777–2433.

SEPTEMBER
Ladies' Getaway Weekend The Chamber of Commerce sponsors tea parties, classes, and demonstrations of jewelry making, cooking, and scrapbook making the second weekend of the month. Men are welcome, too. > Tel. 815/777–9050.

OCTOBER
Galena Country Fair On Columbus Day weekend local artisans, crafters, and performers show their stuff at this old-fashioned country fair. > Tel. 815/777–1048.

NOVEMBER
Nouveau Wine Festival Local winery Galena Cellars goes all out to celebrate the release of its Beaujolais nouveau wine. Special luncheons at Galena eateries, horse-drawn deliveries on Main Street, an afternoon wine-and-cheese party at Benjamin's restaurant, and a dance at the DeSoto House Hotel are traditional activities in honor of the annually produced French wine. > Tel. 815/777–3330.

WHERE TO STAY

Aldrich Guest House Military troops once trained on the grounds of this historic B&B. Built by Cyrus Aldrich, an Illinois state representative, the house has remained structurally unchanged since 1863. Rooms are furnished with antiques and all have fireplaces, private baths with claw-foot tubs, and queen-size beds. > 900 3rd St., Galena 61036, tel. 815/777–3323, www.aldrichguesthouse.com. 5 rooms. Cable TV; no room phones, no smoking. D, MC, V. BP. $–$$

Annie Wiggins Guest House This house, built in 1846, is filled with antiques and overlooks the Galena River. Some rooms include Civil War–era bedroom sets and deep, soaking tubs for two. When not relaxing in your room, sip a summertime lemonade or wintertime hot chocolate on the veranda, or crunch molasses cookies in the 1846 antiques-filled parlor. The Galena ghost tours leave from here. > 1004 Park Ave., Galena 61036, tel. 815/777–0336, www.anniewiggins.com. 7 rooms. AE, MC, V. BP. $–$$$

Avery Guest House Formerly the home of a Union officer, this 1848 building evokes simple charm—its lovely, old-fashioned gazebo makes you long for a glass of something cool by your side and a book of 19th-century short stories on your lap. The house has period decor, with a bay window overlooking the Galena River valley. Antiques-filled guest rooms, each with its own private bathroom, are reminiscent of the mid-1800s; the Sandra Kay Room, for example, is decorated with hand-painted roses and has the original spacious bath with claw-foot tub and shower. > 606 S. Prospect St., Galena 61036, tel. 815/777–3883, fax 815/777–3889, www.averybedandbreakfast.com. 4 rooms. Some in-room VCRs; no kids under 12, no smoking. D, MC, V. BP. $–$$

Best Western Quiet House Suites Each room at this all-suites hotel, ½ mi from downtown Galena, is individually decorated in themes ranging from high tech and art deco to huntsman and Oriental. Most rooms have balconies, and 15 have hot tubs. > 9923 Rte. 20 W, Galena 61036, tel. 815/777–2577, fax 815/777–0584, www.quiethouse.com. 42 suites. Some in-room hot tubs, microwaves, refrigerators, indoor-outdoor pool, gym. AE, D, DC, MC. $–$$$$

Captain Gear Guest House Set on 4 acres in the historic district, this redbrick, pilliard 1855 federal mansion has 12-foot ceilings and a curving staircase that leads to two rooms and one suite. All have private baths, and one has a double shower, another a double whirlpool. The suite is decorated in period colors, with mahogany and period furniture. The home is decorated as in the Victorian era. And if you've never seen a home with crystal gasoliers, now's your chance. > 1000 S. Bench St., Galena 61036, tel. 815/777–0222 or 800/794–5656, fax 815/777–3210, www.captaingearguesthouse.com. 2 rooms, 1 suite. Some in-room hot tubs, cable TV, in-room VCRs; no kids, no smoking. D, MC, V. BP. $$–$$$

Chestnut Mountain Resort The resort resembles a Swiss chalet, sitting atop a bluff above the Mississippi River. The rooms and restaurant overlook the ski slopes. > 8700 W. Chestnut Rd., 8 mi southeast of Galena, Galena 61036, tel. 815/777–1320 or 800/397–1320, fax 815/777–1068, www.chestnutmtn.com. 120 rooms. Restaurant, miniature golf, tennis court, indoor pool, sauna, horseshoes, volleyball, shops, playground. AE, D, DC, MC, V. $–$$$$

DeSoto House Hotel Opened in 1855, the DeSoto House served as presidential campaign headquarters for Ulysses S. Grant, and Lincoln really did sleep here. The spacious rooms recall the 1860s with period furnishings. All bedrooms have balconies or terraces, fireplaces, and private baths. The stately Generals' Restaurant serves steaks, chops, and seafood; the Courtyard Restaurant serves breakfast and lunch; and the Green Street Tavern serves cocktails and snacks. > 230 S. Main St., Galena 61036, tel. 815/777–0090 or 800/343–6562, fax 815/777–9529, www.desotohouse.com. 55 rooms. 3 restaurants, cable TV, no-smoking rooms. AE, D, DC, MC, V. ¢–$$$$

Eagle Ridge Inn and Resort On 6,800 wooded acres, this lakeside resort provides 63 holes of championship golf, canoe and pontoon-boat rentals in its marina, hayrides, sleigh rides and trail rides, as well as a smooth sand beach for sunning. Lodging options are numerous and include one- to three-bedroom town houses and condos, and three- to eight-bedroom homes. Inside the inn, which is perched above 7-mi-long Lake Galena, a spacious common area with a double-sided fireplace unfolds. Rooms have contemporary furnishings with views of the lake or woods. Some rooms have wood-burning fireplaces. > 444 Eagle Ridge Dr., Galena 61036, tel. 815/777–2444 or 800/892–2269, fax 815/777–4502, www.eagleridge.com. 80 rooms. 3 restaurants, room service, some kitchens, minibars, some microwaves, some refrigerators, cable TV, some in-room VCRs, some in-room hot tubs, 4 golf courses, 4 tennis courts, indoor pool, exercise equipment, hot tub, massage, boating, bicycles, bar, children's programs (ages 2–16); no smoking. AE, D, DC, MC, V. $$–$$$$

Goldmoor Inn This idyllic country estate, overlooking the Galena River, is filled with nooks and crannies for settling in with a book and a glass of wine or cup of tea. You can warm by a fireplace, made deliciously comfortable by dozens of pillows on couches and chairs and by hosts who attend to your every need. Little touches are everywhere: rooms and suites are provided with microwave popcorn, standard-size coffee pots and ground coffee, and refrigerators stocked with drinks. The spacious rooms have hot tubs on raised, tiled platforms. The dining room, which looks out onto landscaped grounds and a gazebo, is perfect for sipping steaming cups of coffee and digging into a plate crowded with eggs, fruit, and freshly baked muffins. > 9001 Sand Hill Rd., Galena 61036, tel. 800/255–3925, fax 815/777–3993, www.galena-il.com. 2 rooms, 3 suites, 5 cabins. Some in-room hot tubs, kitchenettes, refrigerators, cable TV, in-room VCRs, massage, spa, mountain bikes. D, MC, V. BP. $–$$$

Hellman Guest House In this Queen Anne Victorian wood- and antiques-filled& house, on a bluff overlooking downtown Galena, you can choose among four rooms with private baths—three with showers only—and wake up to early-morning coffee service. The rooms are plant-filled, with decorative pitchers and washing bowls on the bureaus, Victorian dressing mirrors, and period furniture. All have stained- and beveled-glass windows and coal-burning and gas fireplaces. Downstairs, the living room, with its lacy tablecloth and sheer white curtains, is just the sort of room in which you'd expect to find antique porcelain dolls sipping tea. > 318 Hill St., Galena 61036, tel. 815/777–3638, www.hellmanguesthouse.com. 4 rooms. No room phones, no kids under 10, no smoking. MC, V. BP. $–$$

John Henry Guest House Chances are you may never make it up the walk of this 1996 National Trust Award–winning turn-of-the-20th-century home alone; host Lyndi Huotari will greet at your car before you've turned off the motor. She'll take you through swinging, beveled-glass doors onto handsome wood floors, past original woodwork and built-in cupboards with leaded glass, and upstairs to your suite. Each suite has its own Victorian bedroom, private bathroom, and sitting room with couch, chairs, and a bureau where home-baked cookies appear each night. Comfortable chairs on the porch and a swing for two overlook the river and downtown Galena. > 812 S. Bench St., Galena 61036, tel. 815/777–3595, www.jnhenry.com. 2 suites. MC, V. BP. $

Logan House Inn Above Café Italia, this antebellum inn, built in 1855, at the north end of Galena's historic center, is one of the town's first hotels. Scenes from the movie *Field of Dreams* were filmed here. > 301 N. Main St., Galena 61036, tel. 815/777–0033, fax 815/777–0049. 4 rooms, 2 suites. Restaurant, some in-room hot tubs, some in-room VCRs, cable TV, bar. D, MC, V. Closed Jan. 10–Feb. 13. $

Park Avenue Guest House You're invited to while away a lazy afternoon on the gracefully curving, wraparound porch of this turreted Queen Anne–style home. The inside is just as relaxing; built in 1893, the house has 12-foot ceilings and original, ornate woodwork throughout. Two parlors are filled with period antiques, including dozens of lamps and a turn-of-the-20th-century, hand-cranked Victrola. Each of the four bedrooms has an antique Victorian dresser and other Victorian-era furnishings, a private bathroom with pedestal sink, and ceiling fan. Some rooms have fireplaces. > 208 Park Ave., Galena 61036, tel. 815/777–1075 or 800/359–0743, www.galena.com/parkave. 4 rooms. Cable TV, some in-room VCRs; no kids under 12. D, MC, V. BP. $–$$

Pine Hollow Inn A Christmas tree farm and a babbling brook are included on these 120 acres of rolling hills, 1 mi from town. Each of the five suites has a working wood-burning fireplace, a four-poster bed, a stained-glass window, exposed wood beams and skylights, a garden patio, a private porch, or a spectacular view up the valley. The inn itself has the appearance of a sprawling, old, country home. > 4700 N. Council Hill Rd., Galena 61036, tel. 815/777–1071, www.pinehollowinn.com. 5 rooms. No kids under 12, no smoking. D, MC, V. CP. $–$$

Queen Anne Guest House A candlelight breakfast is served amid antique surroundings in this Queen Anne house, built in 1891. Two parlors beckon readers to curl up and relax; another relaxation possibility is to go to your room and sink into your clawfoot bathtub. > 200 Park St., Galena 61036, tel. 815/777–3849, fax 815/777–3849. 4 rooms. No smoking. D, MC, V. BP. $

Stillman's Country Inn Nestled on a hill across the road from the Ulysses S. Grant home, this inn houses seven themed suites. For example, the Honeymoon Suite has 12-foot ceilings, period decor and antiques, a hot tub for two, and two marble fireplaces. This three-story brick house is also home to Bernadine's Tea Room, which serves authentic English teas as well as lunches and desserts. > 513 Bouthillier St., Galena 61036, tel. 815/777–0557, fax 815/777–8098. 7 rooms. In-room hot tubs, cable TV; no kids. D, MC, V. BP. $–$$$$

Stoney Creek Inn Built in 1996 to resemble a hunting lodge, this inn combines rustic details, such as exposed stone and wood, with modern conveniences. Choose from a selection of themed suites, which include gas-burning stone fireplaces and oversize bathrooms. All are reminiscent of a night in the north woods. Galena's historic district is within walking distance. > 940 Galena Square Dr., Galena 61036, tel. 815/777–2223 or 800/659–2220, fax 815/777–6762, www.stoneycreekinn.com/galena.htm. 66 rooms, 10 suites. In-room data ports, in-room hot tubs, some refrigerators, cable TV, indoor pool, exercise equipment, sauna. AE, D, DC, MC, V. CP. ¢–$$$

Victorian Pines Inn and Spa Nestled among gently rolling hills, this inn (formerly the Princess Motel) invites those who crave ultimate relaxation. A full-service spa provides the latest hair, face, and body treatments, a fully equipped fitness facility, a lap pool, and other elements to both prod and pamper. Twenty acres of landscaped grounds are available for hiking or strolling. The 64 airy rooms, each with private bath, are decorated with country quilts covering wrought-iron beds. Nine king suites, similarly decorated, have whirlpool tubs and gas fireplaces; some have views of the land, others of the private, stocked pond. > 11383 U.S. 20 W, Galena 61036, tel. 815/777–2043, fax 815/777–2625. 64 rooms. Cable TV, exercise equipment, hair salon, hot tub, sauna, spa, steam room, hiking, some pets allowed. AE, D, MC, V. CP. ¢–$$$$

WHERE TO EAT

Benjamin's You are surrounded by antique beer advertisements and memorabilia and photos of Galena's history in this comfy restaurant, where Italian meat loaf, penne Florentine, and rib-eye steaks are the specialties. > 103 N. Main St., Galena, tel. 815/777–0467. Reservations not accepted. AE, D, MC, V. $–$$$

Bubba's Seafood, Pasta, and Smokehouse In both the casual room downstairs and the more formal room upstairs, you can get a taste of New Orleans–style dining at this local favorite spot. Try the Cajun dishes or the hickory-smoked ribs. > 300 N. Main St., Galena, tel. 815/777–8030. AE, D, MC, V. No lunch Mon.–Thurs. $$–$$$$

Café Italia and Twisted Taco Café In a vintage building on historic Main Street, this cozy wood and black-and-white-tiled restaurant serves traditional Italian food with Mexican sides. If you have to wait for a table, the long wooden bar is an inviting place to sit and peruse the extensive wine list. > 301 N. Main St., Galena. D, MC, V. Closed Mon. and Tues. $–$$

Cannova's Pizzeria The homemade bread at Cannova's is just one of the reasons this brick-walled pizzeria is usually packed; the salad, pizza, pasta, and unflappably friendly service are others. > 247 N. Main St., Galena, tel. 815/777–3735. AE, D, MC, V. No lunch Mon.–Thurs. ¢–$$

Fried Green Tomatoes Pasta dishes, Black Angus steaks, and the eponymous vegetables—picked green, then fried—are served in the exposed brick dining room of this old farmstead. A pianist plays Friday and Saturday evenings. > 1301 Irish Hollow Rd., Galena, tel. 815/777–3938. AE, MC, V. No lunch. $$–$$$$

Log Cabin Opened in 1935, Galena's oldest restaurant is a runaway local favorite. Inside its rustic log-cabin exterior, you can choose from among the all-American assortment of steaks, seafood, and chicken, as well as some Greek-inspired dishes. Specials include prime rib, pork chops, Greek salad, and flaming *saganaki*. > 201 N. Main St., Galena, tel. 815/777–0393. Closed Mon. MC, V. $–$$$$

Market House Tavern Restaurant Inside this tavern's black-and-white interior, you can do a little armchair traveling among the many photographs of Ireland on the walls as you dine on grilled salmon or a 12-ounce rib eye. > 204 Perry St., Galena, tel. 815/777–0690. D, MC, V. ¢–$$$$

Perry Street Brasserie The menu changes monthly, but you can always find a mix of such classic dishes as grilled filet mignon or pan-seared Alaskan halibut among more adventurous ones, such as grilled quail on Israeli couscous, at this restaurant furnished with an interesting collection of facsimiles of medieval English brass and Celtic figures. > 124 N. Commerce St., Galena, tel. 815/777–3773. Reservations essential. D, MC, V. Closed Sun. and Mon. No lunch. **$$$–$$$$**

NEARBY

Cove Restaurant Perched on a bluff overlooking Apple Canyon lake, this restaurant serves such contemporary creations as beef tenderloin, baked salmon, and vegetarian dishes such as baked Portobello mushroom. You can dine inside in the Frank Lloyd Wright–style dining room or outside on a porch overlooking the lake. > Apple Canyon Lake, Apple River, tel. 815/492–0123. AE, D, MC, V. **$–$$$**

Timmerman's Supper Club This swanky restaurant has views of the Mississippi River valley and most of Dubuque. A quirky aspect of this all-windows restaurant includes a bunny hut on the front lawn, where you can see anywhere from a half dozen to a dozen bunnies hopping about at any one time. Steaks, crab legs, scallops, and pasta dishes are specials. A DJ spins dance-floor favorites on weekends. > 7777 Timmerman Dr., East Dubuque, tel. 815/747–3316. AE, D, MC, V. **$–$$$**

ESSENTIALS

Getting Here

Driving is the most direct, quickest, and enjoyable way to travel to Galena. Interstates 90 and 94 travel through flatlands, but once you drive a bit on Route 20, the scenery changes into scenic rolling hills. Driving also gives you freedom once you get to Galena. Although the town is compact and walkable, sites outside of town are difficult to get to unless you have a car. Only one bus departs daily from Chicago to Galena, but with eight stops between Chicago and Galena, the trip takes roughly twice as long as driving. You can also take the train, but the nearest station is an hour from Galena—about half the time it takes to drive from Chicago.

BY BUS

Greyhound travels from Chicago to Galena once a day. The 160-mi trip takes 4 hours, 10 minutes; the bus leaves at 8 AM and arrives at 12:10 PM, dropping you off conveniently on Main Street. The cost is $68.40 for a round-trip ticket with discounts available under certain conditions.

BUS LINE **Greyhound Lines** > Tel. 800/229–9424, www.greyhound.com.

BY CAR

From Chicago take I–90 86 mi to Rockford, then Route 20 West 81 mi to Galena.

Visitor Information

CONTACT **Galena/Jo Daviess County Convention and Visitors Bureau** > 101 Bouthillier St., Galena 61036, tel. 815/777–3566 or 888/842–5362, www.galena.org.

Battle Creek & Marshall

160 mi east of Chicago

16

By Kevin Cunningham

VENICE PERFECTED CANALS. PARIS REINVENTED ART. But it took a modest city in the heart of Michigan to revolutionize the most important meal of the day. Battle Creek, "the World's Cereal Bowl," owes its claims of *grrrr*reatness to breakfast cereal. Dr. J. H. Kellogg, culinary inventor extraordinaire, and C. W. Post, advertising genius, built Battle Creek into a food empire. Today their names and their influence are all over the city's streets, parks, buildings, and institutions.

Lying in agricultural land in west-central Michigan, Battle Creek is part of a cluster of towns—Kalamazoo and Holland (to the west), Lansing (to the north), and Ann Arbor (to the west)—essential to the state's fortunes and each known nationwide. Along I–94 and the smaller roads of the area you can see farmland rich enough to grow both cereal grains and the fruit that goes on top. Battle Creek sits in a valley around the confluence of its eponymous creek and the Kalamazoo River, the former once the power source for local industry, the latter a slow-and-steady river flowing through the Fort Custer Recreation Area and on through the neighboring towns of Marshall and Albion.

Battle Creek began its existence in 1831 as a town called Milton. Apparently a battle between a land surveyor and a trespasser impressed the townspeople enough to inspire a change in names. Industry sprang up around the creek and the town was incorporated in 1859. By then, Battle Creek had become a center for abolitionist politics. Local politician Erasmus Hussey, a founder of the Republican Party, served as chief conductor for Battle Creek's crowded stretch of the Underground Railroad. In 1858, anti-slavery crusader Sojourner Truth moved to Battle Creek and lived there until her death in 1883. She is buried in Oak Hill Cemetery.

Another movement, then just gaining strength, would have an even greater effect on the town. The Seventh Day Adventists were a millennial sect that believed in an imminent Second Coming, in keeping Saturday (the seventh day) as the Sabbath, and in the idea that better bodies and souls could be achieved through healthy living—particularly vegetarianism. In 1866, the Adventists founded the Western Health Reform Institute, the first of what would become a system of hospitals and medical facilities around the world. There were no games, but lots of preaching and oatmeal pudding; by 1876, when Dr. John Harvey Kellogg, the son of local Adventists, became superintendent, the institute was sinking. In time, inspired by a new product called Shredded Wheat and by an unhappy patient who'd broken her false teeth on zwieback, Kellogg began experimenting on precooked, flaked foods manufactured from grains. As his brother William worked long weeks on the new ideas, a former institute patient named Charles W. Post cooked up a cereal-based coffee substitute called Postum. Among many advertising gimmicks, Post invented a disease, "coffee neuralgia," and claimed Postum was the cure. In such ways the man destined to give the world Post Toasties (originally called Elijah's Manna) would, along with the Kelloggs, make Battle Creek the breakfast capital of the world.

Today, touring the sites that owe their existence to the Kelloggs' patronage would keep you busy longer than a weekend. Yet while the Kellogg empire has expanded, corporate downsizing has left Battle Creek in search of other options. Downtown has been hit hard by changing economic fortunes and a mall on Beckley Road. However, specialty shops filling a number of niches have kept the area alive. Being close to several attractions makes downtown a good option for restaurants, a surprising number of styles and price ranges. But despite recent efforts to get more people into the area on weekends, many downtown businesses close on Sunday, a concession to the semi-deserted streets.

A trip to the area should also include a drive around Marshall, 13 mi to the east. In the mid-1800s, the town lobbied to become the state capital, and got so far as to win a vote in the House before Lansing won out. Marshall also shared Battle Creek's abolitionist sentiments. In 1846 a runaway slave named Adam Crosswhite, who had lived in Marshall two years, was arrested by slave hunters. The town freed Crosswhite, sent him and his family to Canada, and arrested the slave hunters. Its heyday of making patent medicines is long over, and now Marshall is best known for its magnificent homes and other buildings, some dating from the Civil War era and a few remarkable examples available as lodgings to bed-and-breakfasters. The historic home tour in September provides an excellent showcase.

Albion, another community of vintage houses, is 25 mi from Battle Creek. Though nice enough as a peaceful walk, the town also claims a historical footnote: Juliet Calhoun Blakely, credited as the force behind the creation of Mother's Day, attended Albion's Methodist Episcopal Church. It's also home to Albion College, one of the country's leading liberal-arts schools.

WHAT TO SEE & DO

BATTLE CREEK
Battle Creek Yankees Affiliated with the New York Yankees, this class-A Midwest League team plays at C. O. Brown Stadium. > 1392 Capital Ave. NE, Battle Creek, tel. 616/660–2255, www.battlecreekyankees.com. $6–$8. Apr.–Sept.
Binder Park Zoo A small but highly regarded zoo, Binder Park has exotic and domestic animals, including one of the largest herds of giraffes in the United States, in a natural environment. Elevated boardwalks allow for panoramic (and sometimes up-close) views, and kids can try the hands-on activities at the conservation station. The zoo sponsors special events year-round, but the Halloween and Christmas programs are the most popular. > 7400 Division Dr., Battle Creek, tel. 269/979–1351, www.binderparkzoo.org. $8.50. Late Apr.–early Oct., weekdays 9–5, Sat. 9–6, Sun. 11–6.
Cereal City USA You can, as Toucan Sam said, "Follow your nose," or you can follow the signs to one of Battle Creek's most popular attractions. As much an entertainment complex as a museum—with four theaters, party facilities, and places to eat—Cereal City nonetheless has the history of, and hands-on exhibits about, all your favorite flakes and loops and toaster pastries. > 171 W. Michigan, Battle Creek, tel. 269/962–6230 or 800/970–7020, www.kelloggscerealcityusa.org. $7.95. Tues.–Fri. 10–4, Sat. 10–5, Sun. noon–5.
Kellogg Bird Sanctuary Operated as an experimental facility by Michigan State University, and another example of the Kellogg family largesse, this lush sanctuary

on the shores of Wintergreen Lake includes seasonal visiting wildfowl and permanent residents such as ducks, geese, swans, and birds of prey. Tours on a variety of seasonal topics begin at 10 AM and 11:30 AM (reservations required). > 12685 E. C Ave., Battle Creek, tel. 269/671–2510. $3. May–Oct., daily 9–8; Nov.–Apr., daily 9–5.

Kimball House Museum This 1886 Queen Anne–style house, built by a young doctor from Massachusetts, is furnished with antiques and period exhibits, including appliances, tools, and medical instruments. Special displays honor civil rights activist Sojourner Truth, and cereal magnates C. W. Post and the Kellogg family. In addition to the Sunday hours, the Battle Creek Historical Society conducts special programs Monday evenings 6–8 PM. > 196 Capital Ave. NE, Battle Creek, tel. 269/965–2613 or 269/966–2496, www.kimballhouse.org. $3. Apr.–Dec., Sun. 1–4.

Leila Arboretum More than 70 acres and 3,000 varieties of ornamental trees and shrubs distinguish this arboretum. It's best known for its collection of mature conifers—some date back to the 1920s—and its perennial demonstration gardens. > W. Michigan Ave. at 20th St., Battle Creek, tel. 269/969–0270. Free. Daily dawn–dusk.

Sojourner Truth Grave Battle Creek was a hotbed of abolitionist politics, and Sojourner Truth, the African-American orator and Underground Railroad leader, settled here when freed in the mid-19th century. Born into slavery, Truth escaped in the 1820s and began her public career as a traveling preacher. By 1850 she'd become famous for speeches that described in vivid and heartbreaking detail the lives of slaves. Today her simple grave, near the considerably more ostentatious resting place of cereal magnate C. W. Post, is one of the most visited in Oak Hill Cemetery. > 255 South Ave., Battle Creek. Free. Daily dawn–dusk.

MARSHALL

American Museum of Magic If you've always wanted a look up the proverbial sleeve, then a visit to this small independent museum, which opened appropriately enough on April Fool's Day in 1978, is for you. Housed in a renovated 19th-century building, the museum was conjured by a local collector who wanted to share his fascination with the world of magic. Inside are vintage posters, magician's props, and other intriguing paraphernalia. > 107 E. Michigan Ave., Marshall, tel. 616/781–7674. Free. By appointment.

Honolulu House Museum This lavish Hawaiian-inspired residence with pagodas and island motifs was built in the 19th century for Abner Pratt, a Supreme Court justice who later became U.S. Consul to Hawaii. Outside are pagoda-topped towers, a raised veranda, and other Hawaiian touches; inside are 15-foot murals hand-painted in elaborate Victorian style. > 107 N. Kalamazoo Ave., Marshall, tel. 269/781–8544 or 800/877–5163. $3. May–Sept., daily noon–5; Oct.–Apr., by appointment.

Marshall Historic District Marshall's rich legacy of 19th- and early-20th-century homes and other structures distinguish this town. At the Chamber of Commerce, you can pick up a self-guided tour brochure as well as guides to buildings and the cemeteries. > Marshall, tel. 269/781–5163 or 800/877–5163, www.marshallmi.org. Free.

Marshall Postal Museum A 1931 Model A Ford mail truck and a collection of vintage uniforms highlight this unique collection of Americana, in the basement and annex of a working post office. > 202 E. Michigan Ave., Marshall, tel. 269/979–2719. $3. By appointment.

NEARBY

Fort Custer National Cemetery During World War II, this tranquil 770-acre site, 7 mi from Battle Creek, served as an important army base. In 1985, it became a National Cemetery—Michigan's only—for anyone who has served in the United States Armed Forces. Today, more than 14,000 people are buried here. > 15501 Dickman Rd., Augusta, tel. 269/731–4164, www.fortcusternationalcemetery.com. Free. Daily dawn–dusk.

Fort Custer State Recreation Area This large park, 9 mi west of Battle Creek, is spread out over more than 2,900 acres. It has 22 mi of hiking trails, 4 mi of mountain biking trails, and 16 mi of bridle trails. In winter, trails open up for cross-country skiing. Two minicabins and three rustic cabins are available for rent, but you must call well in advance to reserve them. > Rte. M96, Augusta, tel. 269/731–4200. $4 per vehicle. Daily dawn–dusk. Closed Dec.–Feb.

Gardner House Museum Built by a local hardware magnate, this 1875 Victorian mansion and National Historic Site houses a local heritage museum and has several rooms of Victorian-era furnishings. > 509 S. Superior St., 12 mi from Marshall, Albion, tel. 517/629–5100. Free. May–Sept., weekends 2–4.

Riverside Cemetery In the Victorian spirit of creating cemeteries that served as beautiful parks, Riverside is a leafy place with a fishpond. Its most famous grave is that of Warren G. Hooper, a state senator murdered in 1945. > 1301 S. Superior St., 12 mi from Marshall, Albion, tel. 517/629–2479. Free. Daily.

Save the Date

JUNE

Cereal City Festival The World's Longest Breakfast Table is the highlight of this annual downtown summer event. From 8 AM to 12 PM, more than 60,000 people gather around some 250 tables to feast on cereal, doughnuts, and other breakfast treats. > Tel. 800/397–2240.

JUNE–AUGUST

NASCAR Winston Cup In a pair of rare appearances, NASCAR's elite drivers race twice per season at Michigan International Speedway in Brooklyn, about 70 mi from Battle Creek. > 12626 U.S. 12, Brooklyn, tel. 800/354–1010, www.mispeedway.com.

JULY

Field of Flight Air Show and Balloon Festival Mass balloon launches, the U.S. Air Force Thunderbirds, and the U.S. Team Balloon Championships are part of Battle Creek's big summer event, held at the W. K. Kellogg Airport to coincide with Independence Day. > Tel. 269/962–0592 or 800/397–2240, www.bcballoons.com.

Taste of Battle Creek Thirty local restaurants cook up favorites and specialties during this annual summer festival, held downtown on State Street in mid-July. In addition to the food, live music and a special area for the kids add to the fun. > Tel. 269/963–4407.

Welcome to My Garden Tour This popular citywide garden tour, held in mid-July, takes you behind the scenes and into the backyards of the residences of Marshall's historic district, home to some of the state's best-preserved Victorian-era architecture. > Tel. 269/781–8547, www.marshallmi.org.

AUGUST

Calhoun County Fair The state's oldest county fair is held the second full week in August at the County Fairgrounds, six blocks from downtown Marshall. Parades, livestock competitions, carnival rides, arts-and-crafts booths, and food vendors enrich the experience. > Tel. 269/781–8161, www.calhouncountyfair.org.

Unsolved Mystery

ON JANUARY 16, 1945, NEW STATE SENATOR WARREN G. HOOPER, *having served all of two weeks, was gunned down on M99 north of Springport, Michigan. It remains one of the state's legendary unsolved murders. The night of his murder Hooper stood waist-deep in corruption. How did the great-great-grandson of a signer of the Declaration of Independence come to such an end?*

Hooper owned a gas station before winning election to the Michigan House of Representatives in 1938. In 1939 he took a bribe from the Medical Society in exchange for a favorable vote. By 1943 Hooper had become, coincidentally enough, chairman of the House Public Health Committee, and in 1944 he'd moved up to the state senate. He'd also put himself on the long payroll of Grand Rapids political czar Frank D. McKay. The founder of General Tire, McKay had already been acquitted of rigging municipal bonds, shaking down distillers, and extorting money from Edsel Ford. When he came under suspicion again for corruption, grand jury summonses went out like party invitations. Hooper squealed. McKay, he said, had bribed away unfriendly legislation. Soon after, three bullets ended Hooper's career as a star witness.

Historians lay blame for the murder on McKay, prison officials, and members of Michigan's notorious Purple Gang. Long before becoming the rhythm section in "Jailhouse Rock," the Purples were a band of Detroit gangsters adept at bootlegging and murder. During Prohibition they supplied Capone with "torpedoes," a moniker for hired gunmen, for the St. Valentine's Day Massacre and made liquor the second-biggest business in Detroit (after automobiles). By 1945, even though their glory days were long gone—lost in a string of murder raps and incorporation into the national crime syndicate—the Purples in and out of prison may have still had the connections to arrange a hit. Whatever their role, and that of McKay, the murder remains unsolved. Hooper is buried in Albion's Riverside Cemetery.

SEPTEMBER

Historic Home Tour One of the state's busiest and most popular home tours, this annual event sponsored by the Marshall Historical Society takes the curious inside the city's renowned 19th-century residences. Home styles vary from Eastlake to Shingle to Queen Anne. The tour is held the first weekend after Labor Day, which also includes accompanying dinners, a Civil War reenactment, and other events. > Tel. 269/781–8544 or 800/877–5163.

NOVEMBER–DECEMBER

International Festival of Lights Battle Creek ushers in the holiday season with more than a million tiny, twinkling lights and a lineup of family-oriented events scheduled selected evenings and weekends. The festivities start the weekend before Thanksgiving and run through New Year's Eve. Highlights include holiday train exhibits and lighted animal displays at Binder Park Zoo. > Tel. 800/397–2240.

WHERE TO STAY

BATTLE CREEK
Amerihost Inn & Suites This hotel off Route 37 is near downtown sites and restaurants. Rooms are spacious and have modern furnishings; two of the suites overlook the pool and deck. > 182 W. Van Buren St., Battle Creek 49017, tel. 269/565–0500 or 800/434–5800, fax 269/565–0501, www.amerihostinn.com. 62 rooms, 10 suites. In-room data ports, some in-room hot tubs, microwaves, refrigerators, cable TV, indoor pool, exercise equipment, hot tub, sauna, no-smoking rooms. AE, D, DC, MC, V. CP. ¢–$

Baymont Inn & Suites Free Continental breakfast delivered to your room and in-room coffeemakers make your stay in these spacious rooms extra nice. It is less than ½ mi from shopping and right off I-94. > 4725 Beckley Rd., Battle Creek 49017, tel. 269/979–5400 or 866/999–1111, fax 269/979–3390, www.baymontinns.com. 87 rooms, 8 suites. Some in-room hot tubs, cable TV, indoor pool, business services, no-smoking rooms. AE, D, DC, MC, V. ¢–$

Comfort Inn A loyal business clientele frequents this motel, 3 mi from downtown and Binder Park Zoo. > 2590 Capitol Ave. SW, Battle Creek 49015, tel. 269/965–3201 or 800/465–4329, fax 269/965–0740, www.choicehotels.com. 98 rooms, 9 suites. Some in-room hot tubs, in-room data ports, microwaves, refrigerators, cable TV, indoor pool, exercise equipment, no-smoking rooms. AE, D, DC, MC, V. CP. ¢–$$

Econo Lodge Distinguished by its downtown location, this motel provides easy access to Cereal City and other attractions. Rooms are intimate and quiet; the pool area has a spacious deck. > 165 Capital Ave. SW, Battle Creek 49015, tel. 269/965–3976, fax 269/965–7580, www.choicehotels.com. 54 rooms. Restaurant, kitchenettes, some microwaves, some refrigerators, cable TV, pool, lounge, laundry facilities, business services, no-smoking rooms. AE, D, DC, MC, V. CP. ¢

Greencrest Manor An architectural eye-opener in an area renowned for architecture, this restored Normandy château–style inn, built in 1934 on St. Mary's Lake, is furnished with antiques and surrounded by extensive landscaping. > 6174 Halbert Rd., Battle Creek 49017, tel. 269/962–8633, fax 269/962–7254, www.greencrestmanor.com. 8 rooms, 6 with bath. Some in-room hot tubs, cable TV, business services; no smoking. AE, DC, MC, V. CP. $–$$$$

McCamly Plaza Subdued colors, landscape paintings, metal frames and fixtures, and space to relax are the elegant hallmarks of this mid-rise hotel in the heart of downtown. > 50 Capital Ave. SW, Battle Creek 49017, tel. 269/963–7050 or 888/622–2659, fax 269/963–3880, www.mccamlyplazahotel.com. 239 rooms, 7 suites. Restaurant, minibars, refrigerators, cable TV, indoor pool, exercise equipment, hot tub, bar, shops, business services. AE, D, DC, MC, V. $–$$

MARSHALL
Arbor Inn Pleasant accommodations are available at this motor inn on a busy strip outside of downtown. > 15435 W. Michigan Ave., Marshall 49068, tel. 269/781–7772, fax 269/781–2660. 48 rooms. Some refrigerators, cable TV, indoor pool. AE, D, MC, V. CP. ¢

Holiday Inn Express Opened in autumn 2000, this three-story chain hotel is 2 mi from downtown and a good base for exploring Binder Park Zoo. > 17252 Sam Hill Dr., Marshall 49068, tel. 269/789–9301 or 800/953–6287, fax 269/789–9301, www.ichotelsgroup.com. 66 rooms, 9 suites. In-room data ports, cable TV, indoor pool, exercise equipment, dry cleaning, laundry facilities, business services, no-smoking rooms. AE, D, DC, MC, V. CP. **$**

Joy House Bed & Breakfast A square tower dominates the front of this 1844 home in the historic district, two blocks from downtown. Rooms are antiques-filled and decorated in European motifs reflecting the heritages of the innkeepers. Two porches overlook the surrounding gardens. > 224 N. Kalamazoo Ave., Marshall 49068, tel. 269/789–1323, fax 269/789–1308, www.kephart.com/joyhouse. 3 rooms. No room phones, no TV in some rooms, no smoking. AE, MC, V. BP. **$**

National House Inn Antiques furnish this bed-and-breakfast housed in the state's oldest operating inn. The Victorian-style chambers are adorned with everything from hanging lamps to period prints to elegant wallpaper; the country-style rooms may have a pine rocking chair, burgundy walls, or a fireplace. The original building was a stagecoach stop between Detroit and Chicago. > 102 S. Parkview, Marshall 49068, tel. 269/781–7374, fax 269/781–4510, www.nationalhouseinn.com. 15 rooms. Cable TV, business services, airport shuttle. AE, MC, V. BP. **$–$$**

Rose Hill Inn Bed and Breakfast Once the home of William Boyce, founder of the Boy Scouts of America, this 1860 mansion with a city view is nestled among 100-year-old pines on 3 acres once owned by James Fenimore Cooper. Fireplaces, 12-foot ceilings, Tiffany glass, and antiques fill the interior; down comforters keep you cozy after dark. Three rooms have fireplaces. > 1110 Verona Rd., Marshall 49068, tel. 269/789–1992, fax 269/781–4723, www.rose-hill-inn.com. 6 rooms. Cable TV, tennis court, pool; no pets, no kids under 12, no smoking. AE, MC, V. BP. **$–$$**

WHERE TO EAT

BATTLE CREEK

Arcadia Brewing Company Once a Sears store, and announced by a pub-style sign outside, Arcadia is a working microbrewery where you can Eskimo kiss the big hoppy nose of an English-style ale. The brewery's many award certificates highlight the appropriately dark-wood tavern interior. You can create your own pizza or order a sandwich to go along with your pint, secure in the knowledge everything will be well cooked—all the food comes out of an Italian wood-fire oven, and the usual cooking temperature is 750°F. > 103 W. Michigan Ave., Battle Creek, tel. 269/963–9690. AE, MC, V. Closed Sun. and Mon. **¢–$$**

Clara's on the River Follow the clock tower to this Battle Creek institution, a former Michigan Central Railroad depot that's part museum and part restaurant. Local memorabilia covers the walls and the collection of early cereal boxes provides more than adequate distraction if you must wait for a table. The restaurant presents an eclectic menu with such items as baked Norwegian salmon, several kinds of steaks and chops, and imaginative fare such as Cajun meat loaf. Sandwiches and a long list of salads, many of them not exactly vegetarian, round out the choices. > 44 N. Mc-Camly Pl., Battle Creek, tel. 269/963–0966. AE, D, DC, MC, V. **$–$$$**

Pancake House Two blocks from McCamly Plaza, this restaurant serves their specialty homemade pancakes and leaves the coffee pot on the table, where it belongs. Breakfast is served all day, but late-risers can also order sandwiches and such from the lunch menu. Expect lines on the weekend, especially Sunday. > 185 Capital Ave., Battle Creek, tel. 269/964–6790. D, MC, V. Closed Mon. No dinner. **¢**

Shrank's Cafeteria A midweek visitor can dig in at this downtown institution, open since 1932. Hardly a cafeteria in the military or grade-school sense, Shrank's is small-town Midwest all the way, giving diners a choice of booths or tables and an ongoing sound track of friendly conversation and clattering cutlery. Dinner entrées change throughout the week but often include such staples as perch, liver and onions, and prime rib, plus soul food on Friday. Sandwiches, salads, and old reliables such as macaroni and cheese are also well represented. > 85 W. Michigan Ave., Battle Creek, tel. 269/964–7755, fax 269/964–2940, www.shranks.com. MC, V. Closed Sat. and Sun. ¢

MARSHALL

Copper Bar, Inc. Along with the burgers, televisions are plentiful at this famous local bar with the yellow facade. Inside, exposed beams crisscross the vaulted ceiling. Take time out to drink out of Ball jars and lean back in one of the beat-up wooden chairs to contemplate the animal heads. > 133 W. Michigan Ave., Marshall, tel. 269/781–5400. No credit cards. ¢

Cornwell's Turkeyville Justly considered one of Michigan's quirkier stops, this country restaurant and dinner theater talks turkey daily and serves everything from turkey tacos to turkey stir-fry to classic turkey sandwiches. For dessert try homemade pie or ice cream (*not* turkey-flavored). > 18935 15½ Mile Rd., Marshall, tel. 269/781–4293 or 800/228–4315. MC, V. Closed late Dec.–mid-Jan. $–$$$

Schuler's of Marshall Wise and witty words adorn the dining room rafters in this longtime mid-Michigan favorite, once a bowling alley and livery stable. Four generations of the Schuler family have served up the restaurant's trademark prime rib as well as lighter fare and some vegetarian dishes. A bakery is also on the premises and the menu changes seasonally. > 115 S. Eagle St., Marshall, tel. 269/781–0600 or 877/724–8537. AE, D, DC, MC, V. $$–$$$$

ESSENTIALS

Getting Here

Considering the 12 mi between Battle Creek and Marshall, and the fact both communities are already driving-oriented, a car is the most convenient option for weekenders. Both Amtrak and Greyhound serve Battle Creek and nearby Albion, as does the international airport in Kalamazoo. Battle Creek's mass transit, though reasonable ($1), keeps a sparse schedule on the weekend and hits each stop only about once an hour during the week. It does not run to Marshall or Albion. Air travelers can find cabs and shuttle services to and from the airport.

BY BUS

Greyhound runs a late-afternoon bus once a day from Chicago to Battle Creek, and three times per day from Battle Creek to Chicago (twice in the afternoon, once in the evening). The listed driving time of 4 hours, 10 minutes can be lengthened by delays at intermediate stops or by traffic getting into or out of Chicago. Tickets purchased seven days in advance are usually discounted, but nonrefundable.

Four Greyhound buses serve the Chicago–Albion route, with two morning departures and one afternoon departure. Three buses serve the Albion–Chicago route, with one departure in the morning and two in the afternoon. All have short layovers and transfers to regional buses in Kalamazoo. Travel times are between 4½ and 6 hours, depending on the route. Both the Battle Creek and Albion stations are closed Sunday, meaning tickets must be bought in advance. Passengers with tickets have access to board.

Battle Creek Transit maintains a reliable fleet of buses. Fare is $1 (no change given, transfers free), and it an easy system to learn—all buses are color- and number coded. The system crisscross the area and buses run to most of the major attractions. On weekends service ends at 5:30 PM (earlier on some routes); weekday service ends at 6:45 PM (earlier on some routes).
BUS DEPOTS **Albion Train Depot** > 300 N. Eaton, Albion, tel. 517/629–7373, www.greyhound.com. **Battle Creek Bus Depot** > 104 Capital Ave. SW, Battle Creek, tel. 269/963–1537.
BUS LINE **Greyhound** > Tel. 269/963–1537 or 800/229–9424, www.greyhound.com.

BY CAR
Interstate 94 links Chicago with the Battle Creek/Marshall area. Speed limits are between 55 and 70 mph. Traffic is usually not a problem, with one exception: the merge of I–94 with I–80 near the Indiana state line. Although a 20-mi backup is not typical, it happens and it's never more likely than during a Friday-evening rush hour when commuters, long-haul semis, and vacationers collide. If you're coming from the north you can miss the mess using the I–90 toll road. Otherwise, consider leaving early on Friday. The approximate travel time between Chicago and Battle Creek is three hours.

Access to Battle Creek from the east and west is provided by I–94 (via the north–south I–194 extension), and by U.S. 96 (also called Michigan Avenue), which links it to Marshall. From the north it is served by U.S. 37 and 66. City streets are easy to navigate. Marshall is served east–west by I–94 and U.S. 96, and north–south by I–69. Most of the historic sites are near one another. Once you've parked you can easily find your way around on foot.

BY PLANE
Two airlines serve Kalamazoo to and from Chicago O'Hare. American Eagle has four flights departing Chicago weekdays and Sunday, and three on Saturday; four flights depart Kalamazoo weekdays and Sunday and three on Saturday. United Express has four flights departing Chicago daily and three flights departing Kalamazoo daily. Flights typically take about 50 minutes. Kalamazoo/Battle Creek International is south of I–94 in Kalamazoo, 17 mi from Battle Creek and 29 mi from Marshall. A one-way cab ride to or from Battle Creek costs about $30.
AIRPORT **Kalamazoo/Battle Creek International Airport** > 5235 Portage Rd., Kalamazoo, tel. 269/388–3668, www.kalcounty.com/airport.htm.
CARRIERS **American Eagle** > Tel. 800/433–7300. **United** > Tel. 800/864–8331.

BY TRAIN
Amtrak runs with limited local stops between Chicago Union Station and Battle Creek. Trains depart four times daily from both destinations. The daily 2:10 PM train from Chicago also serves Albion. A train departs Albion for Chicago at 12:45 PM daily. Tickets cannot be purchased at the Albion train stop and must be purchased in advance. Both the Battle Creek and Albion stations are closed Sunday, meaning those traveling that day will need to purchase tickets in advance. Passengers with tickets can access the platform to board.
TRAIN LINE **Amtrak** > Tel. 800/872–7245, www.amtrak.com.
TRAIN STATIONS **Albion Train Depot** > 300 N. Eaton St., Albion, tel. 517/629–7373. **Battle Creek Train Station** > 104 Capital Ave. SW, Battle Creek, tel. 269/963–3351. Closed Sun.

Visitor Information

CONTACTS **Greater Albion Chamber of Commerce** > 416 S. Superior St., Albion 49224, tel. 517/629–5533 or 800/517–9523, www.chamber.albionmi.net. **Greater Battle Creek Visitor and Convention Bureau** > 77 E. Michigan Ave., Battle Creek 49017, tel. 269/962–2240 or 800/397–2240, www.battlecreekvisitors.org. **Marshall Chamber of Commerce** > 424 E. Michigan Ave., Marshall 49068, tel. 269/781–5163 or 800/877–5163, www.marshallmi.org.

Indianapolis

185 mi southeast of Chicago

17

By Joanne Cleaver

HOOSIERS WILL ADMIT THAT THEIR STATE'S BIGGEST CITY wasn't that great a place to visit in the 1970s and much of the '80s. Urban revitalization, however, finally arrived to stay in the mid-'90s. Indianapolis, or "Indy" as the locals affectionately call it, is dotted with historic downtown buildings proudly wearing cream limestone facades that glow as the sun sinks into the prairies. Swaths of redbrick town houses sweep from downtown out to the neighborhoods. And those neighborhoods are roaring back, with urban pioneers reclaiming gracious old Victorians and turn-of-the-20th-century mansions.

Indianapolis's main artery, Meridian Street, runs precisely north and south along the line of longitude. For roughly 2 mi, the street passes stately homes built from the turn of the 20th century through the 1940s. To the east, north of Kessler Boulevard, this residential section bumps up against Broad Ripple, a village that's now filled with restaurants, nightclubs, shops, and galleries. As early as the late 1800s, good eats and good times brought travelers to Broad Ripple, on a horseshoe bend of the White River, 6 mi north of downtown. At the turn of the 20th century, a 5¢ ride on the trolley carried excursionists to Broad Ripple's amusement center at what is now Broad Ripple Park. White City, Indy's Coney Island, labeled itself "the amusement park that satisfied." Broad Ripple is still the destination of choice for nighttime pleasure seekers and pub crawlers. One terminus of the popular 10½-mi Monon Rail Trail is here as well.

Massachusetts Avenue was one of the original diagonal spokes radiating out from the city's hub. It was soon lined with storefronts, factories, and warehouses, and the strip prospered. In the late 1940s, when the streetcar tracks were paved over, the avenue fell into decay. The renovation in the early 1980s of the Hammond Block, a triangular redbrick gem dating from 1874, marked its rebirth. Today, the tall, compact landmark marks the gateway to the district, which has a nucleus of galleries, theaters, storefront eateries, and ethnic restaurants.

Residential and commercial structures alike have been fixed up over the last two decades in the diverse Old Northside Historic District, which runs between 12th Street on the south and 16th Street on the north, and between Pennsylvania Street on the west and just beyond College Street on the east. At the turn of the 20th century, many a local bigwig lived here, including drug company founder Eli Lilly, local department store scion L. S. Ayres, novelist Booth Tarkington, former president Benjamin Harrison, and former vice-president Thomas Riley ("What this country needs is a good five-cent cigar") Marshall; the area declined during post–World War I years, when movers and shakers established other residential neighborhoods farther north and west. Construction of I-465 in the 1960s doomed many gorgeous houses and others were turned into multifamily dwellings. Now, urban homesteaders are hammering new life into the old houses and apartment buildings that survived.

Much of the city's rich jazz and blues heritage is linked to Indiana Avenue, one of the diagonal arteries in the town's original design. Pianist Erroll Grandy, known as the "godfather of Indianapolis jazz," and legendary guitarist Wes Montgomery, among others, are credited with putting the city in the national jazz spotlight. By the 1940s more than 25 jazz clubs stood shoulder to shoulder along the "Grand Ol++CE: '++ Street." The impressive Walker Building presided over the avenue's jazz scene. Named for Madame C. J. Walker, a self-made millionaire, the 950-seat structure is still the place to go for jazz; now called the Madame Walker Urban Life Center and Theatre, it has Jazz on the Avenue every Friday night.

The blues also figured in the Indy music scene early on. By the 1920s, blues greats in the city were playing and recording hits like "Indiana Avenue Stomp." Mandolinist Yank Rachell arrived in town in the 1950s, and over the next 20 years he and other traditional blues players helped attract new interest to the genre. Today the Slippery Noodle Inn, just south of Union Station on South Meridian Street, is synonymous with the blues. The 1850 redbrick building, the oldest commercial structure in the metropolitan area, draws local and national acts, offering basic eats and great music in a no-frills space. Blues lovers know they have arrived when they see the Noodle's red neon sign proclaiming "Dis Is It."

Indy's revitalization has boosted some of its old standbys to best-in-class status. Most surprising are the amount of green space and the number of sports venues that checkerboard the city. One welcome addition to the IndyParks system is the Indy Greenways, 175 mi of marked pedestrian trails and conservation corridors along creeks and canals throughout the metropolitan area. Downtown, there's an abundance of Olympic-class amateur and professional sports facilities including the Conseco Fieldhouse where the Indiana Pacers play.

Indy claims the title "Amateur Sports Capital of the World," having built sports venues such as the track-and-field stadium and the natatorium on the combined campuses of Indiana and Purdue universities. The headquarters of national amateur sports federations governing rowing, track and field, and gymnastics are all here.

For a city that claims to be the "Nation's Crossroads," Indianapolis is curiously overlooked as a weekend getaway destination. It doesn't sound glamorous to say you went to Indianapolis for the weekend; people might assume that you were stuck putting in overtime at a trade show. If the uninformed offer sympathy, you'll be faced with a challenge that might stymie even the most hospitable Hoosier: to let them know that you went to Indy on purpose, and had fun, and will do so again—or you might just smile and nod.

WHAT TO SEE & DO

Children's Museum of Indianapolis The museum is a pacesetter in creating exhibits truly relevant to children of all ages. Throughout its five stories are several protected play spaces for babies and toddlers, as well as ongoing projects at several spacious media and science labs for teens. One strategy for seeing it all is to take the elevator to the top and work your way down. The jolly fifth-level antique carousel runs all day long and rides are only 50¢. The laws of gravity take on a whole new meaning at the enormous water tables, where you can make your own dams and floods. Budding paleontologists can dig into the ongoing project of preparing fossils for display. A 350-seat theater stages performances nearly every day, as does a full-size planetarium. A food court and an educational-toy store flank the entry atrium. A major permanent exhibit on dinosaurs is scheduled to open in 2004. > 3000 N. Meridian St.,

Indianapolis, tel. 317/334–3322 or 800/208–5437, www.childrensmuseum.org. $9.50. Daily 10–5.

Christel DeHaan Fine Arts Center This stunning 500-seat concert hall is renowned for its acoustics. The center hosts a variety of performances and exhibitions. It's on the campus of the University of Indianapolis. > 1400 E. Hanna Ave., Indianapolis, tel. 317/788–3211.

Eagle Creek Park and Greenways The 4,200-acre park is one of the largest municipal parks in the country. Eagle Creek has a nature center and a lake that allows swimming and boating. Seasonal gear—cross-country skis, paddleboats—can be rented at the park. Eagle Creek is connected by biking and walking paths to other parks in the county system. These greenways connect to the riverfront, White River State Park, and downtown. > 7840 W. 56th St., Indianapolis, tel. 317/327–7110, www.indygreenways.org. $3 per vehicle.

Easley's Winery The winery is in an old brick building on the edge of downtown. Chardonnay, Chancellor Noir, and Riesling are a few of the wines you can sample. > 205 N. College Ave., Indianapolis, tel. 317/636–4516, www.easleywine.com. Free. Weekdays 9–6, Sat. 9–5, Sun. noon–4; tours for groups of 12 or more by appointment.

Eiteljorg Museum of American Indians and Western Art You don't have to be a Wild West fan to love the Eiteljorg, but you might be after you visit. The museum started out with a collection of paintings and bronze sculptures by Charles Russell, Frederic Remington, Georgia O'Keeffe, and other members of the original Taos, New Mexico, artists' colony. In 2002, it added a permanent gallery through which Native Americans tell their history in their own voices. Such artifacts as beaded buckskin garments are conveyed in a fresher cultural context than they were before. The museum is at the easternmost point of the White River State Park campus. > 500 W. Washington St., Indianapolis, tel. 317/636–9378, www.eiteljorg.org. $7. Mon.–Sat. 10–5, Sun. noon–5.

Garfield Park and Conservatory This leafy preserve is one of the city's oldest parks. The formal gardens have been restored to their original 1916 design. Urns and planters punctuate the sunken gardens amid the formal gardens. The conservatory contains more than 500 tropical plants and a 15-foot waterfall. Also in the park are a swimming pool, tennis courts, and baseball diamonds. > 2450 S. Shelby St., Indianapolis, tel. 317/327–7184. Free, conservatory $3. Daily 10–5.

Indiana Historical Society State-of-the-art climate-controlled archives, a library, and conservation areas house an extensive collection of rare documents and photographs. In the Cole Porter room, you can listen to a range of Hoosier legends, including Cole Porter, John Mellencamp, Wes Montgomery, Hoagy Carmichael, Michael Jackson, Noble Sissle, and the Hampton Sisters, on a programmable CD jukebox. An exhibit on the early history of flight and how Hoosiers took to the sky opened in 2003. Also here is the William Henry Smith Memorial Library, which houses letters, diaries, business records, maps, architectural drawings, paintings, and other material on the history of Indiana and the Old Northwest. The museum's shop is a go-to source for contemporary Hoosier arts and crafts, as well as history-related goods. The museum is on the northeast border of White River State Park, but is not part of the park. > 450 W. Ohio St., Indianapolis, tel. 317/232–1882, www.indianahistory.org. Free. Tues.–Sat. 10–5, Sun. noon–5 (except library).

Indiana Medical History Museum The museum is housed in the Pathology Department of the former Central State Hospital. When the structure was built in 1896, it was a research and teaching center. It is now the oldest pathology laboratory in the United States. Scientific laboratory equipment and photography, and an assortment of medical equipment and devices, are on display. > 3045 W. Vermont St., Indianapolis, tel. 317/635–7329, www.imhm.org. $5. Thurs.–Sat. 10–4.

Indiana State Museum In 2002, this museum moved from its location in the former city hall to this building on the eastern end of the White River State Park campus. The museum displays exhibits from Native Americans' habitation of the Indiana woodlands to the arrival of pioneers; the rise of the states as an industrial powerhouse; and how its citizens coped with economic and social change in the 20th century. Hands-on activities are incorporated throughout. Though the museum has a café, you can have your history and eat it too at the re-created tearoom of the venerable L. S. Ayres department store. Here, you can eat chicken potpie, warm yeast rolls, and rich desserts in the genteel atmosphere of days gone by. The IMAX theater schedule toggles between two shows and is open late to accommodate movie buffs. > 650 W. Washington St., Indianapolis, tel. 317/232–1637, www.indianamuseum.org. $7. Mon.–Sat. 9–5, Sun. 11–6.

Indiana University–Purdue University Indianapolis The 285-acre campus on the west edge of downtown and immediately north of White River State Park is the city home to both Purdue and Indiana universities. The Indiana University Medical Center is one of the country's top medical research centers. The campus is also home to internationally recognized amateur-sports facilities, including the natatorium, the University Track and Soccer Stadium, and the Indianapolis Tennis Center. Several national and international competitions take place here each year. The National Art Museum of Sport at University Place is also here; it displays works by Winslow Homer and LeRoy Neiman as well as art created by famous athletes. > 425 University Blvd., Indianapolis, tel. 317/274–5555, www.iupui.edu. Free. Daily.

Indianapolis Motor Speedway and Hall of Fame Museum Built in 1909, the famed 2½-mi oval track at the Indianapolis Motor Speedway hosts the Indianapolis 500 every Memorial Day and stock-car races the rest of the year. When it is not being used for competitions or for tire testing or practice, you can take a narrated bus ride around the track. The museum showcases showcases vintage race cars and documents the history of auto racing and winning strategies. The Tony Hulman Theatre screens a film highlighting the history of the racetrack. The complex also has cafés and gift shops. > 4790 W. 16th St., Indianapolis, tel. 317/484–6747, www.indy500.com. Museum $3, track tours $3. Daily 9–5.

Indianapolis Museum of Art Watercolors by J. M. W. Turner and the Eli Lilly Collection of Chinese Art are two of the museum's most in-depth collections. Other highlights of the permanent collection include neo-impressionist art, old-master paintings, African art, and the *Love* sculpture by Robert Indiana. The Oldfields-Lilly House and Gardens is a 22-room 1930s era mansion, which was renovated and reopened in 2002. Beyond the gardens are manicured and wooded grounds and gardens and the Indianapolis Civic Theatre. The museum is in the midst of a multiyear renovation and expansion. > 4000 Michigan Rd., Indianapolis, tel. 317/923–1331, fax 317/920–2660, www.ima-art.org. Free, $5 for Oldfields-Lilly House. Tues., Wed., Fri., and Sat. 10–5, Thurs. 10–8:30, Sun. noon–5.

Indianapolis Zoo The animals aren't caged and you won't feel trapped in this 64-acre zoo, in White River State Park. The dolphin pavilion houses the state's largest aquarium and is the world's second-largest, fully enclosed, controlled-environment, marine mammal facility. More than 3,000 animals in simulated natural habitats make their home on landscaped grounds with 1,700 species of plants. In the Living Deserts of the World, a conservatory covered by a transparent dome, birds and animals roam at will. A children's play area and hands-on animal encounter area are also in the center. > 1200 W. Washington St., Indianapolis, tel. 317/630–2001, www.indyzoo.com. $10.75. Daily 9–4.

James Whitcomb Riley Museum Home One of the more perfectly preserved Victorian houses in the United States, the house, built in 1872, is where the Hoosier poet spent the last 23 years of his life. Many of Riley's personal mementos are displayed. The entire estate looks much the same as Riley left it. > 528 Lockerbie Sq., Indianapolis, tel. 317/631–5885. $3. Tues.–Sat. 10–4, Sun. noon–4.

Madame Walker Urban Life Center and Theatre Madame C. J. Walker was the country's first black female self-made millionaire, and her remarkable life is detailed through exhibits here. African motifs accent this buff-color corner building dating from 1927, and terra-cotta pictures of African symbols embellish the 950-seat hall inside. Jazz and theater performances fill the program. In the spirit of Indiana Avenue's early 1900s heritage as a midwestern jazz center, the theater presents Jazz on the Avenue in the Casino-Ballroom on Friday nights. > 17 Indiana Ave., Indianapolis, tel. 317/236–2099.

Monument Circle A parade of memorials and churches marches northward for blocks along Meridian Street from Monument Circle, the center of downtown. The 1902 **Soldiers' and Sailors' Monument** is the drum major. Its 284-foot limestone spire pays homage to those who served in the Civil War and is crowned by the 30-foot bronze statue *Victory*, better known as *Miss Indiana*. Also on Monument Circle is the city's oldest church, the Episcopalian **Christ Church Cathedral** (55 Monument Circle, tel. 317/636–4577, www.cccindy.org, free), an 1857 Gothic country-style masterpiece, with a spire, steep gables, bell tower, and arched Tiffany windows. Tours are Sunday at noon or by appointment. Farther north in this procession is the **Indiana World War Memorial** (431 N. Meridian, tel. 317/232–7615, www.state.in.us/iwm, free), which pays tribute to fallen Hoosier veterans of World War I, World War II, the Korean War, and the Vietnam War. The circa-1929 Gothic Tudor–style Masonic **Scottish Rite Cathedral** (650 N. Meridian St., tel. 800/489–3579, www.aasr-indy.org, free) contains a 54-bell carillon and a 7,000-pipe organ. The **State Capitol** (200 W. Washington St., tel. 317/233–5293, free, weekdays 9–4) is 1½ blocks west of the Soldiers' and Sailors' Monument downtown on 9 grassy acres. Stop in the rotunda, inside the dome, to pick up self-guided tour brochures.

Morris-Butler House Dark woodwork, Victorian antiques, and chandeliers create a luxurious look in this 16-room house built in 1865 for a well-to-do family. An Indiana-made Wooten desk and paintings by Hoosier painter Jacob Cox are among the striking pieces on view. The house is in the historic Old Northside neighborhood. > 1204 N. Park Ave., Indianapolis, tel. 317/636–5409. $5. Feb.–Dec., Wed.–Sat. 10–4.

NCAA Hall of Champions Visitors to the 40,000-square-foot museum can see college games on a 144-foot video monitor, watch championship games in one of four theaters, and tour the multimedia exhibits to learn about past NCAA champs. The Hall is on the east end of the White River State Park campus. > 700 W. Washington St., Indianapolis, tel. 317/916–4225, www.ncaa.org. $7. Mon.–Sat. 10–5, Sun. noon–5.

President Benjamin Harrison Home Ornate Victorian furnishings, political mementos, and period ball gowns of the nation's 23rd president and first lady fill the circa-1875 house. Even the old carriage house on the grounds is restored to its high Victorian state. > 1230 N. Delaware St., Indianapolis, tel. 317/631–1888, www.presidentbenjaminharrison.org. $5.50. Mon.–Sat. 10–3:30.

White River Gardens Butterflies flit through the garden's conservatory, in which tropical trees brush the three-story glass dome. Outside, themed gardens demonstrate design ideas for shade, sun, and conditions in between; the garden's pros share their tips on slates scattered throughout the grounds. Special events are often held on the croquet-perfect lawn of the wedding garden. The Gardens shares its parking lot with the Indianapolis Zoo, and is on the western end of the White River State Park campus. > 1200 W. Washington St., Indianapolis, tel. 317/630–2001, www.whiterivergardens.com. $6.50. Daily 9–4.

White River State Park This 250-acre park in the heart of downtown is a cultural campus that embraces the Indianapolis Zoo at its west end and is anchored by a clutch of museums at its east end. The White River meanders through the park, which also includes a waterfall and fountains. Gentle banks slope to the river and groves of weeping willows and other trees invite visitors to picnic or just enjoy the view. This 250-acre park in the heart of downtown is the site of numerous landmarks: Victory Field baseball park, the Indianapolis Zoo, the Eiteljorg Museum of American Indians and Western Art, the National Institute for Fitness and Sport, Military Park, River Promenade, Pumphouse Visitors Center, and Celebration Plaza. The historic Central Canal and the Washington Street Bridge, which serves as a pedestrian mall and connects to the ½-mi River Promenade on the northern edge of the Indianapolis Zoo, are also here. The Promenade, which follows the upper banks of the White River, is built from 1,272 blocks of Indiana limestone and is accented with 14 stone tablets carved with renderings of famous buildings made of Indiana limestone, including New York's Empire State Building. A focal point of the Promenade is the hand-carved Rose Window, a limestone frame measuring more than 7 feet in diameter. > 801 W. Washington St., Indianapolis, tel. 317/665–9056. Daily.

Tours

Circle City Tours This company conducts sightseeing tours via bus, van, and limo and specializes in custom itineraries. Popular destinations are the Speedway, historic sites, and the historic districts. Length of tours vary. > Indianapolis, tel. 317/329–0350, www.circlecitytours.com.

Landmarks on Foot Join a group for a walking tour of an Indianapolis historic district. Options include canals and the downtown. Tours are operated by the Historic Landmarks Foundation of Indiana and last approximately 90 minutes. > 340 W. Michigan St., Indianapolis, tel. 317/639–4534, www.historiclandmarks.org.

X-pression Tours Guided bus tours to African-American heritage sites, such as the Madame Walker Theatre Center, are the specialty with this company. > 1075 Broad Ripple Ave., Indianapolis, tel. 317/257–5448.

Save the Date

MAY

Indianapolis 500 Festival A month of events lead up to the running of the Indy 500, including a parade. Events include a parade, an art show, and a Community Day, when kids can meet the drivers. > Tel. 317/927–3378, www.500festival.com.

Indianapolis 500-Mile Race Tradition and high-spirited celebrations surround the granddaddy of all car-racing events; the annual race covers 500 mi on the oval Speedway racetrack. The all-day event, held on Memorial Day weekend, draws roughly 250,000 spectators. > Tel. 317/492–6700, www.indy500.com.

JUNE

Indian Market In late June, Native American artists and artisans from across North America show and sell their wares at this juried market, one of the largest such events east of the Mississippi River. The market also has Native American dancing, food, and kids' activities. > 500 W. Washington St., Indianapolis, tel. 317/636–9378.

JUNE–AUGUST

Symphony on the Prairie The Indianapolis Symphony performs weekly outdoor concerts at the living-history museum Conner Prairie > 13400 Allisonville Rd., Fishers, tel. 317/639–4300, www.indyorch.org.

JULY

Indiana Black Expo Summer Celebration Music stars at this weeklong celebration of black culture, held in mid-July, have included UniverSoul Circus and Drums of West Africa. > 100 S. Capitol Ave., Indianapolis, tel. 317/925–2702, www.indianablackexpo.com.

AUGUST

Indiana State Fair The sixth-oldest fair in the country showcases the talents of youngsters with one of the largest 4-H programs in the country. The big midway has rides, food, a balloon race, and grandstand country-and-western entertainment. The fair runs for 10 days in mid-August. > 1202 E. 38th St., Indianapolis, tel. 317/927–7500, www.indianastatefair.com.

SEPTEMBER

Penrod Art Fair This popular art fair takes place in early September on the grounds of the Indianapolis Museum of Art. More than 250 artists display their work and music, theater, and dance performances are presented. > Tel. 317/923–1331, www.ima-art.org.

OCTOBER

Blue River Valley Pioneer Fair Pioneer craft demonstrations, cooking, and musical presentations are performed by costumed settlers at the Shelby County Fairgrounds in Shelbyville, 33 mi from Indianapolis. > Tel. 317/392–4634.

Heartland Film Festival This film festival, held in mid-October, recognizes and honors filmmakers whose work explores the human journey by expressing hope and respect for positive values of life. > 613 N. East St., Indianapolis, tel. 317/464–9405, www.heartlandfilmfest.org.

DECEMBER

Yuletide Celebration All month, the Indianapolis Symphony Orchestra stages a dazzling holiday show in the elegantly restored Hilbert Circle Theatre. The festive holiday celebration stages music, dance, and classics such as *A Christmas Carol*. > Tel. 317/639–4300 or 800/366–8457, www.indyorch.org.

WHERE TO STAY

Canterbury A member of Preferred Hotels and Resorts Worldwide, this hostelry occupies a landmark structure on the National Register of Historic Places. Built in 1928 of terra cotta–trimmed, brick-faced concrete, the hotel has a private entrance to the Circle Centre Mall. Rooms are small but elegantly furnished with wing chairs and dark-wood furniture. > 123 S. Illinois St., Indianapolis 46225, tel. 317/634–3000 or 800/538–8186, fax 317/685–2519, www.canterburyhotel.com. 74 rooms, 25 suites. Restaurant, bar, meeting rooms. AE, D, DC, MC, V. CP. $$$$

Crowne Plaza–Union Station The second floor of Union Station is comprised of 26 vintage Pullman train cars retrofitted as modern hotel rooms. The hotel's train theme continues throughout its decor, with passenger statues stationed throughout. The hotel is linked to the convention center and RCA Dome, and is one block from Circle Centre Mall and six blocks from the center of downtown. > 123 W. Louisiana St., Indianapolis 46225, tel. 317/631–2221, fax 317/236–7474, www.ichotelsgroup.com. 276 rooms, 28 suites. Restaurant, in-room data ports, cable TV, indoor pool, exercise equipment, hot tub, bar, business services. AE, D, DC, MC, V. $–$$$

Dewolf-Allerdice House Restored inside and out, this Italianate home is in the Old Northside district. Rooms are decorated with Victorian furnishings. The second floor serves as the guest wing and the entire third floor is a single suite. > 1224 Park Ave.,

Indianapolis 46202, tel. 317/822–4299, www.dewolf-allerdicehouse.com. 3 rooms, 1 suite. Library, business services. AE, D MC, V. CP. **$–$$**

Embassy Suites Downtown Lush gardens fill the atrium of this modern, glass-walled hotel. It's downtown, connected to the Circle Centre Mall via a greenery-filled skywalk. Many of the modern rooms have sweeping views of downtown. > 110 W. Washington St., Indianapolis 46204, tel. 317/236–1800, fax 317/236–1816, www.embassysuites.com. 360 suites. Restaurant, in-room data ports, microwaves, refrigerators, cable TV, indoor pool, exercise equipment, hot tub, bar, business services. AE, D, DC, MC, V. BP. **$$–$$$$**

Hyatt Regency Indianapolis This 20-story structure was one of the buildings that inspired Indianapolis's downtown renaissance. Guest rooms open onto corridors that line a soaring 20-story atrium, which is filled with potted plants, shops, several restaurants, and a health club. Rooms come in neutral tones, and many have views of the city. The hotel is linked by skywalk to the convention center, RCA Dome, and Circle Centre. > 1 S. Capitol St., Indianapolis 46204, tel. 317/632–1234, fax 317/616–6079, www.hyatt.com. 497 rooms. 2 restaurants, in-room data ports, cable TV, indoor pool, exercise equipment, hair salon, massage, bar, business services. AE, D, DC, MC, V. **$–$$$$**

Looking Glass Inn A classic-style mansion built in 1905, this establishment is in the Old Northside district of Indianapolis. The home is filled with Victorian and Victorian-style antiques, including queen-size sleigh beds and old Willowware plates on the walls. The Hideaway room spans the entire third floor and is 900 square feet. > 1319 N. New Jersey, Indianapolis 46202, tel. 317/639–9550, fax 317/684–9536. 5 rooms, 1 suite. Some in-room hot tubs, some kitchenettes, cable TV, in-room VCRs. AE, D, MC, V. BP. **$–$$**

Old Northside Bed & Breakfast An imposing brick facade hides a high-Victorian interior with painted ceilings and lots of woodwork. The Hollywood room is papered with a collage of stars. Five rooms have working fireplaces. > 1340 N. Alabama St., Indianapolis 46202, tel. 317/635–9123 or 800/635–9127, fax 317/635–9243. 7 rooms. MC, V. BP. **$–$$$**

Omni Severin Hotel Across from historic Union Station and connected to the Circle Centre Mall, this hotel has crystal chandeliers, a marble staircase, and cast-iron balustrades recalling its 1913 origins. Guest rooms are a blend of traditional and Mediterranean styles. > 40 W. Jackson Pl., Indianapolis 46225, tel. 317/634–6664 or 800/843–6664, fax 317/687–3619, www.omnihotels.com. 424 rooms. 2 restaurants, pool, health club. AE, D, DC, MC, V. **$$–$$$**

Speedway Bed & Breakfast This grand white-columned inn was built in 1906 on the site of Baker's Walnut Grove. Nowadays things rev up in May, during the Indy 500. Rooms have racing themes; you can go for the 500 room, the Nascar room, or the Track Side room, for instance. Some rooms have views of the garden or a pagoda on a goldfish pond. > 1829 Cunningham Rd., Indianapolis 46224, tel. 317/487–6531 or 800/975–3412, fax 317/481–1825, www.bbonline.com/in/speedway. 5 rooms. Some in-room hot tubs, cable TV, business services. AE, D, MC, V. BP. **¢–$$**

Stone Soup Inn Mission-style and Victorian antiques fill the rooms and lofts in this 1901 colonial-revival home on the north side of Indianapolis. The color scheme of the rooms is dark and light green; some have working fireplaces or bay windows that overlook the lily pond. In the lofts, ladders connect sitting and sleeping areas. On weekends you can get hot breakfast foods as well as rolls and muffins. > 1304 N. Central Ave., Indianapolis 46202, tel. 317/639–9550, fax 317/684–9536, www.stonesoupinn.com. 8 rooms. Some kitchenettes, some in-room hot tubs, cable TV, in-room VCRs. AE, D, MC, V. CP. **$–$$**

Tranquil Cherub Bed & Breakfast A grand oak staircase is just inside the front door of this bed-and-breakfast. Each room has either a king- or queen-size bed and antique furnishings. Perennial gardens and lily ponds dot the grounds. It's 1 mi from the Circle. > 2164 Capital Ave., Indianapolis 46202, tel. 317/923–9036, fax 317/923–8676, www.tranquilcherub.com. 4 rooms. No room phones. AE, D, MC, V. BP. $

University Place Conference Center and Hotel On the campus of Indiana University–Purdue University at Indianapolis, this 30,000-square-foot complex includes a hotel, conference facilities, a food court, restaurants, and bars. Rooms have views of the university campus, the hotel courtyard, or downtown Indianapolis. Skywalks connect it to the campus and it's 1¼ mi from downtown. > 850 W. Michigan St., Indianapolis 46202, tel. 317/269–9000 or 800/627–2700, fax 317/231–5168, www.doubletree.com. 264 rooms, 16 suites. Restaurant, in-room data ports, refrigerators, cable TV, bar, business services. AE, D, DC, MC, V. $$

The Villa Renovated in 2001, this turn-of-the-20th-century palazzo was modeled after an Italian villa. The Gothic-arched foyer ceiling is painted blue. Rooms are decorated in a light British-colonial style with pale colors and darker woods. Two rooms are in the adjacent carriage house. A full-service spa with four treatment rooms occupies the basement. The Villa is in the old Northside district. > 1456 N. Delaware, Indianapolis 46202, tel. 317/916–8500, fax 317/917–9086, www.thevillainn.com. 6 rooms. Restaurant, cable TV, spa, Internet. MC, V. BP. $$$$

WHERE TO EAT

Aristocrat Pub Collectibles, antique fixtures, dark paneling, and brass-and-wood booths give this Broad Ripple–area eatery the warmth and charm of an English pub. Fish-and-chips, burgers, and big salads can be washed down with a long list of beers and ales on tap. You can eat outside on the garden patio in good weather. > 5212 N. College Ave., Indianapolis, tel. 317/283–7388. AE, MC, V. $–$$$

Bazbeaux Locally treasured for its pizza (you can choose from 52 toppings), this downtown eatery also serves great sandwiches. It's in an old storefront in the Massachusetts Avenue arts district, and has a covered patio where you can eat outside in warmer weather. > 334 Massachusetts Ave., Indianapolis, tel. 317/636–7662. D, MC, V. No lunch Sun. $–$$$

Hard Times Cafe Chili is the staple here. You get a chili sampler when you are seated, so that you can make educated choices among the Terlingua Red (Texas style with tomato sauce and beef broth), Texas, Cincinnati, and vegetarian chilies. Also available are burgers, dogs, steaks, ribs, and salads. Country-western music plays on the jukebox, and spurs, flags, and license plates fill the walls. > 121 W. Maryland St., Indianapolis, tel. 317/916–8800. AE, MC, V. ¢–$

Hollyhock Hill In the middle of a residential neighborhood, this cheerful restaurant has a loyal following. The family-style service is like Sunday dinner at grandma's house. Plates are heaped with skillet-fried chicken, shrimp, broiled fish, and steak. > 8110 N. College Ave., Indianapolis, tel. 317/251–2294. Reservations essential. AE, MC, V. Closed Mon. $$

Jazz Cooker This big white clapboard house with a Mardi Gras mural outside dishes up Louisiana cuisine in Broad Ripple. The spicy black-bean soup and jambalaya are accompanied by live jazz on weekends, and when the weather's warm, you can eat outside on a brick patio overlooking a colorful tree- and flower-lined street. > 925 E. Westfield Blvd., Indianapolis, tel. 317/575–8312. AE, DC, MC, V. No lunch. $–$$

Magic Moments Restaurant The view of the Indianapolis skyline is particularly mag-ical at this 14th-floor penthouse restaurant. Strolling magicians entertain while you feast on such dishes as ostrich with black bean risotto and wild mushroom duxelles or strawberry chicken. The interior is simple, with mirrors and tea lights. > 1 N. Penn-sylvania St., Indianapolis, tel. 317/822–3400. Reservations essential. AE, D, DC, MC, V. Closed Sun. No lunch. **$$–$$$$**

The Majestic This elegant downtown restaurant in the 1895 Majestic Building is one block east of the Circle Centre Mall and half a block from Conseco Field House. Great steaks vie for attention with oysters and a wide selection of fish. Specialties include the baked pompano, which comes stuffed with scallops, shrimp, and crabmeat, topped with a lobster sherry sauce. > 47 S. Pennsylvania St., Indianapolis, tel. 317/636–5418. AE, DC, MC, V. Closed Sun. **$$$–$$$$**

New Orleans House On the northwest side of Indianapolis, this restaurant is noted for its buffet and bluepoint oysters on the half shell, sautéed scallops, frogs' legs, and escargot. The buffet includes peel-and-eat shrimp, oysters, seafood chowder, king-crab legs, shrimp creole, and jambalaya, as well as chicken and barbecued ribs. A piano bar provides entertainment. > 8845 Township Line Rd., Indianapolis, tel. 317/872–9670. AE, DC, MC, V. Closed Sun. No lunch. **$$$$**

Palomino This upscale, upbeat eatery has vibrantly colored walls, huge oil paintings, handblown glass chandeliers, and a lively clientele. The oven-roasted mussels in rose-mary-lemon butter and authentic paella casserole are not to be missed. > 49 W. Maryland St., Indianapolis, tel. 317/974–0400. AE, D, DC, MC, V. **$$–$$$$**

The Rathskeller This cross between a German inn and a bustling beer hall is in the historic Athenaeum Building. A big Gothic fireplace, stained-glass windows, and stuffed animal heads distinguish the beer hall; live music plays in the Biergarten in summer. The hot and cold appetizers run the gamut of German staples—bratwurst, sauerkraut, red cabbage, and smoked sausage. The *Ochsenschwanz suppe* (soup with oxtails and port wine) is a favorite. > 401 E. Michigan St., Indianapolis, tel. 317/636–0396. AE, D, DC, MC, V. No lunch weekends. **$$–$$$$**

Restaurant at the Canterbury Much more than a typical hotel restaurant, this down-town gem next to Circle Centre is one of the city's best-kept secrets. Crisp white linens contrast with the dark paneling in the intimate dining room, and the menu in-cludes classic fare such as Dover sole and pepper-crusted rack of lamb. Try the chocolate or raspberry soufflé for dessert. > 123 S. Illinois St., Indianapolis, tel. 317/634–3000. AE, MC, V. **$$–$$$$**

Rock Bottom Brewery Beer is brewed on the premises, and you can tour the brewing operation on request. In the basement are small- and large-screen TVs, six pool ta-bles, and two dart alleys. You can eat at the sidewalk tables or in the dining room, which is decorated with photographs of the Southwest. Try the homemade beer bread, served warm, and the Asiago cheese dip for starters; for your main course, try either the brown-ale chicken or the tenderloin with roasted garlic. > 10 W. Washington St., Indianapolis, tel. 317/681–8180. AE, DC, MC, V. **$–$$**

Ruth's Chris Steak House This upscale chain is furnished in old-English style, com-plete with fireplaces and luxurious tapestries. The prime filet mignon is a star on the menu, but you can also order pork chops and seafood, and the side dishes such as potatoes au gratin and steamed asparagus, ample enough to share, are classic. Cig-ars and martinis are also served. > 45 S. Illinois St., Indianapolis, tel. 317/633–1313. Reservations essential. AE, D, DC, MC, V. No lunch. **$$$–$$$$**

Slippery Noodle Inn Indiana's oldest bar is a blues institution, with live music seven nights a week. The redbrick building, built in 1850, is said to have an underground link to Union Station. The backroom was once a livery stable and later a house of prostitution. Now it's a rowdy spot for good eats with a Cajun flair. You can choose from Buffalo wings, garlic wings, teriyaki wings, or wings with cayenne pepper. The voodoo chicken is smothered in onions, peppers, and Cajun spices, with a splash of tequila. > 372 S. Meridian St., Indianapolis, tel. 317/631–6974, fax 317/631–6903. AE, D, DC, MC, V. $–$$$

Something Different/SNAX Tapas at SNAX are just enough to whet your appetite for dinner next door at sister restaurant Something Different. The setting is mod with bright colors, the menu innovative American. > 4939 E. 82nd St., Indianapolis, tel. 317/570–7700. AE, D, MC, V. Closed Sun. No lunch. $–$$

St. Elmo Steak House A city landmark since 1902, this downtown establishment is the place for big steaks, large martinis, and eye-watering shrimp-cocktail sauce. Visiting celebrities often book a table here or stop by the cigar room. > 127 S. Illinois St., Indianapolis, tel. 317/635–0636 or 800/637–1811, www.stelmos.com. AE, MC, V. No lunch. $$$–$$$$

The Villa Inside an oversize dining room of a castlelike inn just north of downtown, the menu reflects the Italian setting, with a Tuscan twist to pasta and sandwiches. > 1456 N. Delaware St., Indianapolis, tel. 317/916–8500. AE, MC, V. Closed Sun. $$–$$$

ESSENTIALS

Getting Here

Indianapolis is easy to get around just about any way you go. Driving is the most convenient option to get here from Chicago, especially if you want to see the surrounding sites, such as Conner Prairie. If you're staying downtown and don't want to drive, you can use local or tourist buses, which circulate from downtown to the museums of White River State Park. If you bring a bike, you have a wealth of trails that connect parks and neighborhoods from which to choose. Keep in mind, though, that winters are cold, so walking and biking are best reserved for warm months.

BY BUS

Greyhound schedules as many as 10 daily trips to Indianapolis, which takes about four hours from Chicago. The Greyhound station is on the south side of downtown.

IndyGo Bus lines serve the main attractions. Some lines and buses provide bike racks for people who are biking the greenways. IndyGo buses run from 4:45 AM to 11:45 PM on heavily traveled routes, with shorter schedules in the suburbs. Fares ($1) are payable upon boarding.

BUS DEPOT **Greyhound Bus Terminal** > 350 S. Illinois St., Indianapolis, tel. 317/267–3071 or 800/231–2222.

BUS LINES **Greyhound Bus Lines** > Tel. 317/267–3071 or 800/231–2222, www.greyhound.com. **IndyGo** > Tel. 317/635–3344, www.indygo.net.

BY CAR

I–65, I–70, and I–74 reach Indianapolis, crossing the city and its surrounding beltway, I–465. Navigation is easy as streets are all organized in a grid, more or less, with just about every other street running one way. Monument Circle—the central reference point of downtown—is 8 mi from the Indianapolis Airport and 6 mi from the Speedway. Street numbers are based on a rectangular coordinate system, with each block roughly equal to 100. The quadrant to the southwest of Monument Circle is largely occupied with hotels and the convention center. An emerging warehouse district is to the southeast; to the northwest is White River State Park, which embraces a cluster of museums and the zoo. To the northeast are hip neighborhoods and the arts district. Two of the most important destinations—the Indianapolis Children's Museum and Conner Prairie—are well north of Monument Circle.

All-day parking at private lots costs around $10, and there is both free and metered street parking, though it's starting to get scarce. Traffic is heaviest during the city's frequent sporting events; unless you're going yourself, it's best to steer clear of the major venues at those times in this sports-crazed town. Weekday rush-hour traffic will slow you down a little as well.

BY PLANE

Seven miles southwest of downtown, the Indianapolis International Airport is served by major and commuter airlines. The flight from Chicago is barely 45 minutes and daily departures are frequent. In 2004, a major expansion to the airport will begin and continue for several years. Be sure to allow extra time for construction delays. Public transportation does not serve the airport; taxis to downtown cost about $17.

AIRPORT **Indianapolis International Airport** > 1500 S. High School Rd., Indianapolis, tel. 317/487–9594, www.indianapolisairport.com.

CARRIERS **Air Canada** > Tel. 800/247–2262, www.aircanada.com. **America West** > Tel. 800/327–7810, www.americawest.com. **American, American Eagle** > Tel. 800/433–7000, www.aa.com. **Continental** > Tel. 800/525–0280, www.continental.com. **Continental Express** > Tel. 800/525–0280, www.continental.com. **Delta, Comair (the Delta Connection)** > Tel. 800/221–1212, www.delta.com. **Frontier** > Tel. 800/432–1359, www.frontierairlines.com. **Northwest** > Tel. 800/225–2525, www.nwa.com. **Southwest** > Tel. 800/435–9792, www.southwest.com. **United** > Tel. 800/864–8331, www.united.com. **United Express** > Tel. 800/864–8331, www.united.com. **US Airways, US Airways Express** > Tel. 800/428–4322, www.usairways.com.

BY TRAIN

Amtrak offers limited service.

TRAIN LINE **Amtrak** > Tel. 800/872–7245, www.amtrak.com.

TRAIN STATION **Union Station** > 350 S. Illinois St., Indianapolis, tel. 317/263–0550 or 800/872–7245.

Visitor Information

CONTACTS **Arts Council of Indianapolis** > Indianapolis, tel. 317/624–2563, www.indyarts.org. **Indianapolis Convention and Visitors Association** > 1 RCA Dome, Suite 100, Indianapolis 46225, tel. 317/639–4282 or 800/958–4639, www.indy.org.

Spring Green & Mineral Point

190 mi northwest of Chicago

By Joanne Cleaver

THE FAME OF SPRING GREEN, a small town on the Wisconsin River, is far greater than its size might warrant. That's because the celebrated architect Frank Lloyd Wright built his home, Taliesin, just outside Spring Green. The town itself has attracted a large community of artisans, as well as a nationally recognized classical theater company. Just south of town is House on the Rock, a former artist's retreat built atop a 60-foot chimney of rock; over time it has grown into a huge complex of buildings housing a museum of oddities and collectibles. The area consists of scenic rolling hills and large tracts of farmland.

Nearby, Mineral Point is home to dozens of potters, painters, metalworkers, sculptors, and others who cherish the long winter for creative immersion and the short, lively summer for selling off winter's production. The main street, High Street, is lined with narrow two-story brick and stone storefronts and cafés. Shops also spill over onto adjacent streets and along Shake Rag Alley, which leads to Pendarvis. The hillsides that surround Mineral Point are dotted with houses that represent nearly every type of vernacular architecture.

A visit to Taliesin can take up an entire day. The House on the Rock is also a time-consuming tour, as it is a 2-mi one-way tromp through the dozens of displays. Taking in Pendarvis and thoroughly exploring Mineral Point can also absorb a day.

Though these disparate sites are worlds apart in philosophy, they make a tidy weekend itinerary. Spring Green itself is about 35 mi west of Madison and Mineral Point is about 20 mi south of Spring Green. If you stay in either Spring Green or Mineral Point/Dodgeville, you are no more than a half hour from the three big attractions. Getting around is easy. Southwest Wisconsin is blanketed with farms and small towns. In between, you can drive through woods and meadows, and over rolling hills.

WHAT TO SEE & DO

American Players Theatre Evening performances of Shakespeare and other classics are staged in a wooded outdoor amphitheater, 3 mi south of downtown. The theater is near Taliesin off Route C. > 5950 Golf Course Rd., Spring Green, tel. 608/588–2361, www.americanplayers.org. June–Sept.
House on the Rock This artist's retreat atop a 60-foot chimney of rock 9 mi south of Spring Green is an architectural wonder, with massive fireplaces inside the building and pools of running water on the premises. Displays include a circus building, a doll building, the world's largest carousel, a mill house, and the Music of Yesterday, which has four rooms with music machines that play tunes like "Dance of the Sugar Plum Fairies." Also here is a Heritage of the Sea building, which has a giant sea creature fighting an octopus. Self-guided tours take four to five hours. The museum is approx-

imately 7 mi south of town. > 5754 Rte. 23, Spring Green, tel. 608/935–3639, www.thehouseontherock.com. $19.50. Mid-Mar.–late Oct.

Mineral Point Historic District The first district in Wisconsin to be listed on the National Register of Historic Places, this area covers the entire city and includes more than 500 structures in various architectural styles, both residential and commercial buildings. Driving and walking tours are available through the visitor center in the heart of downtown. > 225 High St., Mineral Point, tel. 608/987–3201 or 888/764–6894, www.mineralpoint.com. Visitor center: May–Sept., daily 10–4.

Pendarvis State Historical Site At this state historic site, costumed interpreters tell tales of life on Shake Rag Street as they lead you through six restored 19th-century cottages and row houses. The street's name refers to the custom of women shaking dishrags from doorways, signaling the men in the mines across the valley that the noon meal was ready. The tour of the site takes in the row houses, several additional houses that are furnished to reflect points in the site's history, and the hilly grounds. Across the street is the Merry Christmas Mine, which is currently being restored to its originial condition as an operating mine. > 114 Shake Rag St., Mineral Point, tel. 608/987–2122. $8. May–Oct., daily 10–5.

Taliesin Famed architect Frank Lloyd Wright lived in this home on the banks of the Wisconsin River for the last 50 years of his life. The house still has original furniture, art collections, gardens, courtyards, and the tea circle, a dining area. Guided tours are available; strolling the grounds unguided is not allowed. Wright also designed the Hillside Studio and Theatre in 1902 as a boarding school for his aunts to run, which they did for 15 years. In the 1930s it became summer quarters for students at the Frank Lloyd Wright School of Architecture. The interior can be toured. Several other buildings and structures reflect key turning points in the development of Wright's architectural philosophy and techniques. Adjacent to the complex is a small cemetery where Wright is buried. A visitor center has a café and a gift shop that carries books about Wright and items derived from his designs. > 5607 Rte. C, Spring Green, tel. 608/588–7900, fax 608/588–7514, www.taliesinpreservation.org. Prices vary. May–Oct., daily 8:30–5:30.

NEARBY

Blackhawk Lake Recreation Area This recreation area is operated by the Wisconsin Department of Natural Resources and is not a state park. Thus, some of its rules and policies differ from state park rules and regulations. The area has a walleye-stocked lake, hiking trails, campground, playgrounds, and cross-country skiing trails. > 2025 Rte. BH, Highland, tel. 608/623–2707, www.blackhawklake.com. $5. Daily.

Blue Mound State Park This 1,153-acre state park, 33 mi west of Mineral Point, is built atop mounds that have been a southwestern Wisconsin landmark since pioneer days. View the surrounding countryside from the observation towers, and hike or ski the nature trails. There are also scenic picnic areas, and a large swimming pool. > 4350 Mounds Park Rd., Blue Mounds, tel. 608/437–5711, www.dnr.state.wi.us. $10. Daily.

Cave of the Mounds Four miles west of Blue Mounds, 36 mi west of Mineral Point, this registered National Natural Landmark known for the variety, color, and delicacy of its formations is one of the most significant caves in the upper Midwest. Grounds include gardens, picnic areas, a visitor center, and a nature trail. The cave temperature is 50°F year-round. > 2975 Cave of the Mounds Rd., Blue Mounds, tel. 608/437–3038, www.caveofthemounds.com. $12. Mid-Mar.–mid-Nov., daily 10–4; mid-Nov.–mid-Mar., weekends 10–4.

Governor Dodge State Park Wisconsin's second-largest state park 3 mi north of town includes more than 5,000 acres with steep hills, stony bluffs, two man-made lakes, and a waterfall. You can camp, fish, swim, picnic, and use the trails for hiking, mountain biking, horseback riding, cross-country skiing, and snowmobiling. There's even an equestrian campground. > 4175 Rte. 23, Dodgeville, tel. 608/935–2315, www.dnr.state.wi.us. $7. Daily.

Little Norway This farmstead, 38 mi west of Mineral Point, was built by Norwegian settlers in 1856; today, costumed guides lead you through authentically furnished log buildings and a wooden church built for Chicago's 1893 Columbian Exposition. You can climb up, around, and through the small buildings to see how settlers transplanted their agricultural traditions to the new land. The church's many treasures include an original manuscript written in 1873 by Norwegian composer Edvard Grieg. > 3576 Rte. JG N, Blue Mounds, tel. 608/437–8211, www.littlenorway.com. $10. May, June, Sept., and Oct., daily 9–5; July and Aug., daily 9–7.

Mount Horeb Area Museum For a full history of Mount Horeb, this museum has it all: local artifacts, school, church, and regional government records, photographs, textiles, and plot maps from 1860 to the present. The museum is 33 mi west of Mineral Point. > 100 S. 2nd St., Mount Horeb, tel. 608/325–7648, www.trollway.com. Free. Fri.–Sun. 10–4.

Mount Horeb Mustard Museum Pots of mustard from around the world, antique pots that once held mustard, and all manner of mustard lore and advertising occupy this small museum. You can sample mustards, chutneys, hot sauces, salsas, jams, curds, vinegars, marinades, and so on. Discover new ways to use mustard in cooking, and go home with a whimsical "Poupon-U" collegiate T-shirt. > 109 E. Main, Mount Horeb, tel. 608/437–3986 or 800/438–6878, www.mustardmuseum.com. Free. Daily 10–5.

Shopping

Mineral Point Shopaholics could spend a whole day here shopping for antiques, collectibles, textiles, toys, handicrafts, and art on High Street and its adjoining streets.

Mount Horeb Spiffed up in the early 2000s, this pleasant downtown has numerous specialty shops as well as six antiques stores. Several shops specialize in Scandinavian imports, reflecting the heritage of area settlers.

Save the Date

JUNE

Midsummer's Eve Little Norway celebrates the high point of summer, as close to the summer solstice as possible. The day is filled with Norwegian dances, flower wreath weaving, and other traditions that help celebrate the longest, lightest day of the year. > Little Norway, Blue Mounds, tel. 608/437–8211, www.littlenorway.com.

JUNE & SEPTEMBER

Antiques at Shake Rag Alley Dealers from all over the Midwest set up shop in Mineral Point, held in early June and in late September. Wares sold include old pottery, household implements such as corncob-shape baking tins, and vintage commercial signs. > Mineral Point, tel. 888/764–6894, www.mineralpoint.com.

SEPTEMBER

Cornish Festival and Taste of Mineral Point Sample a variety of foods from local restaurants including the area's famous spicy, nut-and-raisin-filled Cornish pastries called "figgy hobbin." Bus tours of the Mineral Point Historic District and Cornish and Celtic entertainment are also part of the festivities. This downtown festival is held the last weekend of the month. > Tel. 888/764–6894.

OCTOBER

Fall Art Tour Local artisans open their studios for a three-day behind-the-scenes peek at the painting, sculpting, potting, weaving, goldsmithing, and quilting processes, held in the middle of October. The tour is a combination walking and driving tour that directs visitors to studios in Mineral Point, Spring Green, and Dodgeville. > Mineral Point, tel. 608/987–3201, www.mineralpoint.com.

DECEMBER

Candlelight Shopping and Gallery Night Come early December, you can see shops and galleries decked out with Christmas merchandise. Galleries hold open houses and sometimes tours of local historic homes decked out for Christmas are given. > Mineral Point, tel. 888/764–6894, www.mineralpoint.com.

WHERE TO STAY

MINERAL POINT

Brewery Creek Inn & Guest House In the heart of Mineral Point, this inn is ideally located for starting walking tours. Rooms with an exposed-brick wall and antique furniture overlook the historic district; three have fireplaces. Nearby is Shake Rag House, a restored miner's cottage with two four-room suites. > 23 Commerce St., Mineral Point 53565, tel. 608/987–3298, www.brewerycreek.com. 7 rooms, 2 suites. Restaurant, cable TV, pub. DC, MC, V. CP. **$$–$$$**

Knudson's Guest House Though the Prairie-style bungalow is spacious, it is on a well-traveled local route on the outskirts of Mineral Point. Oak woodwork, antiques, and restored wooden furniture enrich the rooms. > 415 Ridge St., Mineral Point 53565, tel. 608/987–2733. 3 rooms. No credit cards. BP. **$**

Red Shutters Bed & Breakfast Just blocks from the center of Mineral Point, this federal-style house overlooks its own gardens. The rooms have a homey Prairie-Victorian look, with rocking chairs and patchwork quilts. > 221 Clowney St., Mineral Point 53565, tel. 608/987–2268, www.redshutters.com. 2 rooms without bath. No credit cards. BP. **$**

SPRING GREEN

Hill Street Bed & Breakfast This Queen Anne Victorian is in a residential area just a few blocks from downtown. Standout features include oak woodwork, crown molding, a large staircase at the entryway, two living rooms, and a front porch with swings. > 353 W. Hill St., Spring Green 53588, tel. 608/588–7751, www.hillstreetbb.com. 7 rooms, 5 with bath. MC, V. BP. **¢–$**

Prairie House Built in 1983 in Frank Lloyd Wright Prairie style, this motel has modern, spacious rooms. On the landscaped grounds are a water fountain, evergreens, and hardwood trees. > E4884 U.S. 14, Spring Green 53588, tel. 608/588–2088. 51 rooms. Exercise room, hot tub, sauna, game room. AE, DC, MC, V. **$**

Round Barn Lodge This hostelry started life as a dairy barn in 1914 and housed some two dozen cattle until 1949 when it was converted first into a truck stop and then into a full-service restaurant and bar; you can still see the original rafters 50 feet up. Guest rooms have cathedral ceilings. > U.S. 14, Spring Green 53533, tel. 608/588–2568, fax 608/588–2100, www.roundbarn.com. 44 rooms. Restaurant, cable TV, pool, in-room hot tubs, sauna, no-smoking rooms. DC, MC, V. **$**

Usonian Inn The inn is named after Wright's philosophy of everyday utility. It's an archetypal 1940s-era motel: long and plain with rooms that overlook adjoining farms. The hotel is close to Taliesin and Spring Green. > U.S. 14 at Rte. 23, Spring Green 53565, tel. 608/588–2323 or 877/876–6426, www.usonianinn.com. 11 rooms. MC, V. CP. Closed Nov.–Apr. ¢

NEARBY

Best Western Quiet House & Suites This all-suites hotel is near Mineral Point. Rooms are rustic with wood paneling and old-world coverlets. > 1130 N. Johns St., Dodgeville 53533, tel. 608/935–7739, fax 608/935–7724. 39 suites. Microwaves, refrigerators, cable TV, gym, meeting rooms, no-smoking rooms. AE, D, MC, V. CP. $–$$

Bettinger House Bed & Breakfast North of Spring Green, this Victorian house is in a secluded grove. Victorian and vintage wicker furnishings enrich the rooms. > 855 Wachter Ave. (Rte. 23), Plain 53577, tel. 608/546–2951, fax 608/546–2951, www.bettingerbnb.com. 5 rooms. MC, V. BP. ¢–$

Don Q Inn The lobby of this offbeat motel 2 mi north of town has a large fireplace surrounded by old-style barbershop chairs. The 24 suites have themes—among them a cave, Cupid's corner (with a heart-shape bed), and jungle safari quarters. > 3656 Rte. 23 N, Dodgeville 53533, tel. 608/935–2321 or 800/666–7848, www.fantasuite.com. 36 rooms, 24 suites. Restaurant, some in-room hot tubs, cable TV, indoor-outdoor pool, hot tub. AE, DC, MC, V. CP. ¢–$$$$

House on the Rock Inn Geared for families, this cedar-wood hotel provides suites and rooms in a variety of configurations. The 40-foot submarine and the waterfall in the kids' pool echo the outrageous collections of its namesake museum, 7 mi north of the hotel. > 3591 Rte. 23, Dodgeville 53533, tel. 608/935–3711, www.houseontherock.com. 114 rooms. Restaurant, cable TV, indoor pool, bar. DC, MC, V. CP. $–$$$

CAMPING

Blackhawk Lake Recreation Area Open year-round, this recreation area provides plenty of amenities, including boat mooring sites, sand volleyball, a beach, and a nature center. Campers must buy a weekend pass for $10. > Rte. BH, Highland 53543, tel. 608/623–2707, fax 608/623–2977, www.blackhawklake.com. 78 partial hookups, 82 tent sites. Picnic tables, playground. MC, V. ¢

Governor Dodge State Park Open year-round, this popular state park fills up quickly especially for holiday weekends. Nonresidents must pay a $10 pass to enter the park. There's also a $9.50 reservation fee. The park has hiking, fishing, and boating opportunities. > 4175 Rte. 23 N, Dodgeville 53533, tel. 698/935–2315 or 888/947–2757. 298 sites. Flush toilets, showers. Reservations essential. MC, V. ¢

WHERE TO EAT

MINERAL POINT

Brewery Creek Housed in an 1854 inn, this rustic pub serves oversize burgers and salads. To help you wash down your meal, you can choose from one of its own ales, beers, or sodas. > 23 Commerce St., Mineral Point, tel. 608/987–3298. DC, MC, V. Closed weekdays Nov.–May. No dinner Sun. and Mon. ¢–$$

Miners Point Pasties are the specialty here, with several varieties served daily. You can also get pizza and sandwiches. > 851 Dodge St., Mineral Point, tel. 608/987–3558. MC, V. ¢–$

Red Rooster Café Decorated with a rooster motif, this breakfast-only café is known for its homemade pasties, pastries, bread pudding, and "figgy hobbin"—a Cornish pastry with walnuts, raisins, brown sugar, and cinnamon served with hot caramel and whipped cream. Skillet breakfasts are hearty and inexpensive. > 158 High St., Mineral Point, tel. 608/987–9936. No credit cards. No dinner. ¢–$

Shake Rag Alley Sheltered beneath spreading trees and a short walk from Pendarvis, Shake Rag Alley provides a respite from the rigors of history. The gift and antiques shops and tearoom occupy several stone cottages; when it's warm, tea is served on the adjoining patio among planters tumbling with flowers. > 18 Shake Rag St., Mineral Point, tel. 608/987–3317. MC, V. Closed Nov.–Apr. ¢–$$

SPRING GREEN

General Store Coffee is strong and sandwiches generous at this country café and general store. Try the Polish potato pancakes and tarragon chicken salad. The breakfast menu is expanded on weekends and includes vegetarian options. > 137 S. Albany St., Spring Green, tel. 608/588–7070. MC, V. No dinner. ¢

Post House Home-style cooking reigns supreme here, in one of oldest operating restaurants in the state—the original restaurant was established in 1857. Turkey, leg of lamb, prime rib, and roast duck are the top-selling items in this casual spot. No reservations are accepted on Friday. > 127 W. Jefferson St., Spring Green, tel. 608/588–2595. MC, V. Closed Mon. Nov.–May. No lunch. $–$$

The Shed A hometown favorite, this casual eatery specializes in sandwiches. Try the "Ms. Ruthie," which is a deep-fried haddock fillet loaded with bacon, cheese, and sauce. > 123 N. Lexington, Spring Green, tel. 608/588–9049. MC, V. ¢–$$

NEARBY

Old Feed Mill, LLC On the eastern edge of downtown of Mazomanie, 15 mi east of Spring Green, this restaurant serves hearty country entrées, such as smoked pork chops, in a room reminiscent of an old farmhouse. You can purchase baked goods for takeout. > 114 Cramer St., Mazomanie, tel. 608/795–4909. MC, V. Closed Mon. No dinner Sun. $$–$$$$

ESSENTIALS

Getting Here

The only way to get to the Spring Green and Mineral Point area is by car; no bus or train service is available. The closest airport is Madison's Dane County Airport, at which you would need to rent a car to drive here.

BY CAR

To get to Spring Green, take I–90 north to Madison, where you pick up U.S. 12 (U.S.18) West. Follow U.S. 12 through Madison to U.S. 14 West. Take U.S. 14 West to Spring Green; red barns dot the landscape from this point on. You can also take a tidy circular drive of U.S. 14 from Black Earth to Spring Green; Route 23 South to Mineral Point; Route 18 (Route 151) to Mount Horeb; and Route 78 North again to pick up U.S. 14 in Black Earth. This drive will take you past all the main destinations and through several towns that provide a cornucopia of antiques, art galleries, and offbeat shops. Route 18 (Route 151) between Dodgeville and Mount Horeb includes several side trips, including a small cave complex and an enchanted Norwegian valley. Farms, small hamlets, valleys, and creeks line your route. For the most part, roads are well-maintained, two-lane state and county highways. Parking is plentiful, and either free or metered, for all the destinations.

Visitor Information

CONTACTS **Mount Horeb Area Chamber of Commerce** > 100 S. 1st St., Mount Horeb 53572, tel. 888/767–7929, www.trollway.com. **Uplands** > Box 202, Mount Horeb 53572, tel. 800/279–9472, www.uplands.ws.

Springfield

200 mi southwest of Chicago

19

By Rick Marzec

IF YOU ASK ANYONE WHO LIVES OR WORKS IN SPRINGFIELD, "Why do people visit a city that sits in the middle of cornfields?" the one-word answer you nearly always hear is "Lincoln." After you spend a weekend in Springfield, you may come to realize that the "Lincoln" experience means a whole lot more than you ever imagined.

The first—and obvious—interpretation of Lincoln refers to Abraham Lincoln, the 16th president of the United States. It's in Springfield where you can visit all the historic sites associated with his rise to the presidency. You can see the actual office where he practiced law and stand in the same train depot where thousands of people waved a final good-bye to the president-elect before he boarded a train to the White House.

His assassination had an equal impact on the city. It was here where the cross-country train procession carrying his body ended. His casket was put on display and viewed by more than 75,000 people in two days. And just north of downtown is where you can find the Lincoln Tomb, which serves as the final resting place for both him and his family.

Another part of the Lincoln experience is learning about the man. Lincoln spent six years in nearby New Salem Village, which today has been painstakingly restored to provide you with a glimpse of day-to-day living in the middle of the wilderness during the 1830s. Lincoln later moved to Springfield where he lived for 24 years. His home is now a national monument and is open to the public. After Lincoln's assassination, the town preserved all the Lincoln-related items they could find. Today, you can still visit the family pew and even see his bank ledger.

Another interpretation of the Lincoln experience refers neither to the president nor the man, but rather to politics in general. In 1837 Lincoln and a political group called the Long Nine—so named because all members were more than 6 feet tall—convinced the legislature to move the Capitol from Vandalia to Springfield. Since then, Springfield has been the center of Illinois government and serves as the home of the governor and all the state's highest elected officials. The State Library and State Archives are also here.

Because the town's primary business is government, two distinct Springfields have emerged. The weekday Springfield bustles with activity of the State Assembly and government agencies, but the weekend Springfield becomes peaceful and quiet, since many members of the legislature have left for their respective hometowns. This helps to make a weekend visit to the area even more relaxing and easier to stroll around town.

But there is more to Springfield than all things Lincoln. Non-Abe sights include a zoo, a museum, city parks, a beach on Lake Springfield, and plenty of downtown specialty stores. Historic Route 66 runs through town, and you can find fun sites associated with this road. The once-deserted downtown area on weekends now bubbles with a resurgence of new businesses, restaurants, and bars—all of which are within walking distance of the Old State Capitol Plaza. The city is not without its annual events, which include central Illinois's largest art exhibit, live outdoor theater, and the Illinois State Fair which attracts more than a million people to this city of 110,000.

WHAT TO SEE & DO

Abraham Lincoln Presidential Library This modern, high-tech library houses the state of Illinois's 46,000-item Lincoln Collection, which includes 1,500 documents written or signed by Lincoln, plus the inkwell and desk he used to sign the Emancipation Proclamation. The building also contains Illinois State Historical Library's 12 million items, including books, pamphlets, manuscripts, and other material dating back to the earliest settlers of the state. An adjacent museum includes displays about Lincoln's life and times; a multimedia presentation is shown in the museum's Union Theater. > 112 N. 6th St., Springfield, tel. 217/785–0348, www.alincoln-library.com. Free. Daily 8:30–5.

Dana–Thomas House State Historic Site This Frank Lloyd Wright–designed mansion two blocks south of the governor's mansion is considered one of his finest Prairie-style homes. It is complete with original furniture, art glass doors, light fixtures, and windows. > 301 E. Lawrence Ave., Springfield, tel. 217/782–6776. $3. Wed.–Sun. 9–4.

Daughters of Union Veterans of the Civil War Museum Civil War records of both the Union and Confederate armies are on display at this museum, four blocks from downtown. Other Civil War artifacts are also on display, including photos, medals, currency, and uniforms. > 503 S. Walnut St., Springfield, tel. 217/544–0616. Free. Weekdays 9–noon and 1–4, weekends by appointment.

Edwards Place Once the home of city socialites Benjamin and Helen Edwards, this preserved 1830s Italianate mansion sits in a park six blocks north of downtown Springfield. An adjoining complex houses the Springfield Art Association, an art gallery, and the Michael Victor II Art Library. > 700 N. 4th St., Springfield, tel. 217/523–2631. Donation suggested to house and gallery, library free. House tours by appointment only; art gallery and library weekdays 10–5, Sat. 10–3.

Executive Mansion This is the third-oldest continuously occupied governor's home in the nation. Seven U.S. presidents, including Lincoln, have stayed as guests here. Three levels of the Illinois governor's home are open to the public for viewing. > 410 E. Jackson St., Springfield, tel. 217/782–6450. Free. Tues. and Thurs. 9:30–11 and 2–3:30, Sat. 9:30–11.

Henson Robinson Zoo More than 33 species of rare and exotic animals are housed in naturalistic settings at this zoo, 4 mi southeast of downtown. A petting area and programs for kids round out the attractions. > 1100 E. Lake Dr., Springfield, tel. 217/753–6217, fax 217/529–8748, www.hensonrobinsonzoo.org. $3. Mar.–mid-Oct., weekdays 10–5, weekends 10–6; mid-Oct.–Feb., daily 10–4.

Illinois Korean War Memorial In the Oakridge Cemetery, next to the Vietnam Veterans Memorial, resides this circular, gray granite monument. The memorial pays tribute to the 1,748 citizens of Illinois killed in action in the Korean War. Encircled by the wall are a bell representing liberty and statues of military figures in uniforms of the army, navy, air force, and marines. > 1500 Monument Ave., Springfield, tel. 217/782–2717. Free. Apr.–Oct., daily 7 AM–8 PM; Nov.–Mar., daily 7–5.

Illinois State Capitol Five blocks west of downtown, this center for state government was built from 1868 to 1888. When the Illinois House and Senate are in session, you can watch the proceedings from galleries. The building also houses the offices of the governor, lieutenant governor, secretary of state, comptroller, and treasurer. Across the Capitol's parking lot is the **Capitol Complex Visitors Center** (425 S. College St., tel. 217/524–6620, Mon. 9–3:30, Tues.–Fri. 8–4:30, Sat. 9–4), where you can find information and exhibits on the Capitol, the State Archives, State Library, and state office buildings. A 20-minute video is presented. > 2nd St. and Capitol Ave., Springfield, tel. 217/782–2099. Free. Weekdays 8–4, weekends 9–3.

Illinois State Museum Permanent and changing displays and interactive exhibits tell the story of Illinois land, life, people, and art. Three centuries of family life are represented through both dioramas and interactive displays. A museum store sells crafts made by Illinois artisans, as well as toys, books, and gifts. > 502 S. Spring St., Springfield, tel. 217/782–7386, fax 217/782–1254, www.museum.state.il.us. Free. Mon.–Sat. 8:30–5, Sun. noon–5.

Illinois Vietnam Veterans Memorial A black-and-gray granite structure topped by an eternal flame honors the 2,981 citizens of Illinois who served in the Vietnam War and died or are still missing. Inscribed below the flame are hymns of the army, navy, air force, marines, and coast guard. Memorabilia is often left at the walls by friends and family of those honored. > 1500 Monument Ave., Springfield, tel. 217/782–2717. Free. Apr.–Oct., daily 7 AM–8 PM; Nov.–Mar., daily 7–5.

Lincoln Depot President-elect Lincoln bid farewell to Springfield here as he left for Washington, D.C., in 1861. You can look at two restored waiting rooms (one for women and one for the luggage and tobacco-spitting men), displays of people and places close to Lincoln, and an audiovisual show that re-creates the 12-day trip to his inauguration. > 10th and Monroe Sts., Springfield, tel. 217/544–8695 or 217/788–1356. Free. Apr.–Aug., daily 10–4.

Lincoln–Herndon Law Office Building Lincoln practiced law with William Herndon at this office downtown from 1843 to 1852. On the plaza of the Old State Capitol, this is the only surviving structure in which Lincoln maintained working law offices. Visits to the building are by guided tours only and include a video and a stop at a re-created 1846 post office. > 6th and Adams Sts., Springfield, tel. 217/785–7960 or 217/785–7289. $2 suggested donation. Mar.–Oct., Tues.–Sat. 9–5; Nov.–Feb., daily 9–4 (last tour 45 mins before closing).

Lincoln Home National Historic Site The only home he ever owned, this is where Lincoln's family resided for 17 years. Built in 1839, the home has been restored with furnishings and wallpaper that replicate how it appeared when the Lincolns lived there. Tickets are required to tour the inside of the Lincoln Home and you can only purchase them at the visitor center, one block west at 426 South 7th Street. It's best to arrive early, as tickets are issued on a first-come, first-served basis. > 413 S. 8th St., Springfield, tel. 217/492–4241 Ext. 221. Free. Daily 8:30–5.

Lincoln Memorial Garden and Nature Center Five miles of wooded trails lead you through the same landscape Lincoln walked. Designed by landscape architect Jens Jensen, you can see dogwoods blooming in spring, colorful wildflowers in summer, and the hues of yellow and orange maple leaves in fall. This park is 10 mi south of Springfield, on the south bank of Lake Springfield. > 2301 E. Lake Dr., Springfield, tel. 217/529–1111, www.lmgnc.com. Free. Garden: daily dawn–dusk; nature center: Tues.–Sat. 10–4, Sun. 1–4.

Lincoln Shrines Abe Lincoln's presence is a big part of this town—nowhere more so than in the buildings where he lived and worked. You can learn more about the president—and the man—by visiting many of the buildings that have been preserved for a century and a half.

Lincoln had to pay mortgage and grocery bills like everyone else. Inside Bank One, you can view the **Lincoln Ledger** (Bank One, 1 E. Old State Capitol Plaza, free, weekdays 8–5:30), his original account ledger with Springfield Marine and Fire Insurance. Inside Springfield's first church, the First Presbyterian Church, is the **Lincoln Pew** (321 S. 7th St., free, June–Sept., weekdays 10–4), Abe and Mary Lincoln's family pew. The church, built in 1830, also contains beautiful Tiffany windows.

Lincoln's Tomb (1500 Monument Ave., free, Mar.–Oct., daily 9–5: Nov.–Feb., daily 9–4), in the Oak Ridge Cemetery, is the final resting place of Abraham Lincoln, Mary Todd Lincoln, and three of their four sons. The tomb was paid for with public donations and completed in 1874. A special Civil War Retreat Ceremony is held each Tuesday evening in summer. Serving as the Illinois statehouse from 1839 to 1876, the **Old State Capitol State Historic Site** (1 Old State Capitol Plaza, $2 suggested donation, Mar.–Oct., daily 9–5; Nov.–Feb., daily 9–4) is where Lincoln worked for 23 years trying hundreds of cases and using its law library. It was in the Hall of Representatives where he gave his immortal speech: "A house divided against itself cannot stand." In the same hall, President Lincoln's body lay in state as an estimated 75,000 mourners filed past on May 3 and 4, 1865.

Museum of Funeral Customs At the entrance to Oak Ridge Cemetery, this museum aims to demystify cultural death rites by showcasing the history of American funeral service, grief, and mourning customs. Highlights of the self-guided tour include a scale model of Lincoln's funeral procession, an 1870-era home funeral, a collection of turn-of-the-20th-century mourning jewelry and clothing, and a 1920s embalming room. You can cap off your visit by picking up a few chocolate caskets at the gift shop. > 1440 Monument Ave., Springfield, tel. 217/544–3480, www.funeralmuseum.org. $3. Tues.–Sat. 10–4, Sun. 1–4.

Shea's Gas Station Museum This eclectic collection of gas station and roadside memorabilia has become a favorite photo stop for Route 66 travelers from around the world. Bill Shea himself is happy to share stories about every item in his collection and his 50 years alongside Route 66. You are "required" to sign his guest book, which includes names from as far away as Germany and Thailand. > 2075 Peoria Rd., Springfield, tel. 217/522–0475. Donations accepted. Tues.–Fri. 7–4, Sat. 7–noon.

Springfield Children's Museum Kids and adults alike can enjoy the exhibits on art, architecture, health, and nature at this museum a block east of the Old State Capitol. > 619 E. Washington St., Springfield, tel. 217/789–0679. $3. Mon., Wed., Fri. 10–4, Thurs. 10–7, weekends 11–4.

Thomas Rees Memorial Carillon You can climb the circular staircase or take an elevator to see a spectacular view of the city from the third-largest bell tower in the world. You can also attend a carillon Sunday- or Wednesday-evening concert throughout the summer here, at Washington Park. > 1740 W. Fayette Ave., Springfield, tel. 217/753–6219 or 217/544–1751, www.carillon-rees.org. $2. June–Aug., Tues.–Sun. noon–8; Sept.–May, weekends noon–8.

Vachel Lindsay Home Built around 1850 by the same designer-builder of the Lincoln Home, this Victorian home is the 1987 birthplace of the 20th-century "prairie poet" and

Get Your Kicks from Route 66

IT WAS A RIBBON OF HIGHWAY THAT STRETCHED 2,400 MI, *from Chicago to St. Louis and west to Los Angeles. In the* Grapes of Wrath, *John Steinbeck referred to is as "The Mother Road"—the route to head west in search of the promised land. This compilation of brick, cement, and asphalt would also become immortalized in song and film as the symbol of American's quest for adventure.*

Originally created in 1926 from a patchwork of state and county roads, Route 66 served as the foundation for untold millions of stories. But by the late 1970s, as the need for faster and safer highways increased, the Illinois portion of the old route was replaced by the speedier I–55.

However, neither the memories of Route 66 nor some of the original pavement have been replaced. Today, if you're driving between Chicago and Springfield, you can explore sections of the old route and take an imaginary trip to what it was like to travel several generations ago. In fact, travelers from around the world come here today with the specific purpose of driving on this legendary American highway.

The added bonus for the Chicago–Springfield driver is that it helps break up the monotony of driving on the interstate for over three hours. Though the route originated in Chicago, the best remnants of the route are now found south of Joliet. The road, which is clearly marked Historic Route 66, parallels the east side of I–55 almost the entire way. And because the old route still cuts through the heart of town, Springfield becomes an easy place to either start or end the journey.

Although some stretches are now nothing more than a frontage road for the interstate, other sections veer away and take you through the main streets of such small towns as McLean, Lexington, and Dwight. Along the route are as many shells of businesses that once served drivers in pre-interstate times as there are renovated gas stations and re-created cafés and motels.

You might even find a business that still exists from those long-ago times.

Keep your eyes open for roadside historical markers along the way. In Towanda, for example, the original roadway is preserved for several miles. Though weeds now grow through the pavement's cracks, you can almost imagine hearing a '56 Chevy V-8 convertible rev past you on its way toward nearby "Dead Man's Curve."

This drive along Old Route 66 provides a great diversion during the trek to or from Springfield.

artist, Vachel Lindsay. The house has been restored to look as it would have appeared in 1917. > 603 S. 5th St., Springfield, tel. 217/524–0901. Free. Tues.–Sat. noon–4.

Washington Park Botanical Gardens The domed conservatory in this 20-acre park is one of central Illinois's major horticultural attractions. The surrounding grounds, which you can stroll while the sun is up, include seasonal display beds, rose and shade gardens, a rookery, and perennial borders. > 1740 W. Fayette Ave., Springfield, tel. 217/753–6228. Free. Grounds: daily sunrise–sunset; domed conservatory: weekdays noon–4, weekends noon–5.

NEARBY

George Colin Art Studio & Gallery In the middle of the Illinois River countryside lies this quirky home of nationally known folk artist George Colin and his wife Winne. He still paints, and his colorful works hang in New York's American Museum of Folk as well as in the homes of former President Bush and Oprah Winfrey. The gallery is 10 mi northeast of Springfield on Route 97, roughly halfway to Lincoln's New Salem. > 6111 Mill St., Salisbury, tel. 217/626–2300. Free. Daily 9–5.

Lincoln's New Salem This historic site is a reconstruction of the village where Lincoln spent six years of his early adulthood. Over two dozen houses, workshops, stores, mills, and a school have been reproduced and fully furnished as they might have been in the 1830s. (One building, the Onstot Cooper Shop, is an original building.) You can watch costumed interpreters spin wool and forge horseshoes as they take on the roles of characters who lived and worked in the village. Museum exhibits, with an 18-minute orientation film, are housed in the visitor center. Campgrounds and picnic areas are also available. > Rte. 97, 20 mi northwest of Springfield, Petersburg, tel. 217/632–4000, www.lincolnsnewsalem.com. $2 suggested donation. Mar.–Oct., Wed.–Sun. 9–5; Nov.–Feb., daily 8–4.

Under the Prairie Frontier Archeological Museum At the base of Elkhart Hill, 20 mi northwest of Springfield off I-55, this museum has one of the largest collections of pre–Civil War archaeological artifacts in the Midwest, including earthenware pottery and hand-forged iron tools. A visit to this museum is particularly good following a visit to Lincoln's New Salem to help you better understand the time frame. Adjoining the museum is the Bluestem Bake Shop, which sells freshly made baked goods, soups, and sandwiches. > 109 Governor Ogleby St., Elkhart, tel. 217/947–2522, www.undertheprairie.com. $3. Wed.–Sun. 10–4.

Tours

Springfield Visitors Bureau For groups of 15 or more, the bureau will create a personalized itinerary of Springfield. They will also book your individual tour appointments at each site and provide printed schedule confirmation. > 109 N. 7th St., Salisbury, tel. 800/545–7300, www.visit-springfieldillinois.com.

Save the Date

FEBRUARY & MARCH

Maple Syrup Time Demonstrations of maple syrup–making from sap gathering to sugaring down take place weekends from the middle of February to the middle of March at the Lincoln Memorial Garden and Nature Center. The center is 10 mi south of Springfield on the south bank of Lake Springfield. > 2301 E. Lake Dr., tel. 217/529–1111.

MARCH

Annual Illinois Horse Fair Held on the Illinois State Fairgrounds, on the north side of town, the second weekend of March, this is the largest nonracing horse event in all of Illinois. Clinics on reining and training, plus over 120 vendors selling all kinds of equestrian gear and accessories, round out the fair. > 801 Sangamon Ave., tel. 217/498–8000.

APRIL

International Livestock Exposition Four weeks of events for the whole family, including clowns, horse acts, and trick-riding events come to the Illinois State Fairgrounds. > Tel. 217/787–4653.

MAY

Old Capitol Art Fair The largest juried art fair in central Illinois, this fair displays the work of more 200 national artists at the Old State Capitol Plaza in the middle of May. > 1 Old State Capitol Plaza, tel. 217/528–5785, www.socaf.org.

JUNE

International Carillon Festival Carillon artists from all over the world perform at evening concerts during this weeklong festival at the Thomas Rees Memorial Carillon in Washington Park. > 1740 W. Fayette Ave., tel. 217/753–6219, www.carillon-rees.org.
Municipal Band Concerts The community band performs outdoor concerts in the evening several times a week at Douglas Park, 1 mi north of downtown. > MacArthur and Jefferson Sts., tel. 217/789–2360.

JUNE–AUGUST

114th Infantry Retreat Ceremony Illinois Volunteer Infantry wear authentic period clothing for this event at the Lincoln Tomb State Historic Site in Oak Ridge Cemetery. It takes place every Tuesday evening in June, July, and August. > 1500 Monument Ave., tel. 217/782–2717.

JULY

Capitol City Celebration July Fourth festivities on the New State Capitol lawn include live patriotic music capped off by an evening of fireworks. > 2nd St. and Capitol Ave., tel. 800/545–7300.

AUGUST

Illinois State Fair One of the country's biggest and best state fairs, this 10-day event in the first half of August showcases livestock and produce from all over the state, as well as nationally known performers. Carnival rides, food, and exhibits help keep you going from morning until night. > 801 Sangamon Ave., tel. 217/782–6661.
LPGA State Farm Rail Classic This annual women's golf tournament at the Rail Golf Club, 5 mi north of downtown, attracts some 150 international professional players competing for a purse worth more than $1 million. > I–55, Exit 105, tel. 217/528–5742, www.lpgastatefarmclassic.com.

SEPTEMBER

International Route 66 Mother Road Festival This three-day event—held downtown in late September—includes hundreds of classic vehicles, live entertainment, celebrities, food, one-of-a-kind exhibits, and the world's largest sock-hop. > Tel. 217/422–3733, www.route66fest.com.
Springfield Air Rendezvous Held at Springfield's Capital Airport usually on the third weekend of the month, this celebration provides two days of continuous aviation shows, with everything from skydiving to aerobatics to military jets. Free activities for kids, in the "children's village," add to the fun. > 900 Capital Airport Dr., tel. 217/789–4400.

OCTOBER

Indian Summer Festival Brilliant fall colors make the perfect backdrop for this family fall festival held in mid-October at Lincoln Memorial Gardens on Lake Springfield. Food, crafts, and music add to the festivities. > Tel. 217/529–1111.

WHERE TO STAY

Comfort Inn Eight miles southwest of downtown Springfield, this inn is within walking distance of mall shopping and restaurants. All rooms have queen- or king-size beds. > 3442 Freedom Dr., Springfield 62704, tel. 217/787–2250 or 800/228–5150, www.comfortinn.com. 50 rooms, 16 suites. In-room data ports, some microwaves, some refrigerators, cable TV, indoor pool, hot tub, some pets allowed (fee). AE, D, DC, MC, V. CP. ¢

Country Dreams Bed & Breakfast Ten miles east of Springfield on 16 acres in rural Rochester, this contemporary old-farmhouse-style home has vaulted ceilings, alcoves, cushioned window seats, and a wraparound porch, where you can sit and look out on the surrounding farmland and fruit trees. Country-flavor rooms come with either a fireplace, a deck, or a sitting alcove. > 3410 Park La., Rochester 62563, tel. 217/498–9210, www.countrydreams.com. 4 rooms. Cable TV. AE, D, MC, V. BP. ¢–$$

Courtyard by Marriott Five miles southwest of downtown, this hotel is off I–72 near shopping. Contemporary rooms and a buffet brunch make for an unfussy lodging alternative. > 3462 Freedom Dr., Springfield 62704, tel. 217/793–5300 or 800/321–2211, www.marriott.com. 75 rooms, 3 suites. Restaurant, in-room data ports, microwaves, refrigerators, cable TV, indoor pool, gym, hot tub, bar, laundry facilities, business services. AE, D, DC, MC, V. CP. $

Crowne Plaza Hotel A few miles southeast of downtown, off I–55, this hotel is surrounded by restaurants and a movie theater. Suites come in three styles: executive, western, and business-style with a Murphy bed. > 3000 S. Dirksen Pkwy., Springfield 62703, tel. 217/529–7777 or 800/589–2769. 274 rooms, 14 suites. Restaurant, indoor pool, gym, sauna, bar, gift shop. AE, D, DC, MC, V. $–$$

Hampton Inn & Suites Off I–72 at Route 4, this inn is 5 mi southwest of the downtown area. Rooms are tastefully decorated in hues of greens and golds. The White Oaks Mall and many restaurants are nearby. > 2300 Chuckwagon Dr., Springfield 62707, tel. 217/793–7670 or 800/426–7866, www.hamptoninn.com. 60 rooms, 23 suites. Microwaves, refrigerator, cable TV, indoor pool, hot tub, business center, free parking. AE, D, DC, MC, V. CP. ¢

Henry Mischler House Bed & Breakfast Across from the Lincoln Home National Historic Site, this 1897 Victorian home has original fixtures including hand-carved oak banisters, lace curtains, and Victorian wallpaper. Rooms are furnished with antiques, and all have private baths. > 802 E. Edwards St., Springfield 62703, tel. 217/525–2660, www.mischlerhouse.com. 4 rooms, 1 suite. Cable TV. AE, D, MC, V. BP. ¢–$

Inn at 835 Bed & Breakfast In the heart of Springfield's historic district, this 1909 inn itself is a National Historic Landmark. Rooms are furnished with antiques, such as brass and four-poster beds and claw-foot tubs, and have verandas and ceiling fans. Select wines are served in the sitting room evenings. The inn is within walking distance of many Lincoln historic sites. > 835 S. 2nd St., Springfield 62704, tel. 217/523–4466, fax 217/523–4468, www.innat835.com. 10 rooms, 2 suites. Some in-room hot tubs, cable TV, laundry facilities. AE, D, MC, V. BP. $–$$

Mansion View Inn and Suites At this white-shuttered hotel with motel-like outdoor entrances in the heart of the State Capitol complex, you are directly across from the executive mansion. Room furnishings may be slightly dated, but a free pass to the

YMCA is included in your room rate. > 529 S. 4th St., Springfield 62701, tel. 217/544–7411 or 800/252–1083, fax 217/544–6211, www.mansionview.com. 91 rooms, 2 suites. Restaurant, in-room data ports, some in-room hot tubs, cable TV, bar, laundry facilities, airport shuttle. AE, D, DC, MC, V. CP. ¢–$$

Pear Tree Inn Off I–55 at Exit 94, this motel is about 5 mi southeast of the downtown historic area, amid other motels and chain restaurants. The rooms are comfortably furnished in rich maroon and hunter-green colors. > 3190 S. Dirksen Pkwy., Springfield 62703, tel. 217/529–9100 or 800/378–7946, www.druryhotels.com. 52 rooms. Cable TV, Internet. AE, D, DC, MC, V. CP. ¢

Ramada Limited–North This hotel overlooking a pond is 2 mi northeast of downtown, off I–55 at Exit 100B. A steak house and some shopping are nearby. > 3281 Northfield Dr., Springfield 62702, tel. 217/523–4000, fax 217/523–4080, www.springfieldramada.com. 93 rooms, 4 suites. Cable TV, indoor pool, gym, business services, airport shuttle. AE, D, DC, MC, V. CP. ¢

Renaissance Springfield Hotel This 12-story hotel is in historic downtown Springfield. The interior period decor reflects the Lincoln era with antiques, marble, and crystal appointments. Lincoln historical sites are within easy walking distance of the hotel. > 701 E. Adams St., Springfield 62701, tel. 217/544–8800, fax 217/544–9607, www.renaissancehotels.com. 311 rooms, 15 suites. Restaurant, room service, in-room data ports, some refrigerators, cable TV, indoor pool, gym, hot tub, bar, business services, airport shuttle, parking (fee). AE, D, DC, MC, V. $$

Springfield Hilton The 30-story hotel has city views and spacious rooms. In the heart of downtown, it's within walking distance of Lincoln historical sites. Both lounges, one on the lower floor and one on the top floor with a view of the city, host live music. > 700 E. Adams St., Springfield 62701, tel. 217/789–1530, fax 217/522–5346, www.hilton.com. 366 rooms. 3 restaurants, pool, health club, hair salon, 2 bars, airport shuttle, business services. AE, D, DC, MC, V. BP. $$

WHERE TO EAT

Augie's Front Burner Chef-owner Augie describes his cooking in this airy artsy place on the west side of the Old State Capitol Plaza as "American with an attitude," serving such innovations as macadamia nut–encrusted salmon and pan-roasted ostrich fillet. > 2 W. Old State Capitol Plaza, Springfield, tel. 217/544–6979. AE, D, DC, MC, V. Closed Sun. No lunch Sat. $–$$$

Café Brio Recipes from Mexico, the Caribbean, and the Mediterranean make up this colorful restaurant's menu, where the margaritas are made with fresh lime juice. Try the yellowfin tuna marinated in pineapple and ginger, or chicken-spinach chimichangas. > 524 E. Monroe St., Springfield, tel. 217/544–0574. AE, MC, V. No dinner Sun. $–$$$

Capisce? On the 30th floor of the Springfield Hilton Hotel, this restaurant serves a variety of pasta dishes. Richly decorated in hues of gold with modern furnishings, it has the best views of the city. > 700 E. Adams St., Springfield, tel. 217/789–1530. AE, D, MC, V. Closed Mon. No lunch weekends. $$–$$$

Chesapeake Seafood House You can order steak and barbecued ribs as well as fish (baked orange roughy and fried whole catfish) in this restored 19th-century mansion on the outskirts of town. > 3045 Clear Lake Ave., Springfield, tel. 217/522–5220. AE, D, DC, MC, V. Closed Sun. No lunch Sat. $–$$$$

Coney Island Down the street from the Old State Capitol, this diner is the second-oldest restaurant in the city. Looking nostalgically plain, it's known as a place to get a quick bite. Open at 7 AM, you can grab a breakfast of eggs and bacon before hitting the Lincoln historic sites, or swing by at lunch for a hot dog, burger, or chili. > 210 S. 5th St., Springfield, tel. 217/522–2050. No credit cards. Closed Sun. No dinner. ¢

Cozy Drive In A fixture of Route 66 history and visited by travelers from around the world, this diner is known for its Cozy Dog, or corn dog. Invented by Ed Waldmire in the mid-1940s, Cozy Dogs are now served up by his daughter-in-law and grandson. Be sure to take the time to look at the eclectic Route 66 memorabilia that covers the walls. > 2935 S. 6th St., Springfield, tel. 217/525–1992. No credit cards. Closed Sun. ¢

Lindsay's Gallery Steaks and ribs are the specialties at this casual restaurant on the first floor of the Renaissance Springfield Hotel. Street-level windows provide views of city activity. > 701 E. Adams St., Springfield, tel. 217/544–8800. AE, D, MC, V. $$–$$$

Maldaner's Established in 1883, this is the oldest restaurant in Springfield (it's been at this location in the center of town since 1897). Legislators, lobbyists, and businesspeople come here for the beef Wellington and pistachio-roasted salmon. Other menu items include grilled rib eye, fillet of beef, Portobello mushrooms, roasted chicken, and rack of lamb. You can dine on the sidewalk in summer. > 222 S. 6th St., Springfield, tel. 217/522–4313. AE, MC, V. Closed Sun. No lunch Sat., no dinner Mon. $$–$$$

Sebastian's This late 1800s painted-brick establishment is sandwiched between the old and new Capitol buildings. You can eat in the candlelit dining room, with its brass fixtures and a terrazzo fountain, or take the marble staircase down into the bar and sit at the marble-top tables. Try the shrimp stuffed with jack cheese and chipotle dipping sauce, a signature dish that lures diners from miles away. > 221 S. 5th St., Springfield, tel. 217/789–8988. AE, D, DC, MC, V. Closed Sun. No lunch. $$

ESSENTIALS

Getting Here

Because so many historical attractions in downtown Springfield are within walking distance of each other, driving around Springfield is not an absolute necessity. However, not having a car limits your ability to enjoy those sites that are a short drive away. Driving to Springfield is the best option. Planes and trains run daily between both cities and are viable options. Buses also make daily trips between Chicago and Springfield, but the numerous stops along the way can add 2 hours to a 3½-hour car trip.

BY BUS

Greyhound departs five times each day to Springfield from Chicago. The bus trip, however, can take from four to nearly six hours. This variance depends on the number of stops—ranging from three to nine—that each particular bus route makes along the way.

BUS DEPOT **Greyhound Bus Depot** > 2351 S. Dirksen, Springfield, tel. 217/544–8466.

BUS LINE **Greyhound Lines** > Tel. 312/408–5800, www.greyhound.com.

BY CAR

The easiest route between Chicago and Springfield is via I–55. During non–rush hour times, this trip can take roughly 3½ hours. However, if you leave Chicago during Friday-evening rush hour, you could add as much as 1 hour to your trip. Traffic can move slowly all the way until past Joliet; therefore, it's wise to try to leave Chicago no later than mid-afternoon Friday.

Interstate 55 is a straight, flat road slicing through cornfields the entire distance from Joliet to Springfield. Traffic moves at the posted 65 mph, except in construction zones, which this highway never seems to be free from. To help break up the trip, get off at any exit and take side roads for a stretch. Because Springfield is a weekday kind of town, you will find little traffic to fight on the weekend, unless you happen to visit during the Illinois State Fair. Otherwise, on-street parking and parking lots are plentiful.

BY PLANE

Primarily serving the needs of government and business workers, daily flights are available between Springfield and both Chicago airports: O'Hare and Midway. With morning, afternoon, and early-evening schedules, the flight time is roughly one hour to or from either airport.

AIRPORT **Capital Airport** > 1200 Capital Airport Dr., off Rte. 29, Springfield, tel. 217/788–1060, fax 217/788–8056, www.flyspi.com.

CARRIERS **ATA Connection** > Tel. 800/435–9282, www.ata.com. **United Express** > Tel. 800/864–8331, www.ual.com.

BY TRAIN

Several trains travel each day between Chicago and St. Louis with a stop in Springfield. The station is within six blocks of the heart of downtown area. Because of the concentration of attractions and hotels in the downtown area, a train trip is an alternative to driving to Springfield. However, you will need a car to visit nearby sites.

TRAIN LINE **Amtrak** > Tel. 800/872–7245, www.amtrak.com.

TRAIN STATION **Springfield Amtrak Station** > Washington and 3rd Sts., Springfield, tel. 217/753–2013.

Visitor Information

TOURIST INFORMATION **Springfield Convention and Visitors Bureau** > 109 N. 7th St., Springfield 62701, tel. 217/789–2360 or 800/545–7300, www.visit-springfieldillinois.com.

Baraboo

200 mi northwest of Chicago

20

By Rick Marzec

FOR THE OUTDOORS ENTHUSIAST, BARABOO MAY BE KNOWN AS the access point to numerous state parks that provide incredible hiking, fishing, and camping opportunities. For the parent of a child or the adult three-ring buff, Baraboo may ring a bell as the home of the famous circus museum. For the winter skier, it's the town that's near several excellent downhill options.

But if you visit the town's attractions with a slightly different mind-set, you may find yourself coming away with another impression: Baraboo is a place that understand's the importance of preservation—preservation of land, animal, architecture, and attitude.

This area of Wisconsin was once a great mountain range before a 1,000-mi-long Ice Age glacier swept through. The rock in the area, quartzite, was too strong for even the depth and power of a great glacier to completely wipe away. Unlike the rest of the Midwest that was literally flattened, this area of Wisconsin is abundant with beautiful bluffs and rolling hills. In fact, the stretch that runs through the Baraboo area has one of the best glacial imprints in the country.

In the Wisconsin Dells you can see these quartzite remains only by boat. But in Baraboo—especially at Devil's Lake—you can walk alongside or even climb these bluffs. The state park system has done an outstanding job of acquiring and preserving these lands, protecting them from commercial development.

Wildlife protection is also a large part of the culture here, and nowhere is this more apparent than at the headquarters for the International Crane Foundation. Billed as the world's center for the study and preservation of cranes, its mission is to ensure that these great birds never become extinct. You can find more evidence of preservation in such designated nature areas as scenic Parfrey's Glen where you can look, but not touch.

Like the effort to preserve nature, preserving architecture is also a mainstay here. The historic town square, for examples, reflects how many small towns once appeared in the late 1800s and early 1900s. A lavish 1915 movie palace is currently being restored to its original appearance.

In a sense, the whole small town way of life has been preserved in Baraboo. You can visit stores and restaurants in and around the town square and get a sense of bygone days. Laid-back Baraboo is sure to lower your blood pressure and slow your pulse. By no means is it another Mayberry, but it is a throwback to a gentler way of life.

No discussion of Baraboo is truly complete without reference to the circus. It is here that a group of five of the town's citizens—all brothers named Ringling—jumped on the bandwagon (so to speak) and decided to create their own circus. It's also in Baraboo that you find the Circus World Museum. More than just a place to look at wagons and watch live performances, this famed institution is committed to the preservation of the American circus's heritage. The circus was—and is—one of the country's greatest forms of entertainment, reaching the masses long before movies or broadcast media existed. Much of its history could have been lost forever without the work done by this important institution.

Many benefits result from all these collective efforts toward preservation. Ironically, you may find that your weekend getaway in Baraboo will be a trip that remains well preserved in your own memory.

WHAT TO SEE & DO

Al. Ringling Theater On the National Register of Historic Places, this opulent theater, built in 1915, is the oldest continuously operating movie house in America. Designed by Rapp & Rapp, the architects who would later design and build the equally opulent Chicago Theater, it has high arched ceilings with gold-leaf accents and tall, dramatic red curtains in front of the stage and in doorways. The majestic pipe organ built in 1928 can still make your insides vibrate. Evening movies and live performances are hosted, and 45-minute tours are given daily in summer. > 136 4th Ave., Baraboo, tel. 608/356–8864, www.alringling.com. Tours $3. Tours Memorial Day–Labor Day, daily 11 AM.

Circus World Museum This colorful and fun museum chronicles the history of the circus in America. The museum displays more than 200 circus wagons and show vehicles, the largest collection anywhere. It also preserves more than 10,000 original circus posters dating back to 1832. In summer, the museum stages daily Big Top Circus performances on the grounds. > 550 Water St., Baraboo, tel. 608/356–8341 or 866/693–1500, www.circusworldmuseum.com. $7 Labor Day–mid-May, $14.95 mid-May–Labor Day (includes Big Top performance). Daily 9–5.

Devil's Lake State Park You can camp, swim, rock climb, hike, fish, and scuba dive at this 8,000-acre park, 3 mi south of downtown Baraboo, which includes a 360-acre spring-fed lake surrounded by 500-foot bluffs. Hiking trails run from 1.1 to 5.5 mi. An on-site naturalist program enables you to learn about the natural and human history of the area. Anglers can borrow fishing tackle from the nature center; canoe and rowboat rentals are available. In winter, the park opens 16 mi of cross-country skiing trails. You can pick up maps and information at the park's visitor center. > S5975 Park Rd., Baraboo, tel. 608/356–8301. $10. Daily.

Dr. Evermor's Sculpture Art Park Since 1984, Dr. Evermor (aka scrap artisan Tom Every) has turned local salvage into colossal works of art at this 12-acre sculpture park. One work-in-progress, the Forevertron, stands 65 feet high. With a weight of 320 tons, it's earned a place in the *Guinness Book of World Records*. Also at this working outdoor studio are fields filled with scores of 10-foot-tall birds made out of old musical instruments, as well as hundreds of robotic creatures scattered about. If Tom is not there, his wife Eleanor or son Troy will most likely greet you. > U.S. 12, 10 mi south of Baraboo, Prairie du Sac, tel. 608/592–4735 or 608/219–7830, www.drevermor.org. Free. Daily 10:30–5:30.

Ho-Chunk Casino For some round-the-clock fun, try your luck at Wisconsin's largest casino. It has more than 2,750 slot machines and 78 blackjack tables. Dining options include an elegant restaurant, a buffet, a grill, and a café. The outdoor "Under the Stars" summer concert series hosts popular music artists. The lobby houses a two-story waterfall. > S3214 U.S. 12, Baraboo, tel. 608/356–6210, www.ho-chunk.com. Free. Daily.

International Crane Foundation This foundation focuses on the study and preservation of cranes and the ecosystems on which they depend. On 25 acres in the middle of farm fields, this preserve is the only place in the world where you can see all 15 species of cranes, including the whooping crane, from five different continents. A visitor center showcases the foundation's work. Both self-guided and guided tours are available. > E11376 Shady Lane Rd., Baraboo, tel. 608/356–9462, www.savingcranes.org. $7. Mid-Apr.–Oct., daily 9–5 (last guided tour at 3).

Merrimac Ferry Wisconsin's only free ferry, this seven-minute ferry ride shuttles cars and vans across the Wisconsin River between Merrimac (on the west bank) and Okee (on the east). Bike and pedestrian traffic are also permitted. > Rte. 113 at the Wisconsin River, 11 mi southeast of Baraboo, Merrimac, tel. 608/246–3871. Free. Apr. 15–Nov. 30, daily.

Mid-Continent Railway Museum In North Freedom, 8 mi west of Baraboo, you can explore exhibits on railroad history, ride on an operating steam train, or dine in an old first-class car. A round-trip steam train departs four times each day. The last train departs at 3:30 PM. > E8949 Walnut St., North Freedom, tel. 608/522–4261, www.midcontinent.org. $11. Mid-May–Labor Day, daily 9:30–5; Labor Day–Oct., weekends 9:30–5.

Mirror Lake State Park With a lake partially surrounded by sandstone bluffs, this park has excellent hiking, fishing, camping, swimming, and canoeing. It also has 140 campsites and bike and cross-country ski trails. Within the park is the restored Seth Peterson Cottage, designed in 1958 by Frank Lloyd Wright. It is the only Wright-designed house in the world available for rental occupancy. Guided tours are available; a visitor center has maps and information. > E10320 Fern Dell Rd., Baraboo, tel. 608/254–2333, www.wiparks.net. $10. Daily.

Natural Bridge State Park At this 530-acre park, 12 mi west of U.S. 12, you can hike along scenic, self-guided trails to visit the natural sandstone arch created by the eroding effects of wind and water over thousands of years. Info and maps can be picked up at the information boards near the parking lot. > S5975 Park Rd. (Rte. C), Baraboo, tel. 608/356–8301, www.devilslakewisconsin.com/naturalbridge.html. $10. Daily.

Parfrey's Glen Natural Area Near the eastern outskirts of Devil's Lake State Park, this secluded glen is a local favorite for hikers. The state's first natural area, it serves as a scientific research preserve; hikers are forbidden to remove any plants or animals and must remain on the trail. After creek crossings, the trail passes through a deep gorge and ends at a small waterfall. A 1-mi trail traverses the area. Trail maps are available at information signs near the parking lot. > Rte. DL east of Bluff Rd., Baraboo, tel. 608/356–8301. $10. Daily.

Rocky Arbor State Park At this secluded 225-acre park 9 mi north of downtown Baraboo, hiking trails under white pine trees and sandstone bluffs provide cool relief from the summer sun. The park also has 89 campsites. > U.S. 12 and Rte. 16, Wisconsin Dells, tel. 608/254–8001, 608/254–2333 in winter, www.wiparks.net. $10. Daily.

Sauk County Historical Museum Housed in the Van Orden mansion, the museum is the result of nearly 100 years of donations to the Sauk County Historical Society. Thousands of artifacts and memorabilia relating to Sauk County or its inhabitants are displayed in more than 20 rooms on all four floors of the mansion. These include artifacts of Native Americans and pioneering days, as well as local textile products and geological findings. > 531 4th Ave., Baraboo, tel. 608/356–1001, www.saukcounty.com. Free (donations accepted). Tues.–Sun. noon–5.

Shoppes at Corner on Wisconsin This restored 19th-century building on the town square is home to a dozen unique shops selling books, artwork, candles, quilts, and furniture. On the second floor are more shops and Homer Daehn's studio, where

The Mother of Circuses

IT'S NO SECRET THAT BARABOO WAS NOT ONLY ONCE HOME to the Ringling Brothers but it is also currently the home to the Circus World Museum. But what many people don't know is that Wisconsin was once the center of the circus world, and Baraboo helped create the state's 150-year circus heritage.

The birthplace of the American circus can be traced to Philadelphia in 1793. (The first public performance of people and animals in a ring took place in England 25 years earlier.) At that time, the American circus was performed for extended periods inside wooden amphitheaters. But by the early 1800s the country's population began to shift westward to what is now considered the Midwest. With the East already crowded with traveling circuses, the West became prime territory for this new form of entertainment.

Few amphitheaters, however, existed amid these developing towns, so it became apparent to circus owners that they could reach a greater audience by traveling to a new community each and every day. Thus, the concept of a portable circus tent was born, and it made its first appearance in 1825. What the traveling circuses soon discovered, though, was the change of seasons forced them to make the arduous trek back East to their homes each winter. It was soon decided that a more central location might be more suitable—and there was no better location than Wisconsin. It had plenty of land, and animal feed was affordable. All were key ingredients necessary to support these roaming frontier shows.

The first to make the big move was the Mabie brothers. In 1847, they moved the winter quarters of their Grand Olympic Arena Circus from upstate New York to Delavan, WI. Others quickly followed. By maintaining a Wisconsin-based home, circuses were now able to maximize the length of their season. Over time, circus owners looked for faster ways to move their

shows from town to town. The idea of moving circuses via railway lines got its start in Wisconsin as well. In 1872, William C. Coup helped figure out how to put P. T. Barnum's show on rails. This allowed the entire country to experience "the Greatest Show on Earth."

It wasn't until 1884 that a family of five brothers named Ringling, residents of Baraboo, created the Ringling Bros. Circus. It is on the Ringling's former winter quarters where the Circus World Museum sits today. Serving as the winter haven for elephants and tigers—as well as for the "Thin Man" and the "Tattooed Lady"—Wisconsin was once the home to more than 100 circuses, more than any other state. This is what eventually earned it the nickname, the Mother of Circuses.

you just might see him at work. With hammer and chisel, Homer skillfully shapes wood into everything from merry-go-round horses to life-size James Dean sculptures. > Oak and 4th Sts., Baraboo. Free. Closed Sun.

Village Booksmith and Coffee House By day it's a charming bookstore that serves coffee and tea as well as secondhand, new, and rare books. On Wednesday nights, it hosts live music; Friday nights always bring something new, from folk music to poetry. > 526 Oak St., Baraboo, tel. 608/355–1001. Free. Mon., Tues., Thurs., and Sat. 10–6; Wed. and Fri. 10–10.

Wollersheim Winery You can taste pinot noir, chardonnay, and dry Riesling at this hillside vineyard overlooking the Wisconsin River. Developed by European settlers in 1840, the vineyard shut down in 1899 and switched to regular farming use. In 1972, however, new owners planted grapes, restored the 1840s buildings, and added modern fermentation equipment. One-hour tours are given every hour at 15 minutes past the hour. The last tour is at 4:15 PM. > Rte. 88, 18 mi south of Baraboo, Prairie du Sac, tel. 608/643–6515, www.wollersheim.com. Tasting free, tours $3.50. Daily 10–5.

Tours

Dells Boat Tours Scenic tours along the Wisconsin River take you close to tall sandstone cliffs that were carved by the river over thousands of years. From early April to October, one- and two-hour tours are available, as well as sunset dinner cruises and wine and cheese cruises. > 107 Broadway, Wisconsin Dells, tel. 608/254–8555, www.dellsboats.com.

Sports

SKIING

Cascade Mountain At Cascade Mountain, you can ski on a 460-foot vertical drop, 27 runs, trails up to 1 mi long, 18 of which are lit for night skiing, two terrain parks, and two half-pipes. To refuel, check out the snack bar and cafeteria. The mountain is 13 mi east of Baraboo, within sight of Exit 106, off I–90 (I–94) at Route 33. > 10441 Cascade Mountain Rd., Portage, tel. 608/742–5588, www.cascademountain.com.

Devil's Head Resort Far away from highways and the city, this 250-acre ski and snowboarding area has 31 trails from which to choose and a 500-foot vertical drop. Nearly one-third of the runs are advanced level terrain, the longest of which is 1.5 mi. Snowboarders are allowed access to all trails. Night skiing is permitted on 80% of the skiable terrain. In summer, the resort has a 27-hole golf course, mountain-bike trails, hiking trails, indoor and outdoor pools, tennis, a weight room, two restaurants, a bar, and a lounge. > S6330 Bluff Rd., 15 mi southeast of Baraboo, Merrimac, tel. 800/338–4579 or 800/472–6670, www.devilsheadresort.com.

Save the Date

FEBRUARY

Mid-Continent Railway Snow Train Closed in winter, the railway reopens for one weekend in late February to give a 50-minute, 7-mi train ride across the snow-covered, rolling hills of the Baraboo countryside. You can choose from five departure times. > E8949 Walnut St., 8 mi west of Baraboo, North Freedom, tel. 608/522–4261, www.midcontinent.org.

MAY

Crane Fest This celebration of international Migratory Bird Day, held on the grounds of the International Crane Foundation, welcomes the return of the sandhill and whooping cranes to the Wisconsin skies. The day includes tours of the 25-acre preservation center, speakers, food, music, and "crane dancing." > E11376 Shady Lane Rd., Baraboo, tel. 608/356–9462, www.savingcranes.org.

Faire on the Square Held the third Saturday of May, this fair has 150 arts-and-crafts exhibits from both local and regional artists. A farmers' market rounds out the fair. > Courthouse Sq., Baraboo, tel. 800/227–2266, www.baraboo.com/chamber.

JUNE

Native American Artifact and Antique Show This show held the third weekend in June at the Sauk County fairgrounds displays and sells antique Native American and Civil War–era artifacts such as guns, swords, knives, and decoys. > Sauk County fairgrounds (8th St.), Baraboo, tel. 920/923–3842.

JUNE–AUGUST

Concerts on the Square Starting the second Thursday in June, a free concert is held every Thursday at 7 PM. Dixie, steel drum, Latin, and big bands from local communities and universities have all performed here. > Courthouse Sq., Baraboo, tel. 608/356–8351.

JULY

Circus Train Loading Watch the Circus World Circus Train load up for its annual trip to the Milwaukee Circus Parade. The rest of the Circus World Museum is open as usual, but people gather to watch as each flatbed car is carefully loaded by horse-drawn power, the same way it was done more than 100 years ago. This all-day event takes place in early July. The train leaves the next day. > 550 Water St., Baraboo, tel. 608/356–8341 or 866/693–1500, www.circusworldmuseum.com.

Old Fashioned Day Fire-department water fights, a dunk tank, car show, and food stands add to this July celebration, held the last Saturday of the month. > Baraboo, tel. 800/227–2266, www.baraboo.com/chamber.

Sauk County Fair Usually held on the second week in July, the fair hosts grandstand shows and events from Tuesday to Sunday. Horse shows, livestock exhibits, music, and a beer garden add to the fun. > 8th St., Baraboo, tel. 608/356–8913, www.saukcountyfair.com.

AUGUST

Summer Classic Fine Art Festival A one-day event, usually held the second Saturday of August, is put together by the Sauk County Art Association. The arts festival showcases works by local artisans. > Courthouse Sq., Baraboo, tel. 800/227–2266, www.baraboo.com/chamber.

OCTOBER

Autumn Colors Train Held the first two weekends of October, the 7-mi, 50-minute train rides take you to see the changing colors of the area. Trains depart five times per day. > E8949 Walnut St., North Freedom, tel. 608/522–4261, www.midcontinent.org.

Faire on the Square Held the second Saturday in October, this fair greets fall with 150 arts-and-crafts exhibits from local and regional artisans. Inflatable rides and games add to the fun. > Courthouse Sq., Baraboo, tel. 800/227–2266, www.baraboo.com/chamber.

WHERE TO STAY

Best Western Baraboo Inn This three-story Inn, 2 mi from downtown, has spacious rooms and low rates. Surrounded by fast-food and convenience stores, the hotel provides an economic alternative. > 725 W. Pine St. (U.S. 12), Baraboo 53913, tel.

608/356–1100 or 800/831–3881, www.bestwestern.com. 82 rooms. Restaurant, in-room data ports, cable TV, indoor pool, gym, hot tub, laundry services. AE, D, DC, MC, V. CP. ¢–$

Frantiques Showplace Antiques fill this 25-room Victorian mansion, two blocks from the town square. Suites have brass beds and feather quilts; one has a full kitchen and private entrance. > 704 Ash St., Baraboo 53913, tel. 608/356–5273. 2 rooms. No smoking. No credit cards. BP. ¢

Gollmar Guest House Four blocks from Baraboo's town square, this Victorian home is adorned with beveled glass, chandeliers, antiques, hardwood floors, beaded wood-work, a guest parlor, and an outdoor veranda-patio. > 422 3rd St., Baraboo 53913, tel. 608/356–9432, fax 608/356–3847, www.gollmar.com. 4 rooms. Some in-room hot tubs, library; no smoking. D, MC, V. BP. $–$$

Ho-Chunk Hotel Though a casino adjoins the property, you don't have to gamble to stay at this luxurious alternative to the area's chain motels. The hotel is 5 mi north of downtown Baraboo on U.S. 12. The spacious rooms include balconies, and suites have fireplaces and whirlpools. > S3214 U.S. 12, Baraboo 53913, tel. 800/446–5550, fax 608/355–1501, www.ho-chunk.com. 215 rooms, 100 suites. Restaurant, café, in-room data ports, in-room safes, microwaves, cable TV, indoor pool, gym, lounge, concierge. AE, D, DC, MC, V. $$–$$$

Park Plaza This property, 2 mi west of downtown on U.S. 12, is close to area shop-ping and chain restaurants. Hand-painted murals depicting scenes of ancient Greece embellish the fourth-floor indoor pool. All rooms were renovated in 2003 and deco-rated with modern furnishings. > 630 W. Pine St., Baraboo 53913, tel. 608/356–4869 or 800/355–6422, www.baraboolodging.com. 84 rooms, 12 suites. Restaurant, pool, gym. AE, D, DC, MC, V. CP. $

Pinehaven Bed and Breakfast This rustic, chalet-style bed-and-breakfast, 2½ mi east of downtown Baraboo, is near a spring-fed lake, with the Baraboo Bluffs behind it. If you want to get out on the lake, you can use the inn's rowboat and paddleboat. Each coun-try-inspired guest room has a ceiling fan and private bath. A two-bedroom cottage comes with a double whirlpool, wood-burning stove, and porch swing. > E13083 Rte. 33, Baraboo 53913, tel. 608/356–3489, fax 608/356–0818, www.dells.com/pinehaven. 4 rooms, 1 cottage. Some in-room hot tubs; no smoking. MC, V. BP. $–$$

Rustic Ridge Log Cabins Eleven miles southeast of downtown Baraboo, these luxury log cabins are nestled in the Baraboo Bluffs. The carpeted, wood-beamed cabins in-clude modern appliances, skylights, and satellite TV. > E13981 Rte. DL, Merrimac 53561, tel. 608/493–2440, www.rusticridgecabins.com. 4 cabins. In-room data ports, some in-room hot tubs, kitchens, microwaves; no smoking. MC, V. $$$$

Spinning Wheel This one-story, brick-and-wood motel provides an economic alterna-tive to other accommodations in the area. It's on the east side of town in a residential neighborhood not far from Route 33. Rooms are modern, and were refurbished in 2003. > 809 8th St., Baraboo 53913, tel. 608/356–3933, www.spinningwheelmotel.com. 25 rooms. Microwaves, refrigerators, cable TV, some pets allowed (fee). AE, D, MC, V. ¢

CAMPING

Baraboo Hills Campground Four miles northeast of downtown, this campground rents not only campsites but 19 air-conditioned cabins that can accommodate up to four adults or a family of six. Between Memorial Day and Labor Day, an on-site sports shop provides free sporting equipment for campers, including bikes, fishing poles, soccer, and footballs. > E10545 Terrytown Rd., Baraboo 53913, tel. 608/356–8505, www.baraboohillscampground.com. 24 full hook-up, 76 partial hook-up, 52 tent sites. Flush toilets, laundry facilities, showers, picnic tables, pool. D, MC, V. Closed Oct.–Apr. ¢

Devil's Lake State Park Three separate campground areas are within this 8,000-acre state park, 3 mi south of downtown Baraboo. You can swim in the spring-fed lake or hike along miles and miles of designated trails. Of the 407 sites, 50 are nonreservable and are only available on a first-come, first-served basis. > S5975 Park Rd., Baraboo 53913, tel. 608/356–8301 or 888/947–2757. 124 partial hookups, 283 tent sites. Flush toilets, dump station, drinking water, showers, grills, picnic tables, general store, ranger station. MC, V. ¢

Nordic Pines Resort Across the road from Devil's Lake State Park's main entrance, this campground is within walking distance of swimming, fishing, hiking, and all the other activities found in the park. Six cottages are also available for rent. > E11740 Rte. DL, Baraboo 53913, tel. 608/356–5810, www.nordicpines.com. 20 partial hook-ups, 120 tent sites. Flush toilets, drinking water, showers, fire pits, picnic tables, electricity. D, MC, V. Closed mid-Oct.–mid-May. ¢

Wheeler's Campground This 70-acre, family-owned campground is nestled in Baraboo Bluffs near Devil's Lake. Anglers can try their luck at the on-site pond. > E11329 Rte. 159, Baraboo 53913, tel. 608/356–4877, www.wheelerscampground.com. 27 full hook-ups, 35 partial hook-ups, 64 tent sites. Flush toilets, laundry facilities, showers, general store, playground. MC, V. Closed mid-Oct.–Apr. ¢

WHERE TO EAT

The Cornucopian Perhaps the only restaurant in the Baraboo area with both white tablecloths and a wine list, the entrées served here include fish, meat, and poultry dishes such as stuffed orange roughy, filet mignon, and chicken *portofino*. Windows overlook the scenic Devil's Head Resort. > S6330 Bluff Rd., 11 mi southeast of Baraboo on Rte. 113, Merrimac, tel. 800/338–4579. Reservations essential. AE, D, DC, MC, V. No lunch. **$$–$$$**

Del-Bar Established in 1943, the "Prairie-style" ambience of this roadside steak house was designed by James Dresser, a protégé of Frank Lloyd Wright. Dinners include filet mignon, roasted Long Island duck, and lobster tail. Expect a crackling fire in winter, and the tinklings of live piano year-round. > 800 Wisconsin Dells Pkwy., 10 mi north of Baraboo U.S. 12, Lake Delton, tel. 608/253–1861. AE, D, DC, MC, V. No lunch. **$$$–$$$$**

Java Café & Jive Amid the historic feel of the town square, this café provides a more trendy environment. Original art hangs on the walls. Try the Portobello mushroom sandwich or an apple-pear salad. > 106 4th St., Baraboo, tel. 608/355–1053. MC, V. No dinner. ¢

Jen's Alpine Café This is the oldest restaurant in Baraboo. Its wooden booths, ornate mirrors, and wall decor make it feel as though time has stood still in this storefront café. Five different kinds of homemade soup are made each day, and the wraps are worth trying. A different ice cream sundae is featured each month, and breakfast is served anytime. > 117 4th St., Baraboo, tel. 608/356–4040. MC, V. No dinner. ¢–$

Little Village Café This diner on the square has been here since the 1940s, and is a favorite spot for courthouse clientele and local residents. The menu changes frequently—specials can include Jamaican chicken burritos, sweet-potato pancakes, and Mediterranean Greek salad. > 146 4th Ave., Baraboo, tel. 608/356–2800. MC, V. Closed Sun. and Mon. **$–$$$**

Log Cabin Family Restaurant Home-cooked food is the rule in this replica of an old log cabin with many windows and views of surrounding businesses. Try the country-fried steak or the turkey dinner with potatoes. Pies are homemade and a different flavor is served every month. > 1215 8th St., Baraboo, tel. 608/356–8245. D, MC, V. $–$$

ESSENTIALS

Getting Here

Traveling by car is your best option to get to and around Baraboo. There is no rail or bus service to Baraboo, and no public transportation serves the town. Traffic and parking at major attractions may get congested during peak weekends.

BY CAR

Depending on where you live, you have two ways to get to the Baraboo area. From the south and and west suburbs, take I–90 (the Northwest Tollway) and head west toward Rockford and then north to Madison, where it merges with I–94. Stay on I–90 (I–94) North and exit at Route 33 West. From the north suburbs, take I–94 North toward Milwaukee, where it then turns west. Take this toward Madison, where it merges with I–90 outside the city. Follow I–90 (I–94) North and exit at Route 33. The trip takes about 3½ hours, and gas stations, fast-food outlets, and rest stops every few miles line the route. If you're traveling to Wisconsin on an early Friday-evening and/or returning late afternoon Sunday, add an hour or more to your trip due to weekend travel congestion.

BY PLANE

There is no regular passenger service directly into Baraboo. The closest airport served is Madison, Wisconsin, to the south. But if you consider the time needed to get to O'Hare or Midway, go through airport security, fly to Madison, and get a rental car, driving still is the best option. For those with access to private aircraft or charter service, Baraboo's airport is 5 mi north of the downtown area.

AIRPORT **Baraboo-Wisconsin Dells Municipal Airport** > S3440 Hwy. 12, Baraboo, tel. 608/356–2270.

Visitor Information

CONTACTS **Baraboo Chamber of Commerce** > 600 W. Chestnut St., Baraboo 53913, tel. 800/227–2266, www.baraboo.com/chamber. **Wisconsin Department of Natural Resources** > 101 S. Webster St., Box 7921, Madison 53707, tel. 608/266–2621, www.dnr.state.wi.

Bloomington & Bedford

225 mi southeast of Chicago

21

By Kevin Cunningham

NESTLED IN THE SOUTH-CENTRAL INDIANA HILLS, Bloomington is home to the oldest part of Indiana University, a Big Ten Conference school dating from 1820. In the Old Crescent Historic District of the wooded campus, nine buildings date from 1884 to 1908. One of the city's most recognizable symbols is the fish weather vane atop the dome of the Monroe County Courthouse in the center of the town square. Supposedly first placed atop the 1826 courthouse, it has since been reused on subsequent courthouses. In the early 1990s, the gleam was put back on the current beaux arts–style limestone structure as part of an extensive downtown revitalization.

Pioneers first settled Bloomington in 1815, and five years later the university began with 10 students and one professor. The university struggled along in the early years of its existence, in part because Bloomington's isolation and because the state legislature didn't start funding it until after the Civil War. The town around the university benefited from a number of industries such as furniture making and limestone quarrying.

In the early part of the 20th century IU grew and began to get a national reputation for its education, law, and music programs. Not all of its famous former students were grads—novelist Theodore Dreiser dropped out—but eventually the university's alumni included presidential candidate Wendell Wilkie, who lost to Roosevelt in 1940. Since then, graduates have included TV broadcaster Jane Pauley, actor Kevin Kline, and Nobel prize–winning scientist James Watson.

Few, however, have been more influential than Bloomington native Hoagy Carmichael, the influential writer of pop music standards such as "Stardust," "In the Cool, Cool, Cool of the Evening," and "Georgia on My Mind." Ironically, he graduated from the law school. But obviously something musical floats on the Hoosier air in these parts. IU's school of music is internationally famous, its orchestra perennially praised. Opera lovers visiting during the school year can see both classical and contemporary works performed by some of the best young talent in the country. Even rock has roots here—former Van Halen front man David Lee Roth was born in Bloomington in 1954.

Bloomington's city square sits on a former wheat field, donated in 1818 for that very purpose. The first log building gave way to a brick courthouse, which in turn gave way to the current building, finished in 1908. From the mid-1970s into the 1980s the classical building faced threats of demolition, despite making the National Register of Historic Places. According to one story, the fish on the weather vane represents Christianity. Whichever way the wind blows, it points to a vintage building. None are quirkier than the Masonic Temple, a mix of beaux arts and Egyptian revival with a pyramid roof. At one time the square hosted salesmen and pencil peddlers and grocers selling produce on the sidewalk. Today, the brick storefronts with tall windows and painted trim have all been painstakingly renovated. Bloomington's downtown now has more than 120 specialty shops, galleries, and unusual restaurants.

Limestone Legacy

AN OLD BLACK-AND-WHITE PICTURE hanging at the Land of Limestone shows a caravan of 35-foot limestone columns easing through downtown Bedford on railroad cars in the early 1900s. The mammoth pillars went on to become the building blocks of Pennsylvania's state office building. Cathedrals, Gilded Age mansions of the wealthy (including Cornelius Vanderbilt's Newport, Rhode Island, palace, The Breakers), the Empire State Building, 35 state capitols, and many other notable landmarks in the United States have been built with stone from the Hoosier state. Beginning in the 1820s, quarries centered in Bedford and Oolitic, about 7 mi north, began surrendering the stone that lay in a 10-mi-wide belt between Bloomington and Bedford. "That astonishing material," as one architect called Indiana limestone in the early 1900s, is only found in three Indiana counties.

Indiana's limestone is known for its fine grain and strength, hence its popularity as a building material and a medium for sculptors carving finely detailed ornaments and statues. The former 1926 offices of the Indiana Limestone Company (now Bedford College Center) display tools, more than 200 photographs, architectural renderings, and the geology of Indiana's limestone heritage. That heritage can also be appreciated on downtown walking or driving tours of the area (maps available at the Lawrence County Tourism Commission), one of which passes by the famous Empire Hole, where stone for the Empire State Building was quarried. Surprisingly, some of the best examples of the stone carving can be seen at Bedford's Green Hill Cemetery.

South of Bloomington, a thick belt of limestone stretches across Indiana's midsection, with Bedford at the center. Blocks from Lawrence County's famed "holes," or quarries, have built dozens of state capitols and many of the landmark buildings across the nation. The pride that Bedford takes in its title as Limestone Capital of the World is as durable as the legendary stone itself. You can get a feel for the life of stone, stone, stone on driving and walking tours of Bedford and Lawrence counties. Several major stonecutters still operate in Lawrence County. Underground, caves honeycomb the countryside.

For those who prefer the natural world, the Bloomington/Bedford region has numerous lakes and 200,000 acres of forest. The vast Hoosier National Forest rolls from the shores of Lake Monroe, 10 mi south of Bloomington, to the Ohio River. A half dozen state forests and recreation areas fill in many of the gaps it misses.

WHAT TO SEE & DO

BEDFORD
Antique Auto and Race Car Museum Some 100 antique racing and touring cars are on display in this museum in the center of town, where a gift shop stocks automobile collectibles and limestone gifts. Along with more than a dozen Indy 500 cars are Sprint, Midget, and NASCAR race cars. And because this is Bedford, limestone carvings of cars and historic quarry photos are also part of the museum. > 3348 16th St.,

Stone City Mall, Bedford, tel. 812/275–0556, www.autoracemuseum.com. $3. Apr.–Dec., Mon.–Sat. noon–6.

Bluespring Caverns Inside this network of caverns 4 mi south of the center of Bedford are high-vaulted passageways and one of the world's longest underground streams, the Myst'ry River, which flows for some 20 mi through the main cavern. You can view the main cavern on foot from a paved walkway and viewing platform or by boat on a one-hour guided tour of the underground river where rare blind fish live. > 1459 Bluespring Caverns Rd. (Rte. 11), Bedford, tel. 812/279–9471, www.bluespringcaverns.com. $12. Memorial Day–Oct., daily 9–5; Apr. and May, weekends 9–5.

Green Hill Cemetery The cemetery on the southwest edge of town has some of the finest examples of limestone carving in the county, with ornate and personalized monuments such as the Lewis Baker monument, which depicts the stone carver's workbench and tools. > 1202 18th St., Bedford, tel. 812/275–7637 or 800/798–0769, www.limestonecountry.com. Free. Daily dawn–dusk.

Hoosier National Forest The state's only national forest covers 196,000 acres of south-central Indiana, with two huge parcels near Bloomington and Columbus and the other stretching south from Bedford to the Ohio River. Some 230 mi of hiking, mountain biking, and equestrian trails crisscross hills from 400 feet in height near the Ohio River valley to above 930 feet at Browning Hill. The terrain is surprisingly diverse, from high ridges and hills along the Ohio River to underground cave and karst systems, open meadows, and old-growth forests. A number of geological features in the forest include Wesley Chapel Gulf, an 8-acre collapsed sinkhole, and Shooting Star Cliffs, with native umbrella magnolia and rock shelters. At a horseshoe bend in the Little Blue River called Carnes Mill, a water flume was carved out of the rocky bluff to power a mill. The Clover Lick Barrens is a prairielike area with rock outcroppings and many rare plants, and the Tincher Area is full of caves and other karst features. The forest also includes a box-shape sandstone canyon with waterfalls and rock shelters called Hemlock Cliffs. The forest also provides prime fall color scenic drive opportunities, including Route 46 between Bloomington and Heltonville, Route 135 between Nashville and Freetown, and Route 58 from Bedford on to Heltonville. Near the Ohio River, the scenery is great from Derby to Tell City near the water's edge on Route 66. > 811 Constitution Ave., Bedford, tel. 812/275–5987. Free. Daily.

The state's only federally designated wilderness area, the 13,000-acre **Charles C. Deam Wilderness** (Rte. 446, tel. 812/275–5987, daily) is filled with wooded hills and hollows near Lake Monroe in Jackson, Brown, Lawrence, and Monroe counties and can be reached only on foot or on horseback. Close to 36 mi of trails pass along wooded ridges with scenic views. Also here is the **Hickory Ridge Lookout Tower**, which the Civilian Conservation Corps constructed in 1936 to watch for fires. On the eastern side of the Charles C. Deam Wilderness Area, the tower is on the National Register of Historic Places. From Bedford, take Route 50 East 10 mi to Route 446, then go 10 mi north. Near Paoli (22 mi south of Bedford) at the junction of Route 37 and Route 56, the **Pioneer Mothers Memorial Forest** (free, daily) is an 88-acre preserve within the Hoosier National Forest, which includes an acre of black walnut trees, one of the few such stands in the Midwest. Walnut trees reach 100 feet and measure 40 inches in diameter. Some ancient oaks here are believed to date back to the 15th century.

Jackson-Washington State Forest The 17,000-acre forest spreads across an area known as the Knobs. These are sugarloaf hills that poke up above the flat farm fields—considered miniature mountains in the Hoosier state—affording panoramic vistas from 300 feet above and the 2½-mi Skyline Drive that circles the top of one of them. The 60-foot climb up the fire tower captures strikingly flat 20-mi views. The rugged 1-mi hike to Pinnacle Peak, the most famous of the Knobs, is well worth the effort. Another 20 mi of trails, from moderate to rugged and including a portion of the 57-mi Knobstone Trail, lace the Knobs area. Next to the state forest is **Starve Hollow State Recreation Area,** which is home to Starve Hollow Lake. The lake covers 145 acres and with its boat ramps and canoes provides fishermen and rowers alike plenty of water opportunities. Jackson-Washington is 20 mi east of Bedford. > 1278 E. Rte. 250, Brownstown, tel. 812/358–2160. Free. Daily.

Land of Limestone Exhibit More than 200 vintage black-and-white photographs, stonecutter's tools, architectural drawings, and other artifacts trace Lawrence County's limestone industry. In the 1850s, as quarries were opened in the countryside around Bedford and Oolitic, Lawrence County began supplying the nation with building material for its monuments. The National Cathedral, the Empire State Building, and many of the country's state capitols are built of Indiana limestone. The exhibit is on the north side of Bedford. > Bedford College Center, 405 I St., Bedford, tel. 812/275–7637 or 800/798–0769. Free. Weekdays 9–5, Sat. 9–noon.

Lawrence County Historical Museum In the basement of the county courthouse, this downtown museum houses artifacts and historical materials from the county museum's collection. Glass cases display glassware, antique dolls, a few Native American artifacts, flags, uniforms from the Civil War to World War II, and limestone architectural details and sculptures created by local carvers. > Courthouse Sq., Bedford, tel. 812/275–4141. Free. Weekdays 9–noon and 1–4.

Spring Mill State Park Tucked in the 1,319-acre wooded preserve next to a trickling creek, 13 mi south of Bedford, are a re-created 1814 pioneer village and gristmill built of limestone and timbers. You can explore Twin Cave by boat and Donaldson's Cave on foot. The park also includes 80 acres of virgin forest and woodsy Spring Mill Inn. Leap ahead to the space age at the park's Grissom Memorial, which displays astronaut Virgil "Gus" Grissom's space suit and the Gemini III space capsule. The Spring Mill Inn is in the park along with a range of campsites. > Rte. 60, Mitchell, tel. 812/849–4129. $5 per vehicle. Daily.

BLOOMINGTON

Butler Winery This winery with a tasting room is 9 mi northeast of downtown Bloomington but they have an additional tasting room in a 1903 cream-and-green bungalow-style home on the north edge of downtown. Butler wine comes from Indiana-grown grapes, which include such varietals as Seyval Blanc and Chardonel, plus several sweet wines (blackberry, blueberry) and even port. > In town: 1022 N. College Ave.; outside town: 6200 E. Robinson Rd., Bloomington, tel. 812/339–7233 in town, 812/332–6660 winery, www.butlerwinery.com. Free. In town: Mon.–Sat. 10–6, Sun. noon–6; outside town: Apr.–Nov., Wed.–Sun. noon–6; Dec.–Mar., weekends noon–6.

Fountain Square Mall Set behind nearly a block of historic storefronts facing the courthouse downtown, Fountain Square is a multilevel mall of small, individually owned specialty shops, galleries, ethnic restaurants, delis, and cafés. > 320 W. 8th St., Bloomington, tel. 812/332–0053 or 812/336–7100. Free. Daily.

Indiana University This university has a wooded, 1,860-acre campus in the center of town; many Tudor-style brick buildings here date back to 1820, and the Indiana

Memorial Union, which spans almost an entire city block, is the largest student-union building in the United States. The union and many of the newer buildings are built of Indiana limestone. The art museum, designed by architect I. M. Pei, is made of glass and stone, and a striking red metal sculpture by Alexander Calder stands in front of the Musical Arts Center. > 107 S. Indiana Ave., Bloomington, tel. 812/855–4848, www.indiana.edu. Free. Daily.

The **Glenn A. Black Laboratory of Archaeology** (423 N. Fess St., tel. 812/855–0022 tours, 812/855–9544, free, Sept.–May, Tues.–Fri. 9–4:30, weekends 1–4:30), a major research facility near the center of Bloomington, includes a museum displaying archaeological artifacts and tracing the ethno-history of the Great Lakes and Ohio Valley regions. Tours must be arranged in advance.

The **Hilltop Garden and Nature Center** (2301 E. 10th St., tel. 812/855–2799, free) is a peaceful, 5-acre area near the Indiana University campus, featuring demonstrations from of one of the oldest youth gardening programs in the country, as well as community gardens, a greenhouse, ponds, and flower beds.

The **Indiana Memorial Union** (900 E. 7th St., tel. 812/856–6381, free), the university's student and faculty center, includes a hotel, restaurants, recreational facilities, a bookstore, and plenty of lounge areas. The massive limestone building overlooks an area known as Dunn Meadow in the center of campus.

The international firm of I. M. Pei and Partners designed the soaring, angular **Indiana University Art Museum** (Fine Arts Plaza, 1133 E. 7th St., tel. 812/855–5445, free, Tues.–Sat. 10–5, Sun. noon–5). In addition to temporary exhibits, the museum displays fine arts and artifacts from its 33,000-piece permanent collection representing nearly every major historical culture.

The seven-story **Lilly Library** (Fine Arts Plaza, 1200 E. 7th St., tel. 812/855–2452, free, fall–spring: weekdays 9–6, Sat. 9–1; summer: Mon.–Thurs. 9–6, Fri. 9–5, Sat. 9–1) contains 400,000 books, many of them rare, more than 7 million rare or historical manuscripts, and 100,000 pieces of sheet music. Among the library's holdings on continuing display is a copy of the Gutenberg Bible printed in 1455 and original prints from John James Audubon's *Birds of America*. Special exhibits cover bibliophilia—in 2003 Lilly displayed exhibits devoted to James Bond and to pop-up books. The eclectic collection also includes the Coverdale Bible of 1535 (the first English printed bible), Jefferson's copy of the Bill of Rights, and the complete scripts to *Star Trek: The Next Generation*.

Anthropological and folklore exhibits in the **Mathers Museum** (416 N. Indiana Ave., tel. 812/855–6873, free, Tues.–Fri. 9–4:30, weekends 1–4:30) look at cultures around the world.

The university's highly respected **School of Music** (Musical Arts Center, 3rd St. and Jordan Ave., tel. 812/855–1583 or 812/855–7433) puts on more than 1,000 performances per year. Ballets and shows by the orchestra can usually be seen for $15–$30; opera buffs can attend everything from Verdi to contemporary works for around $20; most student and faculty recitals are free.

Lake Monroe Indiana's largest inland lake, at 10,750 acres, attracts scores of boaters, anglers, campers, and swimmers. The lake, 6 mi south of Bloomington, has two beaches and five state recreation areas totaling 23,952 acres. A section of the Hoosier National Forest borders the lake's southern edge. > 4850 S. Rte. 446, Bloomington, tel. 812/837–9546. $5 per vehicle. Daily.

McCormick's Creek State Park Steep ravines, limestone outcroppings, and waterfalls fill Indiana's oldest state park, part of a health retreat and sanitarium in the late 1800s. The 1,800-acre preserve is in hilly woodlands 14 mi northwest of Bloomington and has a swimming pool, campsites, housekeeping cabins, the Canyon Inn lodge, and a nature center. > Rte. 5, Spencer, tel. 812/829–2235. $5 per vehicle. Daily.

Monroe County Courthouse A distinctive fish weather vane tops this beaux arts–style limestone courthouse atop a knoll in the center of downtown. Inside, a stained-glass window pierces the domed rotunda ceiling. The four murals on local themes are by German artist Gustav A. Brand and were restored in 1992. > Courthouse Sq., Bloomington, tel. 800/800–0037. Free. Weekdays 8–4.

Monroe County Historical Society A Carnegie library dating from 1918 houses this museum near downtown. Permanent exhibits trace the area's natural development and the growth of limestone quarrying, as well as its history from early settlement through the industrial era and up to the present time. Temporary exhibits focus on cultural subjects, including fashion and farming. Be sure to nod a greeting to the famous Schmalz bear, the 9-foot, 4-inch guardian of the second floor. > 202 E. 6th St., Bloomington, tel. 812/332–2517. Free. Tues.–Sat. 10–4, Sun. 1–4.

Oliver Winery The state's oldest and largest winery, 7 mi north of downtown, produces more than 15 varieties of wine, including cabernet and a sweet honey mead. Free tours are conducted on weekends. The grounds include a pond and picnic tables and the winery now has live music on Saturday afternoons, June–August. > 8024 N. Rte. 37, Bloomington, tel. 812/876–5800 or 800/258–2783, www.oliverwinery.com. Free. Mon.–Sat. 10–6, Sun. noon–6.

Tibetan Cultural Center As unlikely as it may sound, Bloomington is a thriving corner of Tibetan culture—the Dalai Lama himself has bestowed a visit on the city. The grounds of the center include the striking Kalachakra Stupa, a 45-foot-high Buddhist shrine decorated with lotus carvings in limestone. Other sites include the Janchub Chorten, a sacred monument consecrated by the Dalai Lama in 1987, four retreat cottages (available for rent), and the center's main building, where a sand mandala and other works of art are displayed. > 3655 Snoddy Rd., Bloomington, tel. 812/331–0014 or 812/334–7046, www.tibetancc.com. Free. Sun. 1–3; grounds: daily 10–4.

Wylie House Museum Six blocks from downtown, the stately 1835 brick Georgian home of the university's first president, Andrew Wylie, is filled with period furnishings, which are described on 45-minute guided tours. The garden dates from the period the house was built. > 317 E. 2nd St., Bloomington, tel. 812/855–6224. Free. Mar.–Nov., Tues.–Sat. 10–2.

Tours

Lawrence County and Bedford Historical and Limestone Heritage Tours Self-guided walking and driving tours take you to stately buildings, including the county courthouse and churches, all made of Indiana limestone. Five tours, which are detailed in brochures available at the tourism commission downtown (after hours, look for the brochure rack in the front of the building), take in limestone-turreted buildings, statues, intricately carved monuments at cemeteries, and former quarries. > Lawrence County Tourism Commission, 1116 16th St., Bedford, tel. 812/275–7637, www.limestonecountry.com. Free. Weekdays 10–4:30.

Save the Date

APRIL

Little 500 Bicycle Race Now more than 50 years old, the Little 500 is the "Breaking Away" bicycle race held on the Indiana University campus on the third Saturday of the month. The women's Little 500 is held on Friday afternoon. Crowds watch teams battle it out on the oval track. > Bill Armstrong Stadium, N. Fee La., Bloomington, tel. 812/855–9152 or 800/558–8311, www.iusf.bloomington.com.

MAY–OCTOBER

Farmers Market at Showers Common Every Saturday morning, local growers sell fresh flowers, fruit, and vegetables at this spot seven blocks from campus. > 7th and Morton Sts.

SEPTEMBER

Annual Persimmon Festival On Main Street in downtown Mitchell, 40 mi south of Bloomington, persimmon pudding is served along with other persimmon novelty dishes. In addition to a bake-off, a parade, and arts-and-crafts booths, a carnival with live entertainment and displays of antique and classic autos adds to the fun. > Tel. 812/849–4441.

4th Street Arts Festival More than 100 artists from Indiana and other states display and sell paintings, woodwork, toys, quilts, and more at this two-day juried event, usually held the first weekend of the month. > 4th and Grant Sts., tel. 812/335–3814.

NOVEMBER–APRIL

University of Indiana Men's Basketball Few if any teams in the country have a following more rabid than the Indiana Hoosiers, a Big Ten power and frequent contender for the national title. Those visiting on nongame days can visit the school's well-stocked trophy cases and Athletic Hall of Fame, open weekdays 8–5. > Assembly Hall, 1001 E. 17th St., tel. 866/487–7678, www.iuhoosiers.com.

WHERE TO STAY

BEDFORD

Bedford Super 8 Motel This two-story motel, housed in a long white building with a blue-green roof, opened in 2000 on the south end of town near Leatherwood Creek. Location is the key here, as it is 3 mi from the Blue Springs Caverns, 10 mi from Spring Mill State Park, and 20 mi from IU. > 501 Bell Back Rd., Bedford 47421, tel. 812/275–8881 or 800/800–8000, fax 812/275–8881, www.super8.com. 47 rooms, 10 suites. In-room data ports, some in-room hot tubs, refrigerators, cable TV, indoor pool, hot tub, laundry facilities, business services, some pets allowed (fee). AE, D, DC, MC, V. CP. ¢

Holiday Inn Express At least four restaurants lie within a mile of this three-story hotel. Interior corridors lead to suites and rooms with one double bed, two queen beds, or one king. It's 1¼ mi from the Antique Auto and Race Car Museum, and 2½ mi from Blue Springs Caverns. > 2800 Express La., at Rte. 37, Bedford 47421, tel. 812/279–1206 or 877/838–6434, fax 812/279–1496, www.ichotelsgroup.com. 64 rooms, 18 suites. In-room data ports, some microwaves, some refrigerators, cable TV, indoor pool, exercise equipment, hot tub, sauna, Internet, business services, some pets allowed (fee). AE, D, DC, MC, V. CP. $

Spring Mill Inn This cozy inn, built in 1937–39 of native limestone, nestles amid tall oaks in Spring Mill State Park, 10 mi from Bedford. The four-story structure has been repeatedly updated over the years but outside looks much the same as it was when it was built. Inside are wood floors, oak paneling, and fireplaces. > Rte. 60 E, Mitchell

47446, tel. 812/849–4081 or 877/977–7464, fax 812/849–4647. 74 rooms. Dining room, indoor pool, shop, no-smoking rooms. AE, D, MC, V. BP. ¢–$

Stonehenge Lodge Open since 1989, this three-story motel, 1 mi west of Bedford, is built of native limestone and dark wood. The lodge offers discounted passes to a nearby fitness club. Rooms are spacious and lean toward light colors. > 911 Constitution Ave., Bedford 47421, tel. 812/279–8111 or 800/274–2974, fax 812/279–0172, www.stonehengelodge.com. 97 rooms. Restaurant, room service, cable TV, pool, lounge, video game room, business services. AE, D, DC, MC, V. CP. ¢

BLOOMINGTON

Canyon Inn The Canyon Inn, now part of McCormick's Creek State Park, was originally the Denkewalter Sanitarium. In the 1920s the building was remodeled and given an exterior veneer of brick. Since then, new wings, a swimming pool, and a recreation center have been added. > Rte. 46, Spencer 47460, tel. 812/829–4881, fax 812/829–1467. 75 rooms. Restaurant, pool, basketball, Ping-Pong, racquetball, shuffleboard, volleyball. AE, D, MC, V. ¢–$

Courtyard by Marriott This five-story hotel is two blocks south of the Courthouse Square shops and restaurants, and within walking distance of campus. Rooms are furnished in dark-wood furniture and have paneled walls. > 310 S. College Ave., Bloomington 47403, tel. 812/335–8000 or 800/321–2211, fax 812/336–9997, www.courtyard.com/bmgcy. 117 rooms, 5 suites. Restaurant, room service, in-room data ports, some microwaves, some refrigerators, cable TV, indoor pool, exercise equipment, hot tub, lounge, laundry facilities, business services. AE, D, DC, MC, V. ¢–$

Eagle Pointe Golf Resort In the hills on the southern edge of Lake Monroe, 13 mi south of downtown Bloomington, you can stay in a condominium with views of the lake, the golf course, or the woods. All have private entrances and a balcony or patio. Also available are loft-style rooms as well as one-, two-, or three-bedroom units and town houses. Many have fireplaces and full kitchens. Golf packages are available. > 2250 E. Pointe Rd., Bloomington 47401, tel. 812/824–4040 or 877/324–7683, fax 812/824–6860, www.eaglepointe.com. 82 condos. 3 restaurants, some kitchenettes, some microwaves, some refrigerators, cable TV, in-room VCRs, driving range, 18-hole golf course, golf privileges, putting green, tennis courts, pro shop, pool, outdoor hot tub, massage, sauna, boating, fishing, bicycles, basketball, 2 bars, laundry facilities, business services, meeting rooms, no-smoking rooms. AE, D, DC, MC, V. $$–$$$$

Fourwinds Resort and Marina Geared toward both couples and families, with a special emphasis on golf and water activities (particularly boating, with many types available for rent), the three-story Fourwinds is on the shore of Lake Monroe, 13 mi south of Bloomington. Furnishings are accented with rustic and contemporary touches, including polished clay floor tiles, woven rugs, and bold patterned fabrics. Many of the rooms have views of the lake. > 9301 Fairfax Rd., Bloomington 47401, tel. 812/824–9904 or 800/824–2628, fax 812/824–9816, www.fourwindsresort.com. 123 rooms. Restaurant, room service, cable TV, tennis courts, indoor-outdoor pool, hot tub, boating, jet skiing, marina, waterskiing, basketball, shuffleboard, bar, playground, business services, meeting rooms, no-smoking rooms. AE, D, DC, MC, V. $–$$

Grant Street Inn The courthouse is five blocks from this two-story clapboard home dating from the late 1800s. The main house was moved lock, stock, and barrel from its original location in 1990. Now it's a bed-and-breakfast with a roofed porch, with wooden rockers and wicker chairs, and the handsomely restored two-tone yellow facade is generously decorated with hanging plants and window boxes. Antique furnishings fill the rooms, some of which have fireplaces. Each is decorated in its own motif and many have tall windows to let in generous amounts of light. > 310 N. Grant St., Bloomington 47401, tel. 812/334–2353 or 800/328–4350, fax 812/331–8673, www.grantsinn.com. 24 rooms. Some in-room hot tubs, cable TV. AE, D, MC, V. BP. **$–$$**

TownePlace Suites by Marriott Aimed at those planning on a longer stay, this three-story all-suites hotel looks more like an apartment complex. It provides kitchens in all units, utensils and cookware, and a dishwasher. Part of the accommodations enclave just off Rte. 37, it's near shopping and 3 mi from the IU campus. Studio, one-, and two-bedroom suites are available > 105 S. Franklin Rd., Bloomington 47404, tel. 812/334–1234 or 800/257–3000, fax 812/334–1995, www.marriott.com. 84 rooms, 62 suites. In-room data ports, kitchenettes, refrigerators, cable TV, in-room VCRs, pool, exercise equipment, laundry facilities, laundry service, business services. AE, D, DC, MC, V. **$–$$$**

University Plaza Hotel Near Route 45 (Route 46), the four-story University Plaza is one of the area's largest hotels and is especially convenient to Cascades Park and to the IU sports facilities at the north end of campus. Though the views of the highway are less than inspiring, the room decor is refreshingly subdued and decent-size wooden desks serve the needs of the hotel's business clientele. For the health-minded, the hotel provides complimentary access to university exercise facilities; and three of the area's golf courses are within a short drive. > 1710 Kinser Pike, Bloomington 47404, tel. 812/334–3252 or 888/406–4262, fax 812/333–1702. 188 rooms. Restaurant, room service, cable TV, indoor pool, hot tub, sauna, lounge, business services, meeting rooms, some pets allowed, no-smoking rooms. AE, D, DC, MC, V. **¢–$$**

WHERE TO EAT

BEDFORD

Mamma's Mexican and Italian Restaurant With choices of Mexican, Italian, and American food on the menu, this small restaurant has one big dining room. It started as a burger joint and now serves sandwiches, shrimp, fish, grilled chicken, rib-eye steaks, grilled chicken salad, and lots of appetizers, including pepperoni bread sticks. Mexican options include chimichangas and burritos—or go Italian with spaghetti or lasagna. > 1707 M St., Bedford, tel. 812/275–0684. Reservations not accepted. D, MC, V. **¢–$**

Stoll's Restaurant Fried chicken is always on the menu at this Amish buffet that has three meats each day such as meat loaf, roast beef, barbecued pork, barbecued beef, barbecued ribs, beef stew, ham and beans, or minute steaks. Friday's buffet includes seafood. You can also order off a menu that has sandwiches, burgers, steaks, pork chops, catfish, shrimp, and baked fish. The main dining room has lots of big tables and booths, but you can also dine in the loft upstairs. > 1801 Plaza Dr., Bedford, tel. 812/279–8150. D, MC, V. Closed Sun. **¢–$$**

BLOOMINGTON

Irish Lion Set behind an old storefront a block from Courthouse Square near the center of town, this lively eatery serves American and Irish fare—and a collection of 57 single-malt Scotches. Dark hardwood floors, old mirrors, and Irish accoutrements make up the interior. Entrées include fresh oysters, mussels, clams, salmon, lamb, beef, poultry, and Irish pub–inspired stews. Beer, cider, and ale are served by the pint, or you might try a "yard" of beer. > 212 W. Kirkwood Ave., Bloomington, tel. 812/336–9076. AE, D, MC, V. **$–$$$**

Limestone Grille In the evening, a neon sign shines above the doorway of this corner storefront restaurant. A hand-carved limestone bas relief covers an entire wall of the restaurant, and the white-linen-covered tables are well spaced and candlelighted. Several menu items make use of contemporary recipes, such as sautéed rainbow trout in a sauce of white wine, oyster mushrooms, and shallots. You can also order Black Angus New York strip steak, pork chops, filet mignon, or chicken française. For dessert, try the bittersweet chocolate almond torte with raspberry sauce or lemon amaretti parfait. > 2920 E. Covenanter Dr., Bloomington, tel. 812/335–8110. AE, D, MC, V. Closed Sun. and Mon. **$$–$$$**

Michael's Uptown Café This popular breakfast spot near the center of Bloomington, reminiscent of a bustling big-city deli, draws crowds for lunch and dinner. Photos and art hang on the walls, and you can either sit in booths or at wooden tables. French, Cajun, and Mediterranean cuisines accent the American menu; the soups are note-worthy, as are the eclectic omelets. Every Tuesday brings live Irish music; McDonough's, an Irish-theme pub, is attached. > 102 E. Kirkwood Ave., Bloomington, tel. 812/339–0900. AE, D, DC, MC, V. No dinner Sun. **$–$$$**

Nick's English Hut Open since 1927, this tavern, a couple of blocks from the Indiana University campus, is a favorite hangout among locals and students. Booths line the perimeter of the room and framed news clippings, photos, and awards hang on the walls. The Back Room is quieter than up front and has a large fireplace; the Attic Room is the place for sports fans. The bar holds more than 30 televisions, four bars, pool tables, and seating for up to 500. Come for burgers, pizza, grilled chicken sand-wiches, and buffalo wings, or entrées such as New York strip steak and jambalaya. The place stays open until 2 AM daily except Sunday, when the doors close at mid-night. > 423 E. Kirkwood Ave., Bloomington, tel. 812/332–4040. Reservations not ac-cepted. AE, D, DC, MC, V. **$–$$$$**

Scholar's Inn Bakehouse Bins of homemade breads and the odor of coffee greet you at this café, across the street from the courthouse. The breads, a meal unto themselves, are free of preservatives and artificial ingredients; sandwiches and salads are available for heartier appetites; and a long list of fresh cakes, pastries, and pies can make for a perfect afternoon break on the café's covered patio. > 125 N. College Ave., Bloomington, tel. 812/331–6029. MC, V. **¢–$**

ESSENTIALS

Getting Here

A car is your best option if you want to travel beyond Bloomington to Bedford, the state parks and forests, or the nearby Columbus/Nashville area. If you're only visiting Bloomington, you can take Greyhound and get around on the city's local transit system. Downtown and the Indiana University campus are within walking distance of each other. Greyhound drops passengers two blocks from the downtown square. If you're flying, Indianapolis International Airport is the closest airport, an hour's drive north of Bloomington. Driving from Chicago to Bloomington takes approximately 4½ hours by car and 6 hours on Greyhound. Combining air travel and no-wait shuttle–rental car serv-ice from Chicago to Bloomington takes approximately 3 hours. No train serv-ice takes you to Bloomington or Bedford from Chicago.

BY BUS

Greyhound runs one bus daily from Chicago to Bloomington. The trip makes multiple stops and take approximately six hours. From Bloomington to Chicago, you can take either a morning or afternoon daily departure, which

21

puts you in Chicago in approximately five hours. Tickets purchased seven days in advance are usually discounted, but nonrefundable. Bloomington Transit maintains a reliable fleet of buses that crisscross the city, with a special concentration on the IU campus area. Fare is 75¢ (transfers free). Bicyclists can load their bikes onto racks on the front of the vehicles.

BUS DEPOT **Greyhound** > 217 W 6th St., Bloomington, tel. 812/332–1522, www.greyhound.com.

BUS LINES **Bloomington Transit** > Tel. 812/336–7433, www.bloomingtontransit.com. **Greyhound** > Tel. 812/332–1522 or 800/229–9424, www.greyhound.com.

BY CAR

Route 37, which links to I–65 in Indianapolis, takes you to Bloomington from the north and south. If you're arriving from the east, take I–65 to Routes 45 and 46; from the west by Routes 45, 46, and 48. Speed limits are 55–65 mph on the interstate, 45–55 mph on Route 37, and approximately 45 mph on the open-road sections of the state roads. Traffic is usually not a problem, with one exception: the merge of I–94 with I–80 near the Indiana state line can see backups, especially during Friday-evening rush hours when commuters, long-haul semis, and vacationers collide. If you're coming from the north you can miss the mess by using the I–90 toll road. Otherwise, consider leaving early. Traffic on the interstates around Indianapolis is usually manageable, compared with Chicago traffic. Bloomington city streets are well marked and easily navigable, with speed limits typically between 25 and 45 mph. Parking weekends and evenings after 5 PM is free. During the week, downtown parking is available in metered parking lots (most 50¢ per hour, some $1 per hour). Some free two-hour parking is available on the street along Kirkwood Avenue and around the square. Parking on-campus is limited. Street parking in Bedford is typically not a problem.

BY PLANE

Bloomington is served by Indianapolis International Airport. Three airlines fly between Indianapolis International Airport and Chicago O'Hare: American, United, and US Airways. Two airlines serve Indianapolis International Airport to and from Chicago Midway: ATA and Southwest (five times a day). Flights can vary but usually take 1 hour and 15 minutes. Check with the airlines for prices and flight times.

AIRPORT **Indianapolis International Airport** > 2500 S. High School Rd., Indianapolis, tel. 317/487–7243, www.indianapolisairport.com/.

CARRIERS **American** > Tel. 800/433–7300. **ATA** > Tel. 317/248–8308 or 800/435–9282. **Southwest** > Tel. 800/435–9792. **United** > Tel. 800/864–8331. **US Airways** > Tel. 800/428–4322.

Visitor Information

CONTACTS **Bloomington/Monroe County Convention and Visitors Bureau** > 2855 N. Walnut St., Bloomington 47401, tel. 812/334–8900 or 800/800–0037, www.visitbloomington.com. **Lawrence County Tourism Commission** > 1116 16th St., Box 1193, Bedford 47421, tel. 812/275–5998, www.limestonecountry.com.

Door County

230 mi north of Chicago

22

By Jenn Q. Goddu

DOOR COUNTY'S NAME IS DERIVED FROM THE MONIKER "Porte des Morts," which French explorers, inspired by the stories told by Potawatomi and Chippewa Indians, gave to the treacherously narrow strait or "death's door" at the north end of this 70-mi-long peninsula. The passage connects Lake Michigan and Green Bay and scores of ships were once stranded or damaged in the turbulent currents of these waters. Today, little danger comes to ships entering these waters, but the name remains a colorful piece of the peninsula's history.

Depending on the season during which you visit, you might find Door County literally awash in color as the fruit trees blossom. Soil conditions and the climate make the peninsula a prime region for cherry and apple production, and its orchards produce more than 20 million pounds of fruit each year. Just seeing the peninsula carpeted in blossoms is enough to merit the drive.

Door County is comprised of quaint towns nestled into the bay or lake shore. Each is filled with shops, restaurants, galleries, and inns. It is easy to make a circle tour of the entire peninsula via Routes 57 and 42. The Lake Michigan side of the peninsula is somewhat less settled and the landscape is more rugged. On the bay side it is busier and more built up.

At the southernmost point of Door County is Sturgeon Bay, the county seat and the only city on the Door County peninsula. Named for the long fish-shape bay it borders, this city has resorts, restaurants, and art galleries. Maritime history is important here and even today the canal linking Lake Michigan to Green Bay is busy with ship activity. Nineteen miles up the bay side of the peninsula is Egg Harbor, a village surrounded by cherry and apple orchards and filled with hops. The community gained its name after a trade flotilla landed in the harbor and had a huge egg-flinging "war" with the spectators on the shore.

Fish Creek is 6 mi farther north. Its harbor is a hub of activity and it also serves as the entrance to Peninsula State Park, where great views and recreational opportunities abound. If you're looking for art, Fish Creek is home to the Peninsula Players (the country's oldest professional summer theater), as well as a music festival and a folklore theater. Nearby Ephraim (pronounced *ee*-frum) is nestled along Eagle Harbor just 5 mi farther up the bay side. This village has a rich Norwegian heritage and has restored a number of buildings that capture the town's history.

A "valkommen" sign greets you as you drive into Sister Bay, Door County's largest community north of Sturgeon Bay. Settled in 1857 by Norwegian immigrants, this community is at the intersection of Routes 57 and 42. Restaurants, shops, and its waterfront keep the community bustling.

With 14,000 acres, Washington Island is the largest of Door County's islands, and it is great for bicycling, boating, golf, leisurely drives, gallery-viewing, and shopping. To get to Washington Island, take Route 42 to the "top o' the thumb," a reference to the County's resemblance to the thumb of a mitten jutting out from the rest of the state. Ellison Bay, Gills Rock, and Rowley's Bay are rugged beauties with bluffs hanging out over the lake or bay. You can get a ferry to the island, which has a permanent population of only 650, from either Gills Rock or Northport, the northernmost point of the peninsula. If you're looking for even more isolation, Rock Island State Park is just a short ferry ride away from the northeast corner of the island.

On the lake side of the peninsula is the peaceful fishing village of Baileys Harbor, 10 mi south of Sister Bay. Here you can take in the waterfront with fewer crowds. Before you even get to the actual Door County peninsula, you might also want to take in Algoma, a lakeside town that is home to one of the state's largest charter fishing fleets. The historic downtown and waterfront districts are the places to see fish shanties, do antique shopping, or visit a fruit winery.

During your trip, be sure to sample one of the vintages pressed at a county orchard or take in one of the region's famed fish boils, one of Door County's culinary delights.

WHAT TO SEE & DO

ALGOMA
Ahnapee State Trail With 15 mi of trail, the Ahnapee runs from Algoma along the Ahnapee River to Sturgeon Bay. The multiuse firm trail surface is great for biking, walking, and snowmobiling. A visitor center at the lake has trail information and maps. > Lake St., Algoma, tel. 920/487–2041 or 800/498–4888. Free. Daily.
Kewaunee County Historical Museum This museum 10 mi south of Algoma in Kewaunee's Court House Square covers local and maritime history. The 1876 building was once the sheriff's residence, office, and the local jail. You can see the original dungeon-style cells. > 613 Dodge St., Kewaunee, tel. 920/388–4410. $2. Memorial Day–Labor Day, daily 9–4:30; Labor Day–Memorial Day, by appointment.
Von Stiehl Winery Housed inside a vintage brewery building, this winery founded in 1965 makes wines following the old German method. Wine tours and tastings, with more than 20 wines to sample, are given. You can also buy foodstuffs, such as wine mustards, wine cheese, and wine sausage. > 115 Navarino St., Algoma, tel. 920/487–5208 or 800/955–5208, www.vonstiehl.com. $3. May, June, Sept., and Oct., daily 9–5; July and Aug., daily 9–5:30; Nov. and Dec., daily 11–5; Jan.–Apr., daily 11–4.

BAILEYS HARBOR
Bjorklunden This 425-acre estate on Lake Michigan serves as Lawrence University's northern campus. Here you can visit the Boynton Chapel, an ancient Norwegian-style *stavkirke*. The small wooden 15th-century-style chapel was handcrafted in the mid-1900s. It is open for guided tours Monday and Wednesday from 1 to 4, from mid-June through August. Inside are ornate Norwegian hand-carved woodwork and murals. > 7603 Chapel La., off Lakeshore Dr., Baileys Harbor, tel. 920/839–2216. $3. June–Aug., Mon. and Wed. 1–4.
Cana Island Lighthouse Be prepared for a little wading as the 500-foot rock walkway to this island's 1869 lighthouse can be covered with water at times. This low dwelling and tall white tower with a two-story cast-iron black lantern is one of Door County's most photographed and painted lighthouses. > Cana Island Rd., 2½ mi off Rte. Q, Baileys Harbor, tel. 920/743–5958. Free. May–mid-Oct., daily 10–5.

Ridges Sanctuary The 1,000-acre sanctuary on the northern outskirts of Baileys Harbor consists of ridges made of sand moved by Lake Michigan currents and wave action. Each ridge took about 30 years to form. Hiking trails follow the crests of the ridges and traverse wooded bogs and boreal forest bursting with wildflowers and rare plants. Within the Sanctuary are the **Ridge Lights,** which were built in 1869 to guide ships into the harbor. These lights, listed on the National Historic Register, were originally fueled by lard and whale oil, but were automated in 1923. They were in use until 1969. > Rte. Q, off Rte. 57, Baileys Harbor, tel. 920/839–1101. $2.

EGG HARBOR
Dovetail Gallery and Studio This gallery is housed in an original dovetail 1873 log home. Particularly unique is the collection of decorated eggs with ethnic and contemporary designs from around the world. Paintings, wood carving, pottery, stained glass, garden art, and art furniture are also on display. Elaborate flower gardens showcase copper garden-art sprinklers. > 7901 Rte. 42, Egg Harbor, tel. 920/868–3987, www.dovetailgallery.com. Free. May–Feb., daily 10–6.

ELLISON BAY
Death's Door Bluff This bluff is at the very tip of the Door County peninsula. The narrow passage, only 6 mi wide, connects Lake Michigan and Green Bay. It has turbulent currents year-round and numerous ships sank here many years ago. > Ellison Bay, tel. 800/527–3529. Free. Daily.
Door County Maritime Museum Commercial fishing, shipwrecks, and navigation are the focus of this seasonal museum 5 mi north of Ellison Bay. You can see models, marine engines, photos, a 1917 Berylume pleasure craft, and a 1930s fishing tug. > 12724 Rte. 42, Gills Rock, tel. 920/743–5958, www.dcmm.org. $4. Memorial Day–Labor Day, daily 10–4.
Newport State Park At this 2,370-acre wild area with 11 mi of Lake Michigan shoreline, northeast of town, you can hike, swim, fish, mountain bike, camp, cross-country ski, and snowshoe. > 475 Rte. NP, Ellison Bay, tel. 920/854–2500, www.dcty.com/newport. $7. Daily.

EPHRAIM
Anderson Barn Museum The community of Ephraim's past is depicted through photographs and artifacts in this 1880 family barn with an unusual square silo. > 3060 Anderson La., Ephraim, tel. 920/854–9688, www.ephraim.org. $2. Mid-June–Oct., Mon.–Sat. 10:30–4.
Anderson Store Museum This 1858 waterfront store, run by the Anderson family for more than 100 years, is now open to the public as a museum of Ephraim's history. It's still set up as an early-20th-century general store, with shelves full of merchandise from that time. Be sure to check out the weathered dock building and its years of graffiti. > 10049 Water St., Ephraim, tel. 920/854–9688, www.ephraim.org. $2, includes barn, schoolhouse, and cabin. Mid-June–Oct., Mon.–Sat. 10:30–4.
Pioneer Schoolhouse and Thomas Goodleston Cabin This big, white 1880 schoolhouse with a bell tower is two blocks up a hill from the main strip. Beside it is a much smaller 1857 log cabin that was originally on Eagle Island and home to a family of seven. The cabin is furnished with period items from Ephraim's early days. > 9998 Moravia St., Ephraim, tel. 920/854–9688, www.ephraim.org. $2. Mid-June–Oct., Mon.–Sat. 10:30–4.

Peninsula Wines

DOOR COUNTY IS NOT OFTEN THE FIRST PLACE that comes to mind when we're thinking of primo wine regions. But as the more than 5,000 acres of cherry and apple orchards prove, the peninsula is an ideal location for growing delicious fruits. The early settlers discovered it was difficult to grow food crops with the thin alkaline soil that's found here but the limestone beneath the soil provides the roots with many nutrients and a mild climate has helped Door County to be a perfect place to foster a fruit industry. And flavorful fruits, not just grapes, can make tasty wines. Although fruit wines make up only about 3% of the wine sales nationally, they represent 75% of wine sales in Wisconsin.

The wines in this region are made from strawberries, blackberries, raspberries, cherries, cranberries, apples, pears, peaches, plums, and, so as not to abandon traditional expectations entirely, grapes. You can find dry or sweet, crisp or tangy, light or full-bodied reds and whites, and even some champagne options, on the shelves of the handful of wineries throughout Door County. Many of these wineries have free guided tours and sample tastings so you can learn about the process of picking, fermenting, and bottling, before deciding whether you're looking for a Chardapple, Blackberry Merlot, or maybe a Holiday Cherry to take home.

Even the buildings that house the winery operations can be interesting. For instance, Von Stiehl's grape and other fruit wines are kept in casks in the underground cellars of an Algoma historic building built around the end of the Civil War. The Door Peninsula Winery outside of Sturgeon Bay uses the thick stone walls of an old schoolhouse cellar to keep its fermenting wines at a constant temperature. Lautenback's Orchard Country Winery & Marketplace is in a restored dairy barn and you can even tour the orchards of this family business outside of Fish Creek.

All this fruit wine activity is also good news for the teetotalers. There are plenty of juice blends and jams available in the winery shops. And when you drive the winding roads of Door County in spring, you're sure to see the beautiful blossoms of a fruit orchard.

FISH CREEK

Edgewood Orchard Galleries This restored stone fruit barn has been displaying the work of county artists in all mediums since 1969. > 4140 Peninsula Players Rd., Fish Creek, tel. 920/868–3579, www.edgewoodorchard.com. Free. Mid-May–Oct., daily 10–5.

Historic Noble House Fish Creek's oldest frame residence was built in 1875 by Alexander Noble, who was town chairman, postmaster, and blacksmith over the years. This example of Greek-revival farmhouse architecture is on the National Register of Historic Places. > Rte. 42 and Main St., Fish Creek, tel. 920/868–2091. $3. Mid-May–mid-June., weekends 11–4; mid-June–Oct., daily 11–4.

Peninsula State Park This 3,762-acre peninsula, with more than 6 mi of shoreline on Green Bay waters, has an 18-hole championship golf course, hiking, bicycle trails, camping, groomed ski trails, snowmobiling, sledding, swimming, boat rentals, a boat ramp, an observation tower, and fishing. You can see the 125-year-old Eagle Bluff lighthouse. Trail maps and other information are available at the park headquarters. The

American Folklore Theatre (tel. 920/854–6117, www.folkloretheatre.com) performs its summer season in the 750-seat park theater from June through August. > 9462 Shore Rd., Fish Creek, tel. 920/868–3258, www.wiparks.net. $7. Daily 6 AM–11 PM.

SISTER BAY

Anderson House Museum When Alex and Emma Anderson moved from Marinette to Sister Bay in 1865, they moved this house with them—across the ice and a mile uphill. The former farmhouse has two stories on one side and one story on the other, and it's furnished with period pieces. The house is on Route 57, on the south end of town. Nearby are three other buildings representing Sister Bay history that are in various stages of restoration. > Rte. 57 at Country La. and Fieldcrest Rd., Sister Bay, tel. 920/854–9242. Free. Mid-May–mid Oct., weekends 11–3.

STURGEON BAY

Door County Historical Museum Inside this museum, Door County history is portrayed through various exhibits, including a fire station replica complete with trucks that kids can climb on and a wildlife exhibit. > 18 N. 4th St., Sturgeon Bay, tel. 920/743–5809. Free. May–Oct., daily 10–4:30; Nov.–Apr., by appointment.

Door County Maritime Museum You can watch ships being built, explore an engine room, study ship models, and learn about Door County lighthouses in this 20,000-square-foot museum on the water's edge. > 120 N. Madison Ave., Sturgeon Bay, tel. 920/743–5958, www.dcmm.or. $6.50. Memorial Day–Labor Day, daily 9–6; Labor Day–Memorial Day, daily 10–5.

The Farm This living museum 4 mi north of the city has a petting zoo with farm animals such as goats, cows, and horses, as well as nature trails and log cabins with farm tools and antiques on display. > 4285 Rte. 57 N, Sturgeon Bay, tel. 920/743–6666. $7. Memorial Day–Labor Day, daily 9–5.

Miller Art Museum Gallery In the same building as the Door County Library, this art museum has changing exhibits as well as a permanent collection of works by 20th-century Wisconsin artists. One wing is devoted to a growing body of the watercolor and egg tempera paintings of Gerhard C. F. Miller. > 107 S. 4th St., Sturgeon Bay, tel. 920/743–6578. Free. Mon.–Thurs. 10–8, Fri. and Sat. 10–5.

Whitefish Dunes State Park This 865-acre park has more visitors than any other day-use park in the state. There's more than a mile of sandy beach, the highest sand dune in Wisconsin, and trails for hiking, biking, and skiing. Bordering Whitefish Dunes on three sides is **Cave Point County Park** (tel. 920/743–4456), where Lake Michigan has carved caves out of dolomite rocks. > 3275 Clark Lake Rd. (Rte. WD), Sturgeon Bay, tel. 920/823–2400, www.wiparks.net.

William S. Fairfield Art Museum The gallery's permanent collection houses maquettes, drawings, and sculptures by Henry Moore; abstract paintings by Kandinsky; and sculpted works by Alberto Giacometti. The museum is housed in 1907 building in the center of the city's historic downtown. > 242 Michigan Ave., Sturgeon Bay, tel. 920/746–0001, fax 920/746–0000, www.fairfieldartmuseum.com. $5. Mon. and Thurs.–Sat. 10–5, Sun. 11–3.

WASHINGTON ISLAND

Art and Nature Center Inside an old schoolhouse, this gallery showcases the work of local artists and houses a nature room, where you can see such displays as an observation beehive. Naturalist-led hikes are available as well. > Main Rd., Washington

Island, tel. 920/847–205 or 920/847–2657. $1. Mid-June–mid-Oct., Mon.–Sat. 10:30–4:30, Sun. 11:30–4:30.

Jackson Harbor Maritime Museum Two former fishing sheds are now a museum dedicated to local maritime history. You can learn about area commercial fishing and shipwrecks. Artifacts, photos, and videos enrich the experience. > Jackson Harbor Rd., Washington Island, tel. 920/847–2179. $1. Late June–Labor Day, daily 10–4; Labor Day–late June, weekends 10–4.

Jacobsen Museum This small museum is dedicated to Jens Jacobsen, a woodworker who immigrated from Denmark in 1881. The museum exhibits pieces he built on a foot-powered scroll saw. Native American artifacts and Icelandic, Norwegian, and Danish memorabilia are also displayed. A small log cabin, once owned by Jacobsen, has been restored with authentic furniture. > Little Lake Rd., Washington Island, tel. 920/847–2213. $1. Mid-May–mid-Oct., daily 10–4.

Rock Island State Park This 905-acre island was once the private estate of million-aire inventor Chester Thordarson, who built several stone buildings on Washington Island between 1918 and 1929. Exhibits in the castlelike boathouse and Viking Hall explore the island's history and natural surroundings. You can hike on 10 mi of trails through deciduous hardwood forests, where backpacking is permitted. To get here, you must take the Rock Island Ferry. > North ferryboat dock, Washington Island, tel. 920/847–2235 summer, 920/847–3156 winter. $7. Daily.

Washington Island Farm Museum On this 3-acre complex, you can visit five original farm buildings that date back to the late 1800s, including a log cabin and a barn. On display is a collection of field machinery, hand tools, photos, and homemaking artifacts. You can tour the museum on your own and watch a demonstration on farm-life techniques, such as weaving or cider pressing. > Jackson Harbor Rd., Washington Island, tel. 920/847–2156. Donations accepted. Memorial Day–mid-Oct., daily 10–5 (grounds and buildings); no building tours rest of yr.

Tours

Cherry Train Tours This 18-mi, 90-minute narrated tour fills you in on the history, folklore, and legends of life on Washington Island. Stops include an ostrich farm, art center, farm museum, and one of the island's earliest settlements. Tours are conducted twice daily in May, June, September, and October. Four tours are led from July to mid-August. The cost is $9. > Tours depart from the Island Ferry Dock, Washington Island, tel. 920/847–2039 or 920/847–2546, www.wisferry.com.

Door County Cruises This two-hour cruise aboard a retired Chicago fireboat departs daily at 11:50 and 2:50. The boat, built in 1937, cruises to Sturgeon Bay Canal Station and, weather permitting, the Sherwood Point Lighthouse. On board, you can visit a small museum dedicated to Chicago's firefighting efforts. The cost is $22. > Docked next to the Door County Maritime Museum at 18 N. 4th St., Sturgeon Bay, tel. 920/825–1112, www.doorcountycruises.com.

Door County Trolley This trolley company runs two different Door County tours. One departs Fish Creek and is a narrated 45-minute tour of the scenic bluffs, during which you hear colorful local stories. The second departs from Sturgeon Bay and is an introduction to the area's shops, wineries, and galleries. The cost to ride this bright red old-style trolley is $10. > 1113 Cove Rd., Sturgeon Bay, tel. 920/868–1100, www.doorcountytrolley.com.

Viking Train Tour This is a 90-minute tram tour of Washington Island. It stops at an ostrich farm, farm museum, a harbor swimming beach, and two Norwegian cottages. Four tours are conducted daily from May to October. An additional tour is added in-

July and August. The cost is $9. > 12731 Rte. 42, Gills Rock, tel. 920/854–2972, www.islandclipper.com.

Sports

BIKING

Ahnapee State Trail More than 15 mi of trail run from Algoma along the Ahnapee River to Sturgeon Bay. > 1226 Lake St., Algoma, tel. 920/487–2041 or 800/498–4888.
Newport State Park Off-road bicycles have access to 16.8 mi of trail. > 475 Rte. NP, Ellison Bay, tel. 920/854–2500, www.wiparks.net.
Peninsula State Park There are 9 mi of off-road bike trails in this 3,776 acres of forest. > 9462 Shore Rd., Egg Harbor, tel. 920/868–3258, www.wiparks.net.
Potawatomi State Park This 1,225-acre park has 4.6 mi of trails open for mountain biking. > 3740 Park Dr., Sturgeon Bay, tel. 920/746–2890.
Rock Island State Park Take a ferry to this Lake Michigan island park that has 10 mi of trails. > Rock Island, tel. 920/847–2235 mid-Apr.–mid-Nov., 920/847–3156 mid-Nov.–mid-Apr., www.wiparks.net.
Whitefish Dunes State Park Trails take in Lake Michigan shoreline, dense upland forest, shoreline on an interior lake, wetlands, and sand dunes. > 3275 Clark Lake Rd. (Rte. WD), Sturgeon Bay, tel. 920/823–2400, www.wiparks.net.
RENTALS **DC Bikes** > 20 N. 3rd Ave., Sturgeon Bay, tel. 920/743–4434, www.doorcountybikes.com. **Edge Of Park Bike & Moped Rental** > Park Entrance Rd., Fish Creek, tel. 920/868–3344. **Nor Door Sport & Cyclery** > 4007 Rte. 42, Fish Creek, tel. 920/868–2275, www.nordoorsports.com.

HIKING

Ahnapee State Trail More than 15 mi of trail, the Ahnapee runs from Algoma along the Ahnapee River to Sturgeon Bay. > 1226 Lake St., Algoma, tel. 920/487–2041 or 800/498–4888.
Newport State Park Nearly 40 mi of hiking trails traverse the park's 2,370 acres of forests. The Brachipod Trail is a 1½-mi interpretive trail; the Pine Plantation trail is a ¼-mi loop through fledgling forest. > 475 Rte. NP, Ellison Bay, tel. 920/854–2500, www.wiparks.net.
Peninsula State Park Amid its 3,776 acres are 20 mi of hiking trails including Eagle Trail, which take you along the water's edge and to highest bluffs in Door County. > 9462 Shore Rd., Egg Harbor, tel. 920/868–3258, www.wiparks.net.
Potawatomi State Park This 1,225-acre park has 17.5 mi of hiking trails. > 3740 Park Dr., Sturgeon Bay, tel. 920/746–2890, www.wiparks.net.
Rock Island State Park Take a ferry to this Lake Michigan island park, which has 10 mi of trails, including a 1-mi interpretive trail. > Rock Island, tel. 920/847–2235 mid-Apr.–mid-Nov., 920/847–3156 mid-Nov.–mid-Apr., www.wiparks.net.
Whitefish Dunes State Park Fourteen miles of trails take in Lake Michigan shoreline, dense upland forest, shoreline on an interior lake, wetlands, and sand dunes. The 11 mi of trails at Whitefish Dunes State Park include a self-guided tour past replicas of the structures used by Native Americans in the area. > 3275 Clark Lake Rd. (Rte. WD), Sturgeon Bay, tel. 920/823–2400, www.wiparks.net.

Save the Date

JANUARY

New Year's Day Parade Despite the weather, New Year's Day is celebrated with this parade, which begins at the south end of Egg Harbor. > Tel. 920/868–2120.

Polar Bear Swim At noon sharp on the first of each year hearty folk gather at Lakeside Park Beach in Jacksonport for this frosty dip in Lake Michigan. > Tel. 920/823–2231.

FEBRUARY

Winter Festival If it's too cold for the contests on the ice and snow of Fish Creek's Clark Park that highlight this festival, check out the carnival-type games in a heated tent. > Tel. 920/868–2316 or 800/577–1880.

APRIL

Baileys Harbor Brown Trout Tournament At this annual event held the last weekend in April, contestants can fish from boats or from the dock. The event includes prizes and an awards ceremony. > Tel. 920/839–2366, www.baileyharbor.com.

MAY

Annual Open-Bass Tournament Held over three days in mid-May, this fishing contest hosts a pro-am event on Friday and a two-day tournament on the weekend in Sturgeon Bay. Family events and a dock dance on Saturday, plus the awards presentation on Sunday, add to the fun. > Tel. 920/743–1100, www.sbobt.org.

Festival of Blossoms A monthlong countywide celebration of spring, the festival highlights blossoming orchards, daffodils, and wildflowers. Communities host guided tours, box socials, fun runs, and more. > Tel. 920/743–4456.

Shipyards Tour The Door County Maritime Museum sponsors a walking tour of Sturgeon Bay's downtown shipyards the second Saturday in May. > Tel. 920/854–5585.

JUNE

American Folklore Theatre Four original musical comedies are presented under the stars in the Peninsula State Park Amphitheater in Fish Creek. > Tel. 920/868–9999.

Fyr-Bal Fest This Scandinavian festival in Ephraim celebrates the beginning of summer with music, dance, crafts, food, a fish boil, beach bonfires, and a sailing regatta. > Tel. 920/854–4989.

Old Ellison Bay Days This late-month community celebration downtown includes food, a talent show, an ice-cream social, a soapbox derby, a parade, an art fair, and music. > Tel. 920/854–5786.

Peninsula Players America's oldest professional resident summer theater group stages performances in an outdoor pavilion 3 mi south of Fish Creek. > Tel. 920/868–3287.

JUNE–AUGUST

Birch Creek Music Performance Center This former barn, 3 mi east of Egg Harbor, hosts approximately 30 summer concerts each year. > Tel. 920/868–3763, www.birchcreek.org.

Midsummer's Music Chamber music for winds, strings, and piano is performed in intimate settings such as churches, galleries, village halls, or historic homes throughout Door County. All concerts are indoors. > Tel. 920/854–7088, www.midsummersmusic.com.

AUGUST

Cherry Fest A fresh crop of cherries is feted with historical displays, fresh baking, arts-and-crafts fair, food, and music on the first weekend of August in Jacksonport. > Tel. 920/823–2231.

Classic Wooden Boat Show and Festival You can spend a day on the waterfront viewing old, restored, or new boats at this event, held the first full weekend in August at the Door County Maritime Museum in Sturgeon Bay. > Tel. 920/743–5958, www.dcmm.org.

Peninsula Music Festival Musicians from orchestras from across the country come together for three weeks and 10 concerts of great classical works, such as the Tchaikovsky symphonies, held at the Door County Community Auditorium in Ephraim. > Tel. 920/854–4060.

Perseid Meteor Shower You can watch a dazzling once-a-year meteor shower in mid-month—sometimes as many as 50 meteors an hour—at Fish Creek's Peninsula State Park, the darkest park on the peninsula. > Tel. 920/854–2500.

Scandinavian Dance Festival Dance, food, desserts, demonstrations, and a tour of a Norwegian church take over Washington Island on the first full weekend of the month. > Tel. 920/847–2179.

OCTOBER

Sister Bay Fall Festival Sister Bay hosts this oldest continuing fall festival in Door County on the third weekend of the month. Activities include a parade, a soapbox derby, a Ping-Pong ball drop, food, entertainment, arts, crafts, and fireworks. > Tel. 920/854–5585.

WHERE TO STAY

ALGOMA

Algoma Beach Motel On the edge of town in a quiet residential neighborhood, this motel has spacious lakeshore rooms and condo units, all with water views. You can grill out on the private beach, have a bonfire, or take a stroll down the town boardwalk. > 1500 Lake St., Algoma 54201, tel. 920/487–2828 or 888/254–6621, fax 920/487–2844, www.harborwalk.com. 28 rooms, 4 condos. Picnic area, some kitchenettes, cable TV, beach, some pets allowed. AE, D, DC, MC, V. CP. ¢–$$

Amberwood Inn This antiques-furnished 1920s Cape Cod–style home has five large suites overlooking Lake Michigan. Each has French doors leading to its own lakefront deck. Breakfast is served in your room or the dining room. The inn also has a 300-foot private beach. > N7136 Rte. 42, Lakeshore Dr., Algoma 54201, tel. 920/487–3471, www.amberwoodinn.com. 5 suites. Picnic area, cable TV, hot tub, sauna, beach. MC, V. BP. $

Harbor Inn Motel This two-story motel in downtown Algoma is on the shores of Lake Michigan by the lighthouse. Every nautical-theme room has a lakefront view. The motel is a favorite of visiting anglers. > 99 Michigan St., Algoma 54201, tel. 920/487–5241. 38 rooms. Refrigerators, cable TV, dock. AE, D, MC, V. Closed Jan.–Mar. ¢

BAILEYS HARBOR

Baileys Harbor Yacht Club Resort The prominent stone fireplace, overstuffed sofas, and vaulted, wood-paneled ceiling of the lobby set the tone of this resort between the Lake Michigan waterfront and a 1,000-acre wildlife preserve. Rooms in the three buildings all have hardwood furniture; some have whirlpool tubs and private porches. > 8151 Ridges Rd., Baileys Harbor 54202-0430, tel. 920/839–2336 or 800/927–2492, www.bhyc.com. 60 rooms, 20 suites. Some kitchenettes, cable TV, indoor-outdoor pool, sauna, dock. AE, D, MC, V. ¢–$$$

Blacksmith Inn This 1912 half-timber inn is on the waterfront and every room has a view of the lake. The inn and the adjacent Harbor House share a private 400-foot sand beach. The inn has fireplaces, patios, wooden floors and beamed ceilings, and, in keeping with its name, a working blacksmith shop. > 8152 Rte. 57, Baileys Harbor 54202, tel.

920/839–9222 or 800/769–8619, fax 920/839–9356, www.theblacksmithinn.com. 15 rooms. In-room hot tubs, in-room VCRs. MC, V. CP. **$$$**

New Yardley Inn This bed-and-breakfast built in 1997 is set on 10 acres in Peninsula Center. Rooms are large and have fireplaces, many large windows, and a screened-in porch. Rooms are decorated with stenciled walls and wood furniture, and you sleep under a comfy quilt. There is one wheelchair-accessible suite. > 3360 Rte. E, between Egg Harbor and Baileys Harbor, Baileys Harbor 54202, tel. 888/492–7353, fax 920/839–9487, www.newyardleyinn.com. 3 rooms, 1 suite. No smoking. D, MC, V. BP. **$–$$$**

Ridges Resort & Guest House Built in 1996, this quiet wood-side resort is adjacent to the Ridges Sanctuary. Wicker furnishings complement the colorfully decorated rooms. The rooms on the second story of the lodge have balconies. Other choices include a three-bedroom guest house and five cottages. The property has 7 mi of hiking trails. > 8252 Rte. 57, Baileys Harbor 54202, tel. 920/839–2127 or 800/328–1710, www.ridges.com. 17 rooms, 5 cottages, 1 house. Some in-room hot tubs, kitchens, cable TV, in-room VCRs. D, MC, V. **$–$$**

EGG HARBOR

Ashbrooke A fireplace, white wicker furniture, paintings, and lots of country charm unfold as you walk into the lobby of this elegant white hotel, 7 mi from Peninsula State Park. The rooms are dressed in French country decor. > 7942 Egg Harbor Rd., Egg Harbor 54209, tel. 920/868–3113 or 877/868–3113, fax 920/868–2837, www.ashbrooke.net. 36 rooms. Some in-room hot tubs, microwaves, refrigerators, cable TV, pool, gym, hot tub, sauna, business services; no kids under 14, no smoking. AE, MC, V. CP. **$–$$$**

Door County Lighthouse Inn A towering lighthouse tops this inn's five suites decorated in nautical themes and named after well-known lighthouses in Door County. A separate log cabin that sleeps up to four people is also available. > 4639 Orchard Rd., Egg Harbor 54209, tel. 920/868–9088 or 866/868–9088, www.dclighthouseinn.com. 5 rooms, 1 cabin. Some in-room hot tubs, in room VCRs. D, MC, V. CP. **$–$$$**

Landing Resort Inside the heart of the village, ensconced in a peaceful wooded setting, this two-story hotel, with its grand stone fireplace in the lobby, feels like a mountain chalet. The bright rooms—with names such as the Flagship, the Spinnaker, the Navigator, or the Captains—are all decorated with a nautical theme. > 7741 Egg Harbor Rd., Egg Harbor 54209, tel. 920/868–3282 or 800/851–8919, www.thelandingresort.com. 61 rooms. Picnic area, microwaves, refrigerators, cable TV, in-room VCRs, tennis courts, 2 pools, hot tub, playground. D, MC, V. **$–$$$$**

Landmark Resort & Conference Center This luxurious four-building, all-suites retreat is nestled in the woods overlooking the waters of Green Bay. The year-round lodgelike resort provides deluxe accommodations and plenty of recreational activities. Homey suites with floral or plaid flourishes have waterside or wood-side views and balconies or porches. > 7643 Hillside Rd., Egg Harbor 54209, tel. 920/868–3205 or 800/273–7877, fax 920/868–2569, www.thelandmarkresort.com. 294 suites. Restaurant, kitchenettes, some minibars, microwaves, refrigerators, cable TV, in-room VCRs, 27-hole golf course, tennis courts, indoor-outdoor pool, health club, hot tub, steam room, basketball, laundry facilities. AE, DC, MC, V. **$–$$$**

Newport Resort The large stone fireplace and forest-green sofas in the lobby and the vaulted, wood-paneled ceiling above the indoor pool lend a country ambiance to this large, cream-color hotel with a front veranda. Every French country decorated suite has a fireplace. > 7888 Church St., Egg Harbor 54209, tel. 920/868–9900. 59 suites.

Some in-room hot tubs, some kitchenettes, cable TV, in-room VCRs, indoor-outdoor pool, gym, sauna, playground, business services; no smoking. D, MC, V. CP. $–$$$$
Wildflower B&B Surrounded by trees and wildflowers, this home, the town's only B&B, is a block from both downtown and the harbor. Each room has a private balcony and fireplace; one has a whirlpool. Floral-theme rooms are cheery and cozy. The common area has a wet bar, refrigerator, and microwave. > 7821 Church St., Egg Harbor 54209, tel. 920/868–9030, www.wildflowerbnb.com. 3 rooms. Cable TV; no room phones. D, MC, V. CP. $–$$

ELLISON BAY

Harbor House This hotel's main building is a turn-of-the-20th-century mansion with a lake view, beach access, a porch with latticework, and many period furnishings. A Scandinavian country wing overlooks the town's fishing harbor and bluffs, and is perfect for sunset views. The Lighthouse Suite, inside 35-foot lighthouse, is a two-room suite with a fireplace and a hot tub. > 12666 Rte. 42, Gills Rock 54210, tel. 920/854–5196, fax 920/854–9717, www.door-county-inn.com. 7 rooms, 6 suites, 2 cottages. Picnic area, some microwaves, refrigerators, hot tub, sauna, playground, some pets allowed; no room phones, no smoking. AE, MC, V. CP. ¢–$$$
Hotel Disgarden Bed and Breakfast This venerable hostelry established in 1902 has waterfront access and lots of country charm. One of the seven suites has two bedrooms, a sitting area, and full kitchen. > 12013 Rte. 42, Ellison Bay 54210, tel. 920/854–9888 or 877/378–3218, fax 920/854–5923, www.dcwis.com/hoteldisgarden. 7 suites. Picnic area, grill, refrigerators, in-room VCRs, boating, bicycles; no smoking. MC, V. CP. ¢–$$
Shoreline Resort This white-frame waterfront motel, the northernmost resort on the Door County peninsula, is on Green Bay and has woods behind it. A seashell-patterned bedspread completes a beach theme in each of the rooms, all of which have waterfront views. You can sun on the rooftop sundeck above the boathouse. This is a good spot to stay if you want to visit Washington Island, as tours depart next door. > 12747 Rte. 42, Gills Rock 54210, tel. 920/854–2606, fax 920/854–5971, www.theshorelineresort.com. 16 rooms. Picnic area, grill, microwaves, refrigerators, dock, business services; no smoking. MC, V. Closed late Nov.–Apr. ¢–$

EPHRAIM

Ephraim Guest House This stained-gray cedar inn with a small lobby is a block from the bay on a little hillside with gardens in the rear. Rooms have dark-wood closets and headboards, and paintings of nature scenes on the walls. Some suites have fireplaces and water views. > 3042 Cedar St., Ephraim 54211, tel. 920/854–2319 or 800/589–8423, www.ephraimguesthouse.com. 16 suites. Picnic area, grill, some in-room hot tubs, kitchenettes, cable TV, in-room VCRs, laundry facilities. AE, D, MC, V. $–$$$$
Ephraim Inn This country home is across the street from a beach in the center of the village. It has a large porch, a fireplace in the lobby, and some rooms with harbor views. A country theme is reflected in the inn's baskets, candles, stenciling, and quilts. > 9994 Pioneer La., Ephraim 54211, tel. 920/854–4515 or 800/622–2193, fax 920/854–1859, www.theephraiminn.com. 16 rooms. Cable TV; no kids under 17, no smoking. AE, D, MC, V. Closed Mon.–Thurs. Nov.–Apr. CP. $–$$$
French Country Inn Built in 1911 as a summer home, this two-story, Prairie-style house is near the bay and the center of town. One of its common rooms has a wood-burning fireplace, and the house is surrounded by an acre of gardens. The cottage

and the rooms of the hotel are all decorated in French country decor. In winter you can rent out the entire inn. > 3052 Spruce La., Ephraim 54211, tel. 920/854–4001, fax 920/854–4001. 7 rooms, 2 with bath; 1 cottage. Some kitchenettes; no kids under 13, no smoking. No credit cards. CP. ¢–$

Hillside Inn of Ephraim This mid-19th-century downtown Victorian guest house is on the National Register of Historic Places and still has its original furnishings. A 100-foot veranda with rocking chairs looks out onto the inn's private beach and Eagle Harbor. Two cottages have hot tubs, fireplaces, kitchens, and front porches with old-fashioned swings. > 9980 Rte. 42, Ephraim 54211, tel. 920/854–7666 or 866/673–8456. 5 suites, 2 cottages. In-room data ports, in-room DVDs, business services; no smoking. AE, D, MC, V. BP. $$$–$$$$

FISH CREEK

Cedar Court Inn One of Door County's oldest resorts, this charmer has several porches, landscaped grounds, and a white picket fence. Inside, it looks like an elegant farm home. The bright motel rooms are decorated with flowers and floral wreaths or framed posters of Fish Creek. > 9429 Cedar St., Fish Creek 54212, tel. 920/868–3361, fax 920/868–2541, www.cedarcourt.com. 14 rooms, 9 cottages. Picnic area, some in-room hot tubs, some kitchenettes, some microwaves, refrigerators, cable TV, some in-room VCRs, pool, business services; no smoking. MC, V. $–$$

Harbor Guest House Originally the carriage house for a large estate, this old-fashioned homey stone inn is on Fish Creek Harbor with a view of Green Bay. The six suites in this Tudor-style building are antiques-filled. Boat slips are available. > 9484 Spruce St., Fish Creek 54212, tel. 920/868–2284, fax 920/868–1535, www.harborguesthouse.com. 6 suites. Kitchenettes, microwaves, cable TV; no kids under 13, no smoking. AE, MC, V. $$$–$$$$

Juniper Inn This updated Gothic-style Victorian with a fireplace in the dining room is set back from the road on a high ridge with a view of cedar and tamarack forest. Stenciling, quilts and rocking chairs add charm to rooms with such names as the Sunflower, the Lilac, and the Red Maple. Two of the rooms have private outdoor decks. A golf course and Peninsula State Park are ¾ mi away. > N9432 Maple Grove Rd., Fish Creek 54212, tel. 920/839–2629 or 800/218–6960, fax 920/839–2095, www.juniperinn.com. 4 rooms. Dining room, some in-room hot tubs, in-room VCRs; no smoking. MC, V. CP. $–$$$

Thorp House Inn, Cottages, and Beach House A turn-of-the-20th-century Victorian home with a library and many antiques is the center of this complex, which overlooks the harbor from atop a hill. The house and its cottages are listed on the National Register of Historic Places. Mountain bikes and a tandem bike are available for guest use. The lavishly decorated rooms have detailed window treatments, wall coverings, and Victorian furnishings. The cottages are more rustic, with exposed wood. > 4135 Bluff Rd., Fish Creek 54212, tel. 920/868–2444, fax 920/868–9833, www.thorphouseinn.com. 6 rooms, 3 suites, 6 cottages. Picnic area, some in-room hot tubs, some kitchenettes, some microwaves, cable TV, in-room VCRs; no a/c in some rooms, no kids, no smoking. No credit cards. CP. ¢–$$$

Whistling Swan Inn Built in 1887, this is the oldest Door County inn on the National and State Register of Historic Places. It was actually built in Marinette and then dragged 22 mi across the frozen bay in 1907. Rooms are filled with antiques and the wicker-filled porch has a great view of the village of Fish Creek. > 4192 Main St., Fish Creek 54212, tel. 920/868–3442, fax 920/868–1703, www.whistlingswan.com. 5 rooms, 2 suites. Cable TV, shops, business services; no smoking. AE, D, MC, V. CP. $–$$$

SISTER BAY

Churchill Inn An English country mood permeates this elegant two-story motel with 34 antiques-filled rooms. Most rooms have four-poster beds and all have private balconies or patios. > 425 Gateway Dr., Sister Bay 54234, tel. 920/854–9462, 920/854–4885, or 800/422–4906. 34 rooms. Cable TV, some hot tubs, pool, gym, spa. MC, V. CP. ¢–$$$

Edge of Town Two buildings make up this quiet and homey motel at the north edge of town. Behind the building is a waterfall and lawn furniture with umbrellas for summertime relaxing on a 3-acre wooded lot. > 11092 Rte. 42, Sister Bay 54234, tel. 920/854–2012. 9 rooms. Microwaves, refrigerators, cable TV, some pets allowed; no room phones. D, MC, V. ¢–$

Nordic Lodge In a quiet, wooded setting opposite a golf course between Ephraim and Sister Bay, this lodge is on 5 landscaped acres; many porches have views of the countryside. > 2721 Rte. 42, Sister Bay 54234, tel. 920/854–5432, fax 920/854–5974, www.thenordiclodge.com. 33 rooms. Picnic area, some microwaves, cable TV, pool, hot tub; no smoking. D, MC, V. Closed Nov.–Apr. CP. ¢–$

Sweetbriar Bed & Breakfast This Cape Cod–style country retreat has both antique and modern furnishings. Guest rooms are all suites; most have fireplaces and whirlpool tubs. Some have four-poster beds. > 102 Orchard Dr., Sister Bay 54234, tel. 920/854–7504, fax 920/854–9885, www.sweetbriar-bb.com. 6 suites. No room phones, no room TVs, no smoking. D, MC, V. BP. $$–$$$

STURGEON BAY

Barbican Olde English Guest House You can choose from three restored late-19th-century houses, all filled with antiques, in the historic waterfront district, one block from the bay or downtown. Two of the homes were owned by L. M. Washburn, a local lumber baron, in the 1870s. The third was built for his daughter as a wedding gift in 1904. Gardens are landscaped with arbors, a fishpond, and a bridge, with wicker furniture on the porches, hanging flower baskets, and some private terraces. Each suite is individually decorated with floral accents and thickly decorated wall coverings. > 132 N. 2nd Ave., Sturgeon Bay 54235, tel. 920/743–4854, www.barbicanbandb.com. 18 suites. Room service, in-room hot tubs, microwaves, cable TV, in-room VCRs; no room phones. MC, V. CP. $$–$$$

Chanticleer Guest House Sheep graze on this B&B's 70 acres of flower gardens, creeks, fishponds, and streams. The guest house and guest barn, each housing four suites, have their original exposed beams, wood floors, fireplaces, and high-back beds; the barn has rafters and hay pulleys. > 4072 Cherry Rd. (Rte. HH), Sturgeon Bay 54235, tel. 920/746–0334, fax 920/746–1368, www.chanticleerguesthouse.com. 8 suites. Picnic area, in-room hot tubs, microwaves, in-room VCRs, pool, sauna, hiking; no kids. D, MC, V. CP. $$–$$$$

Colonial Gardens Bed & Breakfast This 1877 all-suites colonial inn has great views of Sturgeon Bay. All rooms have fireplaces, double whirlpool tubs, and private entrances with porches. Breakfast is delivered right to your room. The rooms are elegantly decorated with period furnishings, oak floors, and patterned handmade quilts. > 344 N. 3rd Ave., Sturgeon Bay 54235, tel. 920/746–9192, fax 920/746–9193, www.colgardensbb.com. 5 suites. Refrigerators, in-room VCRs. D, MC, V. BP. $–$$$

Inn at Cedar Crossing This antiques-filled late-19th-century brick inn is on a historic downtown street. The common areas are elegant and cozy. The restaurant serves regional fare in a Victorian-era setting. Rooms are enriched with antique pine furnishings and boldly patterned fabrics and wallpapers. > 336 Louisiana St., Sturgeon Bay

54235, tel. 920/743–4200, fax 920/743–4422, www.innatcedarcrossing.com. 9 rooms. Restaurant, some in-room hot tubs, cable TV, in-room VCRs, business services, airport shuttle; no smoking. AE, D, MC, V. CP. **$–$$$**

Snug Harbor Inn A dock at your doorstep and 300 feet of parklike shorefront awaits you at this inn, a mile from downtown. Some of the motel rooms have water views. Modern cottages and luxury suites, adjoining the motel, all face the water. > 1627 Memorial Dr., Sturgeon Bay 54235, tel. 920/743–2337 or 800/231–5767, www.snugharbor.com. 5 rooms, 6 suites, 4 cottages. Grills, some in-room hot tubs, cable TV, some pets allowed. MC, V. **¢–$$$**

WASHINGTON ISLAND

Deer Run Resort The rooms of this island resort, 2 blocks south of downtown, are footsteps away from the golf course. The rooms, all of which are on the ground level, are gulf-themed and decorated with antiques. Golf packages are available. The resort also has two lake homes that sleep six to eight people. > Detroit Harbor Rd., Washington Island 54246, tel. 920/847–2017, www.washingtonislandwi.org. 3 rooms, 2 homes. Restaurant, refrigerators, cable TV; no smoking. D, MC, V. CP. **$**

Findlay's Holiday Inn This two-story cedar building, with lattice-trimmed windows, faces Lake Michigan. A grass roof covers the exterior entryway, and Norwegian rosemaling (folk art that depicts roses and other flowers), carvings, and paintings from local artists fill the interior. Wildflower gardens edge the lake side of the building. > Detroit Harbor Rd., Washington Island 54246, tel. 920/847–2526 or 800/522–5469, fax 920/847–2752, www.holidayinn.net. 16 rooms. Restaurant, beach, business services; no a/c in some rooms. AE, MC, V. Closed mid-Nov.–mid-Apr. **$**

CAMPING

BAILEYS HARBOR **Baileys Grove Travel Park & Campground** This large park near Baileys Harbor has grassy sites with shade trees. The amenities, such as a game room, make this more a family's than a backpacker's haven, but the free popcorn each night should appeal to anyone. > Box 198, 2552 Rtes. F and EE, Baileys Harbor 54202, tel. 920/839–2559 or 866/839–2559, fax 920/839–1339. 66 sites, 29 full hook-ups. Dump station, laundry facilities, showers, electricity, general store, pool, playground. MC, V. Closed mid-Oct.–Apr. 30. **¢**

EGG HARBOR **Door County Camping Retreat** Tenters and RV enthusiasts don't have to mix at this camping retreat just south of Egg Harbor with over 200 wooded private sites. At 160 acres, this is the largest private campground in Door County. It has a group camping site as well as camping cabins. Activities include volleyball, basketball, and horseshoes. > 4906 Court Rd., Egg Harbor 54209, tel. 920/868–3151 or 866/830–5145, www.doorcountycamp.com. 12 full hook-ups, 98 partial hook-ups, 50 tent sites. Laundry facilities, showers, general store, playground, pool. MC, V. Closed Nov.–early Apr. **¢**

ELLISON BAY **Wagon Trail Campground** Seven wooded areas accommodating everything from tents to RVs are spread out this northernmost campground on the peninsula. The property's northern boundary is the Mink River Nature Conservancy Preserve and a hiking trail system traverses the grounds. Two log cabins are available for rent, as are yurts, which are circular tentlike structures secured to a finished floor with a skylight dome in the roof's center. > 1190 Rte. ZZ, Ellison Bay 54210, tel. 920/854–4818, www.wagontrailcampground.com. 22 tent sites, 104 partial hook-ups, 12 full hook-ups, 4 cabins, 2 yurts. Dump station, laundry facilities, showers, general store, playground. D, MC, V. Closed Nov.–Mar. **¢**

SISTER BAY **Aqualand Camp Resort** Expect families settled in for the weekend at this seasonal camping site 2 mi south of Sister Bay. A game room, paddleboats, and a heated pool keep the kids occupied. > Box 538, on Rte. Q and Rte. 57, Sister Bay 54234, tel. 920/854–4573, www.aqualandcamping.com. 150 partial hookups. Showers, general store. No credit cards. Closed mid-Oct.–May 15. ¢

STURGEON BAY **Yogi Bear's Jellystone Park** This campground is in the Southern Door County Recreational area, ¼ mi from Green Bay's beaches. Activities include a kiddie pool, game room, minigolf, volleyball, shuffleboard, tetherball, Ping-Pong, and horseshoes. > 3677 May Rd., Sturgeon Bay 54235, tel. 920/743–9001, www.campdoorcounty.com. 255 partial hook-ups, 17 full hook-ups. Dump station, laundry facilities, showers, general store, ranger station, playground, 2 pools. MC, V. Closed Sept. 7–mid-May. ¢

WASHINGTON ISLAND **Washington Island Campground** Just making the trip all the way to Washington Island gives you some privacy but the 101 sites at this camp-ground are also wooded. > Rte. 1, Box 144, Eastside Rd., Washington Island 54246, tel. 920/847–2622. 28 partial hook-ups, 70 tent sites. Laundry, showers, playground, 2 pools. No credit cards. Closed Oct. 15–May 15. ¢

WHERE TO EAT

ALGOMA

Captain's Table Nautical memorabilia fills the two dining rooms here and the salad bar is in a rowboat. It's popular for breakfast as well as for fresh fish lunches and din-ners. Friday night brings a seafood buffet. > 133 N. Water St., Algoma, tel. 920/487–5304. No credit cards. No dinner Dec.–Mar. ¢–$$

Pier 42 Marina Restaurant You can dine on the fresh fish served daily at this marina restaurant or feast on a Friday-night fish fry. Save room for the homemade desserts and sit back and savor the view of the Algoma Harbor and lighthouse. > 70 Church St., Algoma, tel. 920/487–3244. MC, V. Closed Sun. No lunch. ¢–$$

BAILEYS HARBOR

Common House This 1850s wood-frame restaurant was originally a hardware store. Inside, original hardwood floors, tin ceilings, and an authentic woodstove evoke the period. Many dishes use products from Wisconsin, including steak *au bleu* (a grilled fillet served on an eggplant crouton topped with Wisconsin blue-cheese sauce) or the roasted pork tenderloin presented with Door County fruit chutney and an apple-cider reduction. > 8041 Main St., Baileys Harbor, tel. 920/839–2708. D, MC, V. No lunch. $–$$$$

Gordon Lodge Restaurant The dining experience varies depending on the day at this Lake Michigan waterfront restaurant. Monday and Friday, a traditional fish boil is pre-pared and served in the dining room, which has a garden setting. Dinner is served in the Top Deck cocktail lounge with its magnificent water view or in the adjoining din-ing room. The regular menu includes quail, duck, salmon, and pork dishes. > 1420 Pine Dr., Baileys Harbor, tel. 920/839–2331. AE, D, MC, V. No lunch. No dinner Mon. Sept.–June. $$$

Sandpiper This small, modern restaurant on the north end of town is painted bright blue and accented with magenta and yellow. The building is divided into two parts: one is a rustic family-style restaurant specializing in home-cooked German food and pork roasts; the other is a casual restaurant serving up fish boils. Murals of Door

County line the walls. > 8166 Rte. 57, Baileys Harbor, tel. 920/839–2528. Reservations not accepted. MC, V. Closed Nov.–Mar. **$–$$**

Tundra House Green Bay Packers memorabilia fills this supper club with a 100-inch screen TV for watching games. Steaks, seafood, vegetarian dishes, and Italian entrées fill the menu and hand-tossed pizzas are made to order. > 6301 Rte. 57, Jacksonport, tel. 920/823–2542. D, MC, V. Closed Mon–Wed. Nov–Apr. No lunch. **$–$$**

Weisgerbers Cornerstone Pub This downtown family restaurant is filled with Green Bay Packer memorabilia in honor of the owner's father who played for the team more than 50 years ago. The dining room serves steaks, chicken, and burgers. The Friday-night fish fry here is the longest-running panfried fish fry in Door County. > 8123 Rte. 57, Baileys Harbor, tel. 920/839–9001. AE, D, MC, V. **$–$$$**

EGG HARBOR

The Bridge Soups and sandwiches and fresh baked goods are available in this sun-drenched bookstore/eatery on the south end of Egg Harbor. > 7881 Rte. 42, Egg Harbor, tel. 920/868–3221. $4–7. No dinner. ¢

Hof Restaurant Water views are a highlight at this restaurant in the Alpine Resort, where fresh whitefish, aged prime rib, and marinated chicken tarragon are the specialties. At breakfast try the Swiss toast—cream cheese–filled cinnamon bread with Door County cherries. > 7715 Alpine Rd., Egg Harbor, tel. 920/868–3000. AE, D, MC, V. No dinner weekdays Labor Day–June; no lunch. ¢–$$

Landmark Restaurant This modern resort restaurant overlooks a golf course. On the menu: light fare, vegetarian dishes, and such specials as native whitefish or duck breast glazed with honey mustard and topped by a raspberry sauce. On Friday you can try a land-and-sea buffet or a perch fry, and on Saturday a prime-rib dinner. > 7643 Hillside Rd., Egg Harbor, tel. 920/868–3205. MC, V. No lunch Sun. **$–$$$**

Shipwrecked Brewery Restaurant The only microbrewery in Door County, this casual place in the center of town serves burgers, pastas, and steaks to accompany six house brews, including a copper ale, a cherry wheat beer, and a porter. For alfresco dining, try the patio overlooking Egg Harbor. > 7791 Egg Harbor Rd., Egg Harbor, tel. 920/868–2767. AE, D, MC, V. **$$–$$$**

Trio Restaurant Italian dishes such as smoked salmon and roasted red peppers with farfalle as well as such classic French dishes as cassoulet and steak frites highlight the menu in this airy dining room with cathedral ceiling and exposed beams. > Rtes. 42 and E, Egg Harbor, tel. 920/868–2090. AE, D, DC, MC, V. No lunch Nov.–Apr. **$–$$**

ELLISON BAY

Rowleys Bay Restaurant This restaurant in the Wagon Trail Resort 4 mi from Ellison Bay has a view of Lake Michigan. Fish boils are served Monday and Saturday nights. The regular menu specialties include white fish amandine, shrimp scampi, and tenderloin. > 1041 Rte. ZZ, Rowleys Bay, tel. 920/854–2385 Ext. 831. D, MC, V. **$$**

Shoreline Restaurant You can watch the sun set over Green Bay from this restaurant in the Shoreline Resort. Thick burgers, salads, and soups are served at lunch. Nightly specials like crab-stuffed pasta shells are the stars of the menu. > 12747 Rte. 42, Gills Rock, tel. 920/854–2950. D, MC, V. Closed Nov.–Apr. **$$**

T Ashwell A beach-stone fireplace dominates the dining room and a piano player entertains at the wine bar of this sophisticated spot. Dishes on the frequently changing menu have included sautéed duck layered with foie gras and a cherry-and-cranberry reduction. You can also choose to dine on the heated porch. > 11976 Mink River Rd., Ellison Bay, tel. 920/854–4306. AE, D, DC, MC, V. Closed Tues. No lunch. **$$$**

Viking Grill The whitefish boils served daily from mid-May to October at tables in a garden out back are the big draw for this casual downtown restaurant. Otherwise, sandwiches and fried fish are the favorites throughout the year. > 12029 Rte. 42, Ellison Bay, tel. 920/854–2998. AE, D, MC, V. $–$$

EPHRAIM

Old Post Office Restaurant Built at the turn of the 20th century as a post office, this home-style restaurant overlooks Eagle Harbor and many tables have views of the water. Barbecued ribs, chicken, and fish boil are on the dinner menu. Breakfast includes muffins, pancakes, and Belgian waffles, all made with Door County cherries. > 10040 Water St., Ephraim, tel. 920/854–4034. No credit cards. Closed Nov.–Apr. No lunch. $$

Summer Kitchen Restaurant This friendly local favorite on the north side of town is known for its homemade-soup bar, which has included among its ever-changing daily selections French cabbage, tomato dill, and chicken dumpling. Beef tenderloin and pork chops are on the dinner menu. You can eat outside on a patio fenced in with white picket. > 10425 Water St., Ephraim, tel. 920/854–2131. MC, V. $–$$

Wilsons Restaurant Across the street from the water, you can sit outside at this ice cream and burger joint with a red-and-white awning. Established in 1906 this family-owned spot is famous for great milk shakes and enormous ice cream cones. > 9990 Water St., Ephraim, tel. 920/854–2041. MC, V. Closed Mid-Oct.–Apr. ¢

FISH CREEK

Bayside Tavern By day, this spot serves such basic pub fare as burgers and soups; by night it's a hopping club showcasing local bands of all kinds. Friday night there's a perch fry. > 4160 Main St., Fish Creek, tel. 920/868–3441. AE, MC, V. ¢–$

Cookery This family-style restaurant on Fish Creek's main street is surrounded by shops. Large bay windows provide a view of the beach. Try the whitefish chowder, stir-fry dinners, homemade jams, jellies, applesauce, and fruit pies. > Rte. 42, Fish Creek, tel. 920/868–3634. Reservations not accepted. MC, V. Closed weekdays Nov.–Apr. $

Kortes' English Inn This inn on a wooded property a mile north of town has lots of charm, with its beamed ceilings and walls full of work by local artists. The inn serves a Friday seafood buffet, its specialty coffees, and an extensive dessert list. The regular menu has seafood and ribs. > 3713 Rte. 42, Fish Creek, tel. 920/868–3076. MC, V. Closed Nov.–Apr. No lunch. $$–$$$$

Summertime This Prairie-style building looks almost Asian with its curved roofs. Inside, it's casual by day and dressed up after dark. The menu lists South African BBQ ribs, prime rib, pasta, and fresh fish. You can dine inside or outside on a patio overlooking the water. > 1 N. Spruce St., Fish Creek, tel. 920/868–3738. AE, MC, V. $$–$$$$

White Gull Inn The antiques-filled dining room at this downtown inn built in 1896 is elegant yet cozy. You can order the Door County fish boil or sample the raspberry chicken amandine, which is almond-encrusted chicken breast drizzled with raspberry sauce. > 4225 Main St., Fish Creek, tel. 920/868–3517, fax 920/868–2367. AE, D, DC, MC, V. Closed Sun. Nov.–Apr. $$$

SISTER BAY

Al Johnson's Swedish Restaurant and Butik Servers dress in traditional Swedish garb here and, in summer, goats clip the grass that carpets the roof. From the windows in the expansive dining room, you can see the harbor and main street. The kitchen is known for its limpa bread, pickled herring, and fruit soups. > 702–710 N. Bay Shore Dr., Sister Bay, tel. 920/854–2626. AE, D, MC, V. $$

Anne's Corner Café & Catering This deli and café is small, but it does a big business with sandwiches and salads. Popular items are curried-chicken salad; the Islander Sandwich, with turkey, lingonberries, and cheddar cheese; and the Peninsula Sandwich made with roast beef, cucumbers, onions, and cream-cheese-and-chives dressing. Outside dining is available during summer. > 326 Country Walk La., Sister Bay, tel. 920/854–5061. Closed Labor Day–Memorial Day. No dinner weekdays. D, MC, V. ¢

Mission Grille This restaurant, in a former Catholic church, has stained-glass windows and pews for seating. Specialties include Black Angus steak, lamb, duck, pasta, and fresh seafood. > Rtes. 42 and 57, Sister Bay, tel. 920/854–9070. AE, D, MC, V. Closed Mon.–Wed. Nov.–Apr. $–$$$

Sister Bay Café Locals congregate at this small, bright, and cheery restaurant on Sister Bay's main street. Scandinavian memorabilia accents the room and window seats have a great view of passersby. Try the Norwegian farmer's stew and *risegrot* (a hot, creamy, rice pudding–like dish that is a breakfast favorite). You might also try tenderloin of reindeer served with red wine sauce. > 611 Bay Shore Dr., Sister Bay, tel. 920/854–2429. DC, MC, V. Closed Jan.–Mar. $–$$$

STURGEON BAY

Bluefront Cafe They serve a healthy breakfast and lunch in this former retail space a couple of blocks from downtown. Organic pancakes, homemade granola, and quiche are available at breakfast. Lunch is wraps, salads, and quesadillas. > 306 S. 3rd Ave., Sturgeon Bay, tel. 920/743–9218. MC, V. Closed Mon. No dinner. ¢–$

Dal Santo's Restaurant The lighting may be dim but the food tastes good in this former train station. The most popular dishes are pasta in spicy sauces, but meat and fish dinners are served as well. Try the fried ravioli appetizer. > 341½ N. 3rd St., Sturgeon Bay, tel. 920/743–6100. AE, D, MC, V. No lunch. ¢–$$

Grey Stone Castle Popular items here are burgers, steaks, lobster, shrimp, perch, bluegill, and chicken. But the best-selling item is the prime-rib sandwich. The menu is identical for lunch and dinner. You can eat at the counter or at a table underneath mounted displays of area wildlife, including bear, deer, and fish. > 8 N. Madison Ave., Sturgeon Bay, tel. 920/743–9923. AE, D, MC, V. ¢–$

Inn at Cedar Crossing Steaks, ostrich, and quail are served in an 1884 storefront on a shop-filled street in the historic district. Local art hangs from the walls in both the cozy dining area and the equally cozy bar. > 336 Louisiana St., Sturgeon Bay, tel. 920/743–4249. D, MC, V. $$$–$$$$

Perry's Cherry Diner Although this is an All-American 1950s-style diner, Greek specialties are the highlights. For desert try an old-fashioned malt. > 230 Michigan St., Sturgeon Bay, tel. 920/743–9910. AE. D. MC, V. ¢–$

Pudgy Seagull Restaurant This restaurant occupies a modern building in Sturgeon Bay's historic district. The wood-paneled dining room is painted with watercolors and seating is in booths or stacking chairs. Seafood, pressure-fried chicken, and homemade pies made with Door County cherries or apples are the top menu items here. > 113 N. 3rd Ave., Sturgeon Bay, tel. 920/743–5000. Reservations not accepted. MC, V. $–$$

Sage When no one is on hand to play the grand piano in the center of this stylish restaurant, jazz music is usually played. Come relax at the sofa beside the wine bar at the front of this storefront in downtown Sturgeon Bay before settling in for dinner.

Fish, steak, or chops get a fancy treatment with rubs or glazes, from mango to whole-grain Dijon mustard. > 136 N. 3rd Ave., Sturgeon Bay, tel. 920/746–1100. MC, V. No lunch. $$$–$$$$

WASHINGTON ISLAND

Findlay's Holiday Inn Norwegian wood carvings and old Norwegian plates adorn this small restaurant with harbor views. Breads, jams, and soups are all homemade and perch and whitefish anchor the menu; on Friday night a perch dinner is served. Cherry pie made from Door County cherries is a specialty. > 1 Main Rd., Washington Island, tel. 920/847–2526. MC, V. Closed Nov.–Apr. No dinner. ¢–$

Ship's Wheel Restaurant This octagonal-shape restaurant is just beyond the Washington Island ferry dock overlooking Lake Michigan at Krueger's Kap marina. The walleye fry and prime rib are the top-selling items. > Lobdel Point Rd., Washington Island, tel. 920/847–2640. MC, V. ¢–$

ESSENTIALS

Getting Here

A car is essential in Door County as no public transportation exists. Even getting to the peninsula without a car can be difficult as Amtrak only takes you as far as Milwaukee by train. A bus can get you to Green Bay but then you're on your own. There is no ferry to Door County but if you want to get to Washington Island you'll have to take a short cruise with or without your car.

BY CAR

From Chicago take I–94 to Milwaukee. Then, take I–43 North from Milwaukee to Green Bay, then Route 57 North to Sturgeon Bay. You can also take Route 310 East from I–43, then pick up Route 42 North, which will take you to Algoma. The 70-mi-long Door County Peninsula is bordered by Lake Michigan and Green Bay. In Sturgeon Bay you can choose which side of the peninsula you want to explore first. You can do an entire loop of Door County easily as Route 42 (the bay-side highway) and Route 57 (the "quiet side" highway, which borders Lake Michigan) meet near Sister Bay. The stopping points are more spread out on the east side of the peninsula but even on this side it's no more than 10 mi up the road to get to the next town or village. You won't have a shortage of scenery on either side but the bay side gets more traffic. To go farther north from Sister Bay, take Route 42, which will take you to the Washington Island ferry at Northport.

BY FERRY

There are two ways to get to Washington Island. You can either depart from Northport Pier at the end of Route 42 or from Gills Rock. The latter is a narrated crossing aboard the *Island Clipper,* for which you'll have to leave your car behind. The ferry makes four crossings in either direction from late May to mid-October, with an additional crossing late June–late August. The fare is $8 round-trip. If you want to have a car with you on the island, you'll need to cross on a Washington Island Ferry. It departs with greater frequency and runs year-round. The fee is $8 round-trip for each adult passenger. The car is $20. A bicycle is $4. The ride takes 30 minutes. To get from Washington Island over to Rock Island State Park you can take the 10-minute Karfi Ferry from Jackson

Harbor. It runs late May–mid-October and runs $4–$9. This ferry is for passengers and their gear only; it takes no vehicles.

FERRY LINES **Island Clipper** > Tel. 920/854–2972, www.islandclipper.com. **Rock Island Ferry** > Tel. 920/493–6444. **Washington Island Ferry** > Tel. 920/847–2546 or 800/223–2094, www.wisferry.com.

Visitor Information

CONTACTS **Algoma Area Chamber of Commerce** > 1226 Lake St., Algoma 54201, tel. 920/487–2041 or 800/498–4888, www.algoma.org. **Baileys Harbor Business Association** > Box 31, Baileys Harbor 54202, tel. 920/839–2366, www.baileysharbor.com. **Door County Chamber of Commerce** > Box 406, Sturgeon Bay 54235, tel. 920/743–4456 or 800/527–3529, www.doorcounty.com. **Egg Harbor Business Association** > Box 33, Egg Harbor 54202, tel. 920/868–3717, www.eggharbor-wi.com. **Ephraim Foundation** > Box 165, Ephraim 54211, tel. 920/854–4989, www.ephraim.org. **Fish Creek Civic Association** > Box 74, 4097 Main St., Fish Creek 54212-0074, tel. 920/868–2316 or 800/577–1880, www.fishcreek.info. **Sister Bay Advancement Association** > Box 351, Sister Bay 54234-0351, tel. 920/854–2812, www.sisterbaytourism.com. Closed mid-Oct.–mid-May. **Sturgeon Bay Community Development Corporation** > 23 N. 5th Ave., Sturgeon Bay 54235-0212, tel. 920/743–3924, www.sturgeonbay.net. **Washington Island Chamber of Commerce** > Rte. 1, Box 222, Washington Island 54246-9768, tel. 920/847–2179, www.washingtonislandwi.org.

Ann Arbor

230 mi east of Chicago

23

By Kevin Cunningham

ABOVE ALL ELSE, ANN ARBOR IS KNOWN as the home of the University of Michigan. The school, founded in 1837 in Detroit, dominates geographically, culturally, and economically. Atlases may list the population as 114,000 (it can be twice that size on football Saturdays), but Ann Arbor provides enough culture and cuisine to power a fair-size city.

Perhaps because U of M has been a part of Ann Arbor since the city's earliest days, the university and city have a rare synergy you won't find in other college communities. State Street's campus-town vibe rubs against Main Street's commercial downtown, creating a vibrant community of energetic and ambitious U of M students and alumni, who often run the businesses dotting the area.

The town's roots go back to 1824, when John Allen and Elisha Rumsey headed into the forests west of Detroit with their wives Ann and Mary Ann, respectively. When naming their new settlement, they decided to honor (or flatter) their young wives by combining that shared name with "arbor," a word that once meant a grove in the woods. It's still appropriate, today. Because of the university's primacy in the city's economic growth, Ann Arbor was spared the worst of industrial depredation. The deciduous trees on view at the arboretum and along Ann Arbor's streets hint at the richness of the forest in John Allen's time. Much of the city sits on gently rolling land in the Huron River valley, part of a greenbelt surrounding Detroit and part of the 24,000-acre Clinton-Huron Metroparks System.

Like the greenery that surrounds the city, the University of Michigan campus is leafy, its architecture a hodgepodge of styles. Take a ramble around the main campus and its nearest environs and you can see examples of classical revival, Romanesque, Georgian, Italian and French Renaissance, and Gothic styles. English Gothic—particularly the Legal Research Building—dominates the Law Quad, one of the best places on campus for rest or a picnic. Angell Hall, with its row of majestic Doric columns inspired by the beaux-arts classicism of the Lincoln Memorial, would look perfectly at home in Washington, D.C. (or a gladiator movie). The same architect, Alfred Kahn, designed Burton Memorial Tower (on Ingalls Street); its 10 stories of Indiana limestone are visible for miles around.

The university is also the cultural center of the community. If it's happening in Ann Arbor, it's most likely within walking distance of campus, beginning at the shops clustered around the State Street–Liberty Street nexus. Too tidy to be truly bohemian, but undeniably hip and liberal, the State Street area caters primarily to the student body. The music shops stock everything from jazz on vinyl to the latest Icelandic-rock CDs. The city also has the nation's best concentrations of bookstores, ranging from piles-to-the-ceiling firetraps to the Borders flagship store. Two grand movie houses, the State and the Michigan, are local landmarks. And when you need to refuel, you have plenty of places from which to choose, from ice cream and coffee to square meals.

Main Street is Ann Arbor's downtown—more upscale than State, but also more eclectic. Cafés with wireless Internet access stand across the street from microbreweries; crafts stores and new-age teahouses are steps from jazz clubs and steak houses. Many of the buildings, a mix of redbrick and stone, date from the early 1900s. Trees shade the crowds of diners eating lunch or supper outdoors, turning the sidewalk into an obstacle course at noontime but also allowing you to have a look at the eateries—and the meals—in action.

Less flashy is Kerrytown, a historic district just north of downtown. Several redbrick buildings remain from the late 19th and early-20th century, the oldest built in 1874. Nowadays it's a shopping district, more alternative-nation State than trendy Main, and popular for the farmers' market held on Wednesday and Saturday from May to December.

WHAT TO SEE & DO

Ann Arbor Hands-On Museum Five blocks off campus, this kid-oriented museum teaches science with more than 250 loud, tactile, and gadgety exhibits. Particular favorites include the rock-climbing wall and tornado machine; even adults may find the TV studio hard to resist. > 220 E. Ann St., Ann Arbor, tel. 734/995–5439, www.aahom.org. $7. Mon.–Sat. 10–5, Sun. noon–5.

Delhi At this 53-acre park, you can go canoeing, have picnics, and enjoy other outdoor recreation including softball, biking, and hiking. > 3902 E. Delhi Rd., 5 mi northwest of Ann Arbor, Ann Arbor, tel. 734/426–8211 or 800/477–3191. $4 per vehicle. Memorial Day–Labor Day, daily 8 AM–10 PM; Labor Day–Memorial Day, daily 8 AM–9 PM.

Dexter-Huron Spreads across 122 acres along the Huron River, this park is best known for shady picnic areas, fishing, and a canoe launching site into the Huron River. > 6535 Huron River Dr., 7½ mi northwest of Ann Arbor, Dexter, tel. 734/426–8211 or 800/477–3191, www.metroparks.com. $4 per vehicle. Memorial Day–Labor Day, daily 8 AM–10 PM; Labor Day–Memorial Day, daily 8 AM–9 PM.

Hudson Mills At 1,549 acres, this is the largest of the Ann Arbor area parks. Hiking and biking trails, a golf course, picnic areas, playgrounds, a nature trail, canoeing, and cross-country skiing (including rentals) are available. You can rent bicycles, volleyballs, basketballs, and tennis rackets from spring through fall at the Activity Center. Hudson Mills is 12 mi northwest of Ann Arbor. > 8801 N. Territorial Rd., Dexter, tel. 734/227–2757, 734/426–8211, or 800/477–3191, www.metroparks.com. $4 per vehicle. Daily 7 AM–10 PM.

Kempf House Once the home of two prominent local musicians, this 1853 building is a well-restored example of the Greek-revival style. Since 1983, it has served as a museum showcasing life, history, and decoration in Ann Arbor circa 1850–1910 through antique furnishings and other artifacts. > 312 S. Division, Ann Arbor, tel. 734/994–4898. $1. Sun. 1–4.

Main Street The aura around Main Street is refined, amid trees and redbrick and stone buildings that date from the early part of the 20th century. Many independently owned specialty stores here cater to local residents. The restaurants concentrated on Main Street between William and Huron streets, many of them upscale, attract locals, the university community, and visitors. Good weather gives everyone a perfect excuse to dine outdoors. > Ann Arbor.

Nichols Arboretum Part of the University of Michigan campus, this facility contains 123 acres, with some 400 labeled tree species, about half of which are Michigan natives. Don't miss the peony garden in late spring, or the scenic nature trails. Free tours are conducted the third Sunday of each month. > 1610 Washington Heights Rd., Ann Arbor, tel. 734/998–9540. Free. Daily dawn–dusk.

Purple Rose Theatre The small regional theater, 12 mi west of Ann Arbor, is owned and operated by Hollywood actor and native son Jeff Daniels. Performances range from small, intimate plays to world premieres and include both classics and new works from young playwrights. > 137 Park St., Chelsea, tel. 734/433–7673, fax 734/475–0802, www.purplerosetheatre.org.

State Street One of the country's highest concentrations of book and music stores is in this bohemian area near campus. Among them is the flagship **Borders Books and Music** (612 E. Liberty, tel. 734/668–7100), started in 1971 by two University of Michigan graduates. Homes are midwestern style with Victorian flourishes. This area is also home to two handsome movie theaters: the State Theater at State and Liberty streets and the splendid Michigan Theater at Liberty and Maynard streets. > Ann Arbor.

University of Michigan When it moved here from Detroit in 1837, the University of Michigan (U of M) had just 40 donated acres. Today it's among the largest and oldest universities in the Midwest and the main influence on the growth and economy of this city. The nationally regarded U of M campus includes more than 1,300 acres filled with libraries and museums. > 515 E. Jefferson St., Ann Arbor, tel. 734/764–1817, www.umich.edu. Free. Daily.

A campus and area kids' favorite, the **Exhibit Museum of Natural History** (1109 Geddes Rd., tel. 734/764–6085, free, planetarium $3, weekdays 9–5, weekends noon–5) houses a planetarium, dinosaur and prehistoric life exhibits, as well as displays on Michigan wildlife. A distinguished fieldstone building on State Street houses the **Kelsey Museum of Ancient and Medieval Archaeology** (434 S. State St., tel. 734/764–9304, free, Tues.–Fri. 9–4, weekends 1–4), a repository of artifacts gathered from over 110 years of university-sponsored Near Eastern and Mediterranean digs.

The **Gerald R. Ford Presidential Library** (1000 Beal Ave., tel. 734/741–2218, fax 734/741–2341, free, weekdays 8:45–4:45) is primarily a research institution containing papers, photographs, and miscellaneous collections related to the only president from Michigan. Four Gothic-style buildings rim the **Law Quadrangle** (801 Monroe St., free, daily), behind the Legal Research Building on a corner of the bustling campus. For flora and fauna try the **Matthaei Botanical Gardens** (1800 Dixboro Rd., tel. 734/998–7061, fax 734/998–6205, $3, daily 8 AM–dusk). Its conservatory houses year-round blooming exotic plants, and outdoor nature trails spread over 250 acres emphasize local plants and shrubs. The classically inspired **Power Center for the Performing Arts** (121 S. Fletcher, tel. 734/763–3333) seats 1,400 and attracts ballet, theater, and musicians of all kinds.

University of Michigan Museum of Art Ranked among the best university collections in the country, this small but distinguished museum houses western art from the 6th century to the present (Monet, Picasso, Rodin, Whistler, and Tiffany are represented), Near- and Far-Eastern art (including a prime collection of Japanese snuffboxes), African masks and artifacts, and a well-conceived collection of prints and drawings. > 525 S. State St., Ann Arbor, tel. 734/764–0395, fax 734/764–3731. Free. Tues., Wed., Fri., and Sat. 10–5, Thurs. 10–9, Sun. noon–5.

Back in the Day

ASK ANN ARBORITES OF A CERTAIN COLLEGE AGE ABOUT 1940, and they may point you to the archaeology museum. Ridiculous. By 1940, chariots were long gone from Ann Arbor. Sure, the pennies had wheat on them, and the ink-stained wretches at the New Deal–sponsored Works Projects Administration were churning out travel guides. But U of M still had a football team . . . playing in leather helmets. And the players had necks.

Okay, 1940 was a different age. Twelve thousand students came to Ann Arbor during the annual autumn migration; there are 38,000 today. More arrived by train and bus than by "motor-car"; zeppelins were out of service, alas, but airplane flights from home were not unheard-of. Freshmen males danced around a bonfire and flung their caps into the flames. Ah, to be free of home and the threat of liability lawsuits. Formal balls were still part of the calendar, too. The Annual J-Hop, considered the preeminent ball of the season, was held in February in the Intramural Building gymnasium. Intellectuals met at the Unitarian Church to debate politics and weightier issues—just like today, except without the Birkenstocks.

Yet this generation, soon to be the victors of World War II, needed leisure, as do all college types prone to monkeyshines or horseplay or other feral activities. Ann Arbor had five movie houses. Would-be future tycoons could shoot 18 holes of golf for a buck at the Huron Hills Golf Club ($1.50 on Sunday). Outdoors types had canoeing or horseback riding nearby. And those of questionable morals could always get chased out of the Michigan League, the women's student union.

If you plan to climb into the time machine, heed a word of warning: Don't drive. Thirty-five of those wheat pennies will get you a taxi trip anywhere in the city. You see, only faculty cars can park on campus, and double parking in a business area will cost you real dough.

The buildings aren't the only things that never change.

Save the Date

JUNE

Ann Arbor Summer Festival Starting in mid-June through the Fourth of July holiday, this festival hosts national dance and music performances at the Power Center, as well as movies, concerts, and an art show in the adjacent parking structure. > 121 S. Fletcher, tel. 734/647–2278.

JULY

Ann Arbor Art Fairs One of the largest art shows in the country, the Ann Arbor Art Fairs are actually four shows in one, including the Ann Arbor Summer Art Fair, the Ann Arbor Street Art Fair, the Art Fair Village, and the State Street Art Fair. More than 1,000 exhibitors line 26 blocks throughout downtown and east to the edge of campus. Together the fairs attract some 500,000 browsers and buyers. > Tel. 734/995–7281, www.artfair.org.

SEPTEMBER

Ann Arbor Blues and Jazz Festival Held in mid-September, this weeklong festival hosts funky, soul-fired rhythm-and-blues open-air concerts at Gallup Park and indoor concerts at the Michigan Theater and Bird of Paradise jazz club. > Tel. 734/747–9955, a2.blues.jazzfest.org.

SEPTEMBER–DECEMBER

University of Michigan Football Ann Arbor is a legendary football town, and Michigan Stadium is one of the cathedrals of college football. Single-game tickets go on sale in spring (usually May), but don't last long. Latecomers seeking seats at anywhere near the printed ticket price may have the best luck with games against weak nonconference opponents. Note that U of M has instituted a two-tier pricing structure and now charges more for so-called premium games (which most years means Ohio State and Notre Dame). > Tel. 734/764–0247, fax 734/936–8942, www.mgoblue.com.

WHERE TO STAY

Bell Tower Though the building rises only a half block from campus, the fireplace, intimate European style, and low-key lighting in the hotel lobby make it clear from your first step inside that you've left the college bustle behind. Dark woods and soft lighting enhance the rooms. The hotel is also home to the elegant restaurant Escoffier (see Where to Eat). > 300 S. Thayer St., Ann Arbor 48104, tel. 734/769–3010 or 800/562–3559, fax 734/769–4339, www.belltowerhotel.com. 66 rooms, 10 suites. Restaurant, in-room data ports, some minibars, some refrigerators, cable TV, business services. AE, DC, MC, V. CP. $$–$$$

Crowne Plaza Near Briarwood Mall, this hotel feels European, with a large lobby accented by a fireplace, marble, and lace curtains. The rooms reflect the European sensibility with subdued colors and pillow-laden love seats. > 610 Hilton Blvd., Ann Arbor 48108, tel. 734/761–7800, fax 734/761–1040. 198 rooms, 4 suites. Restaurant, room service, in-room data ports, cable TV with video games, indoor pool, exercise equipment, hot tub, sauna, bar, lounge, laundry facilities, business services. AE, D, DC, MC, V. CP. $–$$

Dahlmann Campus Inn Known for its great views of the city and campus, this high-rise hotel is less than 1 mi away from the U of M campus and Medical Center and two blocks from Liberty Street shopping. In the guest rooms the emphasis is on light, with large windows complementing a decor of whites and bright colors. > 615 E. Huron St., Ann Arbor 48104, tel. 734/769–2200 or 800/666–8693, fax 734/769–6222, www.campusinn.com. 208 rooms. Restaurant, in-room data ports, cable TV, pool, exercise equipment, sauna, bar, shop, business services, convention center. AE, D, DC, MC, V. $$$

Fairfield Inn by Marriott A stay at this hotel off I–94 puts you across the street from Briarwood Mall and 3 mi from the U of M. > 3285 Boardwalk, Ann Arbor 48108, tel. 734/995–5200, fax 734/995–5394, www.fairfieldinn.com. 110 rooms. Refrigerators, cable TV, indoor pool, hot tub. AE, D, DC, MC, V. CP. $

Hampton Inn-North This economical four-story chain hotel on the north side of town is a good base for exploring attractions north of Ann Arbor. > 2300 Green Rd., Ann Arbor 48105, tel. 734/996–4444, fax 734/996–0196, www.hampton-inn.com. 130 rooms. Cable TV, indoor pool, hot tub, business services. AE, D, DC, MC, V. CP. $

Hampton Inn-South In the accommodations enclaves near Briarwood Mall and I–94, this chain entry is 2 mi from U of M sports venues and 3 mi from the center of campus. Solid and well kept, it attracts its share of the weekend festival-or-football crowds. > 925

Victors Way, Ann Arbor 48108, tel. 734/665–5000, fax 734/665–8452, www.hampton-inn.com. 149 rooms. Cable TV, indoor pool, exercise equipment, hot tub, laundry facilities, business services, no-smoking rooms. AE, D, DC, MC, V. CP. $–$$

Holiday Inn–North Campus Popular with business travelers, this hotel is 2 mi from downtown restaurants and shopping and the U of M campus. Rooms come with one king- or two queen-size beds. > 3600 Plymouth Rd., Ann Arbor 48105, tel. 734/769–9800 or 800/465–4329, fax 734/761–1290, www.basshotels.com/holiday-inn. 226 rooms. Restaurant, picnic area, room service, cable TV, indoor-outdoor pool, exercise equipment, hot tub, basketball, bar, lounge, video game room, business services, no-smoking rooms. AE, D, DC, MC, V. $–$$

Red Roof Inn-North This budget hotel has some of the best rates in the Ann Arbor area. Part of the cluster around the Route 23/Plymouth Road exit, it is 4½ mi north of Ann Arbor's downtown. > 3621 Plymouth Rd., Ann Arbor 48105, tel. 734/996–5800 or 800/733–7663, fax 734/996–5707, www.redroof.com. 109 rooms. In-room data ports, cable TV, some pets allowed, no smoking rooms. AE, D, DC, MC, V. ¢

Red Roof Inn-South Adjacent to I–94 and 3½ mi south of campus, this location has a few amenities that make it a cut above the usual for the chain. > 3505 S. State, Ann Arbor 48108, tel. 734/665–3500, fax 734/665–3517, www.redroof.com. 119 rooms. In-room data ports, cable TV, laundry facilities, some pets allowed, no-smoking rooms. AE, D, DC, MC, V. CP. ¢

Residence Inn by Marriott Those looking for more space can take advantage of the separate living and sleeping areas in this inn's suites. With fully equipped kitchens, the suites here are ideal for families on a budget, packs of football fans, or those on an extended stay. Rooms are well lighted and have plenty of space to walk or lounge around. > 800 Victors Way, Ann Arbor 48108, tel. 734/996–5666, www.marriott.com. 114 suites. Picnic area, kitchens, cable TV, pool, hot tub, laundry facilities, some pets allowed (fee). AE, D, DC, MC, V. BP. $–$$$

Sheraton Inn Hot-tub suites and its proximity to the mall make this hotel a business and vacationers' favorite. The inn is close to State Street and the heart of campus. > 3200 Boardwalk, Ann Arbor 48108, tel. 734/996–0600 or 800/325–3535, fax 734/996–8136, www.sheraton.com. 197 rooms. Restaurant, room service, in-room data ports, some in-room hot tubs, some microwaves, some refrigerators, cable TV, indoor-outdoor pool, exercise equipment, hair salon, bar, business services. AE, D, DC, MC, V. $–$$$

Weber's Inn Contemporary room furnishings with subdued solid colors distinguish this area favorite, already popular for balcony rooms that overlook the pool and spa area. A substantial family clientele and a position near I–94 keep it busy. At the restaurant, steaks and chops are the specialties. > 3050 Jackson Rd., Ann Arbor 48103, tel. 734/769–2500 or 800/443–3050, fax 734/769–4743, www.webersinn.com. 160 rooms. Restaurant, room service, café, in-room data ports, in-room safes, refrigerators in some rooms, cable TV with movies and video games, indoor pool, exercise equipment, hot tub, sauna, bar, video game room, business services. AE, D, DC, MC, V. CP. $–$$

WHERE TO EAT

Afternoon Delight Oriented toward healthy dishes, but not above serving an Oreo sundae, this popular lunch stop has fruit-heavy smoothies, a long list of creative sandwiches, and a salad bar so big the word "graze" is truly appropriate. Early risers can get a solid breakfast for under $10 (served all day on the weekends). > 251 E. Liberty St., Ann Arbor, tel. 734/665–7513, fax 734/665–0087. AE, D, MC, V. No dinner. ¢

Bella Ciao A half block west of Main Street, this casual trattoria-style eatery has marble tabletops and intimate booths. Try pasta with caramelized sea scallops or lamb osso bucco in tomato sauce with saffron risotto. > 118 W. Liberty St., Ann Arbor, tel. 734/995–2107. AE, D, DC, MC, V. Closed Sun. No lunch. **$$–$$$$**

Conor O'Neill's Charmingly nicked up and frequently raucous with conversation and live traditional Irish music, this pub serves the traditional hearty fare—including Irish stew with Guinness gravy—plus a handful of entrées such as filet mignon and lamb chops. > 318 S. Main St., Ann Arbor, tel. 734/665–2968. AE, D, DC, MC, V. **$–$$$**

The Earle This intimate lower-level eatery is among the city's finest dining spots and is almost always packed. The regularly changing menu often includes entrées such as sautéed lamb chops served on eggplant sautéed with tomatoes and garlic, or grilled fillet of salmon in white wine, shallots, and lemon sauce. The wine cellar has more than 800 bottles. A pianist entertains on weeknights, and a jazz trio performs on weekends. > 121 W. Washington St., Ann Arbor, tel. 734/994–0211. AE, D, DC, MC, V. Closed Sun. June–Aug. No lunch. **$$–$$$$**

Escoffier French-inspired dishes are served in this elegant dining room in the Bell Tower hotel, which is across the street from concert venues and the central campus. Try Continental staples, prime rib, or rack of lamb. Browns, creams, and wood tones provide an intimate setting that hints at homey comfort rather than fine dining. > 300 S. Thayer St., Ann Arbor, tel. 734/995–3800. AE, DC, MC, V. Closed Sun. No lunch. **$$$$**

Gandy Dancer In a 19th-century railroad depot on the edge of town, this flagship of the Muer family's popular seafood chain specializes in fresh seafood and tasty pastas. Try Charley's crab platter (crab legs, Dungeness clusters, fried soft-shell crab, and a Maryland crab cake) or the signature Charley's Chowder, a hearty bouillabaisse-style stew. The Sunday brunch is a lavish, diet-busting spread. > 401 Depot St., Ann Arbor, tel. 734/769–0592. AE, D, DC, MC, V. No lunch Sat. **$$–$$$$**

Paesano's Strolling musicians add a festive air on Friday to this bright and airy casual eatery. Among the many excellent homemade pastas are lasagna or fettuccine alla Bolognese. A daily special includes a fish of the day. You can dine on the patio at tables with umbrellas. > 3411 Washtenaw Ave., Ann Arbor, tel. 734/971–0484. AE, D, DC, MC, V. **$–$$$**

Seva Housed in an old VFW hall, Seva creates vegetarian (and some vegan) dishes, many prepared in Mediterranean or Mexican style. In true Mediterranean fashion, you can dine alfresco on the outdoor deck. The restaurant also emphasizes wine, with a menu that provides suggestions for each dish, and hosts wine-oriented events Tuesday and Thursday. > 314 E. Liberty, Ann Arbor, tel. 734/662–1111. AE, D, DC, MC, V. **$–$$**

Zanzibar What began as a predominantly Asian-inspired restaurant has expanded its outlook for a more global approach, including palm trees, lively music, and booths upholstered in ethnic prints. The menu is equally lively, including Asian greens with fresh veggies, lemongrass vinaigrette, and a warm rice patty, and seafood creations that may include Bengali-style grouper, flash-fried Atlantic cod, or salmon roulade with cucumber-yogurt raita. Though known for Asian and Mediterranean dishes, Italian, Caribbean, and other cuisines are represented. > 216 S. State St., Ann Arbor, tel. 734/994–7777. AE, D, DC, MC, V. No lunch Sat. **$$–$$$**

Zingerman's Noshers and fressers alike swear by the sandwiches at this local institution. Wheels of exotic cheese and a veritable wall of fresh bread flank you as you walk through the door. Though slightly pricey, everything is fresh (the mozzarella is handmade daily, for instance) and the towering made-to-order sandwiches challenge both the biggest eaters and the laws of physics. If you're a true deli fan, compare the strong smoked salmon to that of your favorite haunts. Lunchtime often brings long lines. > 422 Detroit St., Ann Arbor, tel. 734/663–3354 or 888/636–8162. AE, D, DC, MC, V. **$–$$**

ESSENTIALS

Getting Here

Ann Arbor has quite a few choices for a city its size, especially for those who want to leave their car at home. If you choose to come via bus, train, or air, the local mass transit system can take you everywhere. Cab rides from hotel clusters are reasonably priced, especially when you consider parking near campus or downtown will set you back around 80¢ per hour. Both cabs and numerous shuttle services run to Detroit Metropolitan Airport.

BY BUS

Greyhound runs from Chicago to Ann Arbor as part of its service to Detroit. Three morning departures are typically available, but the buses tend to be locals making multiple stops, and that sometimes means a six- or seven-hour ride. For your return trip, you can choose from a number of departures (typically five) throughout the day. When planning for your departure, ask about the express bus. Although it may be crowded, it can save you a couple of hours travel time. The Greyhound Bus Station is six blocks west of campus and close to the Main Street commercial area. The Convention and Visitor's Bureau is steps away. The Ann Arbor Transit Authority (aka the Ride) maintains a reliable fleet of buses that crisscross the city. Fare is $1; exact change is required. Bicyclists can now load their bikes onto racks on the front of the vehicles. Special shuttles (at increased fares) run during the art fairs and on football weekends.

BUS DEPOT **Greyhound Bus Station** > 116 E. Huron St., Ann Arbor, tel. 734/662–5511.
BUS LINE **Greyhound** > Tel. 734/662–5511, www.greyhound.com.

BY CAR

Interstate 94 links Chicago and Ann Arbor. Speed limits are between 55 and 70 mph. Traffic is usually not a problem, with one exception: the merge of I–94 with I–80 near the Indiana state line. Avoid driving on Friday evenings during rush hour, when commuters, long-haul semis, and vacationers collide. If you're coming from the north, you can miss the mess by using the I–90 toll road.

City streets are a good mixture of one-way and two-way, and speed limits range between 35 and 45 mph. If you're parking near the campus, metered spots with limits of between 30 minutes and 4 hours cost 50¢–90¢ an hour. Meters generally need to be fed from 8 AM to 6 PM. Privately owned garages and metered lots around the edge of campus and in the downtown area charge 80¢–$1.20 per hour. University lots have little parking available to visitors. Parking on weekends, however, is quite reasonable. The lot at First and Washington charges $2 for all-day Saturday parking, and the nonuniversity lots are free on Sunday and holidays.

BY PLANE

Flying is a good option, especially for those taking advantage of the lower prices on advance tickets. Numerous airlines operate between Chicago (both O'Hare and Midway) and Detroit Metropolitan airport, including American,

Comair/Delta, Southwest, United, and US Airways; it is also a hub for North-west. Most run multiple flights per day. Ann Arbor is served by the Detroit Metropolitan Airport, 25 mi east of town, off I–94. A one-way cab ride to or from Ann Arbor costs about $40. Many shuttle services are also available, charging anywhere from $25 to $50 one-way.

AIRPORT **Detroit Metropolitan Airport** > 9000 Middlebelt Rd., Detroit, tel. 734/247–7678, www.metroairport.com.

BY TRAIN
Amtrak runs between Chicago and Ann Arbor, with many local stops. Expect youthful company during the school year—with 38,000 students, U of M at-tracts family and friends, and the route serves another major university town (East Lansing, home of Michigan State), as well as such large hometowns as Flint, Battle Creek, and Kalamazoo. Trains depart three times daily from Chicago to Ann Arbor (at 7 AM, 2:10 PM, and 6 PM) and three times daily from Ann Arbor to Chicago (at 8:29 AM, 11:45 AM, and 5:17 PM). Check schedules for changes. The Ann Arbor Train Station is near Kerrytown, two blocks north of downtown.

TRAIN LINE **Amtrak** > Tel. 800/872–7245, www.amtrak.com.

TRAIN STATION **Ann Arbor Train Station** > 325 Depot St., Ann Arbor, tel. 734/994–4906.

Visitor Information

TOURIST INFORMATION **Ann Arbor Convention and Visitors Bureau** > 120 W. Huron St., Ann Arbor 48104, tel. 734/995–7281 or 800/888–9487, www.annarbor.org.

Columbus & Brown County

235 mi southeast of Chicago

24

By Kevin Cunningham

COLUMBUS IS AN ARCHITECTURAL SHOWCASE. Restored vintage buildings stand side by side with innovative modern structures along the brick streets downtown. The 1874 County Courthouse with its clock tower anchors the south edge of town, and 19th-century storefronts line the main street just as in many another Indiana small towns; on the outskirts, strip malls and shopping plazas have sprouted like weeds, as in every other prosperous community in the state.

But that's where the resemblance stops. While at Yale, a local boy named J. Irwin Miller roomed with Eero Saarinen, the son of architect Eliel Saarinen and later a noted architect in his own right. After graduation, Miller built the family business, Cummins Engine, into an international powerhouse, the world's premier manufacturer of diesel engines. With some of the profits, he started the Columbus Engine Foundation, which, to this day, pays the architectural fees for local building projects. As a result, Columbus has become the repository of dozens of buildings by some of the world's best-known contemporary architects, including Harry Weese, Edward Larrabee Barnes, I. M. Pei, Roche Dinkeloo, Cesar Pelli, Robert Venturi, Richard Meier, Skidmore, Owings & Merrill, Gwathney Siegel, and Eliel and Eero Saarinen. In a 1991 American Institute of Architects survey Columbus was ranked sixth among U.S. cities in architectural quality and innovation, following Chicago, New York, Washington, San Francisco, and Boston.

In 1937, Eliel Saarinen was hired to design the **First Christian Church** (531 5th St.), the first contemporary-style building in Columbus and one of the first churches in that style in the United States, which subsequently set the stage for Columbus's architectural renaissance. The interior's pierced brick wall and off-center aisle highlight Harry Weese's **First Baptist Church** (3300 Fairlawn Dr.); a soaring 192-foot spire tops Eero Saarinen's **North Christian Church** (850 Tipton La.); and **Smith Elementary School** (4505 Waycross Dr.) is a vision of the future with its brightly painted connecting "tubes." Also unique is Venturi & Rauch's **Fire Station No. 4,** with an unusual hose-drying tower. I. M. Pei designed the **Cleo Rogers Memorial Library** (536 5th St.), a brick pavilion in his trademark style. The city's dedication to other forms of public art can be seen in the sculpture by Henry Moore presiding over the local public library, and another by Jean Tinguely that dominates the downtown shopping mall.

Roughly 60 mi south of Indianapolis the landscape starts to dip and swell into the hills of Brown County. Artists discovered this lush countryside in the 19th century and made the area something of an artists' colony under the leadership of Adolph Shulz and American impressionist–style painter T. C. Steele, who bought more than 200 acres in 1907 and built his studio and home here. Later, city slickers peppered country lanes in what came to be known as Peaceful Valley with summer cabins in communities such as Bean Blossom, Bear Wallow, and Possum Trot. Steele's home, the House of the Singing Winds, is now a state historic site.

The leafy town of Nashville has welcomed tourists for decades, especially during fall foliage season, when leaf peepers creep through town in bumper-to-bumper traffic. One of the state's top attractions, the town is crammed with shops and restaurants as well as galleries. Throngs notwithstanding, Nashville's charm endures.

Extensive woodlands, particularly thick in Brown County and admired by artists and hikers alike, fill the rest of the county. Brown County State Park and Yellowwood State Forest attract nature lovers and outdoor enthusiasts alike.

WHAT TO SEE & DO

COLUMBUS

Bartholomew County Historical Museum A restored 19th-century Italianate brick house downtown mounts exhibitions in four galleries, and documents the county's history from pioneer times to the 20th century with artifacts, art, and a hands-on area for kids. Past exhibitions have included a tribute to the county's firefighters. Prized artifacts include a vintage Worth from the earliest days of the automobile. Local wood carvings—and some scary taxidermy—are also represented. > 524 3rd St., Columbus, tel. 812/372–3541, www.barthist.com. Free. Tues.–Fri. 9–4.

Columbus Area Visitor Center Two works by internationally recognized glass artist Dale Chihuly, *Yellow Neon Chandelier* and *Persian Window,* ornament this two-story Italianate house built of red brick. Inside the front room is a display showcasing the town's architectural wonders with annotated maps, photography, and blueprints. A gift shop carries souvenirs, handmade pottery, architectural and children's books, jewelry, glass, and clothing. > 506 5th St., Columbus, tel. 812/378–2622 or 800/468–6564, www.columbus.in.us. Free. Mar.–Nov., Mon.–Sat. 9–5, Sun. 10–4; Dec.–Feb., Mon.–Sat. 9–5.

The Commons Architect Cesar Pelli designed this small, one-of-a-kind mall in the center of downtown Columbus in 1973. *Chaos I,* a 7-ton kinetic sculpture by Jean Tinguely, dominates the huge open space at the center. Off to one side is a carpeted play area where kids can climb and slide to their hearts' content. Upstairs are a movie theater and a branch of the Indianapolis Museum of Art. Innovative though it may be, the building continues to lose business to large, glitzier malls on the outskirts of town. > 4th and Washington Sts., Columbus, tel. 812/372–4541. Free. Mon.–Sat. 9:30–7, Sun. noon–5.

Indianapolis Museum of Art–Columbus Gallery The only branch of the Indianapolis Museum of Art was established in 1974 in the Commons, the Cesar Pelli–designed mall in the center of downtown Columbus. The museum mounts traveling exhibits and displays works from the art museum's permanent collections in Indianapolis. > 390 the Commons, 4th and Washington Sts., Columbus, tel. 812/376–2597, www.imacg.org. Free. Tues.–Sat. 10–5, Sun. noon–4.

Irwin Gardens J. Irwin Miller's father, banker William G. Irwin, created these gardens surrounding his former home downtown, a redbrick building dating from 1864. The sunken formal gardens were inspired by the great gardens of Europe, particularly one discovered in the ruins of Pompeii (copies of Pompeiian murals can be found in the garden house). They are filled with sculpted trees and shrubs, flowers, and busts of ancient Greek philosophers. > 540 5th St., Columbus, tel. 812/372–1954. Free. May–Oct., weekends 8–4.

Mill Race Park Where three rivers come together, landscape architect Michael Van Valkenburgh designed an 85-acre park that could withstand periodic flooding and also become, according to its designer, "a small-town equivalent of Central Park." Mill Race includes an outdoor amphitheater, a restored covered bridge, trails, a lake with a fishing pier, and picnic shelters. At Christmas, 2 million lights illuminate holiday sculptures. > 5th and Lindsay Sts., Columbus, tel. 812/376–2680. Free. Daily.

Muscatatuck National Wildlife Refuge The state's only federally designated wildlife refuge covers 7,802 acres of wetlands, woodlands, and open fields that were once primarily farmland. Otters were introduced in 1995 and trumpeter swans in 1998. The refuge attracts waterfowl year-round as well as migrating bald eagles, ospreys, white pelicans, white-faced ibis, American bitterns, and blue herons. It's also a habitat for upland birds including bobwhites and wild turkeys. There are eight short wildlife viewing trails and a small information center with a viewing window. The refuge is 20 mi northeast of Columbus. > 12985 E. U.S. 50, Seymour, tel. 812/522–4352. Free. Feb.–Nov., daily dawn–dusk; Dec. and Jan., daily 6 AM–6 PM.

Otter Creek Golf Course In this architecture-oriented town, it is only fitting that renowned architect Harry Weese designed the golf course clubhouse, which houses a glass-walled dining room. More than 3,000 trees spread across 388 acres shade the 27-hole championship course (open to the public) designed by Robert Trent Jones and his son Rees. This course is 6 mi east of the center of Columbus. > 11522 E. Rte. 50 N, Columbus, tel. 812/579–5227, www.ocgc.com. Mar.–Nov.

NASHVILLE

Bill Monroe Bluegrass Hall of Fame Paying homage to the father of bluegrass, the late Bill Monroe, this gallery, 5 mi north of Nashville, displays memorabilia collected by Mr. Monroe over his epic career. The Bluegrass Hall of Fame room showcases such top artists as Lester Flatt and Earl Scruggs, they of "Foggy Mountain Breakdown" and "Beverly Hillbillies Theme" fame, whom Mr. Monroe recognized for their contribution to the genre. Bluegrass mania climaxes in June during a weeklong annual music festival. > 5163 Rte. 135 N, Bean Blossom 46160, tel. 812/988–6422, www.beanblossom.com. $4. Nov.–Apr., Tues.–Sat. 9–5; May–Oct., Mon.–Sat. 9–5, Sun. 1–5.

Brown County Art Gallery Association Founded in 1926, this association is one of the oldest Midwest art societies, memorializing Glen Cooper Henshaw, a Brown County artist of the early and mid-1900s who turned to impressionism—particularly as a portrait painter—after studying in Europe. > 1 Artist Dr., at E. Main St., Nashville, tel. 812/988–4609. Free. Mon.–Sat. 10–5, Sun. noon–5.

Brown County Art Guild Guild artist-members show their work in the guild's downtown gallery, with a new artist showcase each month and special shows, such as November's Senior Art Show, occasionally scheduled. > 48 S. Van Buren St., Nashville, tel. 812/988–6185. Mar.–Dec., Mon.–Sat. 10–5, Sun. 11–5; Jan. and Feb., by appointment.

Brown County Historical Museum You can watch demonstrations of spinning and weaving in the loom room at this museum, which also displays an 1850s pioneer cabin, an 1879 log jail, an 1897 doctor's office, and a blacksmith shop. > Museum La., Nashville, tel. 812/988–6089. Free. May–Oct., weekends 1–5.

Brown County State Park With 15,500 acres, this rolling woodland preserve is Indiana's largest state park. A covered bridge marks one entrance, and inside are six scenic overlooks along the park's ridgetop roads and a fire tower you can climb for even more amazing hill-behind-hill vistas. Weed Patch Hill is among the tallest summits in Indiana at 1,058 feet. Ten miles of trails skirt two lakes, and a special campground is reserved for equestrians. The rustic, log Abe Martin Lodge serves home-style chicken-and-biscuit dinners; it's so popular that reservations are hard to come by. > Rte. 46, Nashville, tel. 812/988–6406. $5 per vehicle. Daily.

Leaves of Green, Red & Gold

IT SO HAPPENS THAT BROWN COUNTY IS BLESSED *with a generous population of maples, the tree that made New England famous and a species prone to displaying the most dazzling section of the color wheel. When the dark green spears of evergreens split those hillside fields of scarlet, orange, and yellow, the landscape seems to demand that you pick up palette or camera.*

To best enjoy Brown County in October, though, you need to plan ahead. May is good. March is better, especially if you want to stay overnight on a weekend. Though the scenery can be relied upon, so can the crowds. An amble down Old Route 46 is a thrilling display—the thick foliage overhead makes this narrow road east of downtown into an IMAX-like tunnel—but if you want quiet contemplation with your color, consider a drive farther afield, perhaps along the sparser but more scenic Route 135 to Bean Blossom. From Bean Blossom, take Route 45 to Bloomington, where canyons enrich the scenery. In leafy Nashville, you can wander a few blocks west from the shops and walk beneath a colorful canopy.

Brown County State Park is a popular choice among leaf peepers, both for its trails and the miles of winding roads. For escape, veterans recommend the more southerly regions of the park. It's far enough from the highway entrances to thin the crowds somewhat but still provide plenty of vistas. If you're up for a hike, take the No. 5 trail—the only one designated "rugged"—and follow the path around the Ogle Hollow Nature Preserve. Here, you can see wildlife as well as foliage. And don't overlook Yellowwood State Forest, 7 mi west of Nashville. It plays host to the same trees and provides views against the backdrop of Lake Yellowwood.

When in doubt, ask your innkeeper or another local for foliage tips. Everyone has a favorite spot, so you'll have plenty of places to explore.

Little Nashville Opry Boot-stomping fun awaits at this northern relative of the real McCoy. Though the show itself may be dubbed "little," the headliners who appear here are anything but—unless you'd call Loretta Lynn and George Jones minor. You can commemorate your trip with country-music paraphernalia at the concession stands. > 703 Rte. 46, Nashville, tel. 812/998–2235, www.littlenashvilleopry.com. $7. Box office: Mar.–Nov., Tues.–Sat. 9–5.

Nashville/Brown County Convention & Visitors Bureau Here, a collection of brochures, maps, and programs are on hand to help you enrich your visit. Consider buying a Valued Visitors card, valid from January through December of a given year. For $10, you'll receive discounts and freebies at a number of area shops, attractions, and places to stay (some restrictions in October). > Main and Van Buren Sts., Nashville, tel. 812/988–7303 or 800/753–3255, www.browncounty.com. Mon.–Thurs. 9–6, Fri. and Sat. 9–8, Sun. 10–5.

Ski World Recreation Complex The downhill ski resort takes advantage of the hilly terrain with several challenging runs. In summer, music theater and camping are the primary activities. > 2887 W. Rte. 46, Nashville, tel. 812/988–6638, www.skiworldindiana.com. Apr.–Oct. and mid-Dec.–early Mar., daily.

T. C. Steele State Historic Site T. C. Steele moved to Brown County in 1907, with his second wife, Selma Neubacher Steele, and built a home called House of the Singing Winds. As a member of the Hoosier Group of American Regional Impressionist Painters, Steele was inspired by Brown County's tranquil, woodsy landscape, and spent summers here, becoming one of the leading members in the Brown County Art Colony. The hilltop home and studio, surrounded by several acres of gardens first tended by Selma, are filled with personal mementos as well as changing exhibits of paintings from his entire career. Four trails, the Dewar Log Cabin, and the 92-acre Selma Steele Nature Preserve are also part of the 211-acre property. > 4220 T. C. Steele Rd., Nashville, tel. 812/988–2785, fax 812/988–8457, www.tcsteele.org. Free. Apr.–Oct., Tues.–Sat. 9–5, Sun. 1–5.

Yellowwood State Forest At 23,326 acres, Yellowwood is one of the larger state forests, with boat rentals available for fishing its lake. > 772 Yellowwood Lake Rd., off U.S. 46, Nashville, tel. 812/988–7945. Free. Daily.

Tours

Columbus Architecture Tours Those interested in a catch-all spin around the city's most celebrated buildings can take the Columbus Visitors Center's guided bus tour. Tours depart weekdays at 10 AM, Saturday at 10 AM and 2 PM, and Sunday at 10 AM and 4 PM (March–November only). Some walking is included. An additional walking tour is available Friday afternoons in summer. Both one- and two-hour tours are available, the latter of which includes tours inside two buildings. Reservations are required. > 506 5th St., Columbus, tel. 812/378–2622 or 800/468–6564, www.columbus.in.us. $7 1-hr tour, $9.50 2-hr tour.

Nashville Express Train Tours This narrated 20-minute, 2½-mi tour on a simulated steam train takes in the historic sites and local businesses in Nashville. You can watch a video while you're on board. Tours depart every half hour from several hotels in town. > Franklin St. at Van Buren St., Nashville, tel. 812/988–2308 or 812/988–2355. $4. Apr.–Nov., daily.

Save the Date

MAY

Wings over Muscatatuck One of Muscatatuck National Wildlife Refuge's most popular draws, this annual spring event, held the second weekend of May, leads programs on such green activities as birding, attracting wildlife to your yard, and nature photography. Bird walks and guided field trips are also available. Kids can watch puppet shows and even build a birdhouse. > 12985 E. U.S. 50, Seymour, tel. 812/522–4352.

JUNE

Annual Bill Monroe Memorial Bean Blossom Bluegrass Festival Come mid-June in Bean Blossom, the spirit of the legendary father of bluegrass, Bill Monroe, lives on with eight days of music, workshops, and tours of the Bill Monroe Bluegrass Hall of Fame. Past performers include Ralph Stanley and Jimmy Martin. > 5163 Rte. 135 N, Bean Blossom, tel. 812/988–6422 or 800/414–4677, www.beanblossom.com.

Art in the Park Buy or admire the works on display at this art fair, held by a local arts group in Columbus's Donner Park, usually on the last weekend of the month. > 22nd and Sycamore Sts., Columbus, tel. 812/372–4228, www.artcolumbus.org.

Log Cabin Tour Held the first weekend in June, this self-guided annual tour looks at historic and contemporary log cabins tucked among the hills and hollows of scenic Brown County. You can purchase tickets in advance or at the Village Green Gazebo at the corner of Jefferson and Main streets in Nashville. > Tel. 800/753–3255.

JUNE–SEPTEMBER

Brown County Playhouse Each weekend, budding thespians from Indiana University present summer theater in Nashville. Performances include recent off-Broadway hits and comedies. > 70 S. Van Buren St., Nashville, tel. 812/988–2123 box office, 812/855–1103 business office.

SEPTEMBER

Chautauqua of the Arts More than 100 artists from 25 states display and sell fine art and crafts at scenic Mill Race Park. The festival also includes entertainment and food. > 5th and Lindsay Sts., tel. 812/265–5080, www.chautauquaofthearts.com.

SEPTEMBER & OCTOBER

Autumn Festival The turning of the leaves in Brown County is the Midwest's answer to New England or the Smoky Mountains. Admirers descend on Nashville to admire the scenery or paint it *plein air*, or take in the artists' exhibitions, painting demonstrations, plays, and concerts, all against the backdrop of fall foliage. > Tel. 800/753–3255.

NOVEMBER–JANUARY

Winter Park Two million lights illuminate wire-frame sculptures on holiday themes along the road in Mill Race Park every evening from 6 to 10. > 5th and Lindsay Sts., Columbus, tel. 812/378–2622 or 800/468–6564.

WHERE TO STAY

COLUMBUS

Columbus Inn This bed-and-breakfast occupies the renovated 1895 city hall downtown. A redbrick and limestone building in the Romanesque style, it is instantly recognizable for its tower, tall windows, and wide arch over the entryway. Carved woodwork and ornamental tiles decorate the lobby and lounge, and traditional, antique furnishings fill the rooms and suites. Afternoon tea is a daily affair. > 445 5th St., Columbus 47201, tel. 812/378–4289, fax 812/378–4289, www.thecolumbusinn.com. 29 rooms, 5 suites. Some kitchenettes, cable TV, library, meeting rooms; no smoking. AE, D, DC, MC, V. BP. $

Holiday Inn and Conference Center Behind a contemporary facade, this hostelry with a seven-story tower and a couple of smaller wings has a Holidome recreation center, an old-English pub, and a small lobby with striped awnings, touches of brass, and a scattering of Indiana collectibles. It's two blocks off I–65, Exit 68 (Rte. 46), and 1 mi from downtown. > 2480 Jonathan Moore Pike (Rte. 46), Columbus 47201, tel. 812/372–1541, fax 812/378–9049. 253 rooms, 4 suites. Restaurant, patisserie, room service, in-room data ports, some minibars, cable TV, miniature golf, indoor pool, exercise equipment, hair salon, hot tub, saunas, billiards, Ping-Pong, pub, video game room, business services, some pets allowed, no-smoking rooms. AE, D, DC, MC, V. CP. $

Ramada Inn and Conference Center Part of the enclave of hotels off I–65 on Route 46, this stylish three-story building built of fieldstone sits on a fishing lake across from the Holiday Inn. The guest rooms include desks and work areas, and the modest counter space around the refrigerator is a boon to self-caterers. Columbus is a mile to the east. > 2485 Jonathan Moore Pike (Rte. 46), Columbus 47201, tel. 812/376–3051 or 800/842–9832, fax 812/376–0949, www.ramada.com. 78 rooms, 17 suites. Restaurant, room service, in-room data ports, in-room safes, some in-room hot tubs, some minibars, some microwaves, refrigerators, cable TV, exercise equipment, hot tub, bar, business services, no-smoking rooms. AE, D, DC, MC, V. BP. ¢–$

Ruddick-Nugent House Four white columns rise two stories across the front of this three-story colonial-revival house built in 1884. With its expansive front lawn, it occupies an entire city block. William's room and Lizzie's room have gasoliers (a chandelier for both gas and electric). Inez's room is bright with yellow painted walls, an antique wardrobe, and a queen bed. Martha's room holds a queen bed with a headboard made from the original front doors of the house and a marbleized, cast-iron fireplace. You can have your breakfast by candlelight in the dining room, or on the balcony or front porch. No alcohol is allowed on the premises. > 1210 16th St., Columbus 47201, tel. 812/379–1354 or 800/814–7478, fax 812/379–1357, www.ruddick-nugent-house.com. 4 rooms. In-room data ports, cable TV, no smoking. AE, D, MC, V. BP. ¢–$

NASHVILLE

Abe Martin Lodge The lodge takes its name from artist Kin Hubbard's cartoon character Abe Martin, a popular figure with Dogpatch-like quips that appeared in the *Indianapolis News* from 1905 to 1930. Abe Martin Lodge was built of native stone and hand-hewn oak timbers in 1932. Inside are two spacious lobbies with rustic stone fireplaces and a dining room famous for its country-style buffet. Within Brown County State Park, the property includes a main lodge with rooms but also cabins. The rooms tend toward darker, rustic colors on the walls and country-style comforters on each of the two double beds. The cabins, remodeled versions of the 1932 originals, are undeniably woodsy but come with modern bathrooms; the two-story housekeeping cabins have wood-burning stoves and a deck. > Rte. 46, Nashville 47448, tel. 812/988–4418 or 877/265–6343, fax 812/988–7334. 84 rooms, 76 cabins. Dining room, some kitchens, cable TV, video game room, business services, meeting rooms. AE, D, MC, V. ¢–$

Allison House The 1883 yellow-clapboard B&B on the south side of town bustles with downtown shoppers during the day. To accentuate the classic country decor, the innkeepers have contrasted light-friendly whites and creams against strong blocks of blue, reds, and yellows on quilts and carpets—a refreshing change from Victoriana or antiques-heavy rural style. In summer you can eat breakfast beneath the umbrella on the deck. > 90 S. Jefferson St., Nashville 47448, tel. 812/988–0814. 5 rooms. No room phones, no smoking. No credit cards. BP. $

Always Inn A wraparound deck and outdoor gazebo hot tub surrounded by a garden make this B&B a true pastoral escape. Each arboreally named room has antique furnishings—the spacious White Pine Room has a prairie-size brass bed and an uncluttered country style; the honeymoon-oriented Bittersweet is furnished with antiques and a marble fireplace. Some rooms have fireplaces and access to either private patios or decks. > 8072 E. Rte. 46, Nashville 47448, tel. 812/998–2233 or 888/457–2233, fax 812/457–2233, www.alwaysinn.com. 5 rooms. Some in-room hot tubs, in-room VCRs, hot tub. AE, D, MC, V. BP. **$–$$$**

Artists Colony Inn The design of the inn recalls the Pittman Inn, an early 1900s Nashville hostelry frequented by itinerant artists. Built in 1992, this three-story wood-frame building resembles the many oversize early-American clapboard farmhouses seen in the area. Surrounded by gardens and towering trees, the inn sits back off Nashville's busy main street. Reproduction cherrywood and painted furniture, cupboards, Windsor chairs, and woven coverlets furnish the spare yet comfortable rooms in a palette of deep blue, green, burgundy, and cream. Many of the furnishings were made by local artists and each room has been named for one of the early Hoosier School artists. > Van Buren and Franklin Sts., Nashville 47448, tel. 812/988–0600 or 800/737–0255, fax 812/988–9023, www.artistscolonyinn.com. 20 rooms, 3 suites. Restaurant, some in-room hot tubs, some kitchenettes, cable TV, some in-room VCRs, hot tub, no smoking. AE, MC, V. **$–$$**

Brown County Inn Wood siding covers the facade of this motel on the edge of town and about a quarter-mile walk from shops and restaurants. The motel is furnished with antiques, collectibles, and country decor. > 51 State Rd. 46 E, Nashville 47448, tel. 812/988–2291 or 800/772–5249, fax 812/988–8312, www.browncountyinn.com. 99 rooms. Restaurant, cable TV, tennis courts, indoor-outdoor pool, bar, playground. AE, D, DC, MC, V. **$–$$**

Comfort Inn A mile from town and nestling close to Brown County State Park, the Nashville edition of the well-known chain has a lobby with fireplace and more-generous-than-usual amenities. Rooms have space to move and the uncluttered decor reflects the locally popular country style. A ½-mi walk up Van Buren Street lands you in downtown. > 75 W. Chestnut St., Nashville 47448, tel. 812/988–6118, fax 812/988–6118, www2.choicehotels.com. 55 rooms. Some in-room hot tubs, some kitchens, some microwaves, cable TV, indoor pool, exercise equipment, video game room, business services, no-smoking rooms. AE, D, MC, V. CP. **$–$$**

Cornerstone Inn You can sip a cool glass of lemonade in your rocking chair on the balcony at this family-owned B&B. The rooms are named after the innkeepers' Brown County ancestors and each is done in antiques and period decor. The Victorian-style house is steps away from downtown shops and galleries, but set back off the street. > 54 E. Franklin St., Nashville 47448, tel. 812/988–0300 or 888/383–0300, fax 812/988–0200, www.cornerstoneinn.com. 19 rooms, 1 suite. Some in-room hot tubs, cable TV; no smoking. D, MC, V. CP. **$–$$**

Olde Magnolia House In the heart of Nashville, one block from most of the shops, lies this white Victorian mansion. The homey rooms have queen-size beds, antique furnishings, and in some rooms, gas fireplaces. Lace and wallpaper make up some of the fussier rooms. If you are an early riser, you can enjoy a prebreakfast coffee and tea service on the porch. Though some baths are across the hall from their corresponding room, all baths are private. > 213 S. Jefferson St., Nashville 47448, tel. 812/988–2434 or 877/477–5144, www.theoldmagnoliahouse.com. 4 rooms. Some in-room hot tubs, cable TV, in-room VCRs; no smoking. AE, D, MC, V. **$–$$**

Seasons Lodge Set on a hillside off Rte. 46, 1½ mi from downtown and across from Brown County State Park, this hotel is built of native stone with painted timbers in a contemporary style. Eight rooms have wood-burning fireplaces. > 560 Rte. 46 E, Nashville 47448, tel. 812/988–2284 or 800/365–7327, www.seasonslodge.com. 80 rooms. Restaurant, room service, cable TV, indoor-outdoor pool, bar, playground, business services. AE, D, DC, MC, V. **$**

WHERE TO EAT

COLUMBUS

Smith's Row In a brick building near downtown, this fine-dining spot has a long list of wines to complement its menu of steaks, stuffed flounder, and breast of Long Island duck in an orange–port wine sauce. > 418 4th St., Columbus, tel. 812/373–9382. AE, D, DC, MC, V. Closed Sun. $$–$$$

Zaharako's A huge old-fashioned soda fountain with its original pressed-tin ceiling welcomes you to this vintage building. Along with basic cold sandwiches plus dogs and fries, the kitchen serves a grilled-cheese sandwich with chili inside. For dessert, fountain treats such as sundaes are the order of the day. You eat at 1950s Formica-and-chrome tables and chairs. Ask a staffer to crank up the antique orchestra music box in back. > 329 Washington St., Columbus, tel. 812/379–9329. No credit cards. Closed Sun. No dinner. ¢

NASHVILLE

Abe Martin Lodge Generations of visitors to Brown County and the University of Indiana have patronized the dining room at this lodge inside Brown County State Park. Feast on a country-style buffet with such trademark fare as fried chicken and biscuits with apple butter, as well as menu dinners. If you're dining the day, ask to sit in the backroom, which has forest views. > Rte. 46, Nashville, tel. 812/988–4418 or 877/265–6343. AE, D, MC, V. ¢–$$$

Artists Colony Inn People-watch from the porch or eat by lantern light beneath the beamed ceilings of the gallery room at this B&B. The menu lists the wholesome (a fresh strawberry and spinach salad) and the hearty (standards such as meat loaf and country-fried steak), plus excellent fish dinners, including yellowfin tuna and fried catfish. > Franklin and Van Buren Sts., Nashville, tel. 812/988–0600 or 800/737–0255. AE, D, MC, V. Closed Mon. Nov.–Sept. ¢–$$

Hobnob Restaurant Housed in Nashville's oldest commercial building, a big white storefront on a downtown corner, this eatery serves country-style lunches and dinners, including salads, chicken, and steak. It's also a local favorite for breakfast. > 17 W. Main St., Nashville, tel. 812/988–4114. AE, D, MC, V. No dinner Mon. and Tues. Nov.–Sept. ¢–$$

Nashville House Paintings by Brown County artists line the walls and red-checked tablecloths cover the tables within the rustic setting here. In the heart of downtown Nashville, the family restaurant is known for its fried chicken and roast turkey dinners with fried biscuits and apple butter. > 87 N. Van Buren St., Nashville, tel. 812/988–4554. MC, V. Closed late Dec.–early Jan. and Tues. in Nov.–Sept. $$–$$$

The Ordinary Nestled within the 350 shops, galleries, and studios that have sidewalk sales regularly, the restaurant and tavern is dressed in early-American style. Sandwiches are the specialty here—try the pheasant-turkey—but ribs and chops are also worth trying. > N. Van Buren St., Nashville, tel. 812/988–6166. D, MC, V. Closed Mon. Nov.–Sept. ¢–$$

Story Inn Renovated from an 1850s general store, 3½ mi south of Nashville, this old-world enclave serves dinner by candlelight and is considered one of the best restaurants in the state. Filet mignon and bourbon strip steak are menu favorites, with seafood and vegetarian dishes coming in right underneath. For dessert, the turtle cheesecake is legendary. > 6404 S. Rte. 135, Story, tel. 812/988–2273 or 800/881–1183, www.storyinn.com. Reservations essential. MC, V. Closed Mon. $$$–$$$$

ESSENTIALS

Getting Here

A car is the best option if you wish to take advantage of the entire Colum-bus/Brown County area, including Nashville, the state parks, and several sce-nic routes. Greyhound serves Columbus but the closest airport is Indianapolis International Airport, an hour's drive north of Columbus. By car or by bus from Chicago to Columbus takes approximately five hours (if traffic is light). Within Columbus, most of the architecturally significant buildings are spread out across town, but many are accessible via public transportation.

BY BUS

Greyhound runs twice per day between Chicago and Columbus. All buses run with few stops, keeping travel times between 4½ and 5 hours; longer times are generally due to a brief layover in Indianapolis. The ColumBus provides a daily public bus service for Columbus. Fare is 25¢ per ride. Service runs daily from 6 AM to 7 PM. All four ColumBus routes leave from the Commons Mall at :05 after every hour.

BUS DEPOT **ColumBus Bus Depot** > 406 Washington St., Columbus.
BUS LINE **Greyhound** > Tel. 800/229–9424, www.greyhound.com.

BY CAR

A car is recommended, as it affords you the opportunity to fully appreciate Columbus and Brown County's architecture, attractions, and natural splendor. Scenic drives along Routes 46 and 135, and Nashville's Main Street/Old State Road 46 provide some of the best fall foliage in the Midwest.

From Chicago, you can take I–90 or I–80 (I–94) to I–65. The speed limit is typically 65 mph (55 mph in the Indianapolis area). Traffic is usually not a problem, with one exception: the merge of I–94 with I–80 near the Indiana state line. Although a 20-mi backup is not typical, it happens and it's never more likely than during a Friday-evening rush hour when commuters, long-haul semis, and vacationers collide.

A handful of main thoroughfares can take you everywhere quickly. Downtown parking is available at the Commons Mall or on the street. Around the rest of Columbus, street parking is plentiful.

Route 135 provides access to Nashville from the north and east; Route 46 pro-vides access from the south and east. Route 135 becomes Van Buren Street in downtown Nashville. Streets are easy to navigate but tend to be narrow; motor coaches can make things cramped. During summer weekends and just about any time in October, traffic (pedestrian and vehicular) is unavoidable in Nashville and on the foliage-lined roads into and out of town. Park as soon as you can and then walk to where you're going. Street parking is limited and a number of private lots are typically priced around $2–$5 per day, though prices may rise slightly during foliage season.

BY PLANE

Columbus and Nashville is served by Indianapolis International Airport, 50 mi north of Columbus off I–465. Three airlines fly between Indianapolis Interna-tional Airport and Chicago O'Hare: American, United, and US Airways. Two airlines serve Indianapolis International Airport to and from Chicago Midway:

ATA and Southwest. Flights can vary but usually take 1 hour to 1 hour and 15 minutes.

AIRPORT **Indianapolis International Airport** > 2500 S. High School Rd., Indianapolis, tel. 317/487–7243, www.indianapolisairport.com.

CARRIERS **American** > Tel. 800/433–7300. **ATA** > Tel. 317/248–8308 or 800/435–9282. **Southwest** > Tel. 800/435–9792. **United** > Tel. 800/864–8331. **US Airways** > Tel. 800/428–4322.

Visitor Information

CONTACTS **Brown County Convention and Visitors Bureau** > Box 840, 47448, tel. 812/988–7303 or 800/753–3255, fax 812/988–1070, www.browncounty.com. **Columbus Area Visitor Center** > 506 5th St., Nashville 47202, tel. 812/378–2622 or 800/468–6564, www.columbus.in.us.

Michigan Wine Country

354 mi northeast of Chicago

By Linda Packer

ALTHOUGH MANY CHICAGOANS ARE FAMILIAR WITH WINERIES in southwest Michigan, fewer have ventured farther north, where Traverse City branches upward into the Leelanau and Old Mission peninsulas. That's where the streetlights end and the countryside begins and you can drive for a dozen miles and see nothing but rolling land and an occasional sign enticing you with "Country Bread and Pastries" or "Farm-Fresh Fruit."

As you make the six-hour-plus drive here, billboards and fast-food chains give way to the rolling hills of northern Michigan. In autumn, the hills are rich with shades of red and gold. In winter, they sparkle with white blankets of snow and bundled-up kids on toboggans. In spring, the farms come to life with grazing cows and sheep and farmers tending their crops. In summer, the grapes ripen on the vines. By the following spring the best of the grapes will have been nurtured, harvested, and crafted into bottles of excellent wines that are ripe for the tasting in 39 wineries throughout the state.

The climate and soil are excellent for grape growth, and Lake Michigan protects the vines with snow in winter while retarding bud break in spring. Yet another reason for the good wine is a new breed of serious winemakers, some of whom were trained in Europe, others who studied the science of viticulture, and still others who recognize what is required to grow a great crop of grapes and, through science and art, turn it into wines that can compete with California, Oregon, Washington, and even European vintages. The science is understanding the fermentation process, the biology of growing the grapes, the microbiology of the soil. The art is in the nurturing.

Michigan has 13,500 acres of vineyards, about 1,500 of which are devoted to wine grapes. These are primarily vinifera grapes—the classic European varieties such as chardonnay, Riesling (the most widely planted white), pinot noir (the most widely planted red), pinot grigio, and cabernet franc. In 2002 alone, Michigan wines captured medals in more than 350 competitions, including 5 double gold, 41 gold, 90 silver, and 84 bronze medals in such international competitions as the Tasters Guild Awards, San Francisco International Wine Competition, Indy International Wine Competition, Riverside International, Grand Harvest Awards, and the prestigious Los Angeles County Fair.

A weekend of northwest Michigan wine tasting begins with a drive that marks a slow transition from the hectic pace of Chicago to a more relaxed pace. As you get closer to Michigan the flatland changes to rolling hills. On the northern edge of Traverse City is the first winery; thereafter the vineyards are close together. In Suttons Bay on the Leelanau Peninsula, just north of Traverse City, there is a cluster of six wineries within 5 miles of one another. Another two are 11 mi west and one more is 9 mi south of that. In between are small towns worth exploring, with shops, good restaurants, and cozy inns. Traverse City has a number of interesting sights, as do Suttons Bay, Leland, and Glen Arbor, each of which is within 1 mi of a winery.

Once a major lumbering center, Traverse City is now the hub of a flourishing cherry-growing community and northern Michigan's unofficial capital. Each July it hosts the National Cherry Festival, one of the state's largest and best-attended events. Its charming downtown is filled with restaurants and shops selling imported French skin creams, ceramic sushi plates, endlessly popular cherry condiments—and the requisite small-town northern Michigan antiques. For a pleasant diversion follow Route 37 around the Old Mission Peninsula, filled with the cherry orchards and vineyards that are the area's main industry next to tourism (which happened in large part because of the cherry orchards and vineyards). A good time to visit is in spring, when crowds are small.

Nearby Suttons Bay, surrounded by vineyards and cooled by the north arm of the Grand Traverse Bay, is home to most of the wineries on the Leelanau Peninsula. It also has a number of attractive shops and restaurants, and has become a bustling summer getaway. Leland, nestled on a sliver of land between Lake Michigan and Lake Leelanau, is a little village of shops and restaurants with many art galleries and a fantastic wine-and-food fest every June. Glen Arbor, a resort town catering to vacationers with its restaurants, bed-and-breakfasts, and growing gallery trade, is a popular starting point for canoe trips on the nearby Betsie River.

Among the best-known natural attractions is Sleeping Bear Dunes National Lakeshore, near Empire. With some of the largest freshwater dunes in the world and 32 mi of Lake Michigan beach, it's one of the most popular tourist destinations in the state. A National Park Service Visitors Center near the Dune Climb and the parking lot has information, rest rooms, and refreshments.

WHAT TO SEE & DO

GLEN ARBOR

Pleva's Meats Ever since Ray Pleva shared Oprah's stage to talk about Plevalean, a mixture of ground beef and cherries, the "Cherry Burger" has made it on the map. Pleva's sells not only its world-famous hamburger meat but also other delicacies such as cherry pecan sausage and cherry chopped steak. > 8974 S. Kasson St., 12 mi south of Leland, Cedar, tel. 231/228–5000, www.plevas.com. Weekdays 8–6, Sat. 8–5.

Point Betsie Lighthouse This lighthouse once guarded one of northwest Michigan's busiest ports. North of the city of Frankfort, it marks the entrance to the Sleeping Bear Dunes National Lakeshore. You can picnic here, but the lighthouse is not open to the public. > Frankfort, tel. 888/784–7328. Free. Daily dawn–dusk.

Sleeping Bear Dunes National Lakeshore Known for its 400-foot bluffs, 7-mi Pierce Stocking Scenic Drive, and 35 mi of hiking trails, this 75,000-acre preserve is a natural treasure. Sleeping Bear's hills—particularly its challenging Dune Climb—provide breathtaking views of the Lake Michigan shoreline. The visitor center is on Route 72 at the entrance in Empire and has exhibits and slides that shed light on the natural history of the park. It is worth stopping if only to hear how the forests of bleached trees, once covered by the dunes, reappeared as the sands shifted. Within the confines of Sleeping Bear Dunes lies the ghost town of **Glen Haven** (off M-22 in Sleeping Bear Dunes, tel. 231/326–5134). Purchased by the National Park Service in 1975 to ensure the safe future of Sleeping Bear Dunes, the town soon lost its businesses and residents, consequently leaving only a few remnants of once-vital coast-guard town. Today, you can visit a 1920s general store, a working blacksmith shop where all of the park's hooks and nails are made, a boat museum in what used to be the town's cherry cannery, and a maritime museum with exhibits on the work of the U.S. Lifesaving Service before it became the Coast Guard. > Park Headquarters, 9922 Front St., 6 mi south of Glen Arbor, Empire, tel. 231/326–5134, www.nps.gov/slbe/home.htm. $7 per car. Visitor center: Memorial Day–Labor Day, daily 9–6; Labor Day–Memorial Day, daily 9–4; park: daily dawn–dusk.

LELAND

Christmas Cove Farm At this apple farm, 12 mi north of Leland, you won't find just ordinary apples; only "antique apples" are grown here. Included among the more than 200 different varieties are the Lady Apple, which 17th-century French women used as breath fresheners; the Green Newton Pippin, dating from 1722 and thought to be America's oldest apple; and the Spitzenburg, Thomas Jefferson's favorite. > 11573 Kilcherman Rd., Northport, tel. 231/386–5637, www.applejournal.com/christmascove. Sept. 15–Nov., daily.

Fishtown When the Ottawa Indians first established a settlement here by the water, they called the land "Mishi-me-go-bing," which meant "the place where canoes run up into the river to land because they have no harbor." That harbor became Fishtown, and Fishtown became the reason Leland grew. Schooners and steamers brought settlers, most of whom stayed in Leland to lend their skills to the growing community. Today, Fishtown is a small village within Leland, a group of shanties on the river, a scene evoking eerie feelings of time travel. Most of the shanties have been converted to art galleries, clothing stores, and places to take you kayaking. You can buy a hat at Leelanau Leather or pick up handmade chocolates or lollipops from Dam Candy. > Main St., Leland. May–Oct.

Good Harbor Vineyard Tours, both guided and self-guided, are available at this popular vineyard where the tasting room includes many of the wines that have captured medals at the prestigious Los Angeles County Fair and Tasters Guild International competitions. > 34 S. Manitou Tr., 5 mi south of Leland on Rte. 22, Lake Leelanau, tel. 231/256–7165, www.goodharbor.com. Free. May–Oct., Mon.–Sat. 11–5, Sun. noon–5; Nov.–Dec., Sat. noon–5; Jan.–Apr., by appointment.

Whaleback Natural Area It is one of the most recognizable navigation tools for mariners, an important habitat for wildlife, and a calming vista for those in need of a respite. Whaleback, also known as Carp River Point, is a large glacial moraine dating back 10,000 years. The waves of Lake Michigan have since undermined the bluff, causing an erosion in the shape of a whale. Climbing the hill is a great family activity. > From the junction of M-22 and M-204 (just south of Leland), take M-22 north approximately 1 mi. A wooden sign with the profile of the Whaleback exists along the west (left) side of M-22, and marks the entrance to the Whaleback parking area. Leland, tel. 231/256–9665, www.theconservancy.com. Free. Daily.

SUTTONS BAY

Black Star Farms Vinifera wines, fruit brandies, handcrafted artisanal cheeses, a luxurious B&B, and beautiful stables with recreational trails, Black Star Farms is one of the premier destinations in the northwest Michigan wine country. Their wines have won both national and international awards; their 2000 A Capella Ice Wine was given an 87 by *Wine Spectator* magazine. Stop in the tasting room, and don't miss the succulent, distinctive pear brandy. > 10844 E. Revold Rd., Suttons Bay, tel. 231/271–4970, fax 231/271–4883, www.blackstarfarms.com. Free. Mon.–Sat. 11–5; Sun. noon–5.

Chateau de Leelanau The only winery in the state and one of the few in the country that is owned and operated solely by women, Chateau de Leelanau has a tasting room that may appeal to both the adult and the child in you. In addition to their cabernet franc, dry Riesling, late-harvest Riesling, and their proprietary Bianca, the winery's tasting room serves Moomer's ice cream, which is made by a local dairy and is a huge local crowd pleaser. > 5048 Bayshore Dr. SW, Suttons Bay, tel. 231/271–8888, www.cdlwinery.com. Free. Tues.–Sat. 11–5.

Ciccone Vineyard Winery Tony Ciccone had been making wine in his kitchen for years before he decided to quit his "day job" and become a full-time vintner with his wife Joan. Today Ciccone Wines are produced from estate-grown grapes planted and tended by the Ciccone family. All harvesting and wine making is done by hand, since they think modern techniques intrude against the natural balance and delicacy of the sun-ripened fruit. You may even see one of Tony and Joan's many children helping out in the tasting room, but probably not their most famous one—Madonna. > 10343 E. Hilltop Rd., Suttons Bay, tel. 231/271–5551 or 231/271–5553, fax 231/271–5552 or 231/271–5967. Free. Fri.–Sun. noon–5 or by appointment.

Leelanau Sands Casino This Native American–owned, glitzy, Las Vegas–style gaming facility, with two restaurants and an adjacent 51-room hotel, has 825 slots and 16 game tables. > 2521 N.W. Bayshore Dr., Peshawbestown, tel. 231/271–4104, leelanau-sands.casinocity.com. Free. Mid-June–Labor Day, daily 10 AM–2 AM.

Leelanau State Park/Grand Traverse Lighthouse Coastal dunes and a picnic and recreation area surround this scenic 1852 lighthouse, 25 mi north of Traverse City. An 8.5-mi trail, wide and hard-packed, meanders through the park, providing an idyllic spot for walking, hiking, or biking. You're likely to meet some of the park's residents strolling by—porcupines, deer, opossums, and raccoons. Lighthouse tours are given daily 10 AM–7 PM. > 15310 Lighthouse Point Rd., Northport, tel. 231/386–5422 or 800/447–2757. Park: $4 per car, per day; lighthouse: $2. Memorial Day–Labor Day, daily 10 AM–7 PM; Labor Day–Memorial Day, call for hrs.

Leelanau Trail Hikers, mountain bikers, and cross-country skiers travel this trail, a former rail bed. It stretches for 15 mi, from Traverse City to Suttons Bay, winding through woods, open pastures, across several creeks, and beside a small lake. You can in-line skate on the 3 mi near Traverse City that are paved. Entrance to the trail is next to the Town Depot. > Cedar St., Suttons Bay, tel. 231/883–8278. Free.

L. Mawby Vineyards and Winery Larry Mawby prides himself on having a vineyard that produces no more than 3,000 cases of *methode champenoise* sparkling wine each year, which allows him to give hands-on care to every bottle. The vineyard grows vignoles, pinot noir, pinot gris, seyval, chardonnay, pinot meunier, and regent grapes, producing vinifera wines, fruit wines, and hybrids. In summer, the winery hosts Sunday picnics with food from area chefs. > 4519 S. Elm Valley Rd., Suttons Bay, tel. 231/271–3522, fax 231/271–2927, www.lmawby.com. Free. May–Oct., Thurs.–Sun. 1–6; Nov.–Apr., Sat. noon–5 or by appointment.

Shady Lane Cellars Perched on the hilltop between Traverse City and Suttons Bay, this winery was once the site of a fruit farm. The first vines were planted in 1989, and 10 years later the owners transformed a chicken coop into a three-level stone tasting room with a copper roof, Italian-tile floor, elevator, and granite tasting bar. Chardonnay, Riesling, vignoles, and pinot noir are just some of the wines produced here. The sparkling wines are made the traditional French way, with the second fermentation in the bottle, and age a minimum of three years before they are sold. > 9580 Shady La., Suttons Bay, tel. 231/947–8865, www.shadylanecellars.com. Free. May–Oct., daily noon–6; Nov.–Apr., Sat. noon–6.

Willow Vineyard Chardonnay, pinot noir, and pinot gris are the wines of this majestic little vineyard, perched on a windswept hillside with panoramic views of West Traverse Bay. > 10702 E. Hilltop Rd., Suttons Bay, tel. 231/271–4810, www.lpwines.com. Free. Nov. and Dec., weekends or by appointment.

TRAVERSE CITY

Amon Orchards From July through October you can feed and pet goats, pigs, chickens, and rabbits at this family-owned and -operated orchard. In summer, staff will take you on a trolley ride and explain why and how each kind of produce grows. You can also purchase baked goods, jams, and jellies made on the premises. The orchard is 10–15 mi north of downtown Traverse City. > 7404 U.S. 31 N, Acme, tel. 231/938–1644, 231/938–9145, or 800/937–1644, www.amonorchards.com. Free. June–Nov., daily 10–5.

Chateaû Chantal Perched atop a ridge near the northern end of Old Mission Peninsula, overlooking both East and West Grand Traverse bays, this 65-acre estate is home to a vineyard, winery, B&B, and a collection of handcrafted wines that includes chardonnay, pinot gris, pinot noir, merlot, Riesling, and gewürztraminer. Throughout the year the château hosts "Slurpin' Seminars," and the Saturday after Thanksgiving is the annual Macaroni and Cheese Cook-Off. Tastings are held in the great room or in the wine cellar. > 15900 Rue de Vin, Traverse City, tel. 800/969–4009, www.chateauchantal.com. Free. Mid-June–Aug., weekdays 11–8, Sun. noon–5; Sept. and Oct., Mon.–Sat. 11–7, Sun. noon–5; Nov.–mid-June, Mon.–Sat. 11–5, Sun. noon–5.

Dennos Museum Center The center's permanent display of sculpture, prints, and drawings by the Inuit artists of the Canadian Arctic is said to be the largest and most historically complete collection in the country. That's just one of the exciting attractions and exhibits at this vibrant, 40,000-square-foot museum, which also has three changing exhibition galleries, a spacious sculpture court, and a hands-on discovery gallery the kids, especially, will enjoy. The adjacent Milliken Auditorium hosts a family-oriented concert series throughout fall and winter in addition to a lineup of jazz, blues, and classical music concerts. > Northwestern Michigan College, 1701 E. Front St., Traverse City, tel. 231/995–1055, fax 231/995–1597, www.denosmuseum.org. $4. Mon.–Sat. 10–5, Sun. 1–5.

Grand Traverse Dinner Train A beautiful journey through the Boardman River valley is part of the fun on this train; living the elegance of the golden age of railcar dining is another. From the old Traverse City Railway Station, the train travels south through the river valley. The multicourse dinner, whose menu changes seasonally, has included such entrées as chicken breast in puff pastry with mushroom pâté and salmon with shrimp cream sauce. Reservations are essential; departures are at 12:30 and 6:30 PM. > 642 Railroad Pl., Traverse City, tel. 231/933–3768, www.dinnertrain.com. $75. Nov.–May, Sat.; June, Tues. and Thurs.–Sat.; July and Aug., Tues.–Sat.; Sept. and Oct., daily.

Grand Traverse Heritage Center Six independent, nonprofit organizations dedicated to collecting and preserving the artifacts and documents about Grand Traverse and northern Michigan are housed in this single downtown building. The center's archives include photographs, documents, maps, and directories with more than 10,000 items of regional historical significance. Exhibits detail early railroad history, agriculture, the great lumbering era history, and the significance women played in the growth of the area. The Special Collections section displays Native American ethnographic material, with more than 3,000 stone tools and projectiles. > 322 6th St., Traverse City, tel. 231/995–0313. By donation. Mon.–Sat. 10–4.

Peninsula Cellars This winery on the Old Mission Peninsula, 7 mi north of Traverse City, is best known for producing white wines of intense aromas, vibrant acidity, and distinct varietal character. A star among the gewürztraminer, Riesling, pinot blanc, and pinot gris was their 2002 Riesling, which won Best Riesling in the World at the International Riesling Cup. You can taste up to six wines in Peninsula Cellars' tasting room, a 19th-century schoolhouse where you can also purchase such Old Mission agricultural items as cherries, apples, cherry mustard, cherry salsa, vinegar, and chocolate-covered cherries. > 11480 Center Rd. (Rte. 37), Traverse City, tel. 231/933–9787, www.peninsulacellars.com. Free. May–Oct., Mon.–Sat. 10–6; Nov.–Apr., Sat. noon–5.

Tours

By the Bay Tours Three different bus tours, each peppered with anecdotes, stories, and historical facts, are conducted here. A 3-hour Historic City Tour of Traverse City is given on Thursday, Friday, and Sunday; a 3½-hour Old Mission Tour, with wine tasting at each winery, is given on Wednesday and Saturday; and a 4-hour tour takes you to Sleeping Bear Dunes to explore shipwreck artifacts. > Tel. 231/932–1065, www.bythebayshuttle.com.

Traverse City Convention and Visitors Bureau Volunteers here will customize a self-drive day for you. Present a list of sites, ideas, or interests and they'll set up a connect-the-dots route of places to visit that match your tastes. > 101 W. Grandview Pkwy., Traverse City 49615, tel. 231/947–1120 or 800/872–8377, www.tcvisitor.com.

Save the Date

JANUARY

Winterfest This family event in nearby Kalkaska, 20 mi east of Traverse City, takes place on the last weekend of the month. Events include dogsled races, a volleyball tournament, a snowman-building contest, a pancake breakfast, kids' games, and a spicy chili cook-off. > Kalkaska, tel. 231/258–9103, www.kalkaskacounty.com/rec.htm.

FEBRUARY

Taste the Passion Bring your sweetheart and spend Valentine's Day weekend at a romantic wine tasting on the Leelanau Peninsula. Each winery will pair one or more of its wines with chocolate or another sensual treat. > www.lpwines.com.

MAY

Mesick Mushroom Festival The forests in Mesick, 25 mi south of Traverse City, attract thousands of fungi fans hunting for the elusive morel, which grows abundantly here. Mushroom cuisine, a carnival, a rodeo, baseball games, horseshoe tournaments, and a Saturday parade attract all ages during the second week of the month. > Mesick, tel. 231/885–2679, www.mesick-mushroomfest.org.

JUNE

Glen Arbor Antique Show and Festival Exhibitors and enthusiasts from across northern Michigan come to this annual antiques showcase. > Tel. 231/334–3238.

Interlochen Arts Festival A summer-long bonanza of musical talent performs in an open-air theater. Sometime during the evening—between acts, if the timing and weather conditions are right—you'll see a breathtaking sunset over the lake. > 4000 Rte. 137, Interlochen, tel. 231/276–6230, www.interlochen.org. Free. Sept.–May.

Music in the Park Free concerts are held on Traverse City's Marina Park Beach every Friday evening from the end of June through the end of August. > Northport, tel. 231/271–9895, www.leelanauchamber.com.

Old-Fashioned Family Fun Day Family entertainment is the order of the day at the Grand Traverse Zoological Society–sponsored Family Fun Day at the Clinch Park Zoo, held the first Sunday in June. Admission, pop, and popcorn are all just 25¢, and special activities are free. > Traverse City, tel. 231/922–4904.

JULY

Cedar Polka Fest The town lets loose with an annual polka fest each July—four days of polka music, dancing, food, beverages, parades, and other festivities, end-ing with a polka Mass on Sunday at noon. > Cedar, tel. 231/228–3378, www.leelanau.com/cedar/polka.html.

Jazz Fest Professional musicians make magic at this day of classic jazz that draws more than 2,000 fans to Marina Park. > Suttons Bay, tel. 231/271–4444, www.leelanau.com/jazzfest.

National Cherry Festival The country's cherry capital celebrates its harvest the second week of the month with more than 120 events, including three parades, concerts, fireworks, an air show, a Native American powwow, crafts, a rubber ducky race, and family activities. This eagerly anticipated event is one of northern Michigan's most heavily attended. > Traverse City, tel. 231/947–4230, www.cherryfestival.org.

AUGUST

Northwestern Michigan Fair Animals, a carnival midway, harness racing, grandstand events, bands, and log rolling make this fair, held the first Sunday in August, fun for the entire family. > 3606 Blair Townhall Rd., Traverse City, tel. 231/943–4150.

Suttons Bay Art Fair This art exposition, held the first weekend in August at the city's waterfront Marina Park, is one of the most competitive juried art shows in northern Michigan. Treats for the eyes are complemented by treats for the palette. > Suttons Bay, tel. 231/271–5077.

NOVEMBER

Northwoods Festival of Lights A fantasy forest complete with woodland creatures, fairies, elves, and a gingerbread house lights up Grand Traverse Resort for four weeks, starting in mid-November. It's held on the East Grand Traverse Bay shoreline, 8 mi from Traverse City. > Acme, tel. 231/938–2100.

Toast the Season The Leelanau Peninsula vintners conduct a special self-tour wine-tasting weekend, including a wine-and-food pairing. You'll also receive a handcrafted wreath made from vines of the Leelanau Peninsula, and other gifts. > - www.lpwines.com.

WHERE TO STAY

GLEN ARBOR

The Homestead This beautiful, wooded condo resort 2 mi north of town is a four-season favorite and has one- and two-bedroom accommodations with views of Lake Michigan and Sleeping Bear Dunes. Some furnishings are rustic, most are modern. > 1 Woodridge Rd., Glen Arbor 49636, tel. 231/334–5000, 231/334–5100 reservations, fax 231/334–5120, www.thehomesteadresort.com. 77 rooms, 210 condos. 2 restaurants, cable TV, 9-hole golf course, 5 tennis courts, 4 pools, sauna, beach, fishing, bicycles, cross-country skiing, downhill skiing, ice-skating, bar, children's programs (ages 1–10), playground, business services; no a/c in condos. D, MC, V. Closed weekdays Dec. 26–mid Mar., and mid-Mar.–May 1. $$$–$$$$

SUTTONS BAY

Fig Leaf Bed and Breakfast The owner of this 1880 farmhouse has created a unique, romantic place to spend the night. The house, which is filled with original artwork, is within walking distance of shops and restaurants. The waterfall and stream with colorful ducks add charm to the grounds. You can sit on the deck or in peaceful common room. > 9995 E. Duck Lake Rd., Suttons Bay 49682, tel. 231/271–3995, www.leelanau.com/figleaf. 4 rooms, 2 with bath. No smoking, no room TVs. D, MC, V. BP. $$

Inn at Black Star Farms As you enter this former private mansion, part of the Black Star Farms vineyards, a spacious foyer unfolds with a marble floor and huge, sweeping staircase that leads to the second-floor balcony and guest rooms. Once in your room, luxurious pampering with attentive service, furnishings to sink into, and refreshments everywhere you turn await. Other touches include a complimentary wine- and cheese-tasting in Pegasus Lounge before dinner, and complimentary fruit brandies, grappas, or dessert wine served before bed. Packages including romance, kayaking, fishing, and wine tasting are available. > 10844 E. Revold Rd., Suttons Bay 49682, tel. 231/271–4970, fax 231/271–4883, www.blackstarfarms.com. 8 rooms. Sauna, horseback riding, wine shop, library, free parking; no room TVs. AE, D, MC, V. BP. $$$–$$$$

TRAVERSE CITY

Anchor Inn You may feel awash in nostalgia when you see the cottages and motel rooms with knotty-pine furniture. The one-, two-, and three-bedroom cottages have fireplaces and kitchens. > 11998 S.W. Bay Shore Dr., Traverse City 49684, tel. 231/946–7442, fax 231/929–2589, www.anchorin.net. 6 rooms, 8 cottages. Some microwaves, some kitchenettes, refrigerators, cable TV, some pets allowed (fee). AE, D, MC, V. ¢–$

Bayshore Resort This three-story Victorian-theme, yet modern, hotel is 1 mi from downtown Traverse City. You can view the sandy beaches of Lake Michigan's West Grand Traverse Bay from your room's private balcony or patio. If you're visiting in colder months, ask for a room with a fireplace. > 833 E. Front St., Traverse City 49686, tel. 231/935–4400 or 800/634–4401, fax 231/935–0262, www.bayshore-resort.com. 120 rooms. Some in-room hot tubs, cable TV with video games, indoor pool, exercise equipment, beach, laundry facilities, business services, airport shuttle; no smoking. AE, D, DC, MC, V. BP. ¢–$$$$

Grainery Bed and Breakfast Snack on goodies from the dessert and fruit table any time you'd like at this former 1892 gentleman's farm, converted into a B&B in 1990. Just 3 mi south of downtown Traverse City, the Grainery was made for relaxation: sip lemonade while looking at swans, ducks, and wild turkeys in and around the pond. Rooms in the house are appointed with antiques, and all have private baths; rooms in the carriage house have a country flavor and each includes a fireplace. The cottage, decorated with a floral motif, has a private deck and sitting area. > 2951 Hartman Rd., Traverse City 49684, tel. 231/946–8325, www.bbhost.com/thegrainery. 4 rooms, 1 cottage. Some in-room hot tubs, putting green, hot tub; no phones in some rooms, no TVs in some rooms. AE, MC, V. BP. ¢

Grand Beach Resort Hotel A 300-foot sugar-sand beach beckons from this three-story hotel on West Grand Traverse Bay. All rooms have two queen beds or one king and a sofa. Each room either faces the beach or the courtyard with pool. > 1683 U.S. 31 N, Traverse City 49686, tel. 231/938–4455 or 800/968–1992, fax 231/938–4435, www.grandbeach.com. 95 rooms. Refrigerators, cable TV, in-room VCRs with movies, indoor pool, exercise equipment, hot tub, beach, laundry facilities, business services. AE, D, DC, MC, V. CP. $$$

Grand Traverse Resort This top-shelf resort is on 1,400 acres along the shores of Lake Michigan's East Grand Traverse Bay. It's the area's largest all-season resort hotel, known for its 54 golf holes, including a Jack Nicklaus–designed and a Gary Player–designed course. For a little relaxation check out the resort's 7,000-square-foot spa complex. Within the complex you can take advantage of the workout facilities and tennis center. Rooms range from standard to three-bedroom condos. Many rooms have views of the valley or the beach. > 100 Grand Traverse Village Rd., Acme

49610, tel. 231/946–8900 or 800/236–1577, www.grandtraverseresort.com. Some in-room hot tubs, some kitchens, cable TV, in-room VCRs, driving range, 3 golf courses, 1 putting green, 5 indoor and 4 outdoor tennis courts, 4 indoor and 2 outdoor pools, gym, hot tub, massage, sauna, steam room, beach, cross-country skiing, downhill skiing, ice-skating, sleigh rides, tobogganing, bar, children's programs (ages 6–12), laundry facilities, business services, airport shuttle. AE, D, DC, MC, V. **$$$$**

Linden Lea on Long Lake Peace and quiet, a crystal-clear lake, and wild turkeys, white-tailed deer, and woodpeckers may be all you'll notice during your stay at this bed-and-breakfast, 10 mi west of town. An eclectic mix of northern Michigan hand-made items, antiques, and twig furniture outfits the rooms, and window seats over-look the lake. > 279 Long Lake Rd., Traverse City 49684, tel. 231/943–9182, www.lindenleabb.com. 2 rooms. Beach, boating. No credit cards. BP. **$**

Sugar Beach Resort Hotel An all-seasons hotel on East Grand Traverse Bay, Sugar Beach has beachfront rooms with private balconies. Their family suites are small town houses with private entrances and have one bedroom with two king- or queen-size beds, plus a living room with pull-out queen sofa. > 1773 U.S. 31 N, Traverse City 49686, tel. 231/938–0100 or 800/509–1995, fax 231/938–0200, www.sugarbeach.com. 85 rooms, 11 suites. Microwaves, refrigerators, cable TV, in-room VCRs with movies, indoor pool, exercise equipment, hot tub, cross-country skiing, downhill skiing, laundry facilities, business services. AE, D, DC, MC, V. CP. **$–$$$**

Traverse Bay Inn Catering to families is the raison d'être of this mostly suites hotel, which has many family-oriented amenities. One- and two-bedroom suites and studios are available; some have two bathrooms. The Traverse Area Recreational Bike Trail is next door, and bikes are available from the inn at no charge. > 2300 U.S. 31 N, Traverse City 49686, tel. 231/938–2646 or 800/938–2646, fax 231/938–5845, www.traversebayinn.com. 19 suites, 5 studios. Picnic area, in-room data ports, kitch-enettes, cable TV with VCR and movies, hot tub, bicycles, laundry facilities, recreation room, some pets allowed (fee), no smoking rooms. AE, D, MC, V. **$–$$**

Warwickshire Inn This 1902 restored white farmhouse, 2 mi west of town, is across the street from a golf course and close to ski resorts. The inn has a beautiful deck and garden hammock. The interior has some lovely antiques, rooms have queen-size beds, and the pancake-and-bacon breakfast is a big hit. > 5037 Barney Rd., Traverse City 49684, tel. 231/946–7176, www.warwickinn.net. 3 rooms. No credit cards. BP. **¢**

WHERE TO EAT

GLEN ARBOR

Funistrada In a small, old clapboard home, decorated with homey rose and chintz, Funistrada serves garlic chicken and baked whitefish to crowds of both locals and vis-itors. > 4566 MacFarland Rd., 6 mi south of Glen Arbor, Maple City, tel. 231/334–3900. D, MC, V. Closed Mon. and Tues. **$$–$$$**

La Bécasse A tiny, 40-seat restaurant, known as one of the best in the state for su-perb country-French cooking, belies the simplicity of its interior. A few simple paint-ings accent the otherwise whitewashed, rustic interior. Entrées have included grilled *escalopes de veau*, chicken breasts with basil mousse, and whitefish with bread crumbs, black olives, herbs, and lemon beurre blanc, so creatively plated it's almost a shame to eat it. Dine inside all year or alfresco on a summer evening. > 9001 S. Dunn's Farm Rd., Maple City, tel. 231/334–3944. Reservations essential. AE, MC, V. Closed Mon. and Tues. mid-Oct.–mid-June. No lunch. **$$$$**

Western Avenue Grill "Up-north" looks with lodgelike and nautical accessories adorn this laid-back eatery. The menu includes lots of staples such as burgers, salads, and pastas, as well as Lake Superior whitefish and steak. There's open-air dining on an outdoor deck, and a children's menu is available. > 6410 Western Ave., Glen Arbor, tel. 231/334–3362. AE, D, MC, V. **$$**

LELAND

Manitou Though the restaurant has a rustic, "up-north" look, its menu isn't standard "up-north" fare. Try sautéed perch or hazelnut rack of lamb. Extra seating is available at the wine bar, and in warm weather you can enjoy open-air dining on a screened-in patio. A children's menu and early-bird suppers tend to bring in the crowds. Manitou serves beer and wine only. > 4349 Scenic Hwy., Leland, tel. 231/882–4761. MC, V. Closed Jan.–Apr. **$$–$$$**

SUTTONS BAY

Boone's This pub attracts both locals and vacationers with its family-style dining and daily lunch specials. Cozy booths and a wood-and-stone interior add to its rustic appeal. Favorites include whitefish, steaks, and sandwiches. A children's menu is available. > 102 St. Joseph St., Suttons Bay, tel. 231/271–6688. MC, V. **$$–$$$**

Eagle's Ridge Fine Dining The menu at this restaurant, 4 mi north of Suttons Bay, focuses on Native American fare. One of the most popular specials is Indian tacos, made with fried unleavened bread, ground beef, native vegetables, and a special seasoning. Also, try the Indian corn soup and fried cabbage and bacon. The dining room has Native American artwork, stained-glass windows, an arched window in front, and nicely finished wood tables with wood-accent trim. > 2511 N.W. Bay Shore Dr., Suttons Bay, tel. 231/271–7166. MC, V. **¢–$$$**

Hattie's Artwork from local artists accents the spare, elegant interior of this upscale restaurant. You can choose the morel ravioli or Thai-style scallops from the innovative menu. Don't miss the chocolate paradise with raspberries for dessert. > 111 St. Joseph St., Suttons Bay, tel. 231/271–6222. AE, D, MC, V. **$$$$**

TRAVERSE CITY

Apache Trout Grill You can really experience northern Michigan at this rustic, homey eatery. Stuffed fish and wood carvings adorn the walls, lamps are carved in the shape of bears and fishing poles, and a great view of the lake unfolds in front. On the menu are fresh-grilled or sautéed fish, steaks, barbecued ribs, and several pastas. > 13671 Bay Shore Dr., Traverse City, tel. 231/947–7079. AE, D, DC, MC, V. **$$–$$$**

Boat House Blue Water Bistro You may think you're at your cottage when you dine at this restaurant on the Old Mission Peninsula. It's right on the water 10 mi north of Traverse City. Entrées include chicken, steak, seafood, and vegetable specialties. > 14039 Peninsula Dr., Traverse City, tel. 231/223–4030. Closed Mon. and Tues. No lunch Wed. and Thurs. **$$**

Bowers Harbor Inn You get a view of Grand Traverse Bay from this turn-of-the-20th-century mansion, built by a wealthy lumber baron, on the Old Mission Peninsula. High ceilings, a sweeping staircase, and dramatic, unexpected corners and turns add to the mansion's luxurious setting. For dinner, try the fish-in-a-bag and the macadamia nut–encrusted whitefish. Its more casual area, the Bowery, serves ribs, steaks, and chicken and is in the home's former servants' quarters. On weekends you can sip and savor to the strains of an acoustic guitar. > 13512 Peninsula Dr., Traverse City, tel. 231/223–4222. Reservations essential. AE, D, MC, V. No lunch. **$$$–$$$$**

Don's Drive-In If you're looking for a trip down memory lane, head to Don's Drive-In, where Bobby Darin and burger baskets are a reality. Don's has been around since the 1950s, and the people of Traverse City just keep on coming. Whatever American standard you order, don't miss the milk shakes; they're possibly the thickest you've ever had, served in their mixing cups with extra cups and spoons. > 2030 U.S. 31 N, Traverse City, tel. 231/938–1060. D, MC, V. **¢–$**

La Cuisine Amical Café Plants, statuettes, and wall hangings adorn this little in-town bistro that has a patio for summer dining. Braised lamb shank and exquisite French pastries keep customers coming back, but you also have a choice of sandwiches, soups, salads, and pasta. > 229 E. Front St., Traverse City, tel. 231/941–8888. AE, MC. No dinner Sun. **$$–$$$**

La Señorita Bright, eye-catching fixtures complement the zesty fare. It's one of the few places in Traverse City where burritos, chimichangas, and fajitas as well as mesquite-grilled dishes fill the menu. Other favorites include the linguine and any of the eight signature burgers. There's also a children's menu. > 1245 S. Garfield St., Traverse City, tel. 231/947–8820. AE, D, MC, V. **¢–$$**

Minerva's Whatever your entrée at this warm and inviting restaurant—barbecued ribs, filet mignon, and the tortellini chicken breast carbonara in a delicate herbed cream sauce are the most popular—save room for one of Minerva's unforgettable desserts, such as the death by chocolate, bananas Foster, or tiramisu. > 300 E. State St., Traverse City, tel. 231/946–5093, fax 231/946–2772. **$–$$$**

Reflections Stylish fare and an expansive view of East Grand Traverse Bay and Old Mission Peninsula make this restaurant a standout. In addition to the classic prime rib, pecan walleye, and Atlantic char-grilled salmon, you can try one of many sandwiches and entrée-size salads. Try the thick, creamy chowder with rice, corn, and shrimp or the apple chutney chicken. For dessert, sample the Black Forest cheesecake with tangy Traverse City cherries. > 2061 U.S. 31 N, Traverse City, tel. 231/938–2321. AE, D, DC, MC, V. **$$$–$$$$**

Windows With views of the bay from every table and a menu that emphasizes both old favorites and artful, new cuisine, this restaurant serves a memorable dining experience. Try the firecracker pork on bow-tie pasta with cashews, veal Winn Dixie (veal sautéed with shrimp, artichokes, and mushrooms), or duck-and-sausage gumbo. Desserts include chocolate pâté and chocolate mousse Olivia. An extensive wine list rounds out the experience. > 7677 W. Bay Shore Dr., Traverse City, tel. 231/941–0100. DC, MC, V. Closed Nov.–May and Sun. and Mon. **$$$–$$$$**

ESSENTIALS

Getting Here

Cars provide the best means of transportation to and around Traverse City and the surrounding communities. Planes and buses are both possible, but you'll still need to rent a car to explore the small towns on Old Mission Peninsula. Flying will take one hour, driving takes approximately six hours plus breaks, and the bus generally takes a bit over eight hours. If you choose not to rent a car, Bay Area Transportation Authority (BATA) provides door-to-door service approximately five times per day.

BY BUS

Greyhound schedules one bus per day to Traverse City. It leaves downtown Chicago at 10 AM and arrives at 7:10 PM. For the return trip, buses leave Traverse City at 10:15 AM and arrive in downtown Chicago at 5:45 PM. The fare is approximately $110 round-trip. There are many discounts available, so check the Internet or call Greyhound to see which ones apply to you.

Within Traverse City, Bay Area Transportation Authority (BATA) operates a door-to-door service five times a day between 7 AM and 6 PM. Call BATA approximately one hour before you'd like to depart, and they will pick you up during their next regularly scheduled run and drop you off at your destination. The cost is $2.

BUS DEPOTS **Greyhound** > 630 W. Harrison++CE: St.?++, Chicago, tel. 312/408–5800. **Traverse City Greyhound and Indian Trails/BATA** > 3233 Cass Rd., Traverse City, tel. 231/946–5180.

BUS LINES **BATA** > Tel. 231/946–5180, www.bata.net. **Greyhound** > Tel. 800/229–9424, www.greyhound.com.

BY CAR

From Chicago, take I–90 (the Skyway) until it merges again with I–94 in Indiana (you can take I–94 the whole way and skip the tolls, but the Skyway is quicker). Once you're in Michigan, take I–196 North to U.S. 131 North, then go left again onto Route 113. This will be your longest stretch—approximately 113 mi. Your next 20 mi will be a series of 3- and 4-mi stretches.

Most of the expressways have a 70 mph speed limit. Most of the route is dotted with plenty of fast-food places and rest stops but the number of them decreases the farther north you drive. Chicago traffic is unpredictable, particularly on Friday. To best avoid traffic, plan on leaving town at noon or 1 PM. With a couple of rest stops, you can make it to Traverse City in time for a late dinner.

BY PLANE

United Express and American Eagle provide service into Traverse City. Each has several direct and several nondirect flights per day, usually routing through Detroit and Cleveland. The flight takes only an hour, and several are scheduled throughout the day. Cherry Capital Airport is a few miles outside of Traverse City.

CONTACTS **Cherry Capital Airport** > 1330 Airport Access Rd., Traverse City, tel. 231/947–2250, www.tvcairport.com. **O'Hare International Airport** > 10,000 W. O'Hare, Chicago, tel. 800/832–6352, www.ohare.com/ohare/home.asp.

CONTACTS **American Eagle** > Tel. 800/433–7300, www.aa.com. **United Express** > Tel. 800/864–8331, www.ual.com.

Visitor Information

INFORMATION **Benzie County Chamber of Commerce** > 826 Michigan Ave., Box 204, Benzonia 49231, tel. 231/882–5801 or 800/882–5801, fax 231/882–9249, www.benzie.org. **Leelanau Peninsula Vintner Association (LPVA)** > Tel. 231/938–3247, www.lpwines.com. **Suttons Bay Area Chamber of Commerce** > Box 46, Suttons Bay 49682, tel. 231/271–5017, www.suttonsbayarea.com. **Traverse City Convention and Visitors Bureau** > 101 W. Grandview Pkwy., Traverse City 49615, tel. 231/947–1120 or 800/872–8377, www.tcvisitor.com.

Index

Notes